Cultural Sociology

BLACKWELL READERS IN SOCIOLOGY

Each volume in this authoritative series aims to provide students and scholars with comprehensive collections of classic and contemporary readings for all the major subfields of sociology. They are designed to complement single-authored works, or to be used as stand-alone textbooks for courses. The selected readings sample the most important works that students should read and are framed by informed editorial introductions. The series aims to reflect the state of the discipline by providing collections not only on standard topics but also on cutting-edge subjects in sociology to provide future directions in teaching and research.

Forthcoming:

Cultural Sociology

Edited by

Lyn Spillman

BLACKWELL
Publishers

First published 2002

2 4 6 8 10 9 7 5 3 1

Blackwell Publishers Inc.
350 Main Street
Malden, Massachusetts 02148
USA

Blackwell Publishers Ltd
108 Cowley Road
Oxford OX4 1JF
UK

Library of Congress Cataloging-in-Publication Data

Cultural sociology / edited by Lyn Spillman.
    p. cm
   Includes bibliographical references and index.
   ISBN 0–631–21652–9 (alk. paper)—ISBN 0–631–21653–7 (pb. : alk. paper)
   1. Sociology. 2. Culture. I. Spillman, Lyn.

  HM585 .C85 2001
  306—dc21
                                                 2001025204

British Library Cataloguing in Publication Data

A CIP catalogue record for this book is available from the British Library.

Typeset in 10/12 pt Sabon
by Kolam Information Services Pvt. Ltd, Pondicherry, I
Printed in Great Britain by Antony Rowe Ltd, Chipper

This book is printed on acid-free paper.

Contents

Contributors

For biographical information on contributors to Part I, "Key Ideas," see Editor's Notes accompanying each selection.

Jeffrey C. Alexander is Professor of Sociology at Yale University.

Howard S. Becker lives and works in San Francisco.

Mabel Berezin is Visiting Associate Professor in the Department of Geography, University of California, Los Angeles.

Bethany Bryson is Assistant Professor of Sociology at the University of Virginia.

Karen Cerulo is Associate Professor of Sociology at Rutgers University.

Paul DiMaggio is Professor of Sociology at Princeton University.

Nina Eliasoph is Assistant Professor of Sociology at the University of Wisconsin-Madison.

Wendy Griswold is Professor of Sociology, Comparative Literary Studies, and English at Northwestern University.

Darnell Hunt is Associate Professor and Chair of Sociology, and Director of the African American Studies Program at the University of Southern California.

Ronald N. Jacobs is Assistant Professor of Sociology at the University at Albany, State University of New York.

Fredric Jameson is William A. Lane Professor of Comparative Literature and Professor of Romance Studies (French) at Duke University.

Gideon Kunda is Senior Lecturer in the Department of Labor Studies at Tel Aviv University.

Michèle Lamont is Professor of Sociology at Princeton University.

Magali Sarfatti Larson is Professor Emerita of Sociology at Temple University and affiliated with the University of Urbino.

Paul Lichterman is Assistant Professor of Sociology at the University of Wisconsin-Madison.

Christena E. Nippert-Eng is Associate Professor in the Department of Social Sciences, Illinois Institute of Technology.

Richard A. Peterson is Professor of Sociology at Vanderbilt University.

Michael Schudson is Professor of Communication and Adjunct Professor of Sociology at the University of California, San Diego.

Barry Schwartz is Professor Emeritus of Sociology at the University of Georgia.

William H. Sewell, Jr. is Max Palevsky Professor of History and Political Science at the University of Chicago.

Philip Smith is Senior Lecturer in Sociology in the Department of Anthropology and Sociology, the University of Queensland.

Ann Swidler is Professor of Sociology at the University of California, Berkeley.

Robin Wagner-Pacifici is Professor of Sociology and Anthropology at Swarthmore College.

Rhys H. Williams is Associate Professor and Department Head of Sociology at the University of Cincinnati.

Robert Wuthnow is Gerhard R. Andlinger '52 Professor of Sociology at Princeton University.

Eviatar Zerubavel is Professor of Sociology at Rutgers University.

Preface

Even more than most books, an anthology of this sort is only possible because of the work of generations of dedicated scholars, some of them unrecognized. I'm thankful for all their work, which made shaping this collection something like the experience of sculptors who feel that they only release a form which already exists in their material.

General recognition is also due to those who created the intellectual context within which I could follow my own longstanding interest in culture. My teachers at the Australian National University introduced me to epistemological theories in philosophy and to lively theoretical debates about ideology which, I am heartened to think as a teacher now, made a firm foundation. My graduate studies at Berkeley provided unparalleled opportunities to explore cultural theory across the social sciences and humanities; it's notable that no one at Berkeley ever encouraged the shortsighted view that it is necessary to sacrifice intellectual breadth to maintain disciplinary depth. Particular thanks to Neil Smelser, Ann Swidler, Kenneth Bock, Todd Gitlin, and Peter Stromberg for the areas of inquiry about culture they opened to me. At Berkeley, too, the late Leo Lowenthal made an important opportunity for continuous reflection on culture and society in his longstanding reading group, and left me as well as generations of other students with fond memories of his old-world grace and keen critical insight. The Culture Club provided another opportunity to learn more about our shared interests, and the stimulation, curiosity, and good humor of our discussions stay with me to this day; thanks especially to Nina Eliasoph, Richard Kaplan, and Paul Lichterman.

I am fortunate that during my graduate studies the Culture Section of the American Sociological Association was formed; I thank the many people whose work created and maintained such a stimulating intellectual environment and supportive professional context in which to pursue interests in culture. At the University of Notre Dame, the Sociology Department has provided more opportunities and intellectual space than would many other departments, and graduate students in successive Cultural Sociology classes have helped me shape my ideas and shown me new implications of work in the field. My undergraduate students in "Culture and Society" classes in 1999 and 2000 tested many of the selections in this book, and their serious, lively, and interesting responses helped to improve it. I've also been stimulated in the work for this collection by the unusual opportunity of teaching Notre Dame's excellent, year-long interdisciplinary "Core" seminar for sophomores.

Many people have provided more particular support in developing this anthology too. At Blackwell Publishers I'd like to thank Susan Rabinowitz for her ideas and enthusiasm in originating the project, Anthony Grahame for his impressive copyediting, and Ken Provencher for his great help and patience with questions about all the details of putting the book together. I also appreciate the thoughtful responses of authors to questions about the editing of their work. The Institute for Scholarship in the Liberal Arts at the University of Notre Dame provided support which helped speed work on the anthology, and should be commended for the many ways it sustains scholarship. I could not have accomplished the long, complicated tasks of requesting permissions and writing the editor's notes without the heroic labors of Joanna (Asia) Kaftan, Michael Gibbons, and Joe Rumbo, who were devoted in locating and organizing large quantities of obscure information while also pursuing their own interesting research on culture.

Many thanks, too, to Neil Smelser, Ann Swidler, and anonymous reviewers for their helpful input at the beginning of this project. I'm very grateful to Paul Lichterman for his timely and thoughtful suggestions, about both the original plan and the introduction. Mark Chaves and Russell Faeges also made detailed and useful comments on the introduction, and Joe Rumbo, Xiao-ging Wang, and Jamie McClintock helped make it clearer.

This book is dedicated to my husband Russell Faeges, whose scholarly insight, generosity, companionship, and warm support make my work possible.

Acknowledgments

The authors and publishers gratefully acknowledge the following for permission to reproduce copyright material:

Ruth Benedict, "The Diversity of Cultures" excerpted from chapter II in *Patterns of Culture* (Boston: Houghton Mifflin, 1959 [1934]). Copyright © 1934 by Ruth Benedict, © renewed 1961 by Ruth Valentine. Reprinted by permission of Houghton Mifflin Co. All rights reserved;

Georg Simmel, "The Metropolis and Mental Life" from Georg Simmel, *On Individuality and Social Forms: Selected Writings*, edited with an introduction by Donald N. Levine (Chicago and London: University of Chicago Press, 1971). © 1971 by The University of Chicago. All rights reserved;

Max Horkheimer and Theodor Adorno, "The Culture Industry: Enlightenment as Mass Deception" excerpted from *Dialectic of Enlightenment*, translated by John Cumming (New York: Continuum, 1972 [1944]). Reprinted by permission of Continuum Publishers;

Edward Shils, "Center and Periphery," excerpted from chapter 4 in *The Constitution of Society* (Chicago and London: University of Chicago Press, 1982). This essay is acknowledged there as "previously published in a slightly different form in *The Logic of Personal Knowledge: Essays in Honour of Michael Polanyi* (The Free Press of Glencoe, 1961). © The Free Press of Glencoe, 1961. Used with permission of The Macmillan Company;

Raymond Williams, "Base and Superstructure," reprinted from part II, chapter 1 in *Marxism and Literature* (Oxford: Oxford University Press, 1977) by permission of the Oxford University Press. © Oxford University Press 1977;

Clifford Geertz, "Thick Description: Toward an Interpretive Theory of Culture," excerpted from chapter 1, *The Interpretation of Cultures* (New York: Basic Books, 1973), beginning p. 63;

Pierre Bourdieu, "Cultural Power," excerpted from "Social Space and the Genesis of 'Classes,'" translated by Matthew Adamson, chapter 11 in *Language and Symbolic Power*, edited and introduced by John B. Thompson (Cambridge, MA: Harvard University Press, 1991). "Social Space and the Genesis of 'Classes'" was originally published as "Espace social et genèse des 'classes'", *Actes de la recherche en sciences sociales*, 52–53 (June 1984), pp. 3–12. Reprinted by permission of the author, Harvard University Press, and Polity Press;

Christena E. Nippert-Eng, "Boundary Work: Sculpting Home and Work," excerpted from chapter 1 in *Home and Work: Negotiating Boundaries through Everyday Life* (Chicago and London: University of Chicago Press, 1996). © 1995, 1996 by The University of Chicago. All rights reserved;

Gideon Kunda, "Corporate Culture," excerpted from chapter 1 ("Culture and Organization") and chapter 4 ("Presentational Rituals: Talking Ideology") in *Engineering Culture: Control and Commitment in a High-Tech Corporation*

(Philadelphia: Temple University Press, 1992). Reprinted by permission of Temple University Press. © 1992 by Temple University. All rights reserved;

Michèle Lamont, "Symbolic Boundaries and Status," excerpted from chapters 1 and 6 in *Money, Morals, and Manners: The Culture of the French and the American Upper-Middle Class* (Chicago: The University of Chicago Press, 1992). © 1992 by the University of Chicago. All rights reserved. Reprinted by kind permission from the American Sociological Association;

Bethany Bryson, "Symbolic Exclusion and Musical Dislikes," excerpted from "'Anything but Heavy Metal': Symbolic Exclusion and Musical Dislikes," *American Sociological Review* 61 (1996): 884–99;

Darnell Hunt, "Raced Ways of Seeing," excerpted from chapters 2 and 7 in *Screening the Los Angeles "Riots": Race, Seeing, and Resistance* (Cambridge and New York: Cambridge University Press, 1997). © Darnell M. Hunt 1997. Reprinted with the permission of Cambridge University Press;

Nina Eliasoph, excerpted from "'Close to Home': The Work of Avoiding Politics," *Theory and Society* 26 (1997): 605–47. © Kluwer Academic Publishers. Printed in the Netherlands;

Michael Schudson, excerpted from "How Culture Works: Perspectives from Media Studies on the Efficacy of Symbols," *Theory and Society* 18 (1989): 153–80. © Kluwer Academic Publishers. Printed in the Netherlands;

Paul DiMaggio, "Market Structure, the Creative Process and Popular Culture: Toward an Organizational Reinterpretation of Mass-Culture Theory," *Journal of Popular Culture* 11(2), (1977): 436–52. Reprinted with permission of the Publishers, Popular Press;

Richard A. Peterson, "Why 1955? Explaining the Advent of Rock Music," *Popular Music* 9(1), (1990): 97–116. © 1990 Cambridge University Press. Reprinted with the permission of Cambridge University Press;

Howard S. Becker, excerpted from *Art Worlds* (Berkeley and Los Angeles: University of California Press, 1982). Copyright © 1982 The Regents of the University of California;

Wendy Griswold, "American Character and the American Novel: An Expansion of Reflection Theory in the Sociology of Literature," *American Journal of Sociology* 86(4) January 1981: 740–65. © 1981 by the University of Chicago;

Magali Sarfatti Larson, *Behind the Postmodern Façade: Architectural Change in Late Twentieth-Century America* (Berkeley and Los Angeles: University of California Press, 1993). Copyright © 1993 by The Regents of the University of California;

Robin Wagner-Pacifici and Barry Schwartz, "The Vietnam Veterans Memorial: Commemorating a Difficult Past," *American Journal of Sociology* 97(2) September 1991: 376–420. © 1991 by the University of Chicago. All rights reserved;

Eviatar Zerubavel, "The Social Lens," reprinted with the permission of The Free Press, a Division of Simon & Schuster, Inc., from Eviatar Zerubavel, *The Fine Line: Making Distinctions in Everyday Life* (New York: The Free Press, 1991), chapter 4. Copyright © 1991 by Eviatar Zerubavel;

Jeffrey C. Alexander and Philip Smith, "The Discourse of American Civil Society: A New Proposal for Cultural Studies," *Theory and Society* 22 (1993): 151–207. © Kluwer Academic Publishers. Printed in the Netherlands;

Mabel Berezin, "Cultural Form and Political Meaning: State-subsidized Theater, Ideology, and the Language of Style in Fascist Italy," *American Journal of Sociology* 99(5) March 1994: 1237–86. © 1994 by the University of Chicago. All rights reserved;

Karen Cerulo, excerpted from *Deciphering Violence: The Cognitive Structure of Right and Wrong* (New York and London: Routledge, 1998). Copyright © 1998 by Karen Cerulo. Reproduced by permission of Taylor and Francis/Routledge, Inc.;

Ronald N. Jacobs, "Civil Society and Crisis: Culture, Discourse, and the Rodney King Beating," *American Journal of Sociology* 101(5) March 1996: 1238–72. © 1996 by the University of Chicago. All rights reserved;

Rhys H. Williams, "Constructing the Public Good: Social Movements and Cultural Resources," reprinted by permission from *Social Problems* 42(1) February 1995: 124–44. © 1995 by The Society for the Study of Social Problems;

Paul Lichterman, *The Search For Political Community: American Activists Reinventing Commitment* (Cambridge and New York: Cambridge University Press, 1996). © Cambridge University Press 1996. Reprinted with the permission of Cambridge University Press;

Ann Swidler, "Cultural Power and Social Movements," chapter 2 in Hank Johnston and Bert Klandermans (eds.), *Social Movements and Culture* (Minneapolis: University of Minnesota Press, 1995), volume 4 in the "Social Movements, Protest, and Contention" series. Copyright © 1995 by the Regents of the University of Minnesota;

William H. Sewell, Jr., "A Theory of Structure: Duality, Agency and Transformation," *American Journal of Sociology* 98 (1992): 1–29. © 1992 by the University of Chicago. All rights reserved;

Robert Wuthnow, reprinted by permission of the publisher from Robert Wuthnow, *Communities of Discourse: Ideology and Social Structure in the Reformation, the Enlightenment, and European Socialism* (Cambridge, MA: Harvard University Press, 1989). Copyright © 1989 by the President and Fellows of Harvard College;

Fredric Jameson, excepted from "Postmodernism, or The Cultural Logic of Late Capitalism," *New Left Review* 146, July–August 1984: 53–92. Reprinted by permission.

The publishers apologize for any errors or omissions in the above list and would be grateful to be notified of any corrections that should be incorporated in the next edition or reprint of this book.

Introduction: Culture and Cultural Sociology

Lyn Spillman

Cultural sociology is about meaning-making. Cultural sociologists investigate how meaning-making happens, why meanings vary, how meanings influence human action, and the ways meaning-making is important in social cohesion, domination, and resistance. The readings collected here touch on many different topics – from television viewing to volunteering, from rock music to war memorials, from stories of violence to ideals of the public good – but they all contribute to understanding meaning-making processes, and they illustrate key themes and important perspectives in contemporary cultural sociology.

This field of scholarly inquiry is thriving, with an outpouring of innovative research in the last decades of the twentieth century, and promising work in progress for the future. I hope this sampler serves to convey some sense of that richness and possibility, and inspire some readers to look beyond these selections to the books and articles from which they are drawn, and to the other fascinating research which could fill several further volumes like this.

The selections are intended to provide a compact introduction to some classics, developments, and exemplars in cultural sociology for students and scholars unfamiliar with the field. This introduction provides some context for the general reader. I discuss first the slippery yet inescapable idea of culture, and contemporary cultural sociology's angle on it. On that basis, I explain the organization of this book, and conclude with a brief assessment of the opportunities and limitations now shaping cultural sociology. What is distinctive about cultural sociology as a perspective on meaning-making? What are its strengths and its blind spots? How does a cultural sociologist approach a topic like work, or politics, differently from other sociologists, or a topic like novels, or music, differently from scholars in the humanities? What are some of the unresolved issues and neglected topics that should be addressed by cultural sociologists in the future?

"Culture"

When we think about human groups, the idea of culture often seems commonplace and indispensable. But what exactly is "culture?" In common usage, the term has a number of overlapping yet sometimes contradictory connotations. And just as the idea of culture is comfortably capacious, if a little fuzzy, in everyday life, scholars in many different fields in the humanities and social sciences make culture their focus in different ways. Consequently, the idea of culture is notoriously difficult to define, and the concept can seem misty, all-encompassing, and ambiguous – to the extent that some social scientists have found the concept too fuzzy to be useful.[1]

Yet however difficult it is to identify and think clearly about culture, it has seemed to cultural sociologists in the last few decades that the difficulties should be faced head on, rather than avoided. Here, I will sketch the various things we might commonly mean when we refer to culture, explaining why these ambiguities exist. I will suggest that contemporary scholarship on culture in the humanities and social sciences resolves earlier ambiguities by implicitly or explicitly treating culture as *processes of meaning-making*. Cultural sociology, combining interdisciplinary influences with sociological presuppositions, examines meaning-making processes along three specific dimensions; meaning-making in everyday action, the institutional production of meaning, and the shared mental frameworks which are the tools of meaning-making.

Culture as a Feature of Entire Groups and Societies

Sometimes we think of culture as something that connects us to other people in our groups, by contrast with outsiders. If we share with others certain ways of seeing the world, or habits, or shorthand codes and assumptions (for instance, about the way we eat meals, or the heroes we know and admire) we think of ourselves as members of the same culture or subculture.[2] Against this background, we are conscious of "cultural difference" when we encounter a new situation or a new group and find that our usual ways of seeing and acting in the world can no longer be taken for granted (for instance, when commonplace symbols like flags or flowers are used differently, or when informal rules about dating or drugs are different). When we think about culture in this way, we see culture as an attribute of entire groups or societies, and we draw contrasts between the cultures of different peoples.

This idea of culture emerged in nineteenth-century Europe. By that time, new reflection about differences among human populations had been prompted by European exploration and conquest across the globe. This gradually generated a comparative way of thinking about human society which ultimately became commonplace in modern life, and was also crucial to the formation of anthropology as a discipline.[3] In this anthropological sense of the term, the entire way of life of a people is thought to be embedded in, and expressed by, its culture. Cultures are thought to be evident in anything from tools to religion; and different cultures are seen as distinct units.

In the nineteenth century, cultures were rated according to western ideals of social progress, and European cultures were placed at the top of a world hierarchy. But explicit claims about the superiority of western cultures gradually dissipated in the twentieth century. More recently, many scholars have challenged implicit as well as explicit assumptions about western superiority, assumptions embedded in colonial and postcolonial social relations and in relations between cultures of dominant and subordinate groups. Against the belief in cultural hierarchy, the concept of culture was gradually pluralized and relativized, so that different "cultures" were thought to have equal value.[4] We see this connotation very frequently in common usage today, such as when we consider "multiculturalism," or when tourists enjoy visiting "another culture."

Culture as a Separate Realm of Human Expression

Another way we often think of culture has quite different connotations. We can label as "cultural" special activities or material artifacts characteristic of particular groups, like opera, rap music, folk song, novels or haiku, quilts or masks or building styles. In this usage, an implicit contrast is drawn between "culture" and other realms of social life, whether or not we also contrast different societies as well. And we might think of those specialized cultural practices and artifacts as what is most valuable about us or others, what needs to be preserved to express and represent the identity of a group.

Like the way the anthropological sense of culture echoes ideas which emerged in the big social changes associated with European expansion, this second sense in which we use "culture" today also echoes some important social changes, but in a somewhat different way. "Culture" came to refer to the practices and products of a special set of institutions in society in the course of the Industrial Revolution in England. The social differentiation and dissent generated in the transition from premodern to modern social organization accentuated a new contrast between the mundane, pragmatic, and conflict-ridden realms of economics and politics – the new worlds of capitalism, industry, democracy, and revolution – and an ideally purer realm of art and morality expressing higher human capabilities and values than could be seen in modern economic and political life. For some, this separate sphere of culture could serve as a basis for judging what was destructive and superficial in modern society.[5] For others, considering culture as a differentiated realm of expression could encourage the opinion that culture was in some way more trivial, more "epiphenomenal," and, perhaps, more "feminine" than the apparently more consequential spheres of politics or economics. And just as the first understanding of culture was associated with and elaborated by scholars in anthropology, this second sense was associated with and became the core of several forms of scholarship now considered "humanities" – such as the study of literature, art, and music.

When we talk about art, or popular culture, or folk culture, or even mass culture, then, we are echoing an idea which first emerged to help map the massive social changes occurring within European societies as modern economic and political institutions were born. (In earlier, less differentiated societies, "culture" could not be viewed as a separate sphere of life.) When we think of some complex and high status expressive cultural practices and objects – like opera, or sculpture – as "high culture," we are echoing nineteenth-century claims that carved out a set of practices and products which could somehow be set against everyday economic and political life. If we deplore mass culture for its commercialization, we also appeal to a notion that culture is ideally a separate and purer sphere of life. This idea also leaves indirect traces in contemporary thinking which tends to question whether an attachment to "high" culture is anything more than a camouflaged claim to high social status, and in the converse emphasis on the interest and significance of popular or "folk" culture artifacts and practices.

Culture as Meaning-Making

So the commonsense meanings of culture still current today echo the history of the idea. In everyday life, the term might still refer either to that realm of human activity and special artifacts separate from the mundane world of practical social life, or to the whole way of life of a group or a people. And these connotations of the term throughout its history can still resonate dissonantly, adding to its apparent ambiguity or vagueness. Like other disciplines, cultural sociology has been shaped by this sort of wide-ranging difference and development in the understanding of culture.

Confusion can multiply when we consider that even if we restrict our understanding of culture to the sense in which it refers to attributes of whole groups of people, various scholars have taken that to mean many different things. For instance, different scholars might emphasize different analytic dimensions of meaning and value, stressing artifacts, norms, customs, habits, practices, rituals, symbols, categories, codes, ideas, values, discourse, worldviews, ideologies, or principles. And this list is not exhaustive; any list of cultural "things" will necessarily be incomplete, because meaning and interpretation are active and fluid processes. Moreover, such a list conceals some important theoretical disputes between those scholars who emphasize discourses and those who emphasize practices, those who focus on cognitive categories and those who stress values, those who analyze concrete products and those who analyze deep textual patterns – not to mention the many possible combinations of these options.

But many of these confusions and disputes can be resolved if we consider "culture" as referring to *processes of meaning-making* – such processes may operate in different sorts of social locations (in more specialized arenas or more generally) and may be evident in all sorts of social practices and social products. The central concerns of those who study culture are to understand processes of meaning-making, to account for different meanings, and to examine their effects in social life. This view can encompass both culture as specialized realm and culture as an attribute of groups, and can include all the various things, from artifacts to principles, which scholars have thought to be important parts of cultures. Cultural sociologists might investigate culture as "a separate sphere of society," or culture as a "whole way of life" – the examples in this volume cover both territories – but they do it because their key goal is now formulated as understanding processes of meaning-making.[6]

Is this clarification itself too broad? And doesn't that mean that the idea of culture is still confusing? As Eagleton has pointed out, in his discussion of similar problems with the term "ideology," "any word which covers everything loses its cutting edge and dwindles to an empty sound."[7] But while anything may be viewed "culturally" in the sense that anything may indeed be endowed with shared meaning and become the object of human interpretation, other processes also shape and undergird human life. What is distinctive about focusing on culture can be seen if we contrast the study of culture with different sorts of accounts of human action. Most obviously, a focus on culture contrasts with accounts of human action emphasizing nature or biology. It also challenges accounts of social life which focus on universally shared psychological processes or principles. While not denying that biology or psychology profoundly influence human life, creating universal and necessary conditions of social action, cultural explanation brackets those universal conditions and assumes that human forms of thought and ways of doing things are far too diverse and differentiated to be explained by universal features. In addition to differentiating cultural explanation from biological or psychological explanation, many sociologists also contrast cultural accounts with investigation of social structures shaping human life – so, for instance, a study of class consciousness differs from a study of class structure, and a study of organizational culture differs from a study of organizational forms.[8]

I suggest, then, that scholars in many fields concerned with culture all analyze processes of meaning-making, though they may examine different aspects of such processes and use a variety of different tools to do so. Contemporary cultural sociology often draws on anthropology, history, feminist scholarship, literary criticism, media studies, political science, cultural studies, and social psychology for approaches which generate better ways of understanding culture. Indeed, work in the field is often characterized by creative use of the approaches and findings of other fields, as the selections here demonstrate. More than for many areas of sociology, this interdisciplinary awareness seems integral to the vitality of sociological approaches to culture.

"Culture" in American Sociology

But a more specific set of intellectual influences and resources have also shaped cultural sociology. As Smith has pointed out, disciplinary history and institutional pressures have generated a set of sensibilities, assumptions, and questions which ultimately differentiate work in the field from related work in such areas as anthropology and cultural studies, and which also tend to distinguish what he calls "American cultural sociology" from work on culture by sociologists in other countries.[9]

Sociology, like anthropology, was formed in the nineteenth century when concepts of culture were still emerging. But unlike the situation in anthropology, "culture" remained a residual category full of analytic confusion well into the twentieth century in sociological thought. Sociology was especially concerned with conflicts between traditional society and emerging modern society – problems of individual and community, inequality, and power. Early sociologists certainly had a lot to say about culture: for instance, Marx's notion of ideology, Durkheim's ideas about ritual, symbol, and the sacred, Weber's studies of how subjective meanings direct action, and Mead's theory of "significant symbols" in interaction are still essential for research in cultural sociology. But these insights about meaning-making in the work of formative sociological thinkers did not gel to make a theory of culture central in sociological thinking in the way that theories of culture became fundamental to anthropology. Until quite recently, sociology textbooks introducing the idea of culture often turned to anthropology for definitions, explanations, and examples.[10]

Indeed, by the mid-twentieth century some influential traditions in sociological inquiry entirely bracketed reflection on collective meaning-making, and those which did examine culture were somewhat peripheral. Typically, sociology might examine either aspects of society identifiable independently of what they mean to people – e.g. class structure, organizational forms, persistent institutions – or look at more micro-level interactional or social psychological processes "within" a culture – e.g. the life course, or professional socialization – or study aggregations of individual attitudes as potential outcomes of social background and possible determinants of actions – e.g. opinions about racial segregation, or about political parties. Even studies by those sociologists who were explicitly interested in collective meaning-making were marginalized and conducted under many different labels. For instance, studies of the arts and mass culture developed a long tradition, but were distanced from mainstream concerns which engaged the field. So too were ethnographic studies of subcultures, frequently subcultures of the deviant or powerless ("others" might have culture, but mainstream culture was less visible). At least two other traditions of inquiry also addressed culture in different ways at this time: the sociology of knowledge, studying how social context influences ideas, and symbolic interactionism, examining meaning-making in continuous interactional adjustments. All these areas of research continue to be important elements in cultural sociology, but none made "culture" as central in sociological inquiry as it was in anthropology.[11]

Marginalization and fragmentation of sociological studies of culture were exacerbated by a theoretical impasse. By this time, those sociologists interested in broader theories of collective meaning-making took one of two contradictory lines of thought. On the one hand, the anthropological idea of culture as characterizing a whole society was applied, with modifications, to contemporary complex societies, and so culture was treated as relatively or ideally consensual values, norms, and attitudes shared by entire groups. So, for instance, surveys of national attitudes and values were used to investigate "the cultures" of different groups. On the other hand, the idea that meaning-making was about power, a matter of domination or critique, was also widely assumed. So, for instance, critics of the mass media examined how new media could shape consciousness.[12]

Both "consensual values" and "ideology" theories of meaning-making in sociology had well-established theoretical and empirical grounding, but both seemed to speak at cross-purposes, and both seemed inadequate in some ways. If culture was seen as consensual values, then differences within groups and societies were not given enough weight, and power and domination through ideology was ignored. On the other hand, if culture was seen as ideology, then meaning-making seemed relatively unimportant for understanding what was "really" going on in society. While both approaches to analyzing cultures seemed to have some truth, both seemed to overgeneralize about meaning-making processes, to present too "global" a view of culture. Sociological assumptions about meaning-making seemed inadequate for the theoretical weight they had come to bear.

Contemporary cultural sociologists have not been satisfied with these choices, and turned to a wide range of interdisciplinary sources to develop ways of transcending what seemed to be a false dichotomy. They focused on precisely specified investigations which avoided or resolved the apparent contradiction between approaches emphasizing consensual values and those emphasizing ideology, and introduced a variety of conceptual innovations which allowed them to create more particular accounts of meaning-making processes. Including but going beyond a focus on culture as a separate realm of society, they examined meaning-making not only in artifacts and performance but in all corners of social life (as in Nippert-Eng's study of home and work, or Wuthnow's study of historical watersheds like the Enlightenment).[13] Including but going beyond the study of subcultures, they examined meaning-making at the center of society, in major institutions and in dominant groups (as in Kunda's work on a high-technology corporation, or Lamont's study of upper-middle class men). Challenging views that culture is shared values, they worked on developing a better understanding of how shared ideas might also be widely ignored or disputed, paying close attention to difference and conflict and developing a better understanding of how widespread differentiation in common meanings and values coexisted with claims to common culture (as in Hunt's study of how different groups interpret the news, or Wagner-Pacifici and Schwartz's investigation of the origins of the Vietnam Veteran's Memorial). And challenging views that culture was simply a matter of ideology and domination, they showed meaning-making struggles at the center of social change, and examined culture in dissent and conflict (as in the work of Lichterman on activism, or Rhys Williams on claims about the public good).

Culture in Practice, Cultural Production, and Cultural Frameworks[14]

Three sorts of work may be identified in recent cultural sociology, each focusing on meaning-making processes at a different analytic level. Many of the excerpts in this book show that explorations and combinations of these approaches have provided some of the richest recent developments in the field.

The first line of inquiry represented in this volume examines meaning-making processes "on the ground," investigating how interactions constitute meanings and how individuals use them. At this level, culture is treated as a contingent and variable element of the way action is framed. Particular sets of meanings are not assumed to be universally shared, coherent, or consistent within a given group or society; and common norms, values, cognitive frames, and practices are not assumed to be transparent and unambiguous to all. Rather, individuals and social groups may draw fluidly on symbolic repertoires of available meanings according to context, in ways similar to those emphasized by symbolic interactionists. By contrast with earlier views which sometimes treated culture as simply shared, the extent to which meaning-making processes are uniform for different individuals and groups is open to question in each study. Yet by contrast to symbolic interactionism, which has always examined meaning-making in fluid interactional processes, cultural sociologists working at this level also stress the significance of the wider cultural repertoire from which social actors construct their strategies of action. This more fluid approach to culture has the strength of giving analytic purchase on diversity, since a variety of meanings may be embraced by people in the same context, or even by the same person at different times (as in Eliasoph's investigation of the ways people might understand politics). It also creates theoretical space for understanding the importance of culture in structural change, since variant and shifting interpretations may be the mechanisms or conditions of changes in structural patterns (as in the arguments of Swidler about cultural practices, and Sewell about transposable schemas).

The second line of inquiry exemplified here examines meaning-making processes as they occur within fields of institutions or networks of cultural producers, treating culture as a social product like any other and highlighting the specific contexts in which cultural production and innovation occurs. The focus here is on how the particular organizational context in which, for instance, art is created, or a new musical style disseminated, or science practiced, can have important consequences for the emergent cultural product. Much of the research in this area applies this "production of culture" perspective to specialized cultural artifacts and genres. But the perspective can also be used to examine the impact of institutional context on more diffuse sets of symbols, meanings, and values. Like the earlier sociology of knowledge, but unlike earlier approaches which drew very broad connections between culture and society, the point of this approach is to examine more specific, historically located, and contingent meaning-making processes for how their social contexts influence particular cultural outcomes. Thus, for instance, Larson examines how postmodern architecture is a product of particular professional contexts more than large-scale, world-historical changes, and Peterson attributes the emergence of rock music to industry changes rather than to large-scale demographic changes.

If the first two approaches examine meaning-making processes "on the ground," and "in the institutional field," the third approach in cultural sociology investigates meaning-making "in the text," focusing on features of culture intrinsic to meaning-making processes themselves and drawing on insights about textual analysis more familiar in the humanities than in sociology. Cultural repertoires, objects, and texts are analytically distinguished from their social contexts and treated as independent objects of inquiry. By analogy with languages, they are assumed to have their own internal structure; this internal structure is consequential for the ways meanings are generated. Cultural sociologists have drawn analytic tools for understanding deep cultural structure rather freely from a variety of interdisciplinary sources: some common concepts include the notions of symbolic codes, signifiers and sign systems, categorical schemas, genre, and narrative. However, unlike discourse analysis which focused only on textual features, sociologists adopting these tools tend to make close connections between textual properties and the ways in which they are influenced by and influential for individual and institutional meaning-making practices. So, for instance, Jacobs traces the way difference and change in narrative structure was important for the public reaction to the Rodney King beating in Los Angeles.

Of course, exploring meaning-making "on the ground," "in the institutional field," and "in the text" are not mutually exclusive: some of the richest contributions in cultural sociology have carefully combined these levels of analysis. Many of the works excerpted here, though focusing primarily on one aspect of meaning-making, also examine other dimensions in the longer books and articles from which they are drawn. Often, a complete explanation of why aspects of culture vary, or how meaning-making influences human action in particular contexts, will necessarily integrate different levels of analysis. But unless these different levels of analysis are recognized, it is easy to assume that looking at only one dimension can provide a complete cultural account. One of the achievements of recent cultural sociology is that such reductionism – to interactions, institutions, or texts – is now widely resisted as implausible, and dialogues between researchers doing each type of research are fruitful.

Treating meaning-making as occurring simultaneously in these different ways can also help transcend fruitless conflicts between views that culture is essentially consensual and views that culture – ideology – reflects power relations. First, looking at meaning-making "on the ground," as the variable enactment of symbolic repertoires, allows for difference and conflict within and between social groups: the amount of consensus in a particular case is fundamentally open to empirical question (as in Bryson's examination of the ways status conflicts emerge in musical taste). But analyzing culture "on the ground" also challenges views of culture as ideology, because ambiguity in cultural repertoires, human agency, and historical contingency all suggest that cultural domination isn't simply a matter of misleading people about their interests (or as Marx would have called it, creating false consciousness). Second, looking at meaning-making "in the institutional field" and "in the text" also helps identify many sources of variation and indeterminacy in the process which make overgeneralized claims about consensus or ideological domination difficult to sustain (as in Griswold's examination of the "American" novel, or Berezin's study of Fascist theater).

Sociologists have also been divided between those who are most interested in micro-social processes (asking questions about the attitudes of individuals, for instance, or analyzing aspects of interaction) and those who are most interested in macro-social processes (trying to understand the organization and main features of whole groups and societies). Cultural sociology provides ways of thinking about meaning-making which can help bridge this perennial division. For instance, Schudson addresses processes by which individuals' ways of thinking are meshed with broadly available ideas, and Alexander and Smith identify underlying ways of thinking which persistently influence a variety of political attitudes. Like language, meaning-making processes more broadly considered simultaneously encompass both subjective experience and the wider social sphere within which that subjective experience is constructed. So the identities and practices of individuals and small groups are constructed from cultural resources which themselves depend on two wider conditions; the social organization of meaning production, and the discursive frameworks which structure available meanings. And yet these macro-social phenomena are ultimately composed in micro-practices of meaning-making. Thinking of culture as meaning-making at three different levels helps think through how the "micro" and "macro" in society are connected more precisely. One advantage of this greater conceptual precision is a new understanding of how culture is relevant to processes of social change. And, indeed, whereas sociologists formerly considered culture to be mostly a force for the preservation of the status quo, cultural sociologists now make numerous contributions to studies of social change, as in the selections in Part V.

About this Reader

I have suggested here that although ideas about culture are complicated and ambiguous, due to the various historical forces shaping our use of the term, many of these difficulties may be resolved, and the usefulness of the concept retained, if we consider culture as meaning-making. In this sense, understanding cultural processes is important to many scholars, and sociologists interested in meaning-making draw from a variety of interdisciplinary sources. But, especially in the United States, their work is also shaped by a more specific intellectual history and institutional context. This particular institutional history has generated three mid-range approaches which give American cultural sociology a distinctive perspective on cultural analysis compared to the work of cultural analysts in other intellectual contexts. These approaches distinguish between and analyze meaning-making in everyday practice, meaning-making in organized cultural production, and meaning-making as a textual process. Using these approaches cultural sociologists now bridge earlier conceptual divisions with work which provides new insights into social solidarity, conflict, and change.

The excerpts in this volume illustrate the influential ideas and perspectives identified above, and are organized accordingly. Part I introduces some key issues in cultural sociology as discussed in some classics of the field. Part II presents contemporary studies of meaning-making "on the ground," examining some of the ways individuals construct and reconstruct their interpretations of their actions, identities, and groups. Part III treats meaning-making "in the organizational field," providing examples of studies of cultural production. Examples of the work of cultural sociologists who emphasize the ways textual features influence meaning-making possibilities are featured in Part IV. Finally, Part V presents studies of cultural innovation and social change that demonstrate the ways insights from the subfield are now addressing questions at the center of the sociological imagination.

Although selections within each section share an orientation, they differ in empirical topics and methodology, and readers may wish to combine them in different ways. For instance, an introduction to "meaning-making and the media" could begin with readings from Horkheimer and Adorno, Bryson, Hunt, Schudson, Peterson, Cerulo, and Jacobs; an introduction to "class, status, and culture" might include readings from Bourdieu, Kunda, Lamont, Bryson, and Zerubavel; or readers especially interested in ethnographic research could start with excerpts from work by Geertz, Kunda, Eliasoph, and Lichterman. One aim in assembling the collection has been to create flexible options for scholars and students with different interests. Some of the thematic linkages between selections are mentioned in the accompanying editor's notes.

Editor's notes are also included for several other purposes. First, because each excerpt is heavily edited, much of what authors have to say about how they drew on previous work and how they justify their claims cannot be included here. Critical readers should look further into the author's work. Second, each editor's note is intended to provide leads for understanding the wider context in which authors set their works and the intellectual context which makes the work significant or representative. Each excerpt is a portal to broader issues and traditions of investigation and reflection, and the editor's notes point to some of the many intriguing pathways interested readers may follow beyond what can be included here.

Finally, the notes following each selection are intended to allow readers to explore more of the important work currently being done in cultural sociology. Of course, editing a sampler like this involves many selection difficulties. I hope the general benefits of an introductory collection ultimately outweigh problems of exclusion, and I encourage readers to treat this collection as a guide to other studies of the social process of meaning-making, rather than simply a cheat sheet to the field. Editor's notes are settings for small gems and reminders that digging deeper for more riches will be rewarding.

Cultural Sociology as an Agenda

So I exemplify in the following selections what I see as the particular angle of vision with which cultural sociology approaches meaning-making processes, a perspective which shares a lot with common views and with scholarly work in other fields, but a perspective also shaped by sociology, especially American sociology, as an institution. Regrettably, this intellectual context means that some sorts of omissions from this collection are not simply a matter of limited space. First, several genres of contemporary scholarship profoundly concerned with meaning-making – such as science studies, social postmodernism, and cultural studies – are not represented here, even though these fields have a lot to offer any student of culture. Likewise, several long-established angles on cultural analysis, like communications studies, or intellectual history, are not included, even though scholars in such fields could argue that they have been covering similar terrain for a long time. But while cultural sociologists certainly draw on these fields, their institutional base in American sociology means that their approach to similar problems is shaped by different intellectual assumptions, and they speak and write to different colleagues and audiences. As Smith has argued, American cultural sociology ultimately works within disciplinary boundaries, rather than transcending or challenging them, even though it is more interdisciplinary than many other areas of sociology. One future challenge for scholars in the field will be to maintain openness and avoid some of the intellectual blinkers this context could impose, even while preserving the benefits it brings.[15]

Second, some empirical topics have been underemphasized (though not entirely neglected). Cultural sociology as an institutionalized subdiscipline has probably focused until now more on topics like class and status, political culture, and social change than on equally viable topics like gender, crime, religion, or organizations, and this anthology reflects that tendency. It is possible that future work in the field will deal with such topics more frequently. But it is also possible that where sociological research on empirical topics like gender or organizations already has a strong institutional base, the incorporation of cultural approaches is primarily oriented to audiences interested in those particular subjects, rather than in cultural sociology broadly considered. So these omissions, though systematic, are not so much a limitation of the field as an indicator of the wider success of "the cultural turn" in twentieth-century scholarship. Further success in "mainstreaming" cultural analysis in sociology could, ironically, encourage the dissipation of cultural sociology as a specialization.

But there are intellectual as well as institutional reasons why this seems an unlikely outcome. Cultural sociology as an analytic perspective, rather than a particular topic, has generated conceptual innovation on a variety of issues important across sociology, such as problematic assumptions about cultural consensus, links between attitudes and behavior, the implausibility of viewing the powerless as "cultural dopes," and problems in operationalizing the links between big social structures like capitalism and mass culture. I've suggested above that cultural sociologists found new approaches which could help address these issues, approaches which could be applied in a variety of empirical arenas.

Similarly, cultural sociologists are well positioned to offer empirically grounded reflection and new theoretical resolutions for several other general problems now emerging on sociological agendas. These issues could include:

1   pursuing the implications in general sociological research of the observation that whether or not most individuals agree with particular cultural discourses (like "culture wars" or "individualism") the general recognition and circulation of such discourses creates important social facts;

2   incorporating neglected theories of cultural diffusion into theories of large-scale cultural innovation and social change;

3   reconciling two potentially contradictory lines of research currently being integrated into cultural sociology from social psychology, one focusing on cognition, and the other focusing on emotions;

4   developing a richer view of causality which includes extensive attention to meaning-making processes as causal mechanisms;

5   encouraging wider recognition of criteria for designing and assessing qualitative, interpretive, and critical research so that it is neither dismissed as idiosyncratic nor lauded as unreproducibly virtuoso; and

6   communicating research findings and newer ways of thinking about meaning-making in ways that will be useful in activism or policy-making. Understanding what makes things meaningful to people is surely an important step in any attempt at viable and humane social change.

Although this agenda is necessarily sketchy here, it does suggest that cultural sociology can have a wide impact. All these issues – the social consequences of discourse independent of majority belief, cultural diffusion in social change, cognition and emotion in meaning-making processes, causal mechanisms, assessing interpretive research, and meaning-making in sociological practice – are important for furthering general sociological understanding. They also exemplify issues on which cultural sociologists have a lot to contribute, both empirically and theoretically.

But the impact of any future contributions like these will depend on demystifying common confusions about culture and disseminating to a broader audience the conceptual advances and empirical richness in contemporary cultural sociology. I hope that this collection helps in that process.

Notes

1   Some of the ambiguities in the term are discussed in Raymond Williams, "Culture," pp. 76–82 in *Keywords: A Vocabulary of Culture and Society* (New York: Oxford University Press, 1976), and Neil Smelser, "Culture: Coherent or Incoherent," pp. 3–28 in Richard Münch and Neil J. Smelser, eds., *Theory of Culture* (Berkeley: University of California Press, 1992). For an explanation of definitional proliferation see Russell Faeges,

"Why Define?" Paper presented at the American Political Science Association Meetings, Atlanta, August 1999. Social scientists have sometimes dismissed cultural analysis because of their view that earlier approaches lacked conceptual clarity. For instance, some charge that cultural explanations focus on "primordial constants that undergird everything" and thus cannot help to account for change, conflict and difference, or they are "purely ad hoc; they simply do not fit the evidence, and they certainly contradict each other." These particular statements of the view occur in Gary G. Hamilton and Nicole Woolsey Biggart, "Market, Culture, and Authority: A Comparative Analysis of Management and Organization in the Far East," *American Journal of Sociology* (Supplement) 94 (1988): S52–S94: 195, and Margaret Levi, "The Institution of Conscription," *Social Science History* 20 (1996): 154.

2   As Erving Goffman once suggested, "what we think of as a relationship is, in one sense, merely a provision for the use of cryptic expressions." Goffman, "Felicity's Condition," *American Journal of Sociology* 89 (1983): 42.

3   On the development of a comparative way of thinking about culture see George W. Stocking, *Race, Culture and Evolution* (New York: The Free Press, 1968), and John H. Rowe, "The Renaissance Foundations of Anthropology," *American Anthropologist* 67 (1965): 1–20. See also Alfred L. Kroeber and Clyde Kluckhohn, *Culture: A Critical Review of Concepts and Definitions* (New York: Vintage Books, 1963 [1952]) for a detailed though ultimately inconclusive review of concepts of culture in classical anthropology, and more evidence of the definitional proliferation associated with the term.

4   The view that the cultures of different peoples could be arranged in a hierarchy with the cultures of western countries at the pinnacle was clearly demonstrated in the organization of international exhibitions in the late nineteenth century. See Robert Rydell, *All the World's A Fair: Visions of Empire at American International Expositions, 1876–1916* (Chicago and London: University of Chicago Press, 1984); Paul Greenhalgh, *Ephemeral Vistas: The Expositions Universelles, Great Exhibitions, and World's Fairs, 1851–1939* (Manchester: Manchester University Press, 1988), and Lyn Spillman, *Nation and Commemoration: Creating National Identities in the United States and Australia* (Cambridge and New York: Cambridge University Press, 1997), ch. 3. Anthropologist Franz Boas was important in developing an idea of culture which was more plural and relative (Stocking 1968: 198–233), and a significant mentor and colleague of Ruth Benedict, whose work is excerpted in this volume.

5   Simmel, excerpted here, echoes but develops the notion of culture as a separate, more valuable sphere by distinguishing between objective culture (which threatens to overwhelm the individual in modern society) and subjective culture (which expresses higher values of individuality).

6   Characterizing culture as meaning-making *process* echoes the early meaning of the term in English. According to Raymond Williams, "culture" was originally a noun of process – referring to the process of nurturing crops or animals – not a noun referring to an abstract human product. During the Renaissance, the word was applied metaphorically to human development processes – as in "the culture of minds." It was only in the late eighteenth and early nineteenth century that "culture" came to refer to an abstract product.

    The formulation of cultural sociology's primary focus as meaning-making is also suggested in the Symposium on Culture and Meaning in *Contemporary Sociology* 29 (4) July 2000: see especially David R. Maines, "The Social Construction of Meaning," 577–84, Barry Glassner, "Where Meanings Get Constructed," 590–94, and Michèle Lamont, "Meaning-Making in Cultural Sociology: Broadening Our Agenda," 602–7. See also Wendy Griswold, *Cultures and Societies in a Changing World* (Thousand Oaks, CA: Pine Forge Press, 1994), ch. 2.

7   Terry Eagleton, *Ideology: An Introduction* (London: Verso, 1991), 7. For a comprehensive contemporary discussion of many of the definitional issues sketched here see also Terry Eagleton, *The Idea of Culture* (Oxford and Malden, MA: Blackwell, 2000).

8   I have argued elsewhere that processes of meaning-making should be theoretically distinguished from social structures: see Lyn Spillman, "Culture, Social Structure, and Discursive Fields," *Current Perspectives in Social Theory*, 15 (1995): 129–54, and "How are Structures Meaningful? Cultural Sociology and Theories of Social Structure," *Humboldt Journal of Social Relations*, Special Issue, "Recent Advances in Theory and Research in Social Structure," 22 (1996): 31–45. However, distinguishing culture and social structure is more controversial than making the distinction between cultural and biological or psychological explanation. Most cultural sociologists probably lean to the alternative "embeddedness" view, that social structures are fundamentally cultural, represented in this volume by the excerpt from the work of Sewell. Here, it is sufficient to stress that a focus on culture is different from a focus on social structure even if social structures are defined as culturally embedded.

9   Philip Smith, "The New American Cultural Sociology: An Introduction," pp. 1–14 in Philip Smith, ed., *The New American Cultural Sociology* (Cambridge and New York: Cambridge University Press, 1998).

10   On the context and concerns shaping the origins of sociology see Robert A. Nisbet, *The Sociological Tradition* (New Brunswick, NJ: Transaction Publishers, 1993 [1966]). The different emphases in anthropology and sociology are evident in the conceptual division of labor proposed in A. L. Kroeber and Talcott Parsons, "The Concepts of Culture and of Social System," *American Sociological Review* 23 (1958): 582–3.

     For an introduction to classical perspectives on culture see Jeffrey Alexander, "Analytic Debates: Understanding the Relative Autonomy of Culture," pp. 1–27 in Jeffrey C. Alexander and Steven Seidman, *Culture and Society: Contemporary Debates* (Cambridge and New York: Cambridge University Press, 1990). For a useful discussion of culture in early American sociology see Elizabeth Long, "Introduction: Engaging Sociology and Cultural Studies: Disciplinarity and Social Change," pp. 1–32 in Elizabeth Long, ed., *From Sociology to Cultural Studies* (Malden, MA and Oxford: Blackwell, 1997). It is important to note here that although selections from the work of classical sociological theorists have not been included in this volume, this omission does not imply that their work is no longer crucial to cultural sociology. On the contrary, any serious study of the field demands a broader knowledge and deeper understanding of classical cultural arguments than anthologizing allows. Students could begin with Karl Marx, *The German Ideology*, Part One, "Estranged Labour" (from "Economic and Philosophical Manuscripts of 1844") and "The Fetishism of Commodities and the Secret Thereof" (from *Capital*, Volume 1), all reprinted in Robert Tucker, ed., *The Marx–Engels Reader*, 2nd edn. (New York: Norton, 1978), pp. 146–200, pp. 70–81, and pp. 319–29 respectively; Emile Durkheim, *The Elementary Forms of Religious Life* trans. Karen Fields (New York: Free Press, 1995), especially pp. 1–44, 99–126, 207–41 and 303–448; Max Weber, *The Protestant Ethic and the Spirit of Capitalism* 2nd edn. (Los Angeles: Roxbury, 1998), and "The Social Psychology of the World Religions," pp. 267–301 in H. H. Gerth and C. Wright Mills, eds., *From Max Weber: Essays in Sociology* (New York: Oxford University Press, 1946); and George Herbert Mead, *Mind, Self, and Society*, Charles Morris, ed. (Chicago and London: University of Chicago Press, 1962 [1934]), pp. 61–90, 135–64, 173–8, and 192–226.

11   On the sociology of knowledge see Robert Merton, "The Sociology of Knowledge," pp. 510–42 in *Social Theory and Social Structure* (New York: The Free Press, 1968); Peter Berger, *Invitation to Sociology: A Humanistic Perspective* (Doubleday: New York, 1963), 110–18; and for a comparison with contemporary cultural sociology, see Ann

Swidler and Jorge Arditi, "The New Sociology of Knowledge," *Annual Review of Sociology* 20 (1994): 305–29. On symbolic interactionism see for example Herbert Blumer, *Symbolic Interactionism: Perspective and Method* (Englewood Cliffs, NJ: Prentice-Hall, 1969) and Howard Becker and Michal McCall, eds., *Symbolic Interactionism and Cultural Studies* (Chicago and London: University of Chicago Press, 1990).

12 For an example and extension building on what I have labeled here the "consensus" view see excerpt from the work of Shils, this volume; other important scholars worth reading for related work are Talcott Parsons, Seymour Martin Lipset, and (in his early work) Neil Smelser. Examples and extensions building on the "ideology" view can be found in excerpts from the work of Horkheimer and Adorno, and Raymond Williams; important related work includes that of Georg Lukács, Antonio Gramsci, Alvin Gouldner, and Louis Althusser.

13 These and the following examples are excerpted in this collection.

14 This discussion is based on Spillman (1995).

15 Smith (1998), 6–12. For related discussions of science studies, see Chandra Mukerji, "Towards a Sociology of Material Culture: Science Studies, Cultural Studies, and the Meanings of Things," pp. 143–62 in Diana Crane, ed., *The Sociology of Culture* (Oxford and Cambridge, MA: Blackwell, 1994) and Daniel Breslau, "Sociology after Humanism: A Lesson from Contemporary Science Studies," *Sociological Theory* 18 (2000): 289–307. On social postmodernism see Linda Nicholson and Steven Seidman, eds., *Social Postmodernism: Beyond Identity Politics* (Cambridge and New York: Cambridge University Press, 1995) and editor's notes on excerpts from work by Jameson, and Larson, this volume. On cultural studies see the many useful articles in Elizabeth Long, ed. *From Sociology to Cultural Studies* (Malden, MA and Oxford: Blackwell, 1997); Lawrence Grossberg, Cary Nelson and Paula Treichler, eds., *Cultural Studies* (New York and London: Routledge, 1992); and Janet Wolff, "Cultural Studies and Sociology of Culture," *Contemporary Sociology* 28 (1999): 499–507. Wolff criticizes American cultural sociology as too positivist, claiming that it does not sufficiently recognize that "the real" is representation. Although she articulates an important difference in emphasis, many cultural sociologists would argue that both cultural sociology and cultural studies begin with the elementary anti-positivist observation that the real is representation, but go in different directions with the same observation. On why sociologists in general and cultural sociologists in particular should engage more seriously with cultural studies, see Sharon Hays, "Constructing the Centrality of Culture – and Deconstructing Sociology," *Contemporary Sociology* 29 (2000): 594–602.

Part I

Analyzing Culture in Society:
Key Ideas

1 The Diversity of Cultures

Ruth Benedict

A chief of the Digger Indians, as the Californians call them, talked to me a great deal about the ways of his people in the old days. He was a Christian and a leader among his people in the planting of peaches and apricots on irrigated land, but when he talked of the shamans who had transformed themselves into bears before his eyes in the bear dance, his hands trembled and his voice broke with excitement. It was an incomparable thing, the power his people had had in the old days. He liked best to talk of the desert foods they had eaten. He brought each uprooted plant lovingly and with an unfailing sense of its importance. In those days his people had eaten 'the health of the desert,' he said, and knew nothing of the insides of tin cans and the things for sale at butcher shops. It was such innovations that had degraded them in these latter days.

One day, without transition, Ramon broke in upon his descriptions of grinding mesquite and preparing acorn soup. 'In the beginning,' he said, 'God gave to every people a cup, a cup of clay, and from this cup they drank their life.' I do not know whether the figure occurred in some traditional ritual of his people that I never found, or whether it was his own imagery. It is hard to imagine that he had heard it from the whites he had known at Banning; they were not given to discussing the ethos of different peoples. At any rate, in the mind of this humble Indian the figure of speech was clear and full of meaning. 'They all dipped in the water,' he continued, 'but their cups were different. Our cup is broken now. It has passed away.'

Our cup is broken. Those things that had given significance to the life of his people, the domestic rituals of eating, the obligations of the economic system, the succession of ceremonials in the villages, possession in the bear dance, their standards of right and wrong – these were gone, and with them the shape and meaning of their life. The old man was still vigorous and a leader in relationships with the whites. He did not mean that there was any question of the extinction of his people. But he had in mind the loss of something that had value equal to that of life itself, the whole fabric of his people's standards and beliefs. There were other cups of living left, and they held perhaps the same water, but the loss was irreparable. It was no matter of tinkering with an addition here, lopping off something there. The modelling had been fundamental, it was somehow all of a piece. It had been their own.

Ramon had had personal experience of the matter of which he spoke. He straddled two cultures whose values and ways of thought were incommensurable. It is a hard fate. In Western civilization our experiences have been different. We are bred to one cosmopolitan culture, and our social sciences, our psychology, and our theology persistently ignore the truth expressed in Ramon's figure.

The course of life and the pressure of environment, not to speak of the fertility of human imagination, provide an incredible number of possible leads, all of which, it appears, may serve a society to live by. There are the schemes of ownership, with the social hierarchy that may be associated with possessions; there are material things and their elaborate technology; there are all the facets of sex life, parenthood and post-parenthood; there are the guilds or cults which may give structure to the society; there is economic exchange; there are the gods and supernatural sanctions. Each one of these and many more may be followed out with a cultural and ceremonial elaboration which monopolizes the cultural energy and leaves small surplus for the building of other traits. Aspects of life that seem to us most important have been passed over with small regard by peoples whose culture, oriented in another direction, has been far from poor. Or the same trait may be so greatly elaborated that we reckon it as fantastic.

It is in cultural life as it is in speech; selection is the prime necessity. The numbers of sounds that can be produced by our vocal cords and our oral and nasal cavities are practically unlimited. The three or four dozen of the English language are a selection which coincides not even with those of such closely related dialects as German and French. The total that are used in different languages of the world no one has even dared to estimate. But each language must make its selection and abide by it on pain of not being intelligible at all. A language that used even a few hundreds of the possible – and actually recorded – phonetic elements could not be used for communication. On the other hand a great deal of our misunderstanding of languages unrelated to our own has arisen from our attempts to refer alien phonetic systems back to ours as a point of reference. We recognize only one k. If other people have five k sounds placed in different positions in the throat and mouth, distinctions of vocabulary and of syntax that depend on these differences are impossible to us until we master them. We have a d and an n. They may have an intermediate sound which, if we fail to identify it, we write now d and now n, introducing distinctions which do not exist. The elementary prerequisite of linguistic analysis is a consciousness of these incredibly numerous available sounds from which each language makes its own selections.

In culture too we must imagine a great arc on which are ranged the possible interests provided either by the human age-cycle or by the environment or by man's various activities. A culture that capitalized even a considerable proportion of these would be as unintelligible as a language that used all the clicks, all the glottal stops, all the labials, dentals, sibilants, and gutturals from voiceless to voiced and from oral to nasal. Its identity as a culture depends upon the selection of some segments of this arc. Every human society everywhere has made such selection in its cultural institutions. Each from the point of view of another ignores fundamentals and exploits irrelevancies. One culture hardly recognizes monetary values; another has made them fundamental in every field of behaviour. In one society technology is unbelievably slighted even in those aspects of life which seem necessary to ensure survival; in another, equally simple, technological achievements are complex and fitted with admirable nicety to the situation. One builds an enormous cultural superstructure upon adolescence, one upon death, one upon after-life.

The case of adolescence is particularly interesting, because it is in the limelight in our own civilization and because we have plentiful information from other cultures. In our own civilization a whole library of psychological studies has emphasized the inevitable unrest of the period of puberty. It is in our tradition a physiological state as definitely characterized by domestic explosions and rebellion as typhoid is marked by fever. There is no question of the facts. They are common in America. The question is rather of their inevitability.

The most casual survey of the ways in which different societies have handled adolescence makes one fact inescapable: even in those cultures which have made most of the trait, the age upon which they focus their attention varies over a great range of years. At the outset, therefore, it is clear that the so-called puberty institutions are a misnomer if we continue to think of biological puberty. The puberty they recognize is social, and the ceremonies are a recognition in some fashion or other of the child's new status of adulthood. This investiture with new occupations and obligations is in consequence as various and as culturally conditioned as the occupations and obligations themselves. If the sole honourable duty of manhood is conceived to be deeds of war, the investiture of the warrior is later and of a different sort from that in a society where adulthood gives chiefly the privilege of dancing in a representation of masked gods. In order to understand puberty institutions, we do not most need analyses of the necessary nature of *rites de passage*; we need rather to know what is identified in different cultures with the beginning of adulthood and their methods of admitting to the new status. Not biological puberty, but what adulthood means in that culture conditions the puberty ceremony.

Adulthood in central North America means warfare. Honour in it is the great goal of all men. The constantly recurring theme of the youth's coming-of-age, as also of preparation for the warpath at any age, is a magic ritual for success in war. They torture not one another, but themselves: they cut strips of skin from their arms and legs, they strike off their fingers, they drag heavy weights pinned to their chest or leg muscles. Their reward is enhanced prowess in deeds of warfare.

In Australia, on the other hand, adulthood means participation in an exclusively male cult whose fundamental trait is the exclusion of women. Any woman is put to death if she so much as hears the sound of the bull-roarer at the ceremonies, and she must never know of the rites. Puberty ceremonies are elaborate and symbolic repudiations of the bonds with the female sex; the men are symbolically made self-sufficient and the wholly responsible element of the community. To attain this end they use drastic sexual rites and bestow supernatural guaranties.

The clear physiological facts of adolescence, therefore, are first socially interpreted even where they are stressed. But a survey of puberty institutions makes clear a further fact: puberty is physiologically a different matter in the life-cycle of the male and the female. If cultural emphasis followed the physiological emphasis, girls' ceremonies would be more marked than boys'; but it is not so. The ceremonies emphasize a social fact: the adult prerogatives of men are more far-reaching in every culture than women's, and consequently, as in the above instances, it is more common for societies to take note of this period in boys than in girls.

Girls' and boys' puberty, however, may be socially celebrated in the same tribe in identical ways. Where, as in the interior of British Columbia, adolescent rites are a magical training for all occupations, girls are included on the same terms as boys. Boys roll stones down mountains and beat them to the bottom to be swift of foot, or throw gambling-sticks to be lucky in gambling; girls carry water from distant springs, or drop stones down inside their dresses that their children may be born as easily as the pebble drops to the ground.

In such a tribe as the Nandi of the lake region of East Africa, also, girls and boys share an even-handed puberty rite, though, because of the man's dominant role in the culture, his boyhood training period is more stressed than the woman's. Here

2 The Metropolis and Mental Life

Georg Simmel

The deepest problems of modern life flow from the attempt of the individual to maintain the independence and individuality of his existence against the sovereign powers of society, against the weight of the historical heritage and the external culture and technique of life. This antagonism represents the most modern form of the conflict which primitive man must carry on with nature for his own bodily existence. The eighteenth century may have called for liberation from all the ties which grew up historically in politics, in religion, in morality and in economics in order to permit the original natural virtue of man, which is equal in everyone, to develop without inhibition; the nineteenth century may have sought to promote, in addition to man's freedom, his individuality (which is connected with the division of labor) and his achievements which make him unique and indispensable but which at the same time make him so much the more dependent on the complementary activity of others; Nietzsche may have seen the relentless struggle of the individual as the prerequisite for his full development, while Socialism found the same thing in the suppression of all competition – but in each of these the same fundamental motive was at work, namely the resistance of the individual to being levelled, swallowed up in the social-technological mechanism. When one inquires about the products of the specifically modern aspects of contemporary life with reference to their inner meaning – when, so to speak, one examines the body of culture with reference to the soul, as I am to do concerning the metropolis today – the answer will require the investigation of the relationship which such a social structure promotes between the individual aspects of life and those which transcend the existence of single individuals. It will require the investigation of the adaptations made by the personality in its adjustment to the forces that lie outside of it.

The psychological foundation, upon which the metropolitan individuality is erected, is the intensification of emotional life due to the swift and continuous shift of external and internal stimuli. Man is a creature whose existence is dependent on differences, i.e., his mind is stimulated by the difference between present impressions and those which have preceded. Lasting impressions, the slightness in their differences, the habituated regularity of their course and contrasts between them, consume, so to speak, less mental energy than the rapid telescoping of changing images, pronounced differences within what is grasped at a single glance, and the unexpectedness of violent stimuli. To the extent that the metropolis creates these psychological conditions – with every crossing of the street, with the tempo and multiplicity of economic, occupational and social life – it creates in the sensory foundations of mental life, and in the degree of awareness necessitated by our organization as creatures dependent on differences, a deep contrast with the slower, more habitual, more smoothly flowing rhythm of the sensory-mental phase of small town and rural existence. Thereby the essentially intellectualistic character of the mental life of the metropolis becomes intelligible as over against that of the small town which rests more on feelings and emotional relationships. These latter are rooted in the unconscious levels of the mind and develop most readily in the steady equilibrium of unbroken customs. The locus of reason, on the other hand, is in the lucid, conscious upper strata of the mind and it is the most adaptable of our inner forces. In order to adjust itself to the shifts and contradictions in events, it does not require the disturbances and inner upheavals which are the only means whereby more conservative personalities are able to adapt themselves to the same rhythm of events. Thus the metropolitan type – which naturally takes on a thousand individual modifications – creates a protective organ for itself against the profound disruption with which the fluctuations and discontinuities of the external milieu threaten it. Instead of reacting emotionally, the metropolitan type reacts primarily in a rational manner, thus creating a mental predominance through the intensification of consciousness, which in turn is caused by it. Thus the reaction of the metropolitan person to those events is moved to a sphere of mental activity which is least sensitive and which is furthest removed from the depths of the personality.

This intellectualistic quality which is thus recognized as a protection of the inner life against the domination of the metropolis, becomes ramified into numerous specific phenomena. The metropolis has always been the seat of money economy because the many-sidedness and concentration of commercial activity have given the medium of exchange an importance which it could not have acquired in the commercial aspects of rural life. But money economy and the domination of the intellect stand in the closest relationship to one another. They have in common a purely matter-of-fact attitude in the treatment of persons and things in which a formal justice is often combined with an unrelenting hardness. The purely intellectualistic person is indifferent to all things personal because, out of them, relationships and reactions develop which are not to be completely understood by purely rational methods – just as the unique element in events never enters into the principle of money. Money is concerned only with what is common to all, i.e., with the exchange value which reduces all quality and individuality to a purely quantitative level. All emotional relationships between persons rest on their individuality, whereas intellectual relationships deal with persons as with numbers, that is, as with elements which, in themselves, are indifferent, but which are of interest only insofar as they offer something objectively perceivable. It is in this very manner that the inhabitant of the metropolis reckons with his merchant, his customer, and with his servant, and frequently with the persons with whom he is thrown into obligatory association. These relationships stand in distinct contrast with the nature of the smaller circle in which the inevitable knowledge of individual characteristics produces, with an equal inevitability, an emotional tone in conduct, a sphere which is beyond the mere objective weighting of tasks performed and payments made. What is essential here as regards the economic-psychological aspect of the problem is that in less advanced cultures production was for the customer who ordered the product so that the producer and the purchaser knew one another. The modern city, however, is supplied almost exclusively by production for the market, that is, for entirely unknown purchasers who never appear in the actual field of vision of the producers themselves. Thereby, the interests of each party acquire a relentness matter-of-factness, and its rationally calculated economic egoism need not fear any divergence from its must be designated as "the general human character" in the intellectual development of our species. For the correlation, the factual as well as the historical validity of which we are here maintaining, is that the broadest and the most general contents and forms of life are intimately bound up with the most individual ones. Both have a common prehistory and also common enemies in the narrow formations and groupings, whose striving for self-preservation set them in conflict with the broad and general on the outside, as well as the freely mobile and individual on the inside. Just as in feudal times the "free" man was he who stood under the law of the land, that is, under the law of the largest social unit, but he was unfree who derived his legal rights only from the narrow circle of a feudal community – so today in an intellectualized and refined sense the citizen of the metropolis is "free" in contrast with the trivialities and prejudices which bind the small town person. The mutual reserve and indifference, and the intellectual conditions of life in large social units are never more sharply appreciated in their significance for the independence of the individual than in the dense crowds of the metropolis because the bodily closeness and lack of space make intellectual distance really perceivable for the first time. It is obviously only the obverse of this freedom that, under certain circumstances, one never feels as lonely and as deserted as in this metropolitan crush of persons. For here, as elsewhere, it is by no means necessary that the freedom of man reflect itself in his emotional life only as a pleasant experience.

It is not only the immediate size of the area and population which, on the basis of world-historical correlation between the increase in the size of the social unit and the degree of personal inner and outer freedom, makes the metropolis the locus of this condition. It is rather in transcending this purely tangible extensiveness that the metropolis also becomes the seat of cosmopolitanism. Comparable with the form of the development of wealth – (beyond a certain point property increases in ever more rapid progression as out of its own inner being) – the individual's horizon is enlarged. In the same way, economic, personal and intellectual relations in the city (which are its ideal reflection), grow in a geometrical progression as soon as, for the first time, a certain limit has been passed. Every dynamic extension becomes a preparation not only for a similar extension but rather for a larger one and from every thread which is spun out of it there continue, growing as out of themselves, an endless number of others. This may be illustrated by the fact that within the city the "unearned increment" of ground rent, through a mere increase in traffic, brings to the owner profits which are self-generating. At this point the quantitative aspects of life are transformed qualitatively. The sphere of life of the small town is, in the main, enclosed within itself. For the metropolis it is decisive that its inner life is extended in a wave-like motion over a broader national or international area. Weimar was no exception because its significance was dependent upon individual personalities and died with them, whereas the metropolis is characterised by its essential independence even of the most significant individual personalities; this is rather its antithesis and it is the price of independence which the individual living in it enjoys. The most significant aspect of the metropolis lies in this functional magnitude beyond its actual physical boundaries and this effectiveness reacts upon the latter and gives to it life, weight, importance and responsibility. A person does not end with limits of his physical body or with the area to which his physical activity is immediately confined but embraces, rather, the totality of meaningful effects which emanates

from him temporally and spatially. In the same way the city exists only in the totality of the effects which transcend their immediate sphere. These really are the actual
extent in which their existence is expressed. This is already expressed in the fact
that individual freedom, which is the logical historical complement of such extension, is not only to be understood in the negative sense as mere freedom of movement and emancipation from prejudices and philistinism. Its essential characteristic
is rather to be found in the fact that the particularity and incomparability which
ultimately every person possesses in some way is actually expressed, giving
form to life. That we follow the laws of our inner nature – and this is what freedom
is – becomes perceptible and convincing to us and to others only when the expressions of this nature distinguish themselves from others; it is our irreplaceability by
others which shows that our mode of existence is not imposed upon us from the
outside.

Cities are above all the seat of the most advanced economic division of labor. They
produce such extreme phenomena as the lucrative vocation of the *quatorzieme* in
Paris. These are persons who may be recognized by shields on their houses and who
hold themselves ready at the dinner hour in appropriate costumes so they can be
called upon on short notice in case thirteen persons find themselves at the table.
Exactly in the measure of its extension the city offers to an increasing degree the
determining conditions for the division of labor. It is a unit which, because of its
large size, is receptive to a highly diversified plurality of achievements while at the
same time the agglomeration of individuals and their struggle for the customer
forces the individual to a type of specialized accomplishment in which he cannot
be so easily exterminated by the other. The decisive fact here is that in the life of a
city, struggle with nature for the means of life is transformed into a conflict with
human beings and the gain which is fought for is granted, not by nature, but by man.
For here we find not only the previously mentioned source of specialization but
rather the deeper one in which the seller must seek to produce in the person to whom
he wishes to sell ever new and unique needs. The necessity to specialize one's product
in order to find a source of income which is not yet exhausted and also to specialize a
function which cannot be easily supplanted is conducive to differentiation, refinement and enrichment of the needs of the public which obviously must lead to
increasing personal variation within this public.

All this leads to the narrower type of intellectual individuation of mental qualities
to which the city gives rise in proportion to its size. There is a whole series of causes
for this. First of all there is the difficulty of giving one's own personality a certain
status within the framework of metropolitan life. Where quantitative increase of
value and energy has reached its limits, one seizes on qualitative distinctions, so that,
through taking advantage of the existing sensitivity to differences, the attention of
the social world can, in some way, be won for oneself. This leads ultimately to
the strangest eccentricities, to specifically metropolitan extravagances of self-
distanciation, of caprice, of fastidiousness, the meaning of which is no longer to be
found in the content of such activity itself but rather in its being a form of "being
different" – of making oneself noticeable. For many types of persons these are
still the only means of saving for oneself, through the attention gained from others,
some sort of self-esteem and the sense of filling a position. In the same sense there
operates an apparently insignificant factor which in its effects however is perceptibly

cumulative, namely, the brevity and rarity of meetings which are allotted to each individual as compared with social intercourse in a small city. For here we find the attempt to appear to-the-point, clear-cut and individual with extraordinarily greater frequency than where frequent and long association assures to each person an unambiguous conception of the other's personality.

This appears to me to be the most profound cause of the fact that the metropolis places emphasis on striving for the most individual forms of personal existence – regardless of whether it is always correct or always successful. The development of modern culture is characterised by the predominance of what one can call the objective spirit over the subjective; that is, in language as well as in law, in the technique of production as well as in art, in science as well as in the objects of domestic environment, there is embodied a sort of spirit [*Geist*], the daily growth of which is followed only imperfectly and with an even greater lag by the intellectual development of the individual. If we survey for instance the vast culture which during the last century has been embodied in things and in knowledge, in institutions and comforts, and if we compare them with the cultural progress of the individual during the same period – at least in the upper classes – we would see a frightful difference in rate of growth between the two which represents, in many points, rather a regression of the culture of the individual with reference to spirituality, delicacy and idealism. This discrepancy is in essence the result of the success of the growing division of labor. For it is this which requires from the individual an ever more one-sided type of achievement which, at its highest point, often permits his personality as a whole to fall into neglect. In any case this overgrowth of objective culture has been less and less satisfactory for the individual. Perhaps less conscious than in practical activity and in the obscure complex of feelings which flow from him, he is reduced to a negligible quantity. He becomes a single cog as over against the vast overwhelming organization of things and forces which gradually take out of his hands everything connected with progress, spirituality and value. The operation of these forces results in the transformation of the latter from a subjective form into one of purely objective existence. It need only be pointed out that the metropolis is the proper arena for this type of culture which has outgrown every personal element. Here in buildings and in educational institutions, in the wonders and comforts of space-conquering technique, in the formations of social life and in the concrete institutions of the State is to be found such a tremendous richness of crystallizing, depersonalized cultural accomplishments that the personality can, so to speak, scarcely maintain itself in the face of it. From one angle life is made infinitely more easy in the sense that stimulations, interests, and the taking up of time and attention, present themselves from all sides and carry it in a stream which scarcely requires any individual efforts for its ongoing. But from another angle, life is composed more and more of these impersonal cultural elements and existing goods and values which seek to suppress peculiar personal interests and incomparabilities. As a result, in order that this most personal element be saved, extremities and peculiarities and individualizations must be produced and they must be over-exaggerated merely to be brought into the awareness even of the individual himself. The atrophy of individual culture through the hypertrophy of objective culture lies at the root of the bitter hatred which the preachers of the most extreme individualism, in the footsteps of Nietzsche, directed against the metropolis. But it is also the explanation of why indeed they are so passionately loved in the metropolis and indeed appear to its residents as the saviors of their unsatisfied yearnings.

When both of these forms of individualism which are nourished by the quantitative relationships of the metropolis, i.e., individual independence and the elaboration of personal peculiarities, are examined with reference to their historical position, the metropolis attains an entirely new value and meaning in the world history of the spirit. The eighteenth century found the individual in the grip of powerful bonds which had become meaningless – bonds of a political, agrarian, guild and religious nature – delimitations which imposed upon the human being at the same time an unnatural form and for a long time an unjust inequality. In this situation arose the cry for freedom and equality – the belief in the full freedom of movement of the individual in all his social and intellectual relationships which would then permit the same noble essence to emerge equally from all individuals as Nature had placed it in them and as it had been distorted by social life and historical development. Alongside of this liberalistic ideal there grew up in the nineteenth century from Goethe and the Romantics, on the one hand, and from the economic division of labor on the other, the further tendency, namely, that individuals who had been liberated from their historical bonds sought now to distinguish themselves from one another. No longer was it the "general human quality" in every individual but rather his qualitative uniqueness and irreplaceability that now became the criteria of his value.

In the conflict and shifting interpretations of these two ways of defining the position of the individual within the totality is to be found the external as well as the internal history of our time. It is the function of the metropolis to make a place for the conflict and for the attempts at unification of both of these in the sense that its own peculiar conditions have been revealed to us as the occasion and the stimulus for the development of both. Thereby they attain a quite unique place, fruitful with an inexhaustible richness of meaning in the development of the mental life. They reveal themselves as one of those great historical structures in which conflicting life-embracing currents find themselves with equal legitimacy. Because of this, however, regardless of whether we are sympathetic or antipathetic with their individual expressions, they transcend the sphere in which a judge-like attitude on our part is appropriate. To the extent that such forces have been integrated, with the fleeting existence of a single cell, into the root as well as the crown of the totality of historical life to which we belong – it is our task not to complain or to condone but only to understand.

Editor's Notes on Further Reading

Simmel on Modern Culture

Using the illustration of life in the modern city, Georg Simmel (1858–1918) suggests here some distinctive features of culture in modern, complex societies (in contrast with the smaller, premodern societies which anthropologists like Ruth Benedict mostly studied). In large and highly differentiated modern societies, the multiple social circles, the money economy, and the specialized division of labor lead to increasing rationalization and objectification in culture. Simmel also suggests that while the possibilities of individuality and individualism grow, individual experience becomes more shallow, and that objective cultural products multiply and come to dominate subjective meanings and values.

Simmel received his doctorate at the University of Berlin in 1881 and was active for most of his life in Berlin's intellectual circles; he was a prolific writer and popular lecturer on many topics in philosophy, history, and sociology. In addition to other essays published in Georg Simmel, *On Individuality and Social Forms: Selected Writings*, edited with an introduction by Donald Levine (Chicago: University of Chicago Press, 1971), see for instance David Frisby and Mike Featherstone, eds., *Simmel on Culture: Selected Writings* (London and Thousand Oaks: Sage, 1997); Simmel, *Conflict and the Web of Group-Affiliations*, trans. Kurt Wolff and Reinhard Bendix, with a foreword by Everett Hughes (New York: The Free Press, 1955); Simmel, *The Philosophy of Money*, David Frisby, ed., translated by Tom Bottomore and David Frisby from a first draft by Kaethe Mengelberg (London and New York: Routledge, 1990); and *Georg Simmel on Women, Sexuality and Love*, translated with an introduction by Guy Oakes (New Haven: Yale University Press, 1984). For more on Simmel's ideas see Lewis Coser, "Georg Simmel, 1858–1918," pp. 177–215 in *Masters of Sociological Thought: Ideas in Historical and Social Context*, 2nd edn. (Harcourt Brace Jovanovich, 1977); Donald Levine, "Simmel Reappraised: Old Images, New Scholarship," pp. 173–207 in Charles Camic, ed., *Reclaiming the Sociological Classics: The State of the Scholarship* (Malden, MA: Blackwell, 1997); Michael Kaern, Bernard Phillips, and Robert Cohen, eds., *Georg Simmel and Contemporary Sociology* (Dordrecht and Boston: Kluwer Academic Publishers, 1990), Stanley Aronowitz, "The Simmel Revival: A Challenge to American Social Science," *Sociological Quarterly* 35 (1994): 397–414, and the articles collected in *Theory, Culture, and Society* 8 (3) August 1991, "Special Issue on Georg Simmel." For updated discussion of the contrast Simmel draws between objective and subjective culture see Mike Featherstone, "Archiving Cultures," *British Journal of Sociology* 51 (2000): 161–84, and Deena Weinstein and Michael Weinstein, "Simmel and the Dialectic of the Double Boundary: The Case of the Metropolis and Mental Life," *Sociological Inquiry* 59 (1989): 48–59.

Simmel's claims about the cultural impact of modernity resonate here with the themes of alienation, anomie, and rationalization in modern life developed by other classical sociological theorists like Karl Marx, Emile Durkheim and Max Weber. They also prefigure two topics which became increasingly important to students of twentieth-century culture – the impact of mass cultural production, and the impact of increasing individualism. On mass culture see also the excerpt from Horkheimer and Adorno's classic essay and DiMaggio's discussion of mass culture theory in this volume; for discussion of individualism see Lichterman, excerpted this volume, and accompanying notes.

3 The Culture Industry: Enlightenment as Mass Deception

Max Horkheimer and Theodor Adorno

The sociological theory that the loss of the support of objectively established religion, the dissolution of the last remnants of precapitalism, together with technological and social differentiation or specialization, have led to cultural chaos is disproved every day; for culture now impresses the same stamp on everything. Films, radio and magazines make up a system which is uniform as a whole and in every part....

Under monopoly all mass culture is identical, and the lines of its artificial framework begin to show through. The people at the top are no longer so interested in concealing monopoly: as its violence becomes more open, so its power grows. Movies and radio need no longer pretend to be art. The truth that they are just business is made into an ideology in order to justify the rubbish they deliberately produce. They call themselves industries; and when their directors' incomes are published, any doubt about the social utility of the finished products is removed.

Interested parties explain the culture industry in technological terms. It is alleged that because millions participate in it, certain reproduction processes are necessary that inevitably require identical needs in innumerable places to be satisfied with identical goods. The technical contrast between the few production centers and the large number of widely dispersed consumption points is said to demand organization and planning by management. Furthermore, it is claimed that standards were based in the first place on consumers' needs, and for that reason were accepted with so little resistance. The result is the circle of manipulation and retroactive need in which the unity of the system grows ever stronger. No mention is made of the fact that the basis on which technology acquires power over society is the power of those whose economic hold over society is greatest. A technological rationale is the rationale of domination itself. It is the coercive nature of society alienated from itself. Automobiles, bombs, and movies keep the whole thing together until their leveling element shows its strength in the very wrong which it furthered. It has made the technology of the culture industry no more than the achievement of standardization and mass production, sacrificing whatever involved a distinction between the logic of the work and that of the social system. This is the result not of a law of movement in technology as such but of its function in today's economy. The need which might resist central control has already been suppressed by the control of the individual consciousness. The step from the telephone to the radio has clearly distinguished the roles. The former still allowed the subscriber to play the role of subject, and was liberal. The latter is democratic: it turns all participants into listeners and authoritatively subjects them to broadcast programs which are all exactly the same. No machinery of rejoinder has been devised, and private broadcasters are denied any freedom. They are confined to the apocryphal field of the "amateur," and also have to accept organization from above. But any trace of spontaneity from the public in official broadcasting is controlled and absorbed by talent scouts, studio competitions and official programs of every kind selected by professionals. Talented performers belong to the industry long before it displays them; otherwise they would not be so eager to fit in. The attitude of the public, which ostensibly and actually favors the system of the culture industry, is a part of the system and not an excuse for it. If one branch of art follows the same formula as one with a very different medium and content; if the dramatic intrigue of broadcast soap operas becomes no more than useful material for showing how to master technical problems at both ends of the scale of musical experience – real jazz or a cheap imitation; or if a movement from a Beethoven symphony is crudely "adapted" for a film sound-track in the same way as a Tolstoy novel is garbled in a film script: then the claim that this is done to satisfy the spontaneous wishes of the public is no more than hot air. We are closer to the facts if we explain these phenomena as inherent in the technical and personnel apparatus which, down to its last cog, itself forms part of the economic mechanism of selection. In addition there is the agreement – or at least the determination – of all executive authorities not to produce or sanction anything that in any way differs from their own rules, their own ideas about consumers, or above all themselves.

In our age the objective social tendency is incarnate in the hidden subjective purposes of company directors, the foremost among whom are in the most powerful sectors of industry – steel, petroleum, electricity, and chemicals. Culture monopolies are weak and dependent in comparison. They cannot afford to neglect their appeasement of the real holders of power if their sphere of activity in mass society (a sphere producing a specific type of commodity which anyhow is still too closely bound up with easygoing liberalism and Jewish intellectuals) is not to undergo a series of purges. The dependence of the most powerful broadcasting company on the electrical industry, or of the motion picture industry on the banks, is characteristic of the whole sphere, whose individual branches are themselves economically interwoven. All are in such close contact that the extreme concentration of mental forces allows demarcation lines between different firms and technical branches to be ignored. The ruthless unity in the culture industry is evidence of what will happen in politics. Marked differentiations such as those of A and B films, or of stories in magazines in different price ranges, depend not so much on subject matter as on classifying, organizing, and labeling consumers. Something is provided for all so that none may escape; the distinctions are emphasized and extended. The public is catered for with a hierarchical range of mass-produced products of varying quality, thus advancing the rule of complete quantification. Everybody must behave (as if spontaneously) in accordance with his previously determined and indexed level, and choose the category of mass product turned out for his type. Consumers appear as statistics on research organization charts, and are divided by income groups into red, green, and blue areas; the technique is that used for any type of propaganda.

How formalized the procedure is can be seen when the mechanically differentiated products prove to be all alike in the end. That the difference between the Chrysler range and General Motors products is basically illusory strikes every child with a keen interest in varieties. What connoisseurs discuss as good or bad points serve only to perpetuate the semblance of competition and range of choice. The same applies to the Warner Brothers and Metro Goldwyn Mayer productions. But even the differences between the more expensive and cheaper models put out by the same firm steadily diminish: for automobiles, there are such differences as the number of cylinders, cubic capacity, details of patented gadgets; and for films there are the number of stars, the extravagant use of technology, labor, and equipment, and the introduction of the latest psychological formulas. The universal criterion of merit is the amount of "conspicuous production," of blatant cash investment. The varying budgets in the culture industry do not bear the slightest relation to factual values, to the meaning of the products themselves. . . .

The man with leisure has to accept what the culture manufacturers offer him. Kant's formalism still expected a contribution from the individual, who was thought to relate the varied experiences of the senses to fundamental concepts; but industry robs the individual of his function. Its prime service to the customer is to do his schematizing for him. Kant said that there was a secret mechanism in the soul which prepared direct intuitions in such a way that they could be fitted into the system of pure reason. But today that secret has been deciphered. While the mechanism is to all appearances planned by those who serve up the data of experience, that is, by the culture industry, it is in fact forced upon the latter by the power of society, which remains irrational, however we may try to rationalize it; and this inescapable force is processed by commercial agencies so that they give an artificial impression of being in command. There is nothing left for the consumer to classify. Producers have done it for him. Art for the masses has destroyed the dream but still conforms to the tenets of that dreaming idealism which critical idealism balked at. Everything derives from consciousness: for Malebranche and Berkeley, from the consciousness of God; in mass art, from the consciousness of the production team. Not only are the hit songs, stars, and soap operas cyclically recurrent and rigidly invariable types, but the specific content of the entertainment itself is derived from them and only appears to change. The details are interchangeable. The short interval sequence which was effective in a hit song, the hero's momentary fall from grace (which he accepts as good sport), the rough treatment which the beloved gets from the male star, the latter's rugged defiance of the spoilt heiress, are, like all the other details, ready-made clichés to be slotted in anywhere; they never do anything more than fulfill the purpose allotted them in the overall plan. Their whole *raison d'être* is to confirm it by being its constituent parts. As soon as the film begins, it is quite clear how it will end, and who will be rewarded, punished, or forgotten. In light music, once the trained ear has heard the first notes of the hit song, it can guess what is coming and feel flattered when it does come. The average length of the short story has to be rigidly adhered to. Even gags, effects, and jokes are calculated like the setting in which they are placed. They are the responsibility of special experts and their narrow range makes it easy for them to be apportioned in the office. The development of the culture industry has led to the predominance of the effect, the obvious touch, and the technical detail over the work itself – which once expressed an idea, but was liquidated together with the idea. When the detail won its freedom, it became rebellious and, in the period from Romanticism to Expressionism, asserted itself as free expression, as a vehicle of protest against the organization. In music the single harmonic effect obliterated the awareness of form as a whole; in painting the individual color was stressed at the expense of pictorial composition; and in the novel psychology became more important than structure. The totality of the culture industry has put an end to this. Though concerned exclusively with effects, it crushes their insubordination and makes them subserve the formula, which replaces the work. The same fate is inflicted on whole and parts alike. The whole inevitably bears no relation to the details – just like the career of a successful man into which everything is made to fit as an illustration or a proof, whereas it is nothing more than the sum of all those idiotic events. The so-called dominant idea is like a file which ensures order but not coherence. The whole and the parts are alike; there is no antithesis and no connection. Their prearranged harmony is a mockery of what had to be striven after in the great bourgeois works of art. In Germany the graveyard stillness of the dictatorship already hung over the gayest films of the democratic era.

The whole world is made to pass through the filter of the culture industry. The old experience of the movie-goer, who sees the world outside as an extension of the film he has just left (because the latter is intent upon reproducing the world of everyday perceptions), is now the producer's guideline. The more intensely and flawlessly his techniques duplicate empirical objects, the easier it is today for the illusion to prevail that the outside world is the straightforward continuation of that presented on the screen. This purpose has been furthered by mechanical reproduction since the lightning takeover by the sound film.

Real life is becoming indistinguishable from the movies. The sound film, far surpassing the theater of illusion, leaves no room for imagination or reflection on the part of the audience, who is unable to respond within the structure of the film, yet deviate from its precise detail without losing the thread of the story; hence the film forces its victims to equate it directly with reality. The stunting of the mass-media consumer's powers of imagination and spontaneity does not have to be traced back to any psychological mechanisms; he must ascribe the loss of those attributes to the objective nature of the products themselves, especially to the most characteristic of them, the sound film. They are so designed that quickness, powers of observation, and experience are undeniably needed to apprehend them at all; yet sustained thought is out of the question if the spectator is not to miss the relentless rush of facts. Even though the effort required for his response is semi-automatic, no scope is left for the imagination. Those who are so absorbed by the world of the movie – by its images, gestures, and words – that they are unable to supply what really makes it a world, do not have to dwell on particular points of its mechanics during a screening. All the other films and products of the entertainment industry which they have seen have taught them what to expect; they react automatically. The might of industrial society is lodged in men's minds. The entertainments manufacturers know that their products will be consumed with alertness even when the customer is distraught, for each of them is a model of the huge economic machinery which has always sustained the masses, whether at work or at leisure – which is akin to work. From every sound film and every broadcast program the social effect can be inferred which is exclusive to none but is shared by all alike. The culture industry as a whole has molded men as a type unfailingly reproduced in every product. All the agents of this process, from the producer to the women's clubs, take good care that the simple reproduction of this mental state is not nuanced or extended in any way.

The art historians and guardians of culture who complain of the extinction in the West of a basic style-determining power are wrong. The stereotyped appropriation of everything, even the inchoate, for the purposes of mechanical reproduction surpasses the rigor and general currency of any "real style," in the sense in which cultural *cognoscenti* celebrate the organic pre-capitalist past....

By subordinating in the same way and to the same end all areas of intellectual creation, by occupying men's senses from the time they leave the factory in the evening to the time they clock in again the next morning with matter that bears the impress of the labor process they themselves have to sustain throughout the day, this subsumption mockingly satisfies the concept of a unified culture which the philosophers of personality contrasted with mass culture....

[W]hat is new is that the irreconcilable elements of culture, art and distraction, are subordinated to one end and subsumed under one false formula: the totality of the culture industry. It consists of repetition. That its characteristic innovations are never anything more than improvements of mass reproduction is not external to the system. It is with good reason that the interest of innumerable consumers is directed to the technique, and not to the contents – which are stubbornly repeated, outworn, and by now half-discredited. The social power which the spectators worship shows itself more effectively in the omnipresence of the stereotype imposed by technical skill than in the stale ideologies for which the ephemeral contents stand in.

Nevertheless the culture industry remains the entertainment business. Its influence over the consumers is established by entertainment; that will ultimately be broken not by an outright decree, but by the hostility inherent in the principle of entertainment to what is greater than itself. Since all the trends of the culture industry are profoundly embedded in the public by the whole social process, they are encouraged by the survival of the market in this area. Demand has not yet been replaced by simple obedience. As is well known, the major reorganization of the film industry shortly before World War I, the material prerequisite of its expansion, was precisely its deliberate acceptance of the public's needs as recorded at the box-office – a procedure which was hardly thought necessary in the pioneering days of the screen. The same opinion is held today by the captains of the film industry, who take as their criterion the more or less phenomenal song hits but wisely never have recourse to the judgment of truth, the opposite criterion. Business is their ideology. It is quite correct that the power of the culture industry resides in its identification with a manufactured need, and not in simple contrast to it, even if this contrast were one of complete power and complete powerlessness. Amusement under late capitalism is the prolongation of work. It is sought after as an escape from the mechanized work process, and to recruit strength in order to be able to cope with it again. But at the same time mechanization has such power over a man's leisure and happiness, and so profoundly determines the manufacture of amusement goods, that his experiences are inevitably after-images of the work process itself. The ostensible content is merely a faded foreground; what sinks in is the automatic succession of standardized operations. What happens at work, in the factory, or in the office can only be escaped from by approximation to it in one's leisure time. All amusement suffers from this incurable malady. Pleasure hardens into boredom because, if it is to remain pleasure, it must not demand any effort and therefore moves rigorously in the worn grooves of association. No independent thinking must be expected from the audience: the product prescribes every reaction: not by its natural structure (which collapses under reflection), but by signals. Any logical connection calling for mental effort is painstakingly avoided. As far as possible, developments must follow from the immediately preceding situation and never from the idea of the whole. For the attentive movie-goer any individual scene will give him the whole thing....

The culture industry perpetually cheats its consumers of what it perpetually promises. The promissory note which, with its plots and staging, it draws on pleasure is endlessly prolonged; the promise, which is actually all the spectacle consists of, is illusory: all it actually confirms is that the real point will never be reached, that the diner must be satisfied with the menu. In front of the appetite stimulated by all those brilliant names and images there is finally set no more than a commendation of the depressing everyday world it sought to escape. Of course works of art were not sexual exhibitions either. However, by representing deprivation as negative, they retracted, as it were, the prostitution of the impulse and rescued by mediation what was denied. The secret of aesthetic sublimation is its representation of fulfillment as a broken promise. The culture industry does not sublimate; it represses. By repeatedly exposing the objects of desire, breasts in a clinging sweater or the naked torso of the athletic hero, it only stimulates the unsublimated forepleasure which habitual deprivation has long since reduced to a masochistic semblance. There is no erotic situation which, while insinuating and exciting, does not fail to indicate unmistakably that things can never go that far. The Hays Office merely confirms the ritual of Tantalus that the culture industry has established anyway. Works of art are ascetic and unashamed; the culture industry is pornographic and prudish. Love is downgraded to romance. And, after the descent, much is permitted; even license as a marketable speciality has its quota bearing the trade description "daring." The mass production of the sexual automatically achieves its repression. Because of his ubiquity, the film star with whom one is meant to fall in love is from the outset a copy of himself. Every tenor voice comes to sound like a Caruso record, and the "natural" faces of Texas girls are like the successful models by whom Hollywood has typecast them. The mechanical reproduction of beauty, which reactionary cultural fanaticism wholeheartedly serves in its methodical idolization of individuality, leaves no room for that unconscious idolatry which was once essential to beauty. The triumph over beauty is celebrated by humor – the *Schadenfreude* that every successful deprivation calls forth. There is laughter because there is nothing to laugh at. Laughter, whether conciliatory or terrible, always occurs when some fear passes. It indicates liberation either from physical danger or from the grip of logic. Conciliatory laughter is heard as the echo of an escape from power; the wrong kind overcomes fear by capitualting to the forces which are to be feared. It is the echo of power as something inescapable. Fun is a medicinal bath. The pleasure industry never fails to prescribe it. It makes laughter the instrument of the fraud practised on happiness....

Today the culture industry has taken over the civilizing inheritance of the entrepreneurial and frontier democracy – whose appreciation of intellectual deviations was never very finely attuned. All are free to dance and enjoy themselves, just as they have been free, since the historical neutralization of religion, to join any of the innumerable sects. But freedom to choose an ideology – since ideology always reflects economic coercion – everywhere proves to be freedom to choose what is always the same. The way in which a girl accepts and keeps the obligatory date, the inflection on the telephone or in the most intimate situation, the choice of words in conversation, and the whole inner life as classified by the now somewhat devalued depth psychology, bear witness to man's attempt to make himself a proficient apparatus, similar (even in emotions) to the model served up by the culture industry. The most intimate reactions of human beings have been so thoroughly reified that the idea of anything specific to themselves now persists only as an utterly abstract notion: personality scarcely signifies anything more than shining white teeth and freedom from body odor and emotions. The triumph of advertising in the culture industry is that consumers feel compelled to buy and use its products even though they see through them.

Editor's Notes on Further Reading

Horkheimer and Adorno on the Culture Industry

In this famous 1944 essay, Max Horkheimer (1895–1973) and Theodor Adorno (1903–69) examine the rationalized, capitalist organization of cultural production in modern societies. Their rich analysis of mass culture organization and content, and its psychological and political consequences, was among the most wide-ranging and original of scholars' attempts to come to grips with the impact of movies and radio, and continues to offer insights into later forms of mass culture like television. For Horkheimer and Adorno, when art and entertainment are commodified for the mass market in concentrated, rationalized businesses, culture becomes formulaic, commercialized, imaginatively limited, and critically stunted; and audiences became passive, conformist, and uncritical. True individuality is absorbed, true human needs are repressed, and even intimacy is reified.

Horkheimer and Adorno were core members of the Frankfurt School, an interdisciplinary group of German scholars organized as the Institute for Social Research from the 1920s. They aimed to develop Marx's and Weber's ideas about modern exploitation and rationalization in critical theory which applied to twentieth-century problems in western countries, so they incorporated in their critical theory numerous cultural, psychological, and aesthetic themes beyond those typical of traditional Marxism. After fleeing Nazism in 1933, members of the Frankfurt School continued their work in exile; this essay was written while Horkheimer and Adorno were in Santa Monica, California. For examples of other writing on issues raised in this selection see Theodor Adorno, "Culture Industry Reconsidered," *New German Critique* 6 (1975): 12–19; Adorno, "Cultural Criticism and Society," pp. 17–34 in *Prisms*, trans. Samuel and Shierry Weber (Cambridge, MA: MIT Press, 1981 [1967]); "Culture and Administration," *Telos* 97 (1978): 93–111; "The Stars Down to Earth: The Los Angeles Times Astrology Column," *Telos* 19 (1974): 13–90; and "Analytical Study of the NBC *Music Appreciation Hour*," *Musical Quarterly* 78 (1994): 325–77; see also Andrew Arato and Eike Gebhardt, eds., *The Essential Frankfurt School Reader* (New York: Urizen Books, 1978). For further historical and intellectual background see Tom Bottomore, *The Frankfurt School* (London and New York: Tavistock Publications, 1984); Martin Jay, *The Dialectical Imagination: A History of the Frankfurt School and the Institute of Social Research 1923–1950* (Berkeley: University of California Press, 1996 [1973]); Martin Jay, *Adorno* (Cambridge, MA: Harvard University Press, 1984); Robert Witkin, "Why Did Adorno 'Hate' Jazz?" *Sociological Theory* 18 (2000): 145–70; Seyla Benhabib, Wolfgang Bonß, and John McCole, *On Max Horkheimer: New Perspectives* (Cambridge, MA and London: MIT Press, 1993). For some discussion of key Frankfurt School ideas see, for instance, Douglas Kellner, "Critical Theory and the

Culture Industries: A Reassessment," *Telos* #62 (1984–5): 196–206, and Nico Israel, "Damage Control: Adorno, Los Angeles, and the Dislocation of Culture," *Yale Journal of Criticism* 10 (1997): 85–113.

Another member of the Frankfurt School who made substantial contributions on art, literature and popular culture was Leo Lowenthal (1900–93), who taught at the University of California at Berkeley from 1956; see, for instance, "Historical Perspectives of Popular Culture," *American Journal of Sociology* 55 (1950): 323–32; "Sociology of Literature in Retrospect," pp. 11–25 in Philippe Desan, Priscilla Parkhurst Ferguson, and Wendy Griswold, eds., *Literature and Social Practice* (Chicago: University of Chicago Press, 1989) and the essays collected in his *Literature, Popular Culture, and Society* (Palo Alto: Pacific Books, 1961). For an influential early analysis of cultural production in modernity see Walter Benjamin, "The Work of Art in the Age of Mechanical Reproduction," pp. 217–51 in Hannah Arendt, ed., *Illuminations*, trans. Harry Zohn (New York: Schocken Books, 1968). Concerns about modern cultural production are also expressed from a somewhat different point of view by Simmel (see excerpt this volume). Raymond William's work, also excerpted here, demonstrates a different direction in which Marx's theory of ideology was developed in the twentieth century, a direction with more affinities with Antonio Gramsci than with the Frankfurt School.

For a recent general theory and history of the media see John Thompson, *The Media and Modernity: A Social Theory of the Media* (Stanford, CA: Stanford University Press, 1996). Useful collections of twentieth-century debates about American mass culture can be found in Bernard Rosenberg and David Manning White, eds., *Mass Culture: The Popular Arts in America* (Glencoe, IL: The Free Press, 1957) and Rosenberg and White, eds., *Mass Culture Revisited* (New York: Van Nostrand Reinhold Company, 1971); see especially the editors' introductions.

Within cultural sociology, several developments draw on and go beyond Horkheimer and Adorno's theses. First, the concept of the culture industry has been developed and specified to focus on midrange variations in the organizational conditions of cultural production: see DiMaggio's discussion of mass culture theory and Peterson's exemplar of "cultural production" analysis, both in this volume. Second, assumptions about audience effects are challenged by examining the active and critical ways audiences can interpret and respond to mass culture; see, for example, the excerpt from Hunt's *Screening the Los Angeles Riots* in this volume, and accompanying editor's notes. For an application of critical theory which also emphasizes active class conflict see David Gartman, *Auto Opium: A Social History of Automobile Design* (London and New York: Routledge, 1994). For a recent reassessment and new theory of the possibility of aesthetic judgment see Nancy Weiss Hanrahan, *Difference in Time: A Critical Theory of Culture* (Westport CT and London: Praeger, 2000), and for a similar contribution regarding democracy see Orville Lee, "Culture and Democratic Theory: Toward a Theory of Symbolic Democracy," *Constellations* 5 (1998): 433–55.

4 Center and Periphery

Edward Shils

Society has a center. There is a central zone in the structure of society. This central zone impinges in various ways on those who live within the ecological domain in which the society exists. Membership in the society, in more than the ecological sense of being located in a bounded territory and of adapting to an environment affected or made up by other persons located in the same territory, is constituted by relationship to this central zone.

The central zone is not, as such, a spatially located phenomenon. It almost always has a more or less definite location within the bounded territory in which the society lives. Its centrality has, however, nothing to do with geometry and little with geography.

The center, or the central zone, is a phenomenon of the realm of values and beliefs. It is the center of the order of symbols, of values and beliefs, which govern the society. It is the center because it is the ultimate and irreducible; and it is felt to be such by many who cannot give explicit articulation to its irreducibility. The central zone partakes of the nature of the sacred. In this sense, every society has an "official" religion, even when that society or its exponents and interpreters, conceive of it, more or less correctly, as a secular, pluralistic, and tolerant society. The principle of the Counterreformation – *Cuius regio, eius religio* – although its rigor has been loosened and its harshness mollified, retains a core of permanent truth.

The center is also a phenomenon of the realm of action. It is a structure of activities, of roles and persons, within the network of institutions. It is in these roles that the values and beliefs which are central are embodied and propounded.

The larger society appears, on a cursory inspection and by the methods of inquiry in current use, to consist of a number of interdependent subsystems – the economy, the status system, the polity, the kinship system, and the institutions which have in their special custody the cultivation of cultural values, e.g. the university system, the ecclesiastical system, etc. (I use "ecclesiastical" to include the religious institutions of societies which do not have a church in the Western sense of the term.) Each of these subsystems itself comprises a network of organizations which are connected, with varying degrees of affirmation, through a common authority, overlapping personnel, personal relationships, contracts, perceived identities of interest, a sense of affinity within a transcendent whole, and a territorial location possessing symbolic value. (These subsystems and their constituent bodies are not equally affirmative vis-à-vis each other. Moreover the degree of affirmation varies through time, and is quite compatible with a certain measure of alienation within each elite and among the elites.)

Each of these organizations has an authority, an elite, which might be either a single individual or a group of individuals, loosely or closely organized. Each of these elites makes decisions, sometimes in consultation with other elites and sometimes, largely on its own initiative, with the intention of maintaining the organization, controlling the conduct of its members and fulfilling its goals. (These decisions are by no means always successful in the achievement of these ends, and the goals are seldom equally or fully shared by the elite and those whose actions are ordained by its decisions.)

The decisions made by the elites contain as major elements certain general standards of judgment and action, and certain concrete values, of which the system as a whole, the society, is one of the most preeminent. The values which are inherent in these standards, and which are espoused and more or less observed by those in authority, we shall call the *central value system* of the society. This central value system is the central zone of the society. It is central because of its intimate connection with what the society holds to be sacred; it is central because it is espoused by the ruling authorities of the society. These two kinds of centrality are vitally related. Each defines and supports the other.

The central value system is not the whole of the order of values and beliefs espoused and observed in the society. The value systems obtaining in any diversified society may be regarded as being distributed along a range. There are variants of the central value system running from hyperaffirmation of some of the components of the major, central value system to an extreme denial of some of these major elements in the central value system; the latter tends to, but is not inevitably associated with, an affirmation of certain elements denied or subordinated in the central value system. There are also elements of the order of values and beliefs which are as random with respect to the central value system as the value and beliefs of human beings can be. There is always a considerable amount of unintegratedness of values and beliefs, both within the realm of value of representative individuals and among individuals and sections of a society.

The central value system is constituted by the values which are pursued and affirmed by the elites of the constituent subsystems and of the organizations which are comprised in the subsystems. By their very possession of authority, they attribute to themselves an essential affinity with the sacred elements of their society, of which they regard themselves as the custodians. By the same token, many members of their society attribute to them that same kind of affinity. The elites of the economy affirm and usually observe certain values which should govern economic activity. The elites of the polity affirm and usually observe certain values which should govern political activity. The elites of the university system and the ecclesiastical system affirm and usually practice certain values which should govern intellectual and religious activities (including beliefs). On the whole, these values are the values embedded in current activity. The ideals which they affirm do not far transcend the reality which is ruled by those who espouse them.[1] The values of the different elites are clustered into an approximately consensual pattern.[2]

One of the major elements in any central value system is an affirmative attitude toward established authority. This is present in the central value systems of all societies, however much these might differ from each other in their appreciation of authority. There is something like a "floor," a minimum of appreciation of authority in every society, however liberal that society might be. Even the most libertarian and equalitarian societies which have ever existed possess at least this minimum appreciation of authority. Authority enjoys appreciation because it arouses sentiments of sacredness. Sacredness by its nature is authoriative. Those persons, offices, or symbols endowed with it, however indirectly and remotely, are therewith endowed with some measure of authoritativeness.

The appreciation of authority entails the appreciation of the institutions through which authority works and the rules which it enunciates. The central value system in all societies asserts and recommends the appreciation of these authoritative institutions.

Implicitly, the central value system rotates on a center more fundamental even than its espousal by and embodiment in authority. Authority is the agent of *order*, an order which may be largely embodied in authority or which might transcend authority and regulate it, or at least provide a standard by which existing authority itself is judged and even claims to judge itself. This order, which is implicit in the central value system, and in the light of which the central value system legitimates itself, is endowed with dynamic potentialities. It contains, above all, the potentiality of critical judgment on the central value system and the central institutional system. To use Mannheim's terminology, while going beyond Mannheim, every "ideology" has within it a "utopian" potentiality. To use my own terminology, every central value system contains within itself an ideological potentiality. The dynamic potentiality derives from the inevitable tendency of every concrete society to fall short of the order which is implicit in its central value system.

Closely connected with the appreciation of authority and the institutions in which it is exercised, is an appreciation of the *qualities* which qualify persons for the exercise of authority or which are characteristic of those who exercise authority. These qualities, which we shall call secondary values, can be ethnic, educational, familial, economic, professional; they may be ascribed to individuals by virtue of their relationships or they may be acquired through study and experience. But whatever they are, they enjoy the appreciation of the central value system simply because of their connection with the exercise of authority. (Despite their ultimately derivative nature, each of them is capable of possessing an autonomous status in the central zone, in the realm of the sacred; consequently, severe conflicts can be engendered.)

The central value system thus comprises secondary as well as primary values. It legitimates the existing distribution of roles and rewards to persons possessing the appropriate qualities which in various ways symbolize degrees of proximity to authority. It legitimates these distributions by praising the properties of those who occupy authoritative roles in the society, by stressing the legitimacy of their incumbency of those roles and the appropriateness of the rewards they receive. By implication, and explicitly as well, it legitimates the smaller rewards received by those who live at various distances from the circles in which authority is exercised.

The central institutional system may thus be described as the set of institutions which is legitimated by the central value system. Less circularly, however, it may be described as those institutions which, through the radiation of their authority, give some form to the life of a considerable section of the population of the society. The economic, political, ecclesiastical, and cultural institutions impinge compellingly at many points on the conduct of much of the population in any society through the actual exercise of authority and the potential exercise of coercion, through the provision of persuasive models of action, and through a partial control of the allocation of rewards. The kinship and family systems, although they have much smaller radii, are microcosms of the central institutional system and do much to buttress its efficiency.

The existence of a central value system rests, in a fundamental way, on the need which human beings have for incorporation into something which transcends and transfigures their concrete individual existence. They have a need to be in contact with symbols of an order which is larger in its dimensions than their own bodies and more central in the "ultimate" structure of reality than is their routine everyday life. . . .

The need for established and created order, the respect for creativity, and the need to be connected with the center do not exhaust the forces which engender central value systems. To fill out the list, we must consider the nature of authority itself. Authority has an expansive tendency. It has a tendency to expand the order which it represents toward the saturation of territorial space. The acceptance of the validity of that order entails a tendency toward its universalization within the society over which authority rules. Ruling indeed consists in the universalization – within the boundaries of society – of the rules inherent in the order. Rulers, just because of their possession of authority and the impulses which it generates, wish to be obeyed and to obtain assent to the order which they symbolically embody. The symbolization of order in offices of authority has a compelling effect on those who occupy those offices.

In consequences of this, rulers seek to establish a universal diffusion of the acceptance and observance of the values and beliefs of which they are the custodians through incumbency in those offices. They use their powers to punish those who deviate and to reward with their favor those who conform. Thus, the mere existence of authority in society imposes a central value system on that society. I would regret an easy misunderstanding to which the foregoing sentences might give rise. There is much empirical truth in the common observations that rulers "look after their own," that they are only interested in remaining in authority, in reinforcing their possession of authority and in enhancing their security of tenure through the establishment of a consensus built around their own values and beliefs. Nonetheless these observations seem to me to be too superficial. They fail to discern the dynamic property of authority as such, and particularly of authority over society.

Not all persons who come into positions of authority possess the same responsiveness to the inherently dynamic and expansive tendency in authority. Some are more attuned to it; others are more capable of resisting it. Tradition, furthermore, acts as a powerful brake upon expansiveness, as does the degree of differentiation of the structure of elites and of the society as a whole.

The central institutional system of modern societies, probably even in revolutionary crises, is the object of a substantial amount of consensus. The central value system which legitimates the central institutional system is widely shared, but the consensus is never perfect. There are differences within even the most consensual society about the appreciability of authority, the institutions within which it resides, the elites which exercise it, and the justice of its allocation of rewards.

Even those who share in the consensus do so with different degrees of intensity, whole-heartedness, and devotion. As we move from the center of society, the center in which authority is possessed, to the hinterland or the periphery, over which authority is exercised, attachment to the central value system becomes attenuated. The central institutional system is neither unitary nor homogeneous, and some levels have more majesty than others. The lower one goes in the hierarchy, or the further one moves territorially from the locus of authority, the less one appreciates authority. Likewise, the further one moves from those possessing the secondary traits associated with the exercise of authority into sectors of the population which do not equally possess those qualities, the less affirmative is the attitude towards the reigning authority, and the less intense is that affirmation which does exist.

Active rejection of the central value system is, of course, not the sole alternative to its affirmation. Much more widespread, in the course of history and in any particular society, is an intermittent, partial, and attenuated affirmation of the central value system.

For the most part, the mass of the population in premodern societies have been far removed from the immediate impact of the central value system. They have possessed their own value systems, which were occasionally and fragmentarily articulated with the central value system. These pockets of approximate independence have not, however, been completely incompatible with isolated occasions of articulation and of intermittent affirmation. Nor have these intermittent occasions of participation been incompatible with occasions of active rejection and antagonism to the central institutional system, to the elite which sits at its center, and to the central value system which that elite puts forward for its own legitimation.

The more territorially dispersed the institutional system, the less the likelihood of an intense affirmation of the central value system. The more inegalitarian the society, the less the likelihood of an intense affirmation of the central value system, especially where, as in most steeply hierarchial societies, there are large and discontinuous gaps between those at the top and those below them. Indeed, it might be said that the degree of affirmation inevitably shades off from the center of the exercise of authority and of the promulgation of values.

As long as societies were loosely coordinated, as long as authority lacked the means of intensive control, and as long as much of the economic life of the society was carried on outside any market or almost exclusively in local markets, the central value system invariably became attenuated in the outlying reaches. With the growth of the market, and the administrative and technological strengthening of authority, contact with the central value system increased.

When, as in modern society, a more unified economic system, political democracy, urbanization, and education have brought the different sections of the population into more frequent contact with each other and created even greater mutual awareness, the central value system has found a wider acceptance than in other periods of the history of society. At the same time these changes have also increased the extent, if not the intensity, of active "dissensus" or rejection of the central value system.

The same objects which previously engaged the attention and aroused the sentiments of a very restricted minority of the population have in modern societies become concerns of much broader strata of the population. At the same time that increased contact with authority has led to a generally deferential attitude, it has also run up against the tenacity of prior attachments and a reluctance to accept strange gods. Class conflict in the most advanced modern societies is probably more open and more continuous than in premodern societies, but it is also more domesticated and restricted by attachments to the central value system. Violent revolutions and bloody civil wars are much less characteristic of modern societies than of premodern societies. Revolutionary parties are feeble in modern societies which have moved toward widespread popular education, a greater equality of status, etc. The size of nominally revolutionary parties in France and Italy is a measure of the extent to which French and Italian societies have not become modernized in this sense. The inertness, from a revolutionary point of view, of the rank and file of these parties is partially indicative of the extent to which, despite their revolutionary doctrines, the working classes in these countries have become assimilated into the central value system of their respective societies.

The old gods have fallen, religious faith has become much more attenuated in the educated classes, and suspicion of authority is much more overt than it has ever been. Nonetheless in the modern societies of the West, the central value system has gone much more deeply into the heart of their members than it has ever succeeded in doing in any earlier society. The "masses" have responded to their contact with a striking measure of acceptance.

The power of the ruling class derives from its incumbency of certain key positions in the central institutional system. Societies vary in the extent to which the ruling class is unitary or relatively segmental. Even where the ruling class is relatively segmental, there is, because of centralized control of appointment to the most crucial of the key positions or because of personal ties or because of overlapping personnel, some sense of affinity which, more or less, unites the different sectors of the elite.[3]

This sense of affinity rests ultimately on the high degree of proximity to the center which is shared by all these different sectors of the ruling class. They have, it is true, a common vested interest in their position. It is not, however, simply the product of a perception of a coalescent interest; it contains a substantial component of mutual regard arising from a feeling of a common relationship to the central value system.

The different sectors of the elite are never equal. One or two usually predominate, to varying degrees, over the others, even in situations where there is much mutual respect and a genuine sense of affinity. Regardless, however, of whether they are equal or unequal, unitary or segmental, there is usually a fairly large amount of consensus among the elites of the central institutional system. This consensus has its ultimate root in their common feeling for the transcendent order which they believe they embody or for which they think themselves responsible. This does not obtain equally for all elites. Some are much more concerned in an almost entirely "secular" or manipulative way with remaining in power. Nonetheless, even in a situation of great heterogeneity and much mutual antipathy, the different sectors of the elite tend to experience the "transforming" transcendental overtones which are generated by incumbency in authoritative roles, or by proximity to "fundamentally important things." . . .

[G]reater incorporation carries with it also an inherent tension. Those who participate in the central institutional and value systems – who feel sufficiently closer to the center now than their forebears ever did – also feel their position as outsiders, their remoteness from the center, in a way in which their forebears probably did not feel it. The modern trade union movement, which has disappointed those whose revolutionary hopes were to be supported by the organized working classes, illustrates this development. The leaders of the trade unions have come to be part of the central institutional system and accordingly, at least in part, they fulfill the obligations which are inherent in the action within that system. At the same time, the unions' rank and file members also have come to share more widely and intensely in the central value system and to affirm more deeply and continuously than in the past the central institutional system. Nonetheless, the leaders, deriving from sections of the society which have felt themselves to be outside the prevailing society, still and necessarily carry traces of that position in their outlook; the rank and file, less involved in the central institutional system than the leadership, experience even more acutely their position as outsiders vis-à-vis the central value system. The more sensitive among them are the most difficult for the leaders of the unions to hold in check.

Parallel with this incorporation of the mass of the population into society – halting, spotty, and imperfect as this incorporation is – has gone a change in the attitudes of the ruling classes of the modern states of the West. (In Asia and Africa, the process is even more fragmentary, corresponding to the greater fragmentariness of the incorporation of the masses into those societies.) In the modern Western states, the ruling classes have come increasingly to acknowledge the dispersion, into the wider reaches of the society, of the charisma which informs the center. The qualities which account for the expansiveness of authority have come to be shared more widely by the population, far from the center in which the incumbents of the positions of authority reside. In the eyes of the elites of the modern states of the West, the mass of the population have somehow come to share in the vital connection with the "order" which inheres in the central value system and which was once thought to be in the special custody of the ruling classes.

The elites are, of course, more responsive to sectors of society which have voting powers and, therewith, legislative power, and which possess agitational and purchasing powers as well. These would make them simulate respect for the populace even where they did not feel it. Mixed with this simulated respect, however, is a genuine respect for the mass of the population as bearers of a true individuality, and a genuine, even if still limited, appreciation of their intrinsic worth as fellow members of the civil society and, in the deepest sense, as vessels of the charisma which lives at the center of society.

There is a limit to consensus. However comprehensive the spread of consensus, it can never be all-embracing. A differentiated large-scale society will always be compelled by professional specialization, tradition, the normal distribution of human capacities, and an inevitable antinomianism to submit to inequalities in participation in the central value system. Some persons will always be a bit closer to the center; some will always be more distant from the center.

Nonetheless, the expansion of individuality attendant on the growth of individual freedom and opportunity, and the greater density of communications, have contributed greatly to narrowing the range of inequality. The peak at the center is no longer so high; the periphery is no longer so distant.

The individuality which has underlain the entry into the consensus around the central value system might in the end also be endangered by it. Liberty and privacy live on islands in a consensual sea. When the tide rises they may be engulfed. This is another instance of the dialectical relationships among consensus, indifference, and alienation, but further consideration must be left for another occasion.

Notes

1   This set of values corresponds to what Karl Mannheim called "ideologies," i.e., values and beliefs, which are congruent with or embodied in current reality (*seinskongruent*). I do not wish to use the term "ideology" to describe these value orientations. One of the most important reasons is that in the past few decades the term "ideology" has been used to refer to intensely espoused value orientations which are extremely *seinstranszendent*, which transcend current reality by a wide margin, which are explicit, articulated, and hostile to the existing order. (For example, Bolshevist doctrine, National Socialist doctrine, Fascist doctrine, etc.) Mannheim called these "utopias." Mannheim's distinction was fundamental, and I accept it, our divergent nomenclature notwithstanding.
2   The degree of consensuality differs among societies and times. There are societies in which the predominant elite demands a complete consensus with its own more specific values and beliefs. Such is the case in modern totalitarian societies. Absolutist regimes in past epochs, which were rather indifferent about whether the mass of the population was party to a consensus, were quite insistent on consensus among the elites of their society.
3   The segmentation or differentiation in the structure of elites is an important factor in limiting the expansiveness of authority among the elites. A differentiated structure of elites brings with it a division of powers, which can be totally overcome only by draconic measures. It can be done, as the Soviet Union has shown, but it is a perpetual source of strain, as recent Soviet developments have also shown.

Editor's Notes on Further Reading

Shils on Central Value Systems

Edward Shils (1911–95) argued that shared values, beliefs and traditions are essential for social cohesion even in highly differentiated and individualistic modern societies. In every society, central institutions reproduce and promote an authoritative central value system which is both charismatic and functional, ultimately overriding the disintegrative consequences of dissent, apathy, and domination. Moreover, Shils holds that the influence of the central value system has spread further in modern societies than was possible in premodern times.

Among Shils's many influences on American intellectual life was his collaboration with Talcott Parsons and others in developing a theory of culture emphasizing values and focusing on shared values which guide action and pattern differences between groups and societies. Although Shils's ideas ultimately differed from the Parsonian theory of culture (see Turner, cited below), this collaboration was important because value analysis dominated sociological work on culture from the 1950s to the 1980s, and subsequent cultural sociology reacted against value analysis by focusing more on the cognitive and the conflictual in culture. For Parsonian perspectives on culture see Talcott Parsons and Edward Shils, eds., *Toward a General Theory of Action* (Cambridge, MA: Harvard University Press, 1951), especially

"Systems of Value Orientation," 159–89, and Clyde Kluckhohn, "Values and Value-Orientations in the Theory of Action: An Exploration in Definition and Classification," pp. 388–433; and Talcott Parsons, "Introduction to Part Four, Culture and the Social System," pp. 963–93 in Talcott Parsons, Edward Shils, Kaspar Naegele, and Jesse Pitts, eds., *Theories of Society: Foundations of Modern Sociological Theory* (New York: The Free Press, 1961). For an important application see Seymour Martin Lipset, "The Value Patterns of Democracy: A Case Study in Comparative Analysis," *American Sociological Review* 28 (1963): 515–31, and for further examples, summaries, and critiques of value theory see for instance James Spates, "The Sociology of Values," *Annual Review of Sociology* 9 (1983): 27–49, and Ann Swidler, "Culture in Action: Symbols and Strategies," *American Sociological Review* 51 (1986): 273–86. See also Alexander and Smith, excerpted in this volume, for a recent reformulation of value analysis.

Shils divided his time between the University of Chicago and Cambridge. He was a prolific writer whose longstanding interests included macrosociological theory, intellectuals and higher education, mass communication and the arts, Indian society, and the connections between ideology, liberalism, and civility. In addition to other essays by Shils collected in *The Constitution of Society* (Chicago: University of Chicago Press, 1982), see especially "Charisma, Order, and Status," *American Sociological Review* 30 (1965): 199–213; *Tradition* (Chicago: University of Chicago Press, 1981) and his volumes of selected papers in *The Calling of Sociology and Other Essays on the Pursuit of Learning* (Chicago: University of Chicago Press 1980); *Center and Periphery: Essays in Macrosociology* (Chicago: University of Chicago Press 1975); *The Intellectuals and the Powers, and Other Essays* (Chicago: University of Chicago Press 1972). See also Joseph Ben-David and Terry Nichols Clark, eds., *Culture and its Creators: Essays in Honor of Edward Shils* (Chicago: University of Chicago Press, 1977), Liah Greenfeld and Michel Martin, eds., *Center: Ideas and Institutions* (Chicago: University of Chicago Press, 1988), and Stephen Turner "The Significance of Shils," *Sociological Theory* 17 (1999): 125–45. Center–periphery images and theories are also discussed in S. N. Eisenstadt, *Power, Trust and Meaning: Essays in Sociological Theory and Analysis* (Chicago: University of Chicago Press, 1995) and S. N. Eisenstadt, "Cultural Orientations, Institutional Entrepreneurs and Social Change: Comparative Analysis on Traditional Civilizations," *American Journal of Sociology* 85 (1980): 840–69. For a nuanced account of conflicts over a cultural and material center sacred to different groups, see Roger Friedland and Richard Hecht, *To Rule Jerusalem* (Cambridge and New York: Cambridge University Press, 1996).

5 Base and Superstructure

Raymond Williams

Any modern approach to a Marxist theory of culture must begin by considering the proposition of a determining base and a determined superstructure. From a strictly theoretical point of view this is not, in fact, where we might choose to begin. It would be in many ways preferable if we could begin from a proposition which originally was equally central, equally authentic: namely the proposition that social being determines consciousness. It is not that the two propositions necessarily deny each other or are in contradiction. But the proposition of base and superstructure, with its figurative element and with its suggestion of a fixed and definite spatial relationship, constitutes, at least in certain hands, a very specialized and at times unacceptable version of the other proposition. Yet in the transition from Marx to Marxism, and in the development of mainstream Marxism itself, the proposition of the determining base and the determined superstructure has been commonly held to be the key to Marxist cultural analysis.

The source of this proposition is commonly taken to be a well-known passage in Marx's 1859 Preface to *A Contribution to the Critique of Political Economy*:

> In the social production of their life, men enter into definite relations that are indispensable and independent of their will, relations of production which correspond to a definite stage of development of their material productive forces. The sum total of these relations of production constitutes the economic structure of society, the real foundation, on which rises a legal and political superstructure and to which correspond definite forms of social consciousness. The mode of production of material life conditions the social, political and intellectual life process in general. It is not the consciousness of men that determines their being, but, on the contrary, their social being that determines their consciousness. At a certain stage of their development, the material productive forces of society come in conflict with the existing relations of production or – what is but a legal expression for the same thing – with the property relations within which they have been at work hitherto. From forms of development of the productive forces these relations turn into their fetters. Then begins an epoch of social revolution. With the change of the economic foundation the entire immense superstructure is more or less rapidly transformed. In considering such transformations a distinction should always be made between the material transformation of the economic conditions of production, which can be determined with the precision of natural science, and the legal, political, religious, aesthetic or philosophic – in short, ideological – forms in which men become conscious of this conflict and fight it out. (*Selected Works* 1. 362–4)

This is hardly an obvious starting-point for any cultural theory. It is part of an exposition of historical materialist method in the understanding of legal relations and forms of state. The first use of the term 'superstructure' is explicitly qualified as 'legal and political'. (It should incidentally be noted that the English translation in most common use has a plural – "legal and political superstructures" – for Marx's singular "juristicher und politischer Überbau".) 'Definite forms of social consciousness' are further said to 'correspond' to it (*entsprechen*). Transformation of the 'entire immense superstructure', in the social revolution which begins from the altered relations of productive forces and relations of production, is a process in which 'men become conscious of this conflict and fight it out' in 'ideological forms' which now include the 'religious, aesthetic, or philosophic' as well as the legal and political. Much has been deduced from this formulation, but the real context is inevitably limited. Thus it would be possible, simply from this passage, to define 'cultural' ('religious, aesthetic or philosophic') forms in which 'men become conscious of this conflict', without necessarily supposing that these specific forms are the whole of 'cultural' activity.

There is at least one earlier use, by Marx, of the term 'superstructure'. It is in *The Eighteenth Brumaire of Louis Napoleon, 1851–2*:

> Upon the several forms of property, upon the social conditions of existence, a whole superstructure is reared of various and peculiarly shaped feelings (*empfindungen*), illusions, habits of thought and conceptions of life. The whole class produces and shapes these out of its material foundation and out of the corresponding social conditions. The individual unit to whom they flow through tradition and education may fancy that they constitute the true reasons for and premises of his conduct.   (*Selected Works* 1. 272–3)

This is an evidently different use. The 'superstructure' is here the whole 'ideology' of the class: its 'form of consciousness'; its constitutive ways of seeing itself in the world. It would be possible, from this and the later use, to see three senses of 'superstructure' emerging: (a) legal and political forms which express existing real relations of production; (b) forms of consciousness which express a particular class view of the world; (c) a process in which, over a whole range of activities, men become conscious of a fundamental economic conflict and fight it out. These three senses would direct our attention, respectively, to (a) institutions; (b) forms of consciousness; (c) political and cultural practices.

It is clear that these three areas are related and must, in analysis, be interrelated. But on just this crucial question of interrelation the term itself is of little assistance, just because it is variably applied to each area in turn. Nor is this at all surprising, since the use is not primarily conceptual, in any precise way, but metaphorical. What it primarily expresses is the important sense of a visible and formal 'superstructure' which might be analysed on its own but which cannot be understood without seeing that it rests on a 'foundation'. The same point must be made of the corresponding metaphorical term. In the use of 1851–2 it is absent, and the origins of a particular form of class consciousness are specified as 'forms of property' and 'social conditions of existence'. In the use of 1859 it appears in almost conscious metaphor: 'the economic structure of society – the real foundation (*die reale Basis*), on which rises (*erhebt*) a legal and political superstructure (*Überbau*)'. It is replaced, later in the argument, by 'the economic foundation' (*ökonomische Grundlage*). The continuity of meaning is relatively clear, but the variation of terms for one part of the relationship ('forms of property, social conditions of existence'; 'economic structure of society'; 'real basis'; 'real foundation'; *Basis*; *Grundlage*) is not matched by explicit variation of the other term of the relationship, though the actual signification of this term (*Überbau*; superstructure) is, as we have seen, variable. It is part of the complexity of the subsequent argument that the term rendered in English explication (probably first by Engels) as 'base' is rendered in other languages in significant variations (in French usually as *infrastructure*, in Italian as *struttura*, and so on, with some complicating effects on the substance of the argument).

In the transition from Marx to Marxism, and then in the development of expository and didactic formulations, the words used in the original arguments were projected, first, as if they were precise concepts, and second, as if they were descriptive terms for observable 'areas' of social life. The main sense of the words in the original arguments had been relational, but the popularity of the terms tended to indicate either (a) relatively enclosed categories or (b) relatively enclosed areas of activity. These were then correlated either temporally (first material production, then consciousness, then politics and culture) or in effect, forcing the metaphor, spatially (visible and distinguishable 'levels' or 'layers' – politics and culture, then forms of consciousness, and so on down to 'the base'). The serious practical problems of method, which the original words had indicated, were then usually in effect bypassed by methods derived from a confidence, rooted in the popularity of the terms, in the relative enclosure of categories or areas expressed as 'the base', 'the superstructure'.

It is then ironic to remember that the force of Marx's original criticism had been mainly directed against the separation of 'areas' of thought and activity (as in the separation of consciousness from material production) and against the related evacuation of specific content – real human activities – by the imposition of abstract categories. The common abstraction of 'the base' and 'the superstructure' is thus a radical persistence of the modes of thought which he attacked. That in the course of other arguments he gave some warrant for this, within the intrinsic difficulties of any such formulation, is certainly true. But it is significant that when he came to any sustained analysis, or to a realization of the need for such analysis, he was at once specific and flexible in his use of his own terms. He had already observed, in the formulation of 1859, a distinction between analysing 'the economic conditions of production, which can be determined with the precision of natural science' and the analysis of 'ideological forms', for which methods were evidently less precise. In 1857 he had noted:

> As regards art, it is well known that some of its peaks by no means correspond to the general development of society; nor do they therefore to the material substructure, the skeleton as it were of its organization.

His solution of the problem he then discusses, that of Greek art, is hardly convincing, but the 'by no means correspond' is a characteristic practical recognition of the complexity of real relations. Engels, in his essay *Feuerbach and the End of Classical German Philosophy*, still argued specifically, showing how the 'economic basis' of a political struggle could be dulled in consciousness or altogether lost sight of, and how a legal system could be projected as independent of its economic content, in the course of its professional development. Then:

> Still higher ideologies, that is, such as are still further removed from the material, economic basis, take the form of philosophy and religion. Hence the interconnection

between conceptions and their material conditions of existence becomes more and more complicated, more and more obscured by intermediate links. But the interconnection exists.

This relational emphasis, including not only complexity but recognition of the ways in which some connections are lost to consciousness, is of course very far from the abstract categories (though it supports the implication of separate areas) of 'superstructure' and 'base'.

In all serious Marxist analysis the categories are of course not used abstractly. But they may have their effect none the less. It is significant that the first phase of the recognition of practical complexities stressed what are really *quantitative* relations. By the end of the nineteenth century it was common to recognize what can best be described as disturbances, or special difficulties, of an otherwise regular relationship. This is true of the idea of 'lags' in time, which had been developed from Marx's observation that some of the 'peaks' of art 'by no means correspond to the general development of society'. This could be expressed (though Marx's own 'solution' to this problem had not been of this kind) as a matter of *temporal* 'delay' or 'unevenness'. The same basic model is evident in Engels's notion of the relative *distance* ('still further removed') of the 'higher ideologies'. Or consider Engels's letter to Bloch of September 1890:

> According to the materialist conception of history, the *ultimately* determining element in history is the production and reproduction of real life. More than this neither Marx nor I have ever asserted. Hence if somebody twists this into saying that the economic element is the only determining one, he transforms that proposition into a meaningless, abstract, senseless phrase. The economic situation is the basis, but the various elements of the superstructure – political forms of the class struggle and its results, to wit: constitutions established by the victorious class after a successful battle, etc., juridical forms, and even the reflexes of all these actual struggles in the brains of the participants, political, juristic, philosophical theories, religious views and their further development into systems of dogma – also exercise their influence upon the course of the historical struggles and in many cases preponderate in determining their *form*. There is an interaction of all these elements in which, amid all the endless host of accidents (that is, of things and events whose inner interconnection is so remote or so impossible of proof that we can regard it as non-existent, as negligible), the economic movement finally asserts itself as necessary. Otherwise the application of the theory to any period of history would be easier than the solution of a simple equation of the first degree.

This is a vital acknowledgement of real and methodological complexities. It is particularly relevant to the idea of 'determination', which will be separately discussed, and to the decisive problem of consciousness as 'reflexes' or 'reflection'. But within the vigour of his contrast between real history and a 'meaningless, abstract, senseless phrase', and alongside his recognition of a new (and theoretically significant) exception – 'the endless host of accidents' – Engels does not so much revise the enclosed categories – 'the basis' ('the economic element', 'the economic situation', 'the economic movement') and 'the various elements' (political, juridical, theoretical) of 'the superstructure' – as reiterate the categories and instance certain exceptions, indirectnesses, and irregularities which obscure their otherwise regular relation. What is fundamentally lacking, in the theoretical formulations of this important period, is any adequate recognition of the indissoluble connections between material production, political and cultural institutions and activity, and consciousness. The classic summary of 'the relationship between the base and the superstructure' is Plekhanov's distinction of 'five sequential elements: (i) the state of productive forces; (ii) the economic conditions; (iii) the socio-political regime; (iv) the psyche of social man; (v) various ideologies reflecting the properties of this psyche' (*Fundamental Problems of Marxism*, Moscow, 1922, 76). This is better than the bare projection of 'a base' and 'a superstructure', which has been so common. But what is wrong with it is its description of these 'elements' as 'sequential', when they are in practice indissoluble: not in the sense that they cannot be distinguished for purposes of analysis, but in the decisive sense that these are not separate 'areas' or 'elements' but the whole, specific activities and products of real men. That is to say, the analytic categories, as so often in idealist thought, have, almost unnoticed, become substantive descriptions, which then take habitual priority over the whole social process to which, as analytic categories, they are attempting to speak. Orthodox analysts began to think of 'the base' and 'the superstructure' as if they were separable concrete entities. In doing so they lost sight of the very processes – not abstract relations but constitutive processes – which it should have been the special function of historical materialism to emphasize. I shall be discussing later the major theoretical response to this loss: the attempt to reconstitute such processes by the idea of 'mediation'.

A persistent dissatisfaction, within Marxism, about the proposition of 'base and superstructure', has been most often expressed by an attempted refinement and revaluation of 'the superstructure'. Apologists have emphasized its complexity, substance, and 'autonomy' or autonomous value. Yet most of the difficulty still lies in the original extension of metaphorical terms for a relationship into abstract categories or concrete areas *between* which connections are looked for and complexities or relative autonomies emphasized. It is actually more important to observe the character of this extension in the case of 'the base' than in the case of the always more varied and variable 'superstructure'. By extension and by habit, 'the base' has come to be considered virtually as an object (a particular and reductive version of 'material existence'). Or, in specification, 'the base' is given very general and apparently uniform properties. 'The base' is the real social existence of man. 'The base' is the real relations of production corresponding to a stage of the development of material productive forces. 'The base' is a mode of production at a particular stage of its development. Of course these are, in practice, different propositions. Yet each is also very different from Marx's central emphasis on productive *activities*. He had himself made the point against reduction of 'the base' to a category:

> In order to study the connexion between intellectual and material production it is above all essential to conceive the latter in its determined historical form and not as a general category. For example, there corresponds to the capitalist mode of production a type of intellectual production quite different from that which corresponded to the medieval mode of production. Unless material production itself is understood in its specific historical form, it is impossible to grasp the characteristics of the intellectual production

which corresponds to it on the reciprocal action between the two.   (*Theorien über den Mehrwert*, cit. Bottomore and Rubel, 96–7.)

We can add that while a particular stage of 'real social existence', or of 'relations of production', or of a 'mode of production', can be discovered and made precise by analysis, it is never, as a body of activities, either uniform or static. It is one of the central propositions of Marx's sense of history, for example, that in actual development there are deep contradictions in the relationships of production and in the consequent social relationships. There is therefore the continual possibility of the dynamic variation of these forces. The 'variations' of the superstructure might be deduced from this fact alone, were it not that the 'objective' implications of 'the base' reduce all such variations to secondary consequences. It is only when we realize that 'the base', to which it is habitual to *refer* variations, is itself a dynamic and internally contradictory process – the specific activities and modes of activity, over a range from association to antagonism, of real men and classes of men – that we can begin to free ourselves from the notion of an 'area' or a 'category' with certain fixed properties for deduction to the variable processes of a 'superstructure'. The physical fixity of the terms exerts a constant pressure against just this realization.

Thus, contrary to a development in Marxism, it is not 'the base' and 'the superstructure' that need to be studied, but specific and indissoluble real processes, within which the decisive relationship, from a Marxist point of view, is that expressed by the complex idea of 'determination'.

References

Marx, K., *Capital*, London, 1889.
——, *A Contribution to the Critique of Political Economy*, London, 1909.
——, *Economic and Philosophic Manuscripts of 1844*, Moscow, 1961.
——, *Essential Writings* (ed. Caute, D.), London, 1967.
——, *Grundrisse*, London, 1973.
——, *Selected Writings* (ed. Bottomore, T. B., and Rubel, M), London, 1963.
—— and Engels, F., The *Communist Manifesto*, London, 1888.
—— and ——, *The German Ideology*, London, 1963.
—— and ——, *Selected Works*, 2 vols., London, 1962.
Plekhanov, G., *Critical Essays in the History of Materialism*, London, 1934.

Editor's Notes on Further Reading

Raymond Williams on Base and Superstructure

Raymond Williams (1921–88) challenges here one of the most widespread assumptions about culture, the idea that meanings and values are determined by some more objective material reality (a model most well known from the Marxist theories of ideology Williams discusses, but also implicit in many other theories of society). The book develops a more supple model of cultural determination which recognizes cultural elements in material production, material and structural elements of meaning and value, and a relationship of "limits and pressures" rather than strict causal determination between them.

Born in Wales, Williams studied at Cambridge, where he later became Professor of Drama, having previously spent fifteen years teaching adult education classes for the Workers Educational Association. He was also a socialist writer and activist, making notable contributions to the Campaign for Nuclear Disarmament and the New Left in Britain. He wrote over thirty books and hundreds of articles on culture and politics, publishing literary criticism, cultural theory, drama, and novels. Other works important to cultural sociology include *Keywords: A Vocabulary of Culture and Society* (New York: Oxford University Press, 1976); *The Sociology of Culture*, with a new foreword by Bruce Robbins (Chicago: University of Chicago Press, 1995); *Culture and Society 1780–1950* (New York: Columbia University Press, 1983 [1958]); and *Television: Technology and Cultural Form* (New York: Schocken Books, 1975). See also Fred Inglis, *Raymond Williams* (London and New York: Routledge, 1995); Christopher Prendergast, ed., *Cultural Materialism: On Raymond Williams* (Minneapolis and London: University of Minnesota Press, 1995); Terry Eagleton, ed., *Raymond Williams: Critical Perspectives* (Boston: Northeastern University Press, 1989); and Alan O'Connor, *Raymond Williams; Writing, Culture, Politics* (Oxford and New York: Blackwell, 1989).

Williams's work makes a counterpoint both to idealist views that values are the main force driving social action and to theories of ideology which view culture as simply reflecting material and structural forces. In contrast to Horkheimer and Adorno (see excerpt this volume), he introduces influences from Gramsci to critical theories of culture: see for example Quintin Hoare and Geoffrey Nowell Smith, eds., *Selections from the Prison Notebooks of Antonio Gramsci* (London: Lawrence and Wishart, 1971), and Ernesto Laclau and Chantal Mouffe, *Hegemony and Socialist Strategy: Towards a Radical Democratic Politics* (London and New York: Verso, 1985). For useful overviews of the rich variety of Marxist theories of culture, see, for instance, Terry Eagleton, *Ideology: An Introduction* (London: Verso, 1991); Robert Wuthnow, "Infrastructure and Superstructure: Revisions in Marxist Sociology of Culture," pp. 145–70 in Richard Münch and Neil Smelser, eds., *Theory of Culture* (Berkeley and Los Angeles: University of California Press, 1992); Gene Burns, "Materialism, Ideology, and Political Change," pp. 248–62 in Robert Wuthnow, ed., *Vocabularies of Public Life: Empirical Essays in Symbolic Structure* (London and New York: Routledge, 1992), and Albert Bergesen, "The Rise of Semiotic Marxism," *Sociological Perspectives* 36 (1993): 1–22. See also Alvin Gouldner, *The Dialectic of Ideology and Technology: The Origins, Grammar, and Future of Ideology* (New York: Seabury Press, 1976) for another nuanced development of ideology theory, and for a more direct argument against any necessary relationship between ideas and economic structure see Nicholas Abercrombie, Stephen Hill and Bryan Turner, *The Dominant Ideology Thesis* (London: George Allen and Unwin, 1980).

Williams influenced the formation of Cultural Studies as a new intellectual field: see Centre for Contemporary Cultural Studies, *On Ideology* (London: Hutchinson, 1977); Stuart Hall, "Cultural Studies and its Theoretical Legacies," pp. 277–94 in Lawrence Grossberg, Cary Nelson, and Paula Treichler, eds., *Cultural Studies* (New York and London: Routledge, 1992), Richard Johnson, "Reinventing Cultural Studies: Remembering the Best Version," pp. 452–88 in Elizabeth Long, ed., *From Sociology to Cultural Studies: New Perspectives* (Malden, MA and Oxford: Blackwell, 1997), and, for a critique, Kenneth Parker, "Writing Dis-location: Black Writers and Postcolonial Britain," *Social Identities* 4 (1998): 177–201. For a comparison between cultural studies and cultural anthropology built on Williams's work, see Richard Handler, "Raymond Williams, George Stocking and Fin-de-Siècle U.S. Anthropology," *Cultural Anthropology* 13 (1998): 447–63.

6 Thick Description: Toward an Interpretive Theory of Culture

Clifford Geertz

Believing, with Max Weber, that man is an animal suspended in webs of significance he himself has spun, I take culture to be those webs, and the analysis of it to be therefore not an experimental science in search of law but an interpretive one in search of meaning. It is explication I am after, construing social expressions on their surface enigmatical. But this pronouncement, a doctrine in a clause, demands itself some explication . . .

In anthropology, or anyway social anthropology, what the practioners do is ethnography. And it is in understanding what ethnography is, or more exactly *what doing ethnography is*, that a start can be made toward grasping what anthropological analysis amounts to as a form of knowledge. This, it must immediately be said, is not a matter of methods. From one point of view, that of the textbook, doing ethnography is establishing rapport, selecting informants, transcribing texts, taking genealogies, mapping fields, keeping a diary, and so on. But it is not these things, techniques and received procedures, that define the enterprise. What defines it is the kind of intellectual effort it is: an elaborate venture in, to borrow a notion from Gilbert Ryle, "thick description."

Ryle's discussion of "thick description" appears in two recent essays of his (now reprinted in the second volume of his *Collected Papers*) addressed to the general question of what, as he puts it, "*Le Penseur*" is doing: "Thinking and Reflecting" and "The Thinking of Thoughts." Consider, he says, two boys rapidly contracting the eyelids of their right eyes. In one, this is an involuntary twitch; in the other, a conspiratorial signal to a friend. The two movements are, as movements, identical; from an I-am-a-camera, "phenomenalistic" observation of them alone, one could not tell which was twitch and which was wink, or indeed whether both or either was twitch or wink. Yet the difference, however unphotographable, between a twitch and a wink is vast; as anyone unfortunate enough to have had the first taken for the second knows. The winker is communicating, and indeed communicating in a quite precise and special way: (1) deliberately, (2) to someone in particular, (3) to impart a particular message, (4) according to a socially established code, and (5) without cognizance of the rest of the company. As Ryle points out, the winker has not done two things, contracted his eyelids and winked, while the twitcher has done only one, contracted his eyelids. Contracting your eyelids on purpose when there exists a public code in which so doing counts as a conspiratorial signal *is* winking. That's all there is to it: a speck of behavior, a fleck of culture, and – *voilà!* – a gesture.

That, however, is just the beginning. Suppose, he continues, there is a third boy, who, "to give malicious amusement to his cronies," parodies the first boy's wink, as amateurish, clumsy, obvious, and so on. He, of course, does this in the same way the second boy winked and the first twitched: by contracting his right eyelids. Only this boy is neither winking nor twitching, he is parodying someone else's, as he takes it, laughable, attempt at winking. Here, too, a socially established code exists (he will "wink" laboriously, overobviously, perhaps adding a grimace – the usual artifices of the clown); and so also does a message. Only now it is not conspiracy but ridicule that is in the air. If the others think he is actually winking, his whole project misfires as completely, though with somewhat different results, as if they think he is twitching. One can go further: uncertain of his mimicking abilities, the would-be satirist may practice at home before the mirror, in which case he is not twitching, winking, or parodying, but rehearsing; though so far as what a camera, a radical behaviorist, or a believer in protocol sentences would record he is just rapidly contracting his right eyelids like all the others. Complexities are possible, if not practically without end, at least logically so. The original winker might, for example, actually have been fake-winking, say, to mislead outsiders into imagining there was a conspiracy afoot when there in fact was not, in which case our descriptions of what the parodist is parodying and the rehearser rehearsing of course shift accordingly. But the point is that between what Ryle calls the "thin description" of what the rehearser (parodist, winker, twitcher...) is doing ("rapidly contracting his right eyelids") and the "thick description" of what he is doing ("practicing a burlesque of a friend faking a wink to deceive an innocent into thinking a conspiracy is in motion") lies the object of ethnography: a stratified hierarchy of meaningful structures in terms of which twitches, winks, fake-winks, parodies, rehearsals of parodies are produced, perceived, and interpreted, and without which they would not (not even the zero-form twitches, which, *as a cultural category*, are as much nonwinks as winks are nontwitches) in fact exist, no matter what anyone did or didn't do with his eyelids.

Like so many of the little stories Oxford philosophers like to make up for themselves, all this winking, fake-winking, burlesque-fake-winking, rehearsed-burlesque-fake-winking, may seem a bit artificial. In way of adding a more empirical note, let me give, deliberately unpreceded by any prior explanatory comment at all, a not untypical excerpt from my own field journal to demonstrate that, however evened off for didactic purposes, Ryle's example presents an image only too exact of the sort of piled-up structures of inference and implication through which an ethnographer is continually trying to pick his way:

> The French [the informant said] had only just arrived. They set up twenty or so small forts between here, the town, and the Marmusha area up in the middle of the mountains, placing them on promontories so they could survey the countryside. But for all this they couldn't guarantee safety, especially at night, so although the *mezrag*, trade-pact, system was supposed to be legally abolished it in fact continued as before.
>
> One night, when Cohen (who speaks fluent Berber), was up there, at Marmusha, two other Jews who were traders to a neighboring tribe came by to purchase some goods from him. Some Berbers, from yet another neighboring tribe, tried to break into Cohen's place, but he fired his rifle in the air. (Traditionally, Jews were not allowed to carry weapons; but at this period things were so unsettled many did so anyway.) This attracted the attention of the French and the marauders fled.
>
> The next night, however, they came back, one of them disguised as a woman who knocked on the door with some sort of a story. Cohen was suspicious and didn't want to

let "her" in, but the other Jews said, "oh, it's all right, it's only a woman." So they opened the door and the whole lot came pouring in. They killed the two visiting Jews, but Cohen managed to barricade himself in an adjoining room. He heard the robbers planning to burn him alive in the shop after they removed his goods, and so he opened the door and, laying about him wildly with a club, managed to escape through a window.

He went up to the fort, then, to have his wounds dressed, and complained to the local commandant, one Captain Dumari, saying he wanted his 'ar – i.e., four or five times the value of the merchandise stolen from him. The robbers were from a tribe which had not yet submitted to French authority and were in open rebellion against it, and he wanted authorization to go with his *mezrag*-holder, the Marmusha tribal *sheikh*, to collect the indemnity that, under traditional rules, he had coming to him. Captain Dumari couldn't officially give him permission to do this, because of the French prohibition of the *mezrag* relationship, but he gave him verbal authorization, saying, "If you get killed, it's your problem."

So the *sheikh*, the Jew, and a small company of armed Marmushans went off ten or fifteen kilometers up into the rebellious area, where there were of course no French, and, sneaking up, captured the thief-tribe's shepherd and stole its herds. The other tribe soon came riding out on horses after them, armed with rifles and ready to attack. But when they saw who the "sheep thieves" were, they thought better of it and said, "all right, we'll talk." They couldn't really deny what had happened – that some of their men had robbed Cohen and killed the two visitors – and they weren't prepared to start the serious feud with the Marmusha a scuffle with the invading party would bring on. So the two groups talked, and talked, and talked, there on the plain amid the thousands of sheep, and decided finally on five-hundred-sheep damages. The two armed Berber groups then lined up on their horses at opposite ends of the plain, with the sheep herded between them, and Cohen, in his black gown, pillbox hat, and flapping slippers, went out alone among the sheep, picking out, one by one and at his own good speed, the best ones for his payment.

So Cohen got his sheep and drove them back to Marmusha. The French, up in their fort, heard them coming from some distance ("Ba, ba, ba" said Cohen, happily, recalling the image) and said, "What the hell is that?" And Cohen said, "That is my '*ar*." The French couldn't believe he had actually done what he said he had done, and accused him of being a spy for the rebellious Berbers, put him in prison, and took his sheep. In the town, his family, not having heard from him in so long a time, thought he was dead. But after a while the French released him and he came back home, but without his sheep. He then went to the Colonel in the town, the Frenchman in charge of the whole region, to complain. But the Colonel said, "I can't do anything about the matter. It's not my problem."

Quoted raw, a note in a bottle, this passage conveys, as any similar one similarly presented would do, a fair sense of how much goes into ethnographic description of even the most elemental sort – how extraordinarily "thick" it is. In finished anthropological writings, including those collected here, this fact – that what we call our data are really our own constructions of other people's constructions of what they and their compatriots are up to – is obscured because most of what we need to comprehend a particular event, ritual, custom, idea, or whatever is insinuated as background information before the thing itself is directly examined. (Even to reveal that this little drama took place in the highlands of central Morocco in 1912 – and was recounted there in 1968 – is to determine much of our understanding of it.)

There is nothing particularly wrong with this, and it is in any case inevitable. But it does lead to a view of anthropological research as rather more of an observational and rather less of an interpretive activity than it really is. Right down at the factual base, the hard rock, insofar as there is any, of the whole enterprise, we are already explicating: and worse, explicating explications. Winks upon winks upon winks.

Analysis, then, is sorting out the structures of signification – what Ryle called established codes, a somewhat misleading expression, for it makes the enterprise sound too much like that of the cipher clerk when it is much more like that of the literary critic – and determining their social ground and import. Here, in our text, such sorting would begin with distinguishing the three unlike frames of interpretation ingredient in the situation, Jewish, Berber, and French, and would then move on to show how (and why) at that time, in that place, their copresence produced a situation in which systematic misunderstanding reduced traditional form to social farce. What tripped Cohen up, and with him the whole, ancient pattern of social and economic relationships within which he functioned, was a confusion of tongues.

I shall come back to this too-compacted aphorism later, as well as to the details of the text itself. The point for now is only that ethnography is thick description. What the ethnographer is in fact faced with – except when (as, of course, he must do) he is pursuing the more automatized routines of data collection – is a multiplicity of complex conceptual structures, many of them superimposed upon or knotted into one another, which are at once strange, irregular, and inexplicit, and which he must contrive somehow first to grasp and then to render. And this is true at the most down-to-earth, jungle field work levels of his activity: interviewing informants, observing rituals, eliciting kin terms, tracing property lines, censusing households ... writing his journal. Doing ethnography is like trying to read (in the sense of "construct a reading of") a manuscript – foreign, faded, full of ellipses, incoherencies, suspicious emendations, and tendentious commentaries, but written not in conventionalized graphs of sound but in transient examples of shaped behavior.

Culture, this acted document, thus is public, like a burlesqued wink or a mock sheep raid. Though ideational, it does not exist in someone's head; though unphysical, it is not an occult entity. The interminable, because unterminable, debate within anthropology as to whether culture is "subjective" or "objective," together with the mutual exchange of intellectual insults ("idealist!" – "materialist!"; "mentalist!" – "behaviorist!"; "impressionist!" – "positivist!") which accompanies it, is wholly misconceived. Once human behavior is seen as (most of the time; there *are* true twitches) symbolic action – action which, like phonation in speech, pigment in painting, line in writing, or sonance in music, signifies – the question as to whether culture is patterned conduct or a frame of mind, or even the two somehow mixed together, loses sense. The thing to ask about a burlesqued wink or a mock sheep raid is not what their ontological status is. It is the same as that of rocks on the one hand and dreams on the other – they are things of this world. The thing to ask is what their import is: what it is, ridicule or challenge, irony or anger, snobbery or pride, that, in their occurrence and through their agency, is getting said....

The claim to attention of an ethnographic account does not rest on its author's ability to capture primitive facts in faraway places and carry them home like a mask or a carving, but on the degree to which he is able to clarify what goes on in such places, to reduce the puzzlement – what manner of men are these? – to which unfamiliar acts emerging out of unknown backgrounds naturally give rise. This raises some serious problems of verification, all right – or, if "verification" is too strong a word for so soft a science (I, myself, would prefer "appraisal"), of how you can tell a better account from a worse one. But that is precisely the virtue of it. If ethnography is thick description and ethnographers those who are doing the describing, then the determining question for any given example of it, whether a field journal squib or a Malinowski-sized monograph, is whether it sorts winks from twitches and real winks from mimicked ones. It is not against a body of uninterpreted data, radically thinned descriptions, that we must measure the cogency of our explications, but against the power of the scientific imagination to bring us into touch with the lives of strangers. It is not worth it, as Thoreau said, to go round the world to count the cats in Zanzibar.

Editor's Notes on Further Reading

Clifford Geertz on Meaning and Interpretation

Clifford Geertz's essay on "thick description" is an eloquent and famous statement of what makes the study of culture distinctive and difficult – careful attention to meaning and interpretation. He challenges reductionist social explanation which ignores the symbolic dimensions of social life, but also criticizes reified cultural analysis of abstract codes, preferring instead ethnography's close examination of grounded, concrete sequences of action and their contexts. Geertz emphasizes that culture is public and collective, not simply an attribute of individuals; he also makes the important methodological point that cultural analysis should not be treated as idiosyncratic but rather that it should be assessed on criteria appropriate to the subject.

Geertz's work has had a big interdisciplinary impact. William Sewell, in "Geertz, Cultural Systems, and History: From Synchrony to Transformation," pp. 35–55 in Sherry Ortner, ed., *The Fate of "Culture": Geertz and Beyond* (Berkeley: University of California Press, 1999) compares his influence to that of fellow anthropologist Ruth Benedict, also excerpted here. In the 1970s and 1980s his essays became foundational in cultural sociology: for an analysis and assessment see for instance Ann Swidler, excerpt this volume; Swidler, "Geertz's Ambiguous Legacy," *Contemporary Sociology* 25 (1996): 299–302; and Orville Lee III, "Observations on Anthropological Thinking About the Culture Concept: Clifford Geertz and Pierre Bourdieu," *Berkeley Journal of Sociology* 33 (1988): 115–30. Thick ethnographic description of the sort Geertz recommends can be seen in work by Eliasoph, Lichterman, Nippert-Eng, and Kunda, excerpted this volume. Geertz's work invites debate on the key methodological issues in the study of culture; the relative importance of causal explanation and interpretive understanding, the ethics and politics of ethnography, and the relation between particular and general. An entry into these debates, and further commentary, can be found in Aletta Biersack, "Local Knowledge and Local History: Geertz and Beyond," in Lynn Hunt, ed., *The New Cultural History* (Berkeley: University of California Press, 1989); Adam Kuper, *Culture: The Anthropologists' Account* (Cambridge, MA: Harvard University Press 1999), and Ortner, ed., *The Fate of "Culture."*

Born in 1926, Geertz studied at Harvard's Department of Social Relations in the 1950s. He taught at the University of Chicago in the 1960s, and subsequently became Professor of Social Science at Princeton's Institute for Advanced Study for many years. He did ethnographic research in Indonesia and Morocco, and he has published numerous books and articles on religion, economic development, politics, and village life, as well as on cultural theory. In addition to the classic collection of essays from which this excerpt is drawn, *The Interpretation of Cultures* (New York: Basic Books, 1973), see, for instance, *After the Fact: Two Countries, Four Decades, One Anthropologist* (Cambridge, MA: Harvard University Press, 1995); *Local Knowledge: Further Essays in Interpretive Anthropology* (New York: Basic Books, 1983); and *Islam Observed: Religious Development in Morocco and Indonesia* (New Haven: Yale University Press, 1968). For more on Geertz and his work see Richard Handler, "An Interview with Clifford Geertz," *Current Anthropology* 32 (1991): 603–13, and Fred Inglis, *Clifford Geertz: Culture, Customs, and Ethics* (Malden, MA and Oxford: Blackwell, 2000).

7 Cultural Power

Pierre Bourdieu

The Perception of the Social World and Political Struggle

The most resolutely objectivist theory must take account of agents' representation of the social world and, more precisely, of the contribution they make to the construction of the vision of this world, and, thereby to the very construction of this world, via the *labour of representation* (in all senses of the term) that they continually perform in order to impose their own vision of the world or the vision of their own position in this world, that is, their social identity. The perception of the social world is the product of a double social structuring: on the 'objective' side, this perception is socially structured because the properties attached to agents or institutions do not make themselves available to perception independently, but in combinations whose probability varies widely (and just as feathered animals have a greater chance of having wings than furry animals, so the possessors of a substantial cultural capital are more likely to be museum visitors than those who lack such capital); on the 'subjective' side, it is structured because the schemes of perception and evaluation susceptible of being brought into operation at a given moment, including all those which are laid down in language, are the product of previous symbolic struggles and express, in a more or less transformed form, the state of symbolic relations of power. The fact remains, none the less, that the objects of the social world can be perceived and expressed in different ways because, like the objects of the natural world, they always include a certain indeterminacy and vagueness – because, for example, the most constant combinations of properties are never founded on anything other than statistical connections between interchangeable features; and also because, as historical objects, they are subject to variations in time and their meaning, in so far as it depends on the future, is itself in suspense, in a pending and deferred state, and is thus relatively indeterminate. This element of risk, of uncertainty, is what provides a basis for the plurality of world views, a plurality which is itself linked to the plurality of points of view, and to all the symbolic struggles for the production and imposition of the legitimate vision of the world and, more precisely, to all the cognitive strategies of *fulfilment* which produce the meaning of the objects of the social world by going beyond the directly visible attributes by reference to the future or the past. This reference may be implicit and tacit, through what Husserl calls protension and retention, practical forms of prospection or retrospection excluding the positioning of past and future as such; or it may be explicit, as in political struggles in which the past, with the retrospective reconstruction of a past adjusted to the needs of the present ('La Fayette, here we are!'), and especially the future, with the creative foresight associated with it, are continually invoked, in order to determine, delimit, and define the ever-open meaning of the present.

To point out that perception of the social world implies an act of construction is not in the least to accept an intellectualist theory of knowledge: the essential part of one's experience of the social world and of the labour of construction it implies takes place in practice, without reaching the level of explicit representation and verbal expression. Closer to a class unconscious than to a 'class consciousness' in the Marxist sense, the sense of the position one occupies in the social space (what Goffman calls the 'sense of one's place') is the practical mastery of the social structure as a whole which reveals itself through the sense of the position occupied in that structure. The categories of perception of the social world are essentially the product of the incorporation of the objective structures of the social space. Consequently, they incline agents to accept the social world as it is, to take it for granted, rather than to rebel against it, to put forward opposed and even antagonistic possibilities. The sense of one's place, as the sense of what one can or cannot 'allow oneself', implies a tacit acceptance of one's position, a sense of limits ('that's not meant for us') or – what amounts to the same thing – a sense of distances, to be marked and maintained, respected, and expected of others. And this is doubtless all the more true when the conditions of existence are more rigorous and the reality principle is more rigorously imposed. (Hence the profound realism which most often characterizes the world view of the dominated and which, functioning as a sort of socially constituted instinct of conservation, can appear conservative only with reference to an external and thus normative representation of the 'objective interest' of those whom it helps to live or to survive.)

If the objective relations of power tend to reproduce themselves in visions of the social world which contribute to the permanence of those relations, this is therefore because the structuring principles of the world view are rooted in the objective structures of the social world and because the relations of power are also present in people's minds in the form of the categories of perception of those relations. But the degree of indeterminacy and vagueness characteristic of the objects of the social world is, together with the practical, pre-reflexive and implicit character of the patterns of perception and evaluation which are applied to them, the Archimedean point which is objectively made available to truly political action. Knowledge of the social world and, more precisely, the categories which make it possible, are the stakes *par excellence* of the political struggle, a struggle which is inseparably theoretical and practical, over the power of preserving or transforming the social world by preserving or transforming the categories of perception of that world.

The capacity for bringing into existence in an explicit state, of publishing, of making public (i.e. objectified, visible, sayable, and even official) that which, not yet having attained objective and collective existence, remained in a state of individual or serial existence – people's disquiet, anxiety, expectation, worry – represents a formidable social power, that of bringing into existence groups by establishing the *common sense*, the explicit consensus, of the whole group. In fact, this labour of categorization, of making things explicit and classifying them, is continually being performed, at every moment of ordinary existence, in the struggles in which agents clash over the meaning of the social world and their position in it, the meaning of their social identity, through all the forms of speaking well or badly of someone or something, of blessing or cursing and of malicious gossip, eulogy, congratulations, praise, compliments, or insults, rebukes, criticism, accusations, slanders, etc.

It is easy to understand why one of the elementary forms of political power should have consisted, in many archaic societies, in the almost magical power of *naming* and bringing into existence by virtue of naming. Thus in traditional Kabylia, the function of making things explicit and the labour of symbolic production that poets performed, particularly in crisis situations, when the meaning of the world is no longer clear, conferred on them major political functions, those of the war-lord or ambassador. But with the growing differentiation of the social world and the constitution of relatively autonomous fields, the labour of the production and imposition of meaning is performed in and through struggles in the field of cultural production (and especially in the political sub-field); it becomes the particular concern, the specific interest, of the professional producers of objectified representations of the social world, or, more precisely, of the methods of objectification.

If the legitimate mode of perception is such an important stake in different struggles, this is because on the one hand the movement from the implicit to the explicit is in no way automatic, the same experience of the social being recognizable in very different expressions, and on the other hand, the most marked objective differences may be hidden behind more immediately visible differences (such as, for example, those which separate ethnic groups). It is true that perceptual configurations, social *Gestalten*, exist objectively, and that the proximity of conditions and thus of dispositions tends to be re-translated into durable links and groupings, immediately perceptible social units such as socially distinct regions or districts (with spatial segregation), or sets of agents possessing altogether similar visible properties, such as Weber's *Stände*. But the fact remains that socially known and recognized differences exist only for a subject capable not only of perceiving the differences, but of recognizing them as significant and interesting, i.e., exists only for a subject endowed with the aptitude and the inclination to *establish* the differences which are held to be significant in the social world under consideration.

In this way, the social world, particularly through properties and their distribution, attains, in the objective world itself, the status of a *symbolic system* which, like a system of phonemes, is organized in accordance with the logic of difference, of differential deviation, which is thus constituted as significant *distinction*. The social space, and the differences that 'spontaneously' emerge within it, tend to function symbolically as *a space of life-styles* or as a set of *Stände*, of groups characterized by different life-styles. . . .

Distinction – in the ordinary sense of the world – is the difference written into the very structure of the social space when it is perceived in accordance with the categories adapted to that structure; and the Weberian *Stand*, which people so often like to contrast with the Marxist class, is the class adequately constructed when it is perceived through the categories of perception derived from the structure of that space. Symbolic capital – another name for distinction – is nothing other than capital, of whatever kind, when it is perceived by an agent endowed with categories of perception arising from the incorporation of the structure of its distribution, i.e. when it is known and recognized as self-evident. Distinctions, as symbolic transformations of *de facto* differences, and, more generally, the ranks, orders, grades and all the other symbolic hierarchies, are the product of the application of schemes of construction which – as in the case, for instance, of the pairs of adjectives used to express most social judgements – are the product of the incorporation of the very structures to which they are applied; and recognition of the most absolute legitimacy is nothing other than an apprehension of the everyday social world as taken for granted, an apprehension which results from the almost perfect coincidence of objective structures and incorporated structures.

It follows, among other consequences, that symbolic capital is attracted to symbolic capital and that the – real – autonomy of the field of symbolic production does not prevent this field from remaining dominated, in its functioning, by the constraints which dominate the social field as a whole. It also follows that objective relations of power tend to reproduce themselves in symbolic relations of power, in visions of the social world which contribute to ensuring the permanence of those relations of power. In the struggle for the imposition of the legitimate vision of the social world, in which science itself is inevitably involved, agents wield a power which is proportional to their symbolic capital, that is, to the recognition they receive from a group. The authority which underlies the performative effectiveness of discourse about the social world, the symbolic force of visions and pre-visions aimed at imposing the principles of vision and division of this world, is a *percipi*, a being known and recognized (*nobilis*), which allows a *percipere* to be imposed. It is the most *visible* agents, from the point of view of the prevailing categories of perception, who are the best placed to change the vision by changing the categories of perception. But they are also, with a few exceptions, the least inclined to do so.

The Symbolic Order and the Power of Naming

In the symbolic struggle for the production of common sense or, more precisely, for the monopoly of legitimate *naming* as the official – i.e. explicit and public – imposition of the legitimate vision of the social world, agents bring into play the symbolic capital that they have acquired in previous struggles, in particular all the power that they possess over the instituted taxonomies, those inscribed in people's minds or in the objective world, such as qualifications. Thus all the symbolic strategies through which agents aim to impose their vision of the divisions of the social world and of their position in that world can be located between two extremes: the insult, that *idios logos* through which an ordinary individual attempts to impose his point of view by taking the risk that a reciprocal insult may ensue, and the *official naming*, a symbolic act of imposition which has on its side all the strength of the collective, of the consensus, of common sense, because it is performed by a delegated agent of the state, that is, the holder of the *monopoly of legitimate symbolic violence*. On the one hand, there is the world of particular perspectives, of individual agents who, on the basis of their particular point of view, their particular position, produce namings – of themselves and others – that are particular and self-interested (nicknames, insults, or even accusations, indictments, slanders, etc.), and all the more powerless to gain recognition, and thus to exert a truly symbolic effect, the less their authors are *authorized*, either personally (*auctoritas*) or institutionally (by delegation), and the more directly they are concerned to gain recognition for the point of view that they are seeking to impose. On the other hand, there is the authorized point of view of an agent who is personally authorized, such as a great critic or prestigious preface-writer or established author (Zola's '*J'accuse*'), and above all the legitimate point of view of the authorized spokesperson, the delegate of the state, the official naming, or the *title* or qualification which, like an educational qualification, is valid on all markets and which, as an official definition of one's official identity, saves its bearers from the symbolic struggle of all against all, by establishing the authorized perspective, the one recognized by all and thus universal, from which social agents are viewed. The state, which produces official classifications, is to some extent the supreme tribunal to which Kafka was referring when he made Block say, speaking of the advocate and his claim to be among the 'great advocates': 'any man can call himself "great", of course, if he pleases, but in this matter the Court tradition must decide.' The truth is that scientific analysis does not have to choose between perspectivism and what has to be called absolutism: indeed, the truth of the social world is the stake in a struggle between agents who are very unequally equipped to attain absolute, that is, self-verifying, vision and prevision. . . .

But the logic of official naming is most clearly demonstrated in the case of the *title* – whether titles of nobility, educational qualifications or professional titles. This is a symbolic capital that is socially and even legally guaranteed. The nobleman is not only someone who is known, famous, and even renowned for his good qualities, prestigious, in a word, *nobilis*: he is also someone who is recognized by an *official* authority, one that is 'universal', i.e. known and recognized by all. The professional or academic title is a sort of legal rule of social perception, a being-perceived that is guaranteed as a right. It is symbolic capital in an institutionalized, legal (and no longer merely legitimate) form. More and more inseparable from the educational qualification, by virtue of the fact that the educational system tends more and more to represent the ultimate and unique guarantor of all professional titles, it has a value in itself and, although we are dealing with a common noun, it functions like a great name (the name of some great family or a proper name), one which procures all sorts of symbolic profit (and goods that one cannot directly acquire with money). It is the symbolic scarcity of the title in the space of the names of professions that tends to govern the rewards of the profession (and not the relation between the supply of and demand for a certain form of labour). It follows that the rewards associated with the title tend to become autonomous with regard to the rewards associated with the work. In this way, the same work can receive different remunerations depending on the titles and qualifications of the person doing it (e.g. a permanent, official post-holder as opposed to a part-timer or someone acting in that capacity, etc.). The qualification is in itself an *institution* (like language) that is more durable than the intrinsic characteristics of the work, and so the rewards associated with the qualification can be maintained despite changes in the work and its relative value: it is not the relative value of the work which determines the value of the name, but the institutionalized value of the title which acts as an instrument serving to defend and maintain the value of the work.

This means that one cannot establish a science of classifications without establishing a science of the struggle over classifications and without taking into account the position occupied, in this struggle for the power of knowledge, for power through knowledge, for the monopoly of legitimate symbolic violence, by each of the agents or groups of agents involved in it, whether they be ordinary individuals, exposed to the vicissitudes of everyday symbolic struggle, or authorized (and full-time) professionals, which includes all those who speak or write about social classes, and who can be distinguished by the extent to which their classifications involve the authority of the state, as holder of the monopoly of *official naming*, of the right classification, of the right order.

While the structure of the social field is defined at each moment by the structure of the distribution of capital and the profits characteristic of the different particular fields, the fact remains that in each of these arenas, the very definition of the stakes and the trump cards can be called into question. Every field is the site of a more or less openly declared struggle for the definition of the legitimate principles of division of the field. The question of legitimacy arises from the very possibility of this questioning, from this break with the doxa which takes the ordinary order for granted. That being said, the symbolic force of the parties involved in this struggle is never completely independent of their positions in the game, even if the specifically symbolic power of naming constitutes a force which is relatively independent of the other forms of social power. The constraints of the necessity inscribed in the very structure of the different fields still weigh on the symbolic struggles which aim to preserve or transform that structure. The social world is, to a great extent, something which agents make at every moment; but they have no chance of unmaking and remaking it except on the basis of a realistic knowledge of what it is and of what they can do to it by virtue of the position they occupy in it.

In short, scientific work aims to establish an adequate knowledge both of the space of objective relations between the different positions which constitute the field and of the necessary relations that are set up, through the mediation of the habitus of those who occupy them, between these positions and the corresponding stances, i.e. between the points occupied in that space and the points of view on that very space, which play a part in the reality and development of that space. In other words, the objective delimitation of constructed classes, of *regions* of the constructed space of positions, enables one to understand the source and effectiveness of the classificatory strategies by means of which agents seek to preserve or modify this space, in the forefront of which we must place the constitution of groups organized with a view to defending the interests of their members.

Analysis of the struggle over classifications brings to light the political ambition which haunts the gnoseological ambition to produce the correct classification: an ambition which properly defines the *rex*, the one who has the task, according to Benveniste, of *regere fines* and *regere sacra*, of tracing in speech the frontiers between groups, and also between the sacred and the profane, good and evil, the vulgar and the distinguished. If social science is not to be merely a way of pursuing politics by other means, social scientists must take as their object the intention of assigning others to classes and of thereby telling them what they are and what they have to be (herein lies all the ambiguity of forecasting); they must analyse, in order to repudiate it, the ambition of the creative world vision, that sort of *intuitus originarius* which would make things exist in conformity with its vision (herein lies all the ambiguity of the Marxist conception of class, which is inseparably both a being and an ought-to-be). They must objectify the ambition of objectifying, of classifying from outside, objectively, agents who are struggling to classify others and themselves. If they do happen to classify – by carving up, for the purposes of statistical analysis, the continuous space of social positions – it is precisely so as to be able to objectify *all* forms of objectification, from the individual insult to the official naming, without forgetting the claim, characteristic of science in its positivist and bureaucratic definition, to arbitrate in these struggles in the name of 'axiological neutrality'. The symbolic power of agents, understood as a power of making people see – *theorein* – and believe, of producing and imposing the legitimate or legal classification, depends, as the case of *rex* reminds us, on the position they occupy in the space (and in the classifications that are potentially inscribed in it). But to objectify objectification means, above all, objectifying the field of production of the objectified representations of the social world, and in particular of the legislative taxonomies, in short, the field of cultural or ideological production, a game in which the social scientist is himself involved, as are all those who debate the nature of social classes.

Editor's Notes on Further Reading

Bourdieu on Cultural Power

Pierre Bourdieu argues that social explanation must take into account the subjective categories in which people understand their worlds, the pre-conscious practices in which those categories are articulated, the power exercised in social categorization, and the politics of categorical distinctions. Cultural categorization and the power of authoritative categorization are important stakes in social struggles and central to the understanding of inequality and social change. Moreover, intellectuals and social scientists are not only analysts but important participants in symbolic politics, and their work demands an ethic of reflexivity.

   Born in southern France in 1930, Bourdieu studied philosophy at the École normale supérieure in Paris and spent some years in Algeria during the war for independence in the 1950s. He published several books on Algerian society and this work also informed his cultural theory in *Outline of a Theory of Practice*, trans. Richard Nice (Cambridge: Cambridge University Press, 1977) and *The Logic of Practice*, trans. Richard Nice (Stanford: Stanford University Press, 1990). From the 1960s he worked at the École des hautes études en sciences sociales in Paris on a number of collaborative projects on French culture and education, and founded the Centre de sociologie européenne. In 1982 he was appointed Professor of Sociology at the Collège de France in Paris. His many books and articles address numerous aspects of cultural power, treating topics in the sociology of education, art, aesthetics, intellectuals, sport, the media, politics, language, stratification, and status attainment. In addition to his theoretical writing cited above, and the collection of essays from which this selection is drawn, probably the most influential of his writings in the English-speaking world has been *Distinction: A Social Critique of the Judgement of Taste*, trans. Richard Nice (Cambridge, MA: Harvard University Press, 1984), a massive, rigorously analyzed investigation of the relations between social position and cultural taste in France. Other representative or influential works include Pierre Bourdieu and Jean-Claud Passeron, *Reproduction in Education, Society, and Culture*, trans. Richard Nice, foreword by Tom Bottomore (London and Beverly Hills: Sage, 1977); *In Other Words: Essays Towards a Reflexive Sociology*, trans. Matthew Adamson (Stanford: Stanford University Press 1990); Pierre Bourdieu with Luc Boltanski et al., *Photography: A Middle-Brow Art*, trans. Shaun Whiteside (Stanford, CA: Stanford University Press, 1990); Bourdieu and Loïc Wacquant, *An Invitation to Reflexive Sociology* (Chicago: University of Chicago Press, 1992); Bourdieu, *The Field of Cultural Production: Essays on Art and Literature*, edited and introduced by Randal Johnson (Columbia University Press, 1993); Bourdieu et al., *Linguistic Misunderstanding and Professorial Power*, trans. Richard Teese (Stanford: Stanford University Press, 1994); and *On Television*, trans. Priscilla Parkhurst Ferguson (New York: New Press, 1998). Usefully informal reflections can be found in Pierre Bourdieu, "Thinking about Limits," *Theory, Culture, and Society* 9 (1992): 37–49, Pierre Bourdieu and Terry Eagleton, "Doxa and Common Life," *New Left Review* 191 (1992): 111–21, and Loïc Wacquant, "Toward a Reflexive Sociology: A Workshop with Pierre Bourdieu," *Sociological Theory* 7 (1989): 26–63.

Like Geertz, Bourdieu has been influential in many disciplines, and his work has been agenda setting in recent cultural sociology (see Orville Lee III, "Observations on Anthropological Thinking About the Culture Concept: Clifford Geertz and Pierre Bourdieu," *Berkeley Journal of Sociology* 33 (1988): 115–30). Cultural sociologists have been influenced in two ways by Bourdieu: first, his theories of habitus, fields, and symbolic and social capital make culture more central to the investigation of many classic sociological issues; and second, more specifically, his theory of cultural capital has generated a thriving research program on the links between taste, symbolic boundaries and status groups (see excerpts from work by Lamont and Bryson and related editor's notes sections, this volume).

The many reflections on Bourdieu's work include David Swartz, *Culture and Power: The Sociology of Pierre Bourdieu* (Chicago and London: University of Chicago Press, 1997); Bridget Fowler, *Pierre Bourdieu and Cultural Theory: Critical Investigations* (London and Thousand Oaks, CA: Sage, 1997); Craig Calhoun, Edward LiPuma, and Moishe Postone, eds., *Bourdieu: Critical Perspectives* (Chicago: University of Chicago Press, 1993); Richard Jenkins, *Pierre Bourdieu* (London and New York: Routledge, 1992); Vera Zolberg, "Debating the Social: A symposium on and with Pierre Bourdieu," *Contemporary Sociology* 21 (1992): 151–61; Rogers Brubaker "Rethinking Classical Theory: The Sociological Vision of Pierre Bourdieu" *Theory and Society* 14 (1985): 745–75; Nicholas Garnham and Raymond Williams, "Pierre Bourdieu and the Sociology of Culture: An Introduction," *Media Culture and Society* 2 (1980): 209–23; and Paul DiMaggio, "Review Essay: On Pierre Bourdieu," *American Journal of Sociology* 84 (1979): 1460–74.

David Gartman challenges Bourdieu's theory from the point of view of Horkheimer and Adorno's critical theory (see chapter 3 this volume) in "Culture as Class Symbolization or Mass Reification? A Critique of Bourdieu's *Distinction*," *American Journal of Sociology* 97 (1991): 421–47. Some of the many other assessments and challenges from different points of view include T. M. S. Evans, "Bourdieu and the Logic of Practice: Is All Giving Indian-Giving or is 'Generalized Materialism' Not Enough?" *Sociological Theory* 17 (1999): 3–31; Lois McNay, "Gender, Habitus, and the Field: Pierre Bourdieu and the Limits of Reflexivity," *Theory, Culture, and Society* 16 (1999): 95–117; John Myles, "From Habitus to Mouth: Language and Class in Bourdieu's Sociology of Language," *Theory and Society* 28 (1999): 879–901; Rodney Benson, "Field Theory in Comparative Context: A New Paradigm for Media Studies," *Theory and Society* 28 (1998): 463–98; Jeffrey Alexander, "The Reality of Reduction: the Failed Synthesis of Pierre Bourdieu," pp. 128–217 in *Fin de Siècle Social Theory; Relativism, Reduction and the Problem of Reason* (London: Verso, 1995); Leslie McCall, "Does Gender Fit? Bourdieu, Feminism and Conceptions of Social Order," *Theory and Society* 21 (1992): 837–68, and Christian Joppke, "The Cultural Dimensions of Class Formation and Class Struggle: On the Social Theory of Pierre Bourdieu," *Berkeley Journal of Sociology* 31 (1986): 53–78.

Part II

Cultural Repertoires: Identities and Practices

8 Boundary Work: Sculpting Home and Work

Christena E. Nippert-Eng

In general "boundary work" consists of the strategies, principles, and practices we use to create, maintain, and modify cultural categories. I focus on a specific case of boundary work: the process through which we organize potentially realm-specific matters, people, objects, and aspects of self into "home" and "work," maintaining and changing these conceptualizations as needed and/or desired. Through boundary work, we impose our views of "home," "work," and their relationship on a fairly malleable world of possibilities.

Boundary work is first and foremost a mental activity, but it must be enacted and enhanced through a largely visible collection of essential, practical activities. It is this physical side of boundary work (e.g., wearing different or similar clothes at home and work; using "personal" money for "work" expenses, or not; listing work and home engagements on the same or different calendars; having co-workers over for dinner, or not; bringing children to the workplace, or not; putting a family photo on one's desk or colleagues' pictures on the fireplace mantel, or not; changing clothes upon arriving home each day, or not; consuming differently drugged drinks in the morning and evening, or not) that helps us tangibly reinforce and even challenge cognitive and situational distinctions between "home" and "work."

Accordingly, boundary work is the key process that reflects and helps determine how much we integrate/segment home and work. It is what ultimately allows each of us to repeatedly define and refine the essence of and relationship between our home and work realms – what is unique to each place and what is shared between them. It is the process that lets us create, challenge, defend and change categories of social existence within the mental and structural constraints of that existence.

There are two kinds of boundary work. The first focuses on boundary placement. The second focuses on boundary transcendence. Both are essential to place and maintain boundaries. The former more visibly draws the line between realms and the latter helps keep it in place by allowing us to jump back and forth over it. The activities associated with both forms may be continually adjusted to accommodate different conceptualizations of these realms.

Both forms of boundary work are affected by and reflected in three components: (1) the degree to which the people of either realm overlap, (2) the degree to which the objects (ranging from task-specific "tools," in the most general sense of the word, to decorations) and ambiance of surroundings are similar/different; and (3) the degree to which we think, act, and present ourselves in either realm in similar/different ways....

Of course, what we do along one of these fronts is often heavily influenced in the same integrating or segmenting direction by the same factors that guide our actions along other fronts. Nevertheless, any one of us might be highly segmenting in how we manage the people of both realms, extremely integrating via the inanimate objects of both realms, and more in the middle ranges in how we manage our appearance, talk styles, and eating habits. One's position along the continuum at a certain time is a composite, a summation of how one manages each of these broad components and their multiple dimensions.

For example, Irene is a scientist who engages in wage labor work at home at almost any time of the day or night. She has similar reading materials, computers, telephones, artwork, writing supplies, lights, and furniture in her workplace and home offices. She regularly brings her children into institutional workspace, entertains mostly colleagues at home, and is married to her collaborator.... [T]hese strategies place Irene toward the integration pole of the continuum.

Yet Irene also maintains numerous pockets of privacy, reflecting more selective distinctions between "home" and "work." These distinctions are encouraged simply because she possesses a separate workplace and residence. In addition, she does certain work and leisure and domestic activities only at home, while others occur only at the work place. Only her spouse is privy to certain thoughts and behavior. Only family attends certain social functions. Certain workmates are engaged only outside the home. These more segmenting distinctions offset her more integrating influences and practices and keep Irene from approaching the integration pole more closely.

Sal is a machinist who also has a policy about mixing "home" and "work," but his efforts...are designed to keep them separate. He never brings coworkers or wage labor tasks home, and he strictly adheres to a 7:30 to 4:30 workday, Monday through Friday. There are no common objects between his home and his workplace except himself, his lunch box, his underwear, and his jeans. (He wears different shoes and shirts in both places, even keeping his home and work shirts in separate drawers at home.)

Yet Sal makes and receives personal phone calls at work. He occasionally shares bits of more impersonal information between coworkers and family and attends colleagues' retirement parties and the funerals of their relatives. He brings the family to an annual workplace picnic and has a family portrait hanging at his workspace. So, while Sal is far more segmenting than Irene, he too falls short of an extreme type, some practices off-setting the segmenting effects of others.

Integrating through these three components presents three possibilities in terms of the direction of integration. First, we may create an overall effect in which "work" is heavily infused with elements conventionally associated with "home." Or we may heavily infuse "home" with the traditional elements of "work." Or, of course, we may obtain a fairly even balance in our integrating efforts, interweaving both realms with ways of being, people, activities, and artifacts commonly associated with another realm.

The amount of discretion we have for personal boundary work is a most important constraint on the direction and forms of our integration. For reasons I discuss later, the discretion to infuse work with home-related elements is often much less than the discretion to infuse or absorb home with work. Nonetheless, theoretically, and for some people even practically, the integrating of realms may be a fairly well-balanced endeavor, or one in which *either* side of the commute claims more turf from the other.

Wherever we currently fall along the continuum, however, we use, different practices in many different ways to create, preserve and change the experiential categories of "home" and "work." The process is like sculpting. In its classical, artistic sense, sculpting is an activity in which boundaries are physically imposed on matter, creating new forms and evoking new interpretations of raw material in the process. If an artist is working with stone, for instance, she carves out negative and positive spaces, defining each from and with the other, to form a new, critically interrelated whole. Hence, the sculptor's activity is a kind of "boundary work," in which matter is envisioned, divided up, and related to itself with virtually endless possibilities. This boundary work transforms relatively undifferentiated material into artificial, socially embedded "works of art."

Delineating and relating the concepts "home" and "work" is similarly a mental and physical sculpting process, and it too can result in endless different experiences. Consider a raw chunk of stone that represents all the items potentially divided into "home" and "work": people, objects, activities, even ways of thinking and being. Like the marble worker whose creations emerge from undifferentiated lumps, each of us must mentally carve out our own categories and relationships of "home" and "work" from an otherwise amorphous social existence. The process is embedded in the systems of cultural concepts and demands we are born into, as well as those we consciously choose or are forced to embrace later on. These ideas are reflected and modified through the tangible, physical side of boundary work, like the presence or absence of phone calls from home while at work, talking about work with one's family, using a briefcase or computer modem to bring personal reading materials and children's fund-raising forms to work or wage work to home, or carrying bag lunches from home to work.

In the extremely segmented approach to home and work, material is purposefully transformed into two distinct categories, "home" and "work" (i.e., negative and positive space), each inversely defining the other. The fully integrated "home–work" category lacks further internal boundaries, though, remaining an undifferentiated lump. It is enacted through people, objects, activities, and a self that are utterly interchangeable across time and space. It pointedly resists subdividing matter into "negative" and "positive" space.

At some point, however, the sculptor's job turns from the placement of boundaries to their maintenance. He must stop chiseling, stop imposing new variations on the boundary between negative and positive space. At first, he does this sequentially, perhaps repeatedly returning and adjusting what he's done in some places, while leaving others alone. Eventually, though, he must do whatever is necessary in order to uphold all of what he's done, allowing the boundaries to exist as a particular, final arrangement of negative and positive space. To maintain this boundary, he might sell the sculpture, so he's not tempted to keep tapping away forever. He might make sure that another chunk of stone will be ready to go, diverting his energy from the old to the new. He may (re)train himself to simply accept the ways these particular negative and positive spaces join at each juncture. Whatever it takes, this, too, is part of the work the sculptor must do in order for the work to exist.

In the same way, home–work negotiators must turn to different forms of boundary work whenever we are, or must be, satisfied with the boundary we've imposed. Whenever we finish with the work of *placing* the boundary, we must turn to the work of *transcending* it. Rather than continuing to chisel away, we work on making transitions between realms, in order to preserve both "home" and "work" as they currently exist. . . .

Of course, any sculptor faces certain constraints, so that often unseen influences limit how she approaches, fashions, and leaves each stone. Creating a work of art is not simply a matter of exercising personal choice or "free will." Many constraints take the form of social expectations about what is culturally meaningful to both artist and audience and what sculpting is all about: what should the process be like and what kind of an outcome should we expect. The thoughts of the sculptor's teachers and commissioners will be especially important to her regarding cultural, conceptual issues of what "works of art" look like and how they are made. Other constraints are much more tangible, like the shape and physical characteristics of the stone, the tools the artist has to shape it, the dimensions of her studio, and how much and how soon she's relying on the income a work might generate.

Because of these constraints, some choices are already made for the artist before he even begins his work, especially choices about what the stone will *not* become. These choices are largely made at the unconscious level, reflecting the fact that boundary work occurs here, according to internalized principles, as well as at a more conscious level. The sculptor embraces some options yet does not even consider others. (This may be, as Steven Lukes argues, the most insidious form of social control.) Social, cognitive constraints thus manifest in personal experience, imagination, and others' expectations. This makes boundary work both visible and invisible, conscious and unconscious.

Accordingly, while there is plenty of room for personal innovation in sculpting, the most basic rules that guide the sculptor's hand are predetermined and virtually impossible to ignore. These rules may be so fundamental that they are taken for granted; only the most systematic exploration uncovers them. Like a good cook, experimental scientist, or home–work negotiator, a sculptor takes her mental constraints and the physical resources at hand and produces a wonderfully synergistic result. And, as is the case with these other people, the end product causes the sculptor to reflect back on the concepts, understandings, techniques, and material situations that originally guided her hand. Through her practical sculpting activity and the artifact it produces, new light is shed on the way she sees these things, the importance they have for her work, and the way she might negotiate them next time.

Likewise, sociocognitive and social-structural constraints abound for us as we practically negotiate the meaning of "home," "work," and their "proper" relationship. First of all, individual thinking is nothing less than the embodiment of group thinking. This is the common thread of the works of Emile Durkheim, Max Weber, Karl Marx, Alfred Schutz, Schutz and Thomas Luckmann, Peter Berger and Luckmann, Michel Foucault, Karl Mannheim, Ludwig Fleck, and Thomas Kuhn, for instance. All students of philosophy and the sociology of knowledge and science, they note the primacy of the social group for personal thought. "Worldviews," "thoughtstyles," "paradigms," "class consciousness," etcetera, shape any individual's conceptual framework.

Hence, one person's conceptualization of "home" and "work" and their proper relationship is predicated on cultural understandings of these terms. But, as Durkheim reminds us, while cultural constructs precede and inform personal ones, personal ones are never the mere embodiments of social ones. Raymond Williams explicitly argues that the perpetuation of a multiplicity of meanings for cultural concepts is a result of variations in personal experience. A concept must be commensurate with a person's experience for her or him to cognitively embrace it, in whole or in part. This mutually constraining effect results in cultural categories like "home" and "work" that inform and are informed by personal experience.

In addition to more mental, conceptual social constraints, more readily apparent social factors influence what each of us can understand home and work to be, as well as what we can shape them to look like. For instance, just as a sculptor's teacher encourages him to chisel in a certain way, so do spouses' and children's demands influence the way we divide our time between wage and domestic work. If an artistic school of thought leads the sculptor to envision a piece in a certain way, so too do a work group's expectations guide the home–work negotiator. For instance, formal and informal workplace rules about making "personal" phone calls, taking "personal" breaks, and using "work" equipment, materials, and money for "personal" reasons undoubtedly shape the way we distinguish between home and work. The size of a studio limits the dimensions of a sculptor's work of art, just as workplace danger may prohibit the otherwise integrating presence of children or spouses. An artist may not have enough money to buy better tools or study with a more eminent teacher, which would allow him to change his understanding of sculpture. Similarly, the single mother living on her wages and possessing few marketable skills may not have the chance to move beyond her present boss's boundary expectations, whatever they are. Even cultural norms about things like the ideal relationship between parents and children and the forms of day care that should be available shape possible juxtapositions of home and work.

The process of socialization regarding what "home" and "work" mean starts with models presented during childhood. As we grow, our own employment and education experiences provide confirmation or alternatives to these ideas. Soon, spouses', employers', and coworkers' expectations – even children's demands – are crucial in shaping our decisions of what can and will belong to each sphere, or even if there will be two spheres. These classificatory negotiations largely result from expectations about how and why one does certain kinds of wage and domestic work, and the kinds of family, work group, and daily lives we and significant others desire and require of ourselves.

As a result of these factors, for instance, the occupations of university professor, diplomat, family business owner, cleric, and medical doctor and those in cottage industries push members toward the integration end of the spectrum. So do the home-related constraints of people married to coworkers or highly wage work-supportive spouses. Part-time cashiers, insurance claim processors, construction laborers, and "job shop" machinists, however, are examples of occupations that tend to make us segment home and work more. So do the constraints of new parents, those who do most of the daily domestic work, and those whose spouses steadfastly insist that we draw the home–work line at the front doorstep.

Sociologically, the home–work boundary varies for any given person largely according to expectations associated with the following: occupation, work organization, work group, and hierarchical position held within these, gender, family structure, spouse's wage work, one's parenting role, and domestic labor role. Each of these social statuses encapsulates historical, cultural norms about the meaning of home and work, the kinds of activities and ways of being each entails, and the ways each "kind" of person should experience these realms. These normative guidelines are part of what we internalize during our lifelong socialization in making classificatory distinctions.

Furthermore, any individual negotiates these statuses within specific physical environments. The selves, roles and activities institutionally and personally associated with certain statuses are carried out within the real world. A laboratory feels very different from a living room, while a powerful administrator's office may be quite similar to it. Thus, physical, ambient conditions also constrain the way we experience either realm and the extent to which we perceive differences between them.

Change in these statuses, the activities associated with them or the environments in which they are carried out is thus likely to bring about change in the way someone categorizes and experiences "home" and "work." This is because these changes frequently invoke new, modified understandings of what home and work mean. They may also change the available ways in which we may carry out these understandings. . . .

[E]ach of us responds to changing constraints on the ways we see and experience home and work. If a sculptor's arthritis causes him to abandon certain forms of stone working, so may the onset of a parent's or child's terminal or chronic illness cause us to become more segmentist in the interweaving of our home and work. Or, bosses and family permitting, our own illness may promote a more flexible approach to the time and space of both realms, as we try to work and recuperate simultaneously. The adoption of workplace policies like flex-time and flex-place can offer far more integrating possibilities. The sudden institution of bureaucratic workplace policies, however, encourages a more segmentist approach to home and work, demanding that we remove "personal" items and activities from workspace and time. A promotion to management may mean expectations of greater investment of self in work. It may require and promote more thinking about work while at home, more extra-workplace socializing with coworkers and more business travel. A new job in a work group with fairly segmentist expectations, though, can lead us to become more segmenting, as people repeatedly refuse invitations to chat about domestic matters or socialize "on the outside." On the other hand, a likable coworker's enthusiasm can just as easily rope us into playing on a departmental softball or bowling team, extending our relationships with coworkers into the physical and social space and time outside the workplace proper. Likewise, marriage to a spouse who positively throws herself into furthering our career by networking, entertaining, and typing on our behalf may greatly increase a previous level of integration.

Over time, certain realm and boundary expectations and ambient conditions generally hold constant. But new expectations and physical arrangements demand or allow us to change home and work arrangements beyond our previous conceptualizations. We abandon or adopt specific segmenting and integrating practices along numerous dimensions as needed and desired. At the same time, these new practices react back on the social influences that give rise to them, causing us to modify both our visions of "home" and "work" and the temporal and spatial territories they previously encompassed.

Sometimes the change in our home–work configurations will be quite radical. Other times it will be more of a fine-tuning of present configurations. It depends on the changes we experience and how severely these test and constrain the previous conceptual framework and practical ways of distinguishing between home and work.

Of course, while boundary work is firmly and consistently embedded in the social structure, it also allows for discretion in personal responses to these constraints. For example, if it is not required in our job descriptions, we must still decide if we will have nothing to do with our colleagues outside the workplace and workday. Will we socialize with them in a neutral, social place like a softball field or a restaurant? Will we invite them into our homes? How often and for what kinds of occasions? And if we make a decision about these things today, what will we do tomorrow, if a new, quite likable colleague joints the department or our marriage hits a low point?

Boundary work thus gives us room for personal innovation as well as the accommodation of cultural and sociostructural expectations. It allows us to constantly modify our understandings and experiences of home and work, providing an important link between self and society, what is personal and cultural. In this respect, the home–work negotiator is no different from the artistic sculptor, whose work links him and his unique propensity for creation with the rest of the art community.

Thus, each person may move in any direction along the continuum, reflecting the new ways she or he is asked by others and herself or himself to perceive and enact "home" and "work." Integration and segmentation are not personality types. They are typifications of the ways we classify and juxtapose items, acts, thoughts, and aspects of self to accommodate social and personal expectations.

For a given person, however, there may well be differing levels of social-psychological comfort with certain positions on the continuum. Yet that comfort is more a function of two situational factors. First, how closely are we allowed by others to enact our socialized views about the "proper" relationship between home and work? Second, how well can we muster the resources that allow us to adjust when we're forced to abandon old views and adopt new ones?

For instance, Didi grew up as an important presence in her parents' prestigious family business. In its purest form, the presence of family and business were inseparable in this social unit, whether its members were at home or the office. Now a wife and mother of two, Didi still helps run the company. Her husband, however, shares no such integrated background. Despite a highly lucrative, professional career and long hours at work, he is far more segmentist in his views, as are his colleagues. He is quickly annoyed if even the smallest amount of paperwork from Didi's job lays on the living room coffee table. Alan firmly believes that when she's at home, Didi should do only "home" things. Of course, throughout Didi's childhood, "home" things included "work" things and vice versa. The definition of "home" things was an early and continuous point of contention for this couple.

Didi now finds she is more segmentist too, a result of the births of her two children within one year, her acceptance of most of the family's domestic and child-related work, and the desire to dedicate their small amount of shared time to family activities. She still "sneaks in" a little "wage work" in the evenings, however, after the kids are in bed. Through evening thoughts, paperwork, and phone calls, Didi retains some of her old ideas about home, work, and their relationship. At the same time, she's adopted some new practices to handle the changes in her personal situation and in what "home" and "work" mean to her and those around her.

References

Berger, Peter L., and Thomas Luckmann. 1968. *The Social Construction of Reality.* Garden City, N.Y.: Anchor Press.

Durkheim, Emile. [1912] 1965. *The Elementary Forms of the Religious Life.* New York: Free Press.

Fleck, Ludwig. (1935) 1981. *Genesis and Development of a Scientific Fact.* Chicago: University of Chicago Press.

Foucault, Michel. [1966] 1973. *The Order of Things.* New York: Vintage Books.

Kuhn, Thomas S. [1962] 1970. *The Structure of Scientific Revolutions.* Chicago: University of Chicago Press.

Lukes, Steven. 1974. *Power: A Radical View.* London: Macmillan.

Mannheim, Karl. [1936] 1985. *Ideology and Utopia.* San Diego: Harvest/HBL.

———. 1972. *Essays on the Sociology of Knowledge*, 5th ed. London: Routledge, Kegan Paul.

———. 1982. *Structures of Thinking.* London: Routledge, Kegan Paul.

McLellan, David, ed. 1977. *Karl Marx: Selected Writings.* Oxford: Oxford University Press.

Schutz, Alfred. 1973. "On Multiple Realities." In *Collected Papers*, 4th ed., 1:207–59. The Hague: Martinus Nijhoff.

Schutz, Alfred, and Thomas Luckmann. 1973. *The Structures of the Life World.* Evanston: Northwestern University Press.

Shibutani, Tamotsu. 1955. "Reference Groups as Perspectives." *American Journal of Sociology* 60: 562–69.

———. 1962. "Reference Groups and Social Control." In *Human Behavior and Social Processes*, edited by A. Rose, 128–47. Boston: Houghton Mifflin.

Weber, Max. [1904] 1976. *The Protestant Ethic and the Spirit of Capitalism.* New York: Charles Scribner's Sons.

Williams, Raymond. [1976] 1985. *Keywords.* New York: Oxford University Press.

Editor's Notes on Further Reading

Nippert-Eng on Boundary Work

Christena Nippert-Eng investigates the complicated meaning-making behind the apparently simple cognitive categories of "home" and "work." Her book, based on an intensive study of 72 workers in a large scientific institution, elaborates the mundane symbolic markers creating these categories, the processes of moving between realms, and the influences on how much people integrate work and home. The research sparked widespread public discussion when it first appeared because it offered a new perspective on topics like gender and work, telecommuting, and contemporary work organization. On culture and work organization see also Kunda, this volume, and associated editor's note; for a cultural analysis of the home see Mihaly Csikszentmihalyi and Eugene Rochberg-Halton, *The Meaning of Things: Domestic Symbols and the Self* (Cambridge and New York: Cambridge University Press, 1981). On the particularly intense issues of home/work boundaries for family women, see for example Arlie Russell Hochschild, *The Second Shift* (New York: Avon Books, 1997) and Sharon Hays, *The Cultural Contradictions of Motherhood* (New Haven and London: Yale University Press, 1996), pp. 145–78.

More generally, Nippert-Eng contributes to the theory of symbolic boundaries, which has its origins in the classical sociological concern with social classification (e.g. Emile Durkheim, *The Elementary Forms of Religious Life*, trans. Karen Fields (New York: Free Press, 1995), pp. 8–18). In recent years, cognitive categories and symbolic boundaries (rather than values or attitudes) have been seen by many cultural sociologists as the key elements of culture. On symbolic boundaries see, for example, excerpts from work by Lamont and Bryson, this volume and Michèle Lamont and Marcel Fournier, eds., *Cultivating Differences: Symbolic Boundaries and the Making of Inequality* (Chicago and London: University of Chicago Press, 1992); Cynthia Fuchs Epstein, *Deceptive Distinctions: Sex, Gender, and the Social Order* (New Haven and London: Yale University Press, and New York: Russell Sage Foundation, 1988); Judith Gerson and Kathy Peiss, "Boundaries, Negotiation, Consciousness: Reconceptualizing Gender Relations," *Social Problems* 32 (1985): 317–31; and Thomas Gieryn, "Boundary Work and the Demarcation of Science from Non-Science: Strains and Interests in Professional Ideologies of Scientists," *American Sociological Review* 48 (1983): 781–95. On cognitive categories see Zerubavel, this volume, and the accompanying notes.

Nippert-Eng also emphasizes the active and creation and re-creation of cognitive categories in "boundary work"; she pays attention to individual agency and processes of cultural construction, as well as the more static, transindividual analysis of cultural categories, and in doing so links cultural analysis to the symbolic interactionist tradition in sociology. See, for instance, Howard Becker and Michal McCall, eds., *Symbolic Interaction and Cultural Studies* (Chicago and London: University of Chicago Press, 1990), especially John Hall, "Social Interaction, Culture, and Historical Studies," pp 16–45; Norman Denzin, *Symbolic Interaction and Cultural Studies* (Cambridge, MA and Oxford: Blackwell, 1992), and Gary Alan Fine and Sherryl Kleinman, "Network and Meaning: An Interactionist Approach to Structure," *Symbolic Interaction* 6 (1983): 97–110.

9 Corporate Culture

Gideon Kunda

Tech Culture: A Managerial Perspective

On this randomly selected workday, the Lyndsville engineering facility is the stage upon which practical managerial concerns with "the culture" are acted out. A few miles away, in a fairly spacious but still modest office at Tech's corporate head-quarters, Dave Carpenter is preparing a presentation to be given at Lyndsville later in the day. He is one of the more senior managers in the Engineering Division, and has been with the company a long time. Like many Tech managers, Dave Carpenter works extremely hard. He has recently gone on a strictly enforced seven-to-seven schedule that includes working breakfasts and dinners, but it is still difficult to get onto his calendar. He has just finished a series of long-scheduled "one-on-ones." The last one was with a Harvard professor wearing a fancy business suit and a prom-inently displayed visitor's badge, who has just been ushered out after exactly half an hour. ("Some kind of case study interview – culture and productivity; everybody wants to know what we're up to.") Dave has a few minutes to get his presentation together. The group at Lyndsville has recently been made part of his organization – "his world" – in one of the frequent reorganizations that are a way of life for Tech managers, or, as he would say, "a part of the culture."

For Dave, as for many managers, cultural matters are an explicit concern. Dave considers himself an expert. One wall of his office is covered with a large bookcase holding many managerial texts. Japanese management, in particular, intrigues him, and books on the subject take up a whole shelf. ("They know something about putting people to work – and we better find out what it is.") Dave has a clear view of what the culture is all about and considers it his job not only to understand, but to influence and shape it for those whose performance he believes to be his responsi-bility.

A key aspect of Tech culture, Dave often points out, is that formal structure tells you nothing. Lyndsville is a case in point. "It's typical Tech. The guys up there are independent and ambitious. They are working on state-of-the-art stuff – really neat things. Everyone, including the president, has a finger in the pot. The group is potentially a revenue generator. That they are committed there is no doubt. But they are unmanageable." How then, he wonders, can he make them see the light? Work in the *company's* interest? Cooperate? Stop (or at least channel) the pissing contests? And not make him look bad? Dave knows that whether he controls it or not, he "owns" it – another aspect of the culture. And as he reads the company, his own future can be influenced by the degree to which he is credited with the group's success. And he is being watched, just as he watches others. His strategy is clear. "Power plays don't work. You can't *make 'em* do *anything*. They have to *want* to. So you have to work through the culture. The idea is to educate people without them knowing it. Have the religion and not know how they ever got it!"

And there are ways to do this. Today Dave will make his first appearance at Lyndsville. He will give a presentation about the role of Lyndsville's various technical projects in Tech's long-term business strategy. "Presentations are important in this culture," he says. "You have to get around, give them the religion, get the message out. It's a mechanism for transmitting the culture." Sending and interpreting "messages" are a key to working the culture. Dave is clear about what he wants to accomplish: generate some enthusiasm, let them work off some steam, celebrate some of the successes, show them that they are not out on their own, make his presence felt. And maybe give them an example of the right "mindset." In "the trenches" (a favorite expression), he is sure, there must be considerable confusion caused by "the revolving door" – the frequent changes of management. Lyndsville reputedly has quite a few good and committed people. It is a creative group. But it is also considered a tough, competitive environment. Some say it reminds them of the early days of Tech, when commitment and burnout went hand in hand. Perhaps. The company has been changing. But some things stay the same. Dave remembers life in the trenches. He was "there" years ago, he has paid his dues – including a divorce – and he still feels an affinity for the residents of the trenches, some of whom he will meet today. And, as always, he is prepared. He reaches for the tools of the culture trade – the "road show" color slides used at yesterday's strategy presentation to the executive committee – and selects the ones for today.

Concern with the culture is not just the domain of senior managers; it has also spawned a small internal industry that translates global concerns, ideas, and messages into daily activities. Near the front lobby of the Lyndsville building, a large conference room is being prepared for more routine "cultural shaping." Alone in the room, Ellen Cohen is getting ready to run her "Culture Module" for the "Introduction to Tech" workshop for new hires, also known as "bootcamp." It will take two hours, and if everything runs smoothly, she will stay for Dave Carpenter's presentation. ("It's a must for Tech-watchers. You can learn a lot from attending.") She is an engineer who is now "totally into culture." Over the last few years she has become the resident "culture expert." "I got burnt out on coding. You can only do so much. And I knew my limits. So I took a management job and I'm funded to do culture now. Some people didn't believe it had any value-added. But I went off and made it happen, and now my workshops are all oversubscribed! I'm a living example of the culture! Now I do a lot of work at home. Isn't this company super?"

She is preparing her material now, waiting for the participants to arrive. On one table she is sorting the handout packages. Each includes copies of her paper "A Culture Operating Manual – Version II"; some official company materials; a copy of the latest edition of *Tech Talk*, with an interview with the president and extensive quotations from his "We Are One" speech; a review of academic work on "corporate cultures" that includes a key to the various disguised accounts of Tech; a glossary of Tech terms; and a xeroxed paper with some "culture exercises" she has collected for her files over the years. "It covers it all. What is a Techie. Getting Ahead. Networking. Being a Self-Starter. Taking Charge. How to Identify Burnout. The Subcultures. Presentations. Managing Your Career. Managing Your Boss. Women. Over the years I've gathered dynamite material – some of it too sensitive to show anyone. One day I'll write a thesis on all of this. In the meanwhile I'm funded to document and preserve the culture of Engineering. It's what made this company great. 'Culture' is really a 'people issue' – a Personnel or OD [Organization Development] type of thing, but they have no credibility in Engineering, and I'd rather stay here, close to the action. It's a fascinating company. I could watch it forever. Today I'm doing culture with the new hires. I tell them about how to succeed here. You can't just do the old nine-to-five thing. You have to have the right mindset. It's a gut thing. You have to get the religion. You can push at the system, you drive yourself. But I also warn them: 'Win big and lose big. You can really get hurt here. This place can be dangerous. Burnout City.' And I tell them the first rule: 'Do What's Right.' It's the company slogan, almost a cliche, but it captures the whole idea. 'Do What's Right.' If they internalize that, I've done my job. My job? They come in in love with the technology; that's dangerous. My job is to marry them to the company."

What does "Tech's strong culture" mean to Dave Carpenter and Ellen Cohen? First, and most broadly speaking, it is the context of their work life, a set of rules that guides the relationship between the company and "it's people." At one level, the culture offers a description of the social characteristics of the company that also embodies a specification of required work behavior: "informality," "initiative," "lack of structure," "inherent ambiguity," "hard work," "consensus seeking," "bottom-up decision making," "networking," "pushing against the system," "going off, taking risks, and making things happen." But, as the frequently heard metaphors of "family," "marriage," and "religion" suggest, the rules run deeper. The culture also includes articulated rules for thoughts and feelings, "mindsets" and "gut reactions": an obsession with technical accomplishment, a sense of ownership, a strong commitment to the company, identification with company goals, and, not least, "fun." Thus, "the culture" is a gloss for an extensive definition of membership in the corporate community that includes rules for behavior, thought, and feeling, all adding up to what appears to be a well-defined and widely shared "member role."

But there is more. For Dave Carpenter and Ellen Cohen, as well as many others, the culture has a dual nature: it is not just the context but also the object of their work lives. The culture means not only the implicit and explicit rules that guide and shape their own behavior and experience of work; it is also the vehicle through which they consciously try to influence the behavior and experience of others. The "culture," in this sense, is something to be engineered – researched, designed, developed, and maintained – in order to facilitate the accomplishment of company goals. Although the product – a member role consisting of behavior, thoughts, and feelings – is not concrete, there are specified ways of engineering it: making presentations, sending "messages," running "bootcamp," writing papers, giving speeches, formulating and publishing the "rules," even offering an "operating manual." All are work techniques designed to induce others to accept – indeed, to become – what the company would like them to be.

This duality reflects a central underlying theme in the way culture is construed by many Tech managers: the "culture" is a mechanism of control. Its essence is captured in Dave Carpenter's words: "You can't make 'em do anything; they have to want to." In this view, the ability to elicit, channel, and direct the creative energies and activities of employees in profitable directions – to make them want to contribute – is based on designing a member role that employees are expected to incorporate as an integral part of their sense of self. It is this desire and the policies that flow from it, many insiders feel, that makes Tech "something else."

The use of culture in the service of control in a modern corporation might seem at first strange, even unique, to those for whom culture is a concept more meaningfully applied to Bornean headhunters or to the urban literati. Tech managers, however, are not alone. A practical concern with culture and its consequences is widely shared among those for whom the corporate jungle is of more than passing interest....

"It's not just work – it's a celebration!" is a company slogan one often hears from members attempting to describe life at Tech. Less formally, many refer to Tech as "a song and dance company." And, more privately, some agree, that "you have to do a lot of bullshitting in groups." Like much of the self-descriptive conventional wisdom that permeates the company, these observations – whether offered straightforwardly or cynically – contain a valid observation: everyday life at Tech is replete with ritual.

Ritual, most generally speaking, is "a rule-governed activity of a symbolic character which draws the attention of participants to objects of thought and feeling which they hold to be of special significance."[1] At Tech, as insiders well know, members regularly participate in a variety of such structured face-to-face gatherings: speeches, presentations, meetings, lectures, parties, training workshops, and so forth. Dave Carpenter's planned appearance at Lyndsville and Ellen Cohen's culture seminar are examples, along with more routinely occurring events such as [a] weekly team meeting with the members of the ABC project. Whatever else they are intended to accomplish, these events are also occasions where participants, speaking as agents for the corporate interest, use familiar symbols – presentational devices, stylized forms of expression, company slogans and artifacts – to articulate, illustrate, and exemplify what members in good standing are to think, feel, and do. In short, these gatherings, which I will refer to as presentational rituals, are where the organizational ideology – the managerial version of Tech culture and the member role it prescribes – is dramatized and brought to life....

Presentational rituals at Tech are an integral and ongoing feature of members' work lives. In one form or another they are a pervasive presence on the Tech scene and constantly make demands on the way members present themselves. Most generally speaking, the performance of the ritual – whether in large and festive settings or on smaller and less formal occasions – is a framing device: members, acting as agents of the corporate interest, attempt to establish a shared definition of the situation within which reality claims derived from the organizational ideology are experienced as valid. To this end, participants are presented with slogans and metaphors ("Tech is a bottom-up company," "We are like a football team") with which the complex reality that is Tech is to be expressed. In particular, a distinct and somewhat abstract view of the member role and its appropriate behaviors ("doing what's right," "working hard," "he who proposes does"), cognitions ("the importance of technological accomplishment," "the centrality of profit"), and emotions ("commitment," "having fun," "enthusiasm") is presented or implied, and, more crucially, specific instances of their correct application are dramatized, noted, and rewarded. In short, like all rituals, these occasions are used as vehicles for the exertion of what Pierre Bourdieu (1977) refers to as symbolic power – the power to define reality.

Tech rituals, however, have two distinct features. First, they are characterized by a decentralization of power. Symbolic power, as one might expect, is clearly possessed by those invested with formal authority and high status, and most effectively applied when the status gap between participants is large or the power of reward or sanction well defined. But in the context of ritual life at Tech, this type of power may accrue to those who possess other resources as well: the power of numbers found in the pooled resources and the concerted action of groups; temporarily assigned formal roles; acknowledged technical expertise or relevant experience; an open endorsement of the organizational interest; the threat that in Tech's open and shifting environment, reputation, status, and real rewards are in the hands of numerous, often unknown, others; and, if nothing else, a fluency in the language, mode of thinking, and style of ideological discourse. In short, from the point of view of the individual participant, agents of control are everywhere: one is surrounded and constantly observed by members (including oneself) who, in order to further their own interests, act as spokespersons and enforcers of the organizational ideology.

Second, since the ideology is one of openness, informality, individual initiative, and real feelings, symbolic power is exerted, for the most part, quite subtly: overt, centralized control and forced compliance would belie the messages of the ideology. Nevertheless, its presence is revealed in brief episodes that resemble a small-scale version of what Turner (1974) calls "social drama." In Turner's view, a social drama is a fundamental and recurring part of the process of group life that unfolds in predictable stages: a public and dramatic breach or a challenge to the prevailing order is followed by a sense of mounting crisis and a series of attempts at redressive action, and culminates in either an unbridgeable schism between the opposed parties or reintegration and reestablishment of order. At Tech, mini-dramas of control are an ever-present part of presentational rituals. Although they vary in length and intensity, these mini-dramas follow a predictable pattern: a challenge to the ritual frame causes the tension to rise, and members acting as agents for the corporate interest (in the rituals we have observed, these roles are widely shared by participants) use various techniques – Bourdieu (1977) refers to these as "symbolic violence" – to suppress or redefine dissent, silence the deviants, and gain the participants' support. Thus, collective support for the ritual frame is bolstered by the organization's symbolic power, exerted through particular members.

The most dominant response to the exertion of symbolic power in the context of ritual life at Tech is the expression of role embracement; participants express their acceptance of the member role, including not only the prescribed behaviors but, more crucially, the beliefs one must espouse and the emotions one is to experience and display. This occurs to different extents in the various types of presentational rituals: it appears whole-hearted and festive in top management presentations; reserved and tentative in training workshops; and pragmatic, conflictual, and continuous in work group meetings. Despite the subtle and occasionally overt pressures to conform, many members, if asked, would claim that this stance – whether an expression of sincerely held convictions or a scripted role – is freely chosen. Such a response may reflect the participants' experience, but it is also consistent with the ideological depiction of the company: the open community, freedom of expression, "bottom-up decision making," informality, and so forth.

Whatever their causes, displays of role embracement may have a considerable impact on those who perform them. Public expressions of support for an ideological point of view may cause cognitive dissonance: members who, under pressure, publicly espouse beliefs and opinions they might otherwise reject tend to adopt them as an authentic expression of their point of view. Moreover, as Arlie Hochschild (1983) suggests, when institutionally prescribed roles include definitions of appropriate emotions, they require "deep acting": the performer must try to "feel" rather than feign role-prescribed emotions. Consequently, participation in ritual enactments of the member role at Tech – no matter how tentative – may lead to what she calls emotive dissonance: members are inclined to experience the emotions they display as authentic. Over time, cognitive and emotive dissonance may blur the boundary between the performers' perception of an acted role and the experience of an "authentic self." This, in principle, should occur for all displays of role embracement, but it is probably more acute for sustained and scrutinized performances. Particularly susceptible in this regard are those members who perform the various spokesperson roles and those who act as agents of control, whether in their capacity as possessors of authority, as temporary volunteers, or as individuals recognizing the advantages of speaking for the company interest. The performance of such roles, Lewis Coser (1974) points out, is a particularly effective mechanism for instilling commitment to ideological principles among those who perform them. Thus, extensive and ongoing participation in ritual life at Tech, may, as Mills (1940: 908) put it, induce people to become what at first they merely sought to appear.

There are limits, however, to the power of ritual to elicit the expression of role embracement. Some members – perhaps at some cost to their reputation – minimize their participation in ritual events. Others participate as a "secondary audience," excluded from the actual event but aware of it and participating after the fact through reports and reenactments. Such secondary participants may share in some of the potential for "deep acting" of the member role offered by presentational rituals. But in many cases their form of participation is also an indication and a demonstration of lower status, marginality, passivity, or lack of interest. Many members experience both primary and secondary participation at different times, and their effects might not always reinforce each other. More extremely, for many in support and service roles – mainly members of Wage Class 2 and temporary workers – such ritual performances make clear their status as what Goffman (1959) calls "nonpersons": individuals who are present in body only and not considered a relevant part of the scene. Here, too, there might be potential for deep acting, albeit of marginal or alienated roles.

More crucially, however, the ritual form itself contains built-in opportunities for temporary suspension of role embracement: transitional phases and timeouts that bracket and intersperse the ritual frame. These episodes resemble those stages of ritual that Turner (1969) has called "liminal": a relatively unstructured period that occurs between structured modes of relating where the participants' relationship is characterized by "communitas," a relatedness temporarily unmediated by social structure. Liminal phases of ritual, Turner suggests (1969: 167), tend to highlight the most significant dimensions of a specific culture. For example, in his exemplary studies of tribal societies, liminality was shown to be the occasion for role reversals between subordinate and superordinate members: dramatized exchanges between up and down, strong and weak, having and not having authority (Turner, 1969). These he saw as variations on the theme of hierarchy.

At Tech, however, the liminal phases of ritual have a different flavor: not role reversal, but role distancing is their central attribute. These episodes are occasions

Douglas, M. 1966. *Purity and Danger: An Analysis of Concepts of Pollution and Taboo.* London: Routledge and Kegan Paul.

Goffman, E. 1959. *The Presentation of Self in Everyday Life.* New York: Doubleday.

——. 1961. *Asylums.* Garden City, N.Y.: Anchor.

——. 1967. *Interaction Ritual.* New York: Doubleday Anchor.

Hochschild, A. R. 1983. *The Managed Heart.* Berkeley: University of California Press.

Kanter, R. M. 1977. *Men and Women of the Corporation.* New York: Basic Books.

——. 1983. *The Change Masters.* New York: Simon and Schuster.

Kaufman, H. 1960. *The Forest Ranger.* Baltimore: Johns Hopkins University Press.

Kertzer, David. 1988. *Ritual, Politics, and Power.* New Haven: Yale University Press.

Lukes, S. 1975. "Political Ritual and Social Integration." *Sociology* 9: 289–308.

Meyer, J. W., and B. Rowan. 1977. "Institutionalized Organizations: Formal Structure as Myth and Ceremony." *American Journal of Sociology* 83: 340–63.

Miller, M. C. 1988. *Boxed-In.* Evanston, Ill.: Northwestern University Press.

Mills, C. W. 1940. "Situated Actions and Vocabularies of Motive." *American Sociological Review* 5: 904–13.

——. 1956. *White Collar.* New York: Oxford University Press.

Moore, S. F., and B. G. Meyerhoff. 1977. "Secular Ritual: Forms and Meaning." In S. F. Moore and B. G. Meyerhoff (eds.), *Secular Ritual.* Atlantic Highlands, N.J.: Humanities Press.

Trice, H. M., and J. M. Beyer. 1984. "Studying Organizational Cultures Through Rites and Ceremonials." *Academy of Management Review* 9: 653–69.

Trilling, L. 1972. *Sincerity and Authenticity.* Cambridge, Mass.: Harvard University Press.

Turner, V. 1969. *The Ritual Process.* Chicago: Aldine.

——. 1974. *Dramas, Fields, and Metaphors.* Ithaca, N.Y.: Cornell University Press.

Van Maanen, J., and G. Kunda. 1989. "'Real Feelings': Emotional Expression and Organizational Culture." In L. L. Cummings and B. M. Staw (eds.), *Research in Organizational Behavior*, vol. 11. Greenwich, Conn.: JAI Press.

Editor's Notes on Further Reading

Kunda on Organizational Rituals

In contemporary organizations like the high-tech corporation Kunda studied, shared cognitions, norms, and values may be promoted in symbols and rituals aimed at creating and maintaining internalized employee motivation. Kunda's book is an in-depth investigation of corporate ideology, organizational ritual, normative control, and their consequences for employees' ambivalent sense of self.

Other studies investigating organizations, paid work, and culture include Gideon Kunda and John Van Maanen, "Changing Scripts at Work: Managers and Professionals," *Annals of the American Academy of Political and Social Sciences* 561 (1999): 64–80; Wendy Nelson Espeland, *The Struggle for Water: Politics, Rationality, and Identity in the American Southwest* (Chicago and London: University of Chicago Press, 1998); Carol Heimer and Lisa Staffen, *For The Sake of the Children: The Social Organization of Responsibility in the Hospital and the Home* (Chicago and London: University of Chicago Press, 1998); Barbara Czarniawska, *Narrating the Organization: Dramas of Institutional Identity* (Chicago and London: University of Chicago Press, 1997); Diane Vaughan, *The Challenger Launch Decision: Risky Technology, Culture, and Deviance at NASA* (Chicago and London: University of Chicago Press, 1996); Gary Alan Fine, *Kitchens: The Culture of Restaurant Work* (Berkeley: University of California Press, 1996); Calvin Morrill, *The Executive Way: Conflict Manage-*

ment in Corporations (Chicago and London: University of Chicago Press, 1995); Jennifer Pierce, *Gender Trials: Emotional Lives in Contemporary Law Firms* (Berkeley: University of California Press, 1995); Richard Biernacki, *The Fabrication of Labor: Germany and Britain 1640–1914* (Berkeley: University of California Press, 1995); Frank Dobbin, "Cultural Models of Organizations: The Social Constructions of Rational Organizing Principles," pp. 117–41 in Diana Crane, ed., *The Sociology of Culture: Emerging Theoretical Perspectives* (Oxford and Cambridge, MA: Blackwell, 1994); Dobbin, *Forging Industrial Policy: the United States, France, and Britain in the Railway Age* (Cambridge and New York: Cambridge University Press, 1994); Stephen Barley and Gideon Kunda, "Design and Devotion: Surges of Rational and Normative Ideologies of Conrol in Managerial Discourse," *Administrative Science Quarterly* 37 (1992): 363–99; John Van Maanen and Gideon Kunda, "'Real Feelings': Emotional Expression and Organization Culture," in L. L. Cummings and B. M. Staw, eds., *Research in Organizational Behavior* 11 (1989): 43–103; Paul Hirsch, "From Ambushes to Golden Parachutes: Corporate Takeovers as an Instance of Cultural Framing and Institutional Integration," *American Journal of Sociology* 91 (1986): 800–37; Eric Eisenberg, "Ambiguity as Strategy in Organizational Communication," *Communication Monographs* 51 (1984): 227–42; and John Meyer and Brian Rowan, "Institutionalized Organizations: Formal Structure as Myth and Ceremony," *American Journal of Sociology* 83 (1977): 340–63.

More generally, Kunda uses the "thick description" of signification called for by Geertz to investigate the sort of power relations implicit in commonsense practices Bourdieu is concerned with (see excerpts this volume). In its focus on the consequences of normative control for the sense of self, his work also builds on Goffman's dramaturgical analysis of interaction (e.g. Erving Goffman, *The Presentation of Self in Everyday Life* (Garden City, NY: Doubleday, 1959). Background on the nature and importance of ritual for creating "solidarity without consensus" is provided in David Kertzer, *Ritual, Politics, and Power* (New Haven: Yale University Press, 1989).

10 Symbolic Boundaries and Status

Michèle Lamont

What is primarily at issue here is the nature of the criteria that people use to define and discriminate between worthy and less worthy persons, i.e., between "their sort of folks" and "the sort they don't much like." To identify these criteria I scrutinize symbolic boundaries – the types of lines that individuals draw when they categorize people – and high-status signals – the keys to our evaluative distinctions. More specifically, different ways of believing that "we" are better than "them" are compared by analyzing both the standards that underlie status assessments and the characteristics of symbolic boundaries themselves – their degree of rigidity, for instance. This contributes to developing a more adequate and complex view of status, i.e., of the salience of various status dimensions across contexts. It also helps us to understand how societies and social classes differ culturally. By contrasting the cultures of members of the French and American upper-middle classes, we will see that the disapproval that New Yorkers often express toward Midwestern parochialism, the frequent criticisms that the French address to American puritan moralism, the scorn that businessmen voice toward intellectualism, and the charges that social and cultural specialists frequently make against materialism and business interests can be interpreted as specific instances of a pervasive phenomenon (i.e., as boundary work) rather than as incommensurable manifestations of national character, political attitudes, regionalism, etc. Using the framework presented here, it will be possible to view prejudices and stereotypes as the supraindividual by-products of basic social processes that are shaped by the cultural resources that people have at their disposal and by the structural situations they live in. . . .

[M]y study focuses on these three standards or types of symbolic boundaries:

Moral boundaries are drawn on the basis of moral character; they are centered around such qualities as honesty, work ethic, personal integrity, and consideration for others. . . . *Socioeconomic boundaries* are drawn on the basis of judgments concerning people's social position as indicated by their wealth, power, or professional success. . . . *Cultural boundaries* are drawn on the basis of education, intelligence, manners, tastes, and command of high culture. . . .

I show that whereas in both France and the United States sociological studies of high status signals have focused almost exclusively on cultural boundaries, and more specifically on a small subset of the cultural signals that are used to draw cultural boundaries, . . . evidence suggests that members of the French upper-middle class draw boundaries on the basis of moral and socioeconomic standing almost as frequently as they do on the basis of cultural standing. Second, . . . whereas sociologists also have often argued that cultural capital is a major basis of exclusion in the United States, the data I collected indicates that American upper-middle-class members stress socioeconomic and moral boundaries more than they do cultural boundaries; this is not the case in France where moral and cultural boundaries are slightly more important than socioeconomic boundaries; these differences are becoming less accentuated: data suggest that socioeconomic boundaries are gaining in importance in both countries while cultural boundaries appear to be losing in importance in the United States and possibly in France. . . .

The national boundary patterns . . . conceal important internal cultural variations within both the French and the American upper-middle classes. To unearth them, I compare groups of individuals who, due to their occupation or social trajectory, have different market conditions and different relationships with economic rationality: social and cultural specialists with for-profit workers, intellectuals with non-intellectuals, the upwardly with the downwardly mobile, and those whose family has been part of the upper-middle class for several generations with those who have recently entered the group. Examining these internal variations helps us gain a better knowledge of the role played by proximate structural conditions in shaping boundaries. It also permits obtaining richer knowledge concerning variations in the boundary work of various groups. While exploring such differences, I discuss further the causes of the greater French orientation to culture and American materialism. I show that national patterns in boundary work reinforce occupational patterns, distinct occupational groups having an impact on strengthening or weakening cultural and socioeconomic boundaries in their society.

Social and Cultural Specialists and For-Profit Workers

[O]ccupation is one of the main dimensions that define the identities of upper-middle-class men. It seems likely that patterns of boundary work will vary considerably across occupational groups, and my interviews suggest that indeed they do.

Profit Making and Boundary Work

In *Economy and Society*, Max Weber distinguished between economic and value rationalities: economic rationality dominates contemporary life by organizing it around a systematic orientation toward profit and efficiency. In contrast, value rationality, which is antithetical to economic rationality, is "determined by a conscious belief in the value for its own sake of some ethical, aesthetic, religious or other form of behavior" [Vol. 1, p. 25].

In trying to explain fluctuations in level of political liberalism, social scientists have pointed out how political attitudes vary with the structural relationship that people have with economic rationality and with economic necessity more generally. For instance, some have suggested that people who grew up during periods of economic prosperity are more prone to favor postmaterialist values such as self-actualization, environmentalism, sexual permissiveness, and opposition to nuclear power and armament: these people have had more "formative security," i.e., they (or their families) had a strong market position during their growing-up years and are, therefore, less concerned with materialist values and with economic rationality. Along the same lines, Seymour Martin Lipset has argued that intellectuals (in his definition, social and cultural specialists) have dissenting attitudes toward capitalism and the business class because their work requires that they maintain a certain independence from commercialism. Following Lipset's lead, I have suggested that the political liberalism and dissent of professionals and managers varies with the degree to which their work is instrumental to profit making (i.e., is directed to and justified by the creation of goods and services that realize a profit), and with the degree to which these upper-middle-class workers depend upon the market system for their livelihoods (whether they are employed in the private sector or in the public and nonprofit sectors)....

I generalize this hypothesis to other cultural realms to suggest that the boundary-drawing activities of the members of the upper-middle class varies with the degree to which their occupation is instrumental to, and dependent on, profit making: because the professional energies of artists, social workers, priests, psychologists, scientific researchers, and teachers are oriented toward attaining cultural, spiritual, or humanitarian goals, and because their professional achievements cannot be measured primarily in economic terms, one can expect these people to put more emphasis on cultural or moral standards of evaluation. On the other hand, because the labor of accountants, bankers, marketing executives, realtors, businessmen, and others like them is more dominated by the pursuit of economic rationality as they set goals based on cost/benefit analysis, and because their success is measured in economic terms, these individuals are more likely to value socioeconomic standards of evaluation. For similar reasons, intellectuals might draw stronger cultural boundaries and weaker socioeconomic boundaries than nonintellectuals.

To examine these hypotheses, the respondents were divided in two groups: (1) those involved in capitalist production and distribution, i.e., in the institutional mechanisms of profit making (business ownership, management, sales and applied technology), and in market enhancement (banking and finance), and (2) those that are not involved in these mechanisms, i.e., those who work in occupations in the media, the academe, the arts, etc. I further divided interviewees into two groups based on their sector of employment, positing that nonprofit and, to a greater extent, public sector employees are provided by their organizations with relative freedom from profit-making concerns, given that these organizations often depend on public funding and/or on donations for their existence and are not as directly dependent on the laws of supply and demand. On the basis of these distinctions, I classified respondents into four occupational aggregates depending on their sector of activity and the contribution of their work to the realization of profit. These four categories could be represented as a spectrum of increasing dependency on, and utility for profit making....

Patterns of Exclusion Across Occupational Groups

The conversations I had reveal that...social and cultural specialists and for-profit workers express somewhat critical attitudes toward one another. Indeed, by drawing antisocioeconomic boundaries in favor of cultural ones, social and cultural specialists often reject for-profit workers as impure: they often are critical of business types for their excessive materialism and lack of concern for cultural issues. For instance, a university professor in New York expressed his disappointment in his son, a business school student, for not being intellectual enough:

It's very frustrating to see your own son walk away from all of your own values . . . [H]e can't read a novel and be impressed by it. He can't see something in the newspaper and recognize it as important. Even when he does well in school, it's purely a manipulative or mechanistic approach . . . He is probably well suited for the business culture. But I would prefer if he had ideas. If he went to Princeton, where he could pursue cultural wealth and achievement . . . Even when he rebels, he rebels in the way that is prescribed by the movies.

For-profit workers are not different: many expressed their dislike for the cultural style of social and cultural specialists, rejecting the cultural purity principle at the same time. For instance, a senior manufacturing executive who manages a large plant and several thousand employees in Clermont remarked that ideologues and intellectuals "have a bad reputation in France. They live on a cloud. They are not realists. They isolate themselves through their language." Likewise, a self-employed insurance agent who lives in St. Cloud criticized technocrats because "to tell you that this pen is red, they will talk for two hours, and at the end, we will learn that the pen is red. They like to listen to themselves." Along the same lines, a sporty-looking Clermont-Ferrand architect whom I interviewed in his stylish postmodern apartment explained to me that those who specialize in abstract thought are inadequate: "Intellectuals are disconnected from reality. They are too much into the cerebral dimension, they don't get out of it. This gets on my nerves. I think that the intellectual who only gets stuck in intellectual things does not try to help others. He is happy in his own little universe."

The opposition between the two groups is often expressed under the cover of political attitudes, symbolic and political boundaries being drawn at one and the same time. This came up often during our conversations, but rarely as clearly as when a right-wing Clermont-Ferrand hotel manager described to me his hatred for the Socialists. He said: "I am anti-Socialist, completely. [Socialists] are all teachers . . . intellectuals. They have a bad attitude. They are bourgeois, i.e., very attached to their privileges . . . They are jealous, interested. I find in them many bad qualities."

The extent to which political attitudes and symbolic boundaries overlap cannot be explored here (this could well be the topic of an entirely separate study). Suffice it to say that attitudinal patterns such as opposition to capitalism, the business class, and unregulated economic activities as well as support for urban beautification, environmentalism, self-actualization, and income distribution could be taken as expressions of symbolic boundaries, i.e., as a way of drawing cultural (and moral) boundaries and of rejecting socioeconomic boundaries. On the other hand, opposition to a strong welfare state might indicate a defense of socioeconomic boundaries and of another type of moral boundary based not on human solidarity but on a belief in the importance of strong work ethics. Just as social and cultural specialists (or intellectuals) differ from for-profit workers in their political orientation, they also adopt different definitions of high status signals.

A comparison of individual scores on the moral, cultural, and socioeconomic dimensions reveals that social and cultural specialists are somewhat more culturally exclusive than for-profit workers, that the latter group is slightly more likely to draw strong socioeconomic boundaries than social and cultural specialists and that moral boundaries are equally valued by both groups. I am suggesting that the proximate structural positions of the men I talked to, as revealed by their relationship with the realization of profit, do shape their boundary work. This is again confirmed by a comparison of the boundary work of intellectuals and nonintellectuals, the first group having a lower instrumentality for the realization of profit: the vast majority of intellectuals draw strong cultural boundaries compared to less than a quarter of the interviewees who are considered nonintellectuals. Such occupational patterns might be reinforced by the market position of social and cultural specialists and that of intellectuals: those whose work is less instrumental to, and dependent on, profit making generally have market positions that are inferior to those of for-profit workers as their opportunities for mobility are often less abundant and their income generally lower. This might lead them to value forms of prestige other than socio-economic status.

Additional evidence suggests that proximate structural position affects boundary work: compared to social and cultural specialists in public on non-profit sections, those working in the private sector draw boundaries that are more similar to the boundaries drawn by for-profit workers. This reflects their higher dependency on and instrumentality to the realization of profit as these interviewees are involved in the public sector or are for-profit workers. Likewise, the self-employed for-profit workers score slightly higher than the salaried for-profit workers on the socioeconomic scale. These patterns persist when the two occupational categories are compared within each site. Further studies, however, based on larger data sets are needed before firm conclusions can be drawn on such comparisons. . . .

[Some] evidence suggests that intellectuals feel more marginal to American mainstream culture than French intellectuals do in France. Similarly, American social and cultural specialists seem to be more marginal in American culture than are their French counterparts in their own culture. Steven Brint indicated that in the United States, liberal sentiments are highly focused in a few predictable groups in the middle class, making these groups more different from the rest of the population than they would otherwise be in societies such as France where liberal and social-democratic views are more spread across various middle-class segments. This pattern can probably be extrapolated to attitudes other than political attitudes: strong cultural boundaries are likely to be characteristic of only a relatively small segment of the American population, whereas in France such boundaries might be found among wider groups, including among for-profit workers. The next section provides support for these hypotheses.

National Patterns and the Dynamics of Occupational Groups

The national patterns [distinguishing France and the US] reinforce boundary-drawing patterns across groups. Interviews and the quantitative ranking of respondents on the three dimensions confirm this:

1. French social and cultural specialists draw stronger cultural boundaries than American social and cultural specialists do. In this context, it is hardly surprising that they often have a very charismatic view of their work, as is most tellingly expressed by Jean Lebleu, a bearded philosophy professor who lives in Clermont in a small house cluttered with books. Talking to me through the heavy smoke of his Gitane cigarettes, he describes his *métier* with great gestures and emphasis:

I thought I could give young people the pleasure of discovering the company of others, of intellectual giants, the company of poets, novelists, philosophers and eruditi, the very men who helped me to understand life in a new light at the time when I was really discouraged...I would like to do for [the students] what my masters did for me. I had teachers who were almost gods for me, because of the depth of their minds, their intellectual limpidity, their humor, their irony, the way they were able to synthesize, their ability to help me discover unsuspected things. My teachers are the ones who gave me faith in myself, who opened new horizons for me, who forced me to go further, to be more demanding toward myself.

Not a single American cultural specialist expressed half as strongly his devotion to the value rationality that animates his professional vocation.

2. The same French social and cultural specialists draw much weaker socio-economic boundaries than their American counterparts. Conversely, French teachers expressed fewer regrets for not having chosen a more lucrative occupation. Most take their small income to be the result of an active and positive choice on their part and of their decision to put freedom and self-actualization above money, as explained here by the literature professor who teaches in a *lycée* in the Paris region...

I prefer to make what I make and be free rather than make twice as much and have to be subservient. I could not bear to be a butcher...the dependency on the customers, the fact of having to say "yes, miss; no, miss," of having to pay attention to her dog, while you should tell her to leave the dog outside because of hygiene. Or of having to be nice to a person who takes half an hour to get what she needs while there is a line of people waiting outside...But even more generally I don't like the notion that how you are doing financially depends on how you behave toward other people, with more or less insincerity...because it means a loss of freedom...I know that I make much less than my neighbors, including those whose professions require less of them intellectually. But this really leaves me indifferent. They can try to impress me with their Mercedes, but I go on my bicycle, no problem...For me, the value of things is not measured this way.

Along the same lines, a Versailles priest whose family is part of the most trad-itional French bourgeoisie explains that in his view his small income

is a question of independence...The fact of not having a high salary allows me to choose to do what I do independently of what it gives me monetarily. When I worked in the corporate world, I made five or six times what I make now...But today I don't take money into consideration in choosing what I do or don't do, in deciding what activities I will get involved in...This allows me to avoid falling into mediocrity, and it allows me to do something interesting with my life...not to be only a widget in a large machine ...to go further in experiencing things and in getting totally involved in what I do.

A French social worker whom I interviewed in the bare office of a charitable organization located in the Sixth Arrondissement offers a similar explanation for his professional choices when he says that

the nonprofit sector gives you a chance to invest yourself personally in many ways...It gave me a chance to live according to my Catholic faith, my Christian faith. I made the decision to have an effect, even if a limited one, on our society, and more particularly on social inequality...Making money is not my professional motivation. I experience everyday how difficult it is for a family to live in Paris with a small salary...but I accepted that when I chose to work for the nonprofit sector...Honestly, I do not regret it. I believe that it is good to reduce income inequality. So in theory I personally live in coherence with that.

Like the Clermont-Ferrand philosophy professor, these men stress the value rationality that motivated their vocational choice over the economic rationality emphasized by "mainstream" society. This conviction that their comparatively low salaries are compensated by exceptional opportunities not available in the business world for service or personal fulfillment – are compensated by the fact that they are getting more out of life – was less frequently communicated by American social and cultural specialists. Indeed, members of the latter group more often denigrated their profession and voiced regrets for not having chosen a more lucrative occupation. Several told me that they hope to change their career course "because of the money issue." For instance, a second-generation Italian who works as a recreation specialist in New Jersey explained that he was in the process of finishing college courses in financial planning to pursue a new career because "I have to try to financially secure myself and my little boy." Along the same lines, a Scarsdale science teacher told me that "I think if I had to do it all over again, I would put myself in a position where I had more opportunities to demonstrate my individualism...such as business..."A sizable number of American social and cultural specialists seem to believe that people who are really smart "go for the money" and that only "losers," people who are not "totally with it," and people who could not pay for the training that would qualify them for higher-paying work, would take a job with low monetary rewards. Along the same lines, echoing the Indianapolis minister... for whom money was the main yardstick of his "professional success," this New York teacher has also totally absorbed the principles of economic rationality, transposing them onto the educational and cultural worlds:

> I am not one of those sacrificial-teachers types that will spend inordinate amounts of time working for almost nothing. I really don't do anything in life, or hardly anything right now, that I don't get paid for, I'm a professional vocalist, and I never sing in any church or temple or concert hall without being paid. Also, a lot of teachers do an awful lot of volunteer work of all kinds. It's not doing their professionalism very much good. I have to admire them to a certain extent that they're willing to spend that much time, but I have a family and other interests, and I just really can't see spending the extra time. I work efficiently enough so that they're impressed enough with my work to pay me a lot. But I wouldn't be there if they didn't pay me, and if I change jobs it would be because of a combination of cost of living and a salary and so on.

While these few individuals do not represent the full repertoire of interpretations through which social and cultural specialists understand their place in American society, their views echo perspectives voiced frequently. They all hint at the fact that this group has not developed an alternative subculture as highly coherent as that of its French counterpart, an alternative subculture that would legitimate value rationality over economic rationality and clearly support cultural standards of status assessment. In this context, it is hardly surprising that American social and cultural specialists draw stronger socioeconomic boundaries than their French counterpart.

3. The comparison of scores on the three dimensions shows that French for-profit workers draw considerably stronger cultural boundaries than their American counterparts. Accordingly, various French for-profit workers have joined social clubs and associations where they can maintain a certain level of intellectual activity. The Freemasons are particularly popular because this organization puts a strong emphasis on philosophical and spiritual issues and provides individuals a forum in which "to ask oneself important questions beyond how to balance a budget or which car to buy... questions on the meaning of life, the meaning you give to your life, what actions you should carry out" (financial advisor, Clermont-Ferrand). An unusually charming and articulate Paris lawyer explains in similar terms that it is crucial for him to share ideas with people who have

> a similar search for truth, for spirituality, a detachment from materialism which is invading us more and more. [We need to] be able to take distance toward this, to attach more importance to other-worldly things that make us human... What I miss in my everyday professional life is the stimulation to push further certain ideas and topics that are not related to everyday life. I need to think about things like "Truth," otherwise I am living like an animal. I can't live only for my work. I have professional satisfaction when I win a trial, but this is only a technical satisfaction. The rest of my time is spent developing argumentations, and this is quite banal.

Not a single American working in the private sector indicated participation in organizations that would be the intellectual equivalent of the Freemasons, whereas at least ten Frenchmen revealed that they were involved with this group – largely for intellectual and spiritual reasons – despite the fact that as members they were sworn to secrecy.

4. Finally, a comparison of scores shows that American for-profit workers are on average considerably more socioeconomically exclusive than their Parisian counterparts and slightly more socioeconomically exclusive than the Clermontois. This, along with the trends described above, clearly suggests that national patterns in boundary work reinforce the patterns typical of occupational groups in both countries, French for-profit workers being more culturally inclined than their American counterparts, while American social and cultural specialists are more materialistic than their French counterparts. More generally, the dynamic between social and cultural specialists and for-profit workers in both countries reflects the dynamic between cultural and socioeconomic boundaries in France and the United States: cultural boundaries are strongest and are most stressed by a wider population in the context where intellectuals and social and cultural specialists themselves play a more active role in promoting value rationality and legitimating cultural standards of evaluation.

References

Brint, Stephen. 1988. "The Social Bases and National Contexts of Middle-Class Liberalism and Dissent in Western Societies: A Comparative Study." Unpublished paper, Department of Sociology, Yale University.

Lipset, Seymour Martin. 1977. "Why No Socialism in the United States?" In *Sources of Contemporary Radicalism*, edited by S. Bialer and S. Sluzar Boulder, Colo.: Westview Press, 31–149.

—— 1979. *The First New Nation: The United States in Historical and Comparative Perspective*. New York: Norton.

—— 1981. *The Political Man: The Social Bases of Politics*. Chapter 10 of expanded ed. Baltimore: Johns Hopkins University Press.

—— 1990. *Continental Divide: The Values and Institutions of the United States and Canada*. New York and London: Routledge.

Weber, Max. 1946. "The Protestant Sects and the Spirit of Capitalism." In *From Max Weber: Essays in Sociology*, edited by Hans Gerth and C. Wright Mills. New York: Oxford University Press, 302–22.

—— 1964. *L'éthique protestante et l'esprit du capitalisme*. Paris: Librairie Plon.

—— 1978. *Economy and Society*. Vol. 1. Berkeley: University of California Press.

Editor's Notes on Further Reading

Lamont on Symbolic Boundaries and Status

Michèle Lamont explores cultural variation in status judgments in interviews with 160 upper-middle class men in the United States and France. The concept of symbolic boundaries (see Nippert-Eng excerpt this volume) helps analyze the meanings underlying status assessments. The book compares symbolic boundaries cross-nationally, and also assesses differences between residents of major and provincial cities, between upwardly mobile men and others, and, as in this selection, between men in different types of occupations.

To some extent this study may be seen as a response to Bourdieu's investigation of the relations between social position and cultural taste in France in *Distinction: A Social Critique of the Judgement of Taste*, trans. Richard Nice (Cambridge, MA: Harvard University Press, 1984). Lamont's view that Bourdieu overstates the nature and importance of "high culture" status markers is echoed in various ways in Bryson (excerpted this volume), and in the findings of Richard Peterson and his colleagues that high status groups in the US now base status claims on a relatively indiscriminate "ability to appreciate": see for example Richard Peterson and Roger Kern, "Changing Highbrow Taste: From Snob to Omnivore," *American Sociological Review* 61 (1996): 900–7. David Halle challenges the notion that art functions as cultural capital in the United States in *Inside Culture: Art and Class in the American Home* (Chicago and London: University of Chicago Press, 1993). See also Michèle Lamont and Marcel Fournier, eds., *Cultivating Differences: Symbolic Boundaries and the Making of Inequality* (Chicago: University of Chicago Press, 1992); Helmut Anheier, Jurgen Gerhards, and Frank Romo, "Forms of Capital and Social Structure in Cultural Fields: Examining Bourdieu's Social Topography," *American Journal of Sociology* 100 (1995): 859–903; Bonnie Erickson, "Culture, Class and Connections," *American Journal of Sociology* 102 (1996): 217–51; Paul DiMaggio, "Classification in Art," *American Sociological Review* 52 (1987): 440–55; DiMaggio, "Cultural Capital and School Success," *American Sociological Review* 47 (1982): 189–201; and Douglas Holt, "Distinction in America? Recovering Bourdieu's Theory of Tastes from its Critics," *Poetics* 25 (1997): 93–120.

For other studies of symbolic boundaries see editor's note to excerpt from work by Nippert-Eng and Michèle Lamont, ed., *The Cultural Territories of Race: Black and White Boundaries* (Chicago: University of Chicago Press and New York: Russell Sage Foundation, 1999); Lamont, *The Dignity of Working Men: Morality and the Boundaries of Race, Class, and Immigration* (Cambridge, MA: Harvard University Press and New York: Russell Sage Foundation, 2000); Michèle Lamont and Laurent Thevenot, eds., *Rethinking Comparative Cultural Sociology: Repertoires of Evaluation in France and the United States* (New York: Cambridge University Press, 2000); and Cynthia Fuchs Epstein, *Deceptive Distinctions: Sex Gender and the Social Order* (New Haven and London: Yale University Press and New York: Russell Sage Foundation, 1988). On the way moral boundaries have been linked to class reproduction in moral crusades see Nicola Beisel, *Imperiled Innocents: Anthony Comstock and Family Reproduction in Victorian America* (Princeton: Princeton University Press, 1997); "Morals Versus Art: Censorship, The Politics of Interpretation, and the Victorian Nude," *American Sociological Review* 58 (1993): 145–62, and "Class, Culture, and Campaigns against Vice in Three American Cities, 1872–1892," *American Sociological Review* 55 (1990): 44–62. On intra-class differences between service and for-profit workers, see also for example Steven Brint, "'New Class' and Cumulative Trend Explanations of the Liberal Political Attitudes of Professionals," *American Journal of Sociology* 90 (1984): 30–71.

11 Symbolic Exclusion and Musical Dislikes

Bethany Bryson

Background

Music as a Symbolic Resource

Music has long been considered an important part of social life. Its symbolic and ritual powers are used to explain both social cohesion and cultural resistance (Willis 1977; Hebdige 1979; Rose 1994). Furthermore, music is an important cultural and communicative medium. For instance, Cerulo (1995) describes how national anthems represent identity and communicate a nation's position in the world system. Likewise, Weinstein (1991) demonstrates that heavy metal music generates community and solidarity among fans while sending an unmistakable message to its detractors.

Music contains a complex set of dimensions, sounds, lyrics, visual cues, social relations, and physical acts (DeNora 1991; Dowd 1992). Music also permits many levels of engagement, from humming to oneself to screaming above the music with 30,000 fans. Given its symbolic and social potency, it is no wonder that music is such an important part of human society, that nearly every nation has an anthem, that most religious ceremonies involve music, and that singing is so frequently a part of political rallies. The importance of music to group identity and social differentiation, then, suggests that musical taste provides a good test for questions about symbolic boundaries. Therefore, I use musical taste to examine a more general theory of cultural exclusion.

High-Status Exclusiveness

Most sociologists of culture agree that some forms of cultural consumption serve as markers of social status (Weber [1968] 1978). For instance, knowledge of fine arts, literature, and upper-class etiquette signals wealth and prestige. Such knowledge may also serve as a passkey for entrance into elite social life. Bourdieu (Bourdieu 1984; Bourdieu and Passeron 1977) calls this passkey *cultural capital* because it is cultural knowledge that can be translated into real economic gains, for example, by allowing access to elite social networks and clubs where business deals often are made (Kanter 1977).

By restricting access to resources, social status can be translated into market position and political status. This process can be seen as the result of two interrelated levels of exclusion. First, *social exclusion* is a process of social selection that is based on a previously determined set of cultural criteria and is exercised by people with high levels of income, education, and occupational prestige (Bourdieu and Passeron 1977). Social exclusion occurs at the level of social relations and is the sort of "social closure" that Weber ([1968] 1978: 342, 933, 935) addresses as the monopolization of resources and inclusion in social intercourse.

The second level, *symbolic exclusion*, is the source of those "previously determined cultural criteria." Whereas social exclusion refers to the monopolization of human interactions, symbolic exclusion depicts the subjective process that orders those social interactions – taste. This process, then, is a form of "boundary-work" (Gieryn 1983; Lamont 1992) that continuously recreates the positive, negative, and neutral attitudes toward cultural cues and that define these cues as more or less acceptable in various situations. The present study focuses on symbolic exclusion. The analytical distinction between social exclusion and symbolic exclusion highlights an important empirical difference between behavior and attitudes. Note, however, that symbolic systems are social and that social exclusion can occur without physical interaction.

Music is one type of cue that can be used to construct symbolic boundaries between groups or individuals. Therefore, I analyze *musical exclusion* as a type of symbolic exclusion and operationalize it as dislike for various music genres. I use the terms *musical tolerance* or *cultural tolerance* to refer to the absence of dislike for a cultural cue or music genre. Musical tolerance, then, is operationalized as the complement of musical exclusiveness – not its opposite.

The crux of symbolic exclusion is dislike, and according to Bourdieu, the exercise of dislike and exclusion is more important to high-status individuals than to others:

> Tastes (i.e., manifested preferences) are the practical affirmation of an inevitable difference. It is no accident that, when they have to be justified, they are asserted purely negatively, by the refusal of other tastes. In matters of taste more than anywhere else, all determination is negation; and tastes are perhaps first and foremost distastes.... The most intolerable thing for those who regard themselves as the possessors of legitimate ["highbrow"] culture is the sacrilegious reuniting of tastes which taste dictates shall be separated   (Bourdieu 1984: 56–7).

For Bourdieu, the relationship between the symbolic level and the social level is reciprocal (Bourdieu and Wacquant 1992). While they shape each other, other material and subjective factors intervene to prevent the two levels from being perfectly aligned. Symbolic exclusion and social exclusion are assumed to work in a manner similar to another pair of terms more familiar to American sociologists – prejudice and discrimination.

Bourdieu's (1984) main exposition on what I have called "symbolic exclusion" argues that knowledge about fine arts is a status cue while popular taste is rejected. "The higher the level of education, the greater is the proportion of respondents who, when asked whether a series of objects would make beautiful photographs, refuse the ordinary objects of popular admiration ... as 'vulgar' or 'ugly'" (Bourdieu 1984: 35). Bourdieu's perspective, then, expects high-status individuals to be the most culturally exclusive. That is, they distinguish themselves with an exclusive culture that rejects the cultural patterns and tastes of other groups.

Educated Tolerance

When the well-documented finding that education increases political tolerance (Adorno et al. 1950; Stouffer 1955; Davis 1975; Nunn, Crockett, and Williams

1978; Lipset 1981) is extended to cultural tolerance, the predicted effect of education is the opposite of that expected by theories of high-status exclusiveness.

To the extent that political tolerance is a belief that civil liberties should be extended to nonconformist groups (Stouffer 1955), political intolerance is a measure of symbolic exclusion. That is, political tolerance refers to the willingness to include specified groups within the boundary of "citizen" – or "us" as opposed to "them" (Gamson 1995). In the realm of public opinion, then, the term "political tolerance" can be seen as a general reluctance to symbolically exclude nonconformists from the category "citizen."

To link these two literatures, I propose that dislike of social groups is associated with dislike of music genres. My specific expectations are twofold. First, political intolerance – the general tendency to exclude social groups symbolically – should be positively related to musical exclusiveness – the general tendency to exclude music genres symbolically. Second, because I see both political intolerance and musical exclusiveness as forms of symbolic exclusion, contra Bourdieu's prediction, I expect education to reduce musical exclusiveness, just as it reduces political intolerance, and income and occupational prestige are expected to have little or no effect on musical exclusiveness when the impact of education is held constant (Davis 1975).

Symbolic Racism

Kinder and Sears (1981) propose a two-stage description of racism and public opinion. Termed *symbolic racism*, the model suggests, first, that racism shapes cultural (value) orientations and, second, that racism and the resulting set of orientations together may explain public opinion about interracial issues. Whites' stereotypes about African Americans, which can be considered symbolic exclusion, may be good predictors of Whites' discomfort with residential integration, which can be considered an estimate of social exclusion (Farley et al. 1994).

I provide a theoretical foundation and an empirical test for the relationship between racism and cultural orientations that has been named *symbolic racism*. Here, "stereotypes" are understood as symbolic boundaries between social groups that reinforce simple dislike. These "stereotypes" or cultural differentiations are, furthermore, extended from the realm of values (usually relating to work, family, and economics) to the field of musical taste. Thus, racism is expected to predict dislike for the types of music that are disproportionately liked by Hispanic Americans or African Americans.

Patterned Tolerance

Recent research on political tolerance raises new questions about the reason for and universality of education's liberalizing effect (Phelan et al. 1995). Jackman and Muha (1984) critique the earlier assertions of Stouffer (1955), Davis (1975) and others that education increases democratic liberalism through simple enlightenment. Jackman and Muha claim that highly educated people have only a superficial commitment to the rhetoric of democratic liberalism, and oppose real social changes if the changes threaten their status. Jackman and Muha show that the strong effects of education on abstract beliefs about the importance of racial equality are not present for attitudes about concrete actions intended to foster racial inequality. Their work suggests that the political tolerance displayed by educated respondents is, in fact, only a carefully cultivated status symbol.

In a new formulation of the superficial ideology explanation, Schuman and Bobo (1988) show that opposition to neighborhood racial integration may be based on perceived class differences between Whites and African Americans rather than a lack of commitment to racial equality. In abstract form and when the class status of an African American family is at least equal to that of the respondent, racial integration is approved, but in concrete form, respondents often see residential integration as the entrance of lower-class families into middle-class neighborhoods. Thus, respondents displayed a commitment to democratic liberalism with respect to racial integration but continued to resist class integration.

If my proposition that dislike of a social group is evidenced by dislike of that group's perceived culture is correct, Schuman and Bobo's (1988) findings suggest that the apparently tolerant tastes of educated respondents may mask a systematic dislike of music genres whose audiences have lower than average levels of education. This prediction has important implications for our understanding of the wide-ranging tastes of highly educated cultural "omnivores" (Peterson 1992; Peterson and Simkus 1992; Peterson and Kern 1996). That is, rather than being indiscriminately broad, omnivorous taste may include high-status types of music that are popular among non-Whites, especially "world music" (Peterson 1990) genres like reggae and Latin music, while excluding low status genres like gospel and country regardless of their association with race or ethnicity. (See DiMaggio and Peterson 1975 for a discussion of country music's status and audience.) Identifying boundaries around broad taste would allow us to more confidently interpret Peterson and Kern's (1996) findings as a specific pattern of taste, rather than as evidence against the existence of high-status culture (Halle 1993).

A tendency for patterns of broad taste to exclude low-status genres would suggest that cultural breadth, or tolerance, could itself be a source of cultural capital. Unlike the refined form of cultural capital that Bourdieu (1984) documented in France, however, this contemporary American emphasis on breadth and tolerance would be more accurately described as *multicultural capital* – the social prestige afforded by familiarity with a range of cultural styles that is both broad and predictably exclusive. I add the term "multi" to "cultural capital" in order to specify a content of cultural capital, not to modify its meaning. That is, multicultural capital should not be included in a list of "types" of capital (e.g., social capital, cultural capital, and economic capital). However, the term could be used in an as yet nonexistent list of types of *cultural* capital (e.g., multicultural capital, high-cultural capital, counter-cultural capital, techno-cultural capital, etc.). (See Lamont 1992 and Erickson 1991 for work in this direction.)

This specific pattern of broad taste can be considered a form of cultural capital to the extent that it meets three criteria (Lamont and Lareau 1988). First, cultural tolerance and openness are widely recognized as symbols of social status among upper-middle-class Americans (Lamont 1992), and that recognition is evident, though less pervasive, in the working class (Lamont 1997). Second, familiarity with this cultural style must, nevertheless, be at least somewhat restricted. Using

Bourdieu's (1984, chap. 8) methodology, then, the frequency of "don't know" responses to questions about musical taste is expected to decrease with education. The third characteristic of cultural capital is that it can serve as the basis of social exclusion. In this case, the potential for exclusion would be evidenced by a class-based distribution of cultural tolerance, on one hand, and a predictable pattern of symbolic exclusion (more dislike of low-status genres), on the other.

Hypotheses

High Status Exclusiveness
H_1: People with high levels of education, income, and occupational prestige dislike more types of music than do people with low levels of education, income, and prestige.
Educated Tolerance
H_2: People with high levels of education dislike fewer types of music than do people with medium and low education, controlling for income and occupational prestige.
H_3: People who are reluctant to extend civil liberties to stigmatized groups dislike more types of music than do people with more tolerant political attitudes.
Symbolic Racism
H_4: Whites who have high racism scores dislike the types of music that are disproportionately liked by people of color more than do people who report less racist attitudes.
Patterned Tolerance
H_5: People who dislike few music genres will dislike those types of music that are liked by people with low levels of education more than other types of music, when education is controlled.
H_6: People who have high levels of education are less likely to report that they are unfamiliar with any music genre.

Measures

Dependent Variables

The General Social Survey (GSS) is a nearly annual survey of noninstitutionalized adults in the United States conducted by the National Opinion Research Center using a stratified random sampling method. The 1993 GSS includes a set of questions about culture, including musical tastes as well as leisure activities and values (Davis and Smith 1993; Marsden and Swingle 1994). These new data make information on musical *dislikes* available for the first time. Like other surveys of taste and participation in the arts, this survey presented respondents with a list of musical categories, but rather than having them choose their favorite or mark all they like, the GSS asked all 1,606 respondents to evaluate each of 18 music genres on a five-point Likert scale ranging from "like very much" to "dislike very much". Using these data, I derive a measure of musical exclusiveness by counting the "dislike" and "dislike very much" responses given by each respondent. . . .

Conclusion

Summary. I seek to resolve the contradiction between two widely accepted theories of culture by highlighting the neglected notion of cultural *exclusion* or dislike. The first perspective posits that people with high social status are the most culturally exclusive and intolerant. The second perspective claims that education increases tolerance, openness, and cultural acceptance. If the most highly educated Americans were ever the most culturally exclusive, this clearly is not the case today.

By analyzing dislikes of 18 types of music, I show that education significantly decreases exclusiveness in musical taste. Thus, the *high-status exclusion* hypothesis (Hypothesis 1) does not accurately describe the distribution of musical taste in the contemporary United States: Respondents with high levels of education reported more tolerant musical taste than those with less education. This supports the first *educated tolerance* hypothesis (Hypothesis 2).

Furthermore, I show that cultural exclusiveness is associated with political intolerance (Hypothesis 3) and that negative attitudes toward social groups result in negative attitudes toward the types of music associated with that group (Hypothesis 4). These findings not only demonstrate that some theories of political tolerance may be extended to cultural attitudes, they also show that patterns of taste are related to group conflict. However, I do not assume that rising levels of education will decrease cultural exclusiveness, as Stouffer (1955) did when he predicted that rising education would obliterate political intolerance. Instead, I draw on recent developments in the study of political tolerance to scrutinize musical tolerance.

I find that highly educated people in the United States are more musically tolerant, but not indiscriminately so. I provide evidence of class-based exclusion in that the genres most disliked by tolerant people are those appreciated by people with the lowest levels of education. Therefore, I suggest that *cultural tolerance should not be conceptualized as an indiscriminate tendency to be nonexclusive, but as a reordering of group boundaries that trades race for class*. If a person with average taste were injected with a serum to encourage broad taste, the first three genres that would disappear from that person's list of dislikes (Latin music, jazz, and blues/rhythm and blues) are significantly associated with non-dominant racial or ethnic groups, while the types of music that are most likely to remain on that person's list of musical dislikes (rap, heavy metal, country, and gospel music) are the four most strongly associated with low education. Furthermore, two of those four most excluded genres – gospel and rap – lie at the intersection of race and education. Their fans tend to be Black and have less education than the general population.

Together with the finding that less educated people more frequently reported being unfamiliar with one or more of the 18 genres, results show that cultural breadth has become a high-status signal that excludes low-status cultural cues and is unevenly distributed by education in the United States. Therefore, I suggest that the phenomenon be understood as *multicultural capital*.

Limitations. With this large data set, I have demonstrated a connection between intergroup affect and musical taste. However, the proportion of variance explained is relatively modest. Therefore, I do not argue that musical dislike is *only* a tool of symbolic exclusion. Cultural taste may also be shaped by the extent to which a particular work or genre resonates with the cultural orientations of its listeners (Griswold 1992). This can cause taste for the genre to be patterned by social location that, in turn, would reinforce the tendency for the genre to appeal to one group more than others. Also, symbolic exclusion treats cultural cues as "tools" (Swidler 1986), but music can be *used* in other ways as well. Anderson (1990), for example, shows how young African American men use rap music (at high volumes) to gain control of public spaces.

A second limitation of this study is that these data cannot tell us what respondents have in mind when they think of each genre. One of the categories, for instance, is labeled "new age/space music." While 18.2 percent of the respondents reported that they didn't know much about the genre, we cannot tell how the remaining respondents understand the category. . . .

As with most survey data on opinions and attitudes, the GSS imposes cultural categories on respondents (Marsden and Swingle 1994). The bias introduced by this method may be unimportant when "real world" choices are constrained ("For whom do you plan to vote in the upcoming election?"), but an important task in the sociology of culture is to *discover* salient cultural categories rather than assume them. The list used by the GSS vaguely resembles the major categories of music used by popular music distributors, but we cannot be sure how the results would differ if the list were altered. . . .

Finally, it is unclear whether the inconsistency between my findings and Bourdieu's (1984) are due to differences in time, national culture, or methodology. Peterson and Kern (1996) show that the status value of cultural breadth has increased over time in the United States, but Lamont (1992) finds that upper-middle-class Americans are much more reluctant than their French counterparts to draw class boundaries on the basis of cultural taste. Likewise, Weil (1985) finds that the effect of education on anti-Semitism is not constant cross-nationally. In either case, Bourdieu (1984) does not provide much evidence that educated respondents were more *or less* exclusive because, with one exception, he does not ask them about their distastes. His finding that the upper classes have more knowledge about and appreciation for high culture does not contradict the concept of a tolerance line. In fact, support of multiculturalism is positively associated with – rather than opposed to – an appreciation for traditional high culture (DiMaggio and Bryson 1995). Cross-national research is needed to separate theoretical generalities from local strategies of symbolic exclusion.

Contributions. By exploring the connections between literatures on cultural taste, political tolerance, and racism, this analysis contributes to each field. In the political tolerance literature, I address the central question of why there is a relationship between education and democratic liberalism. Researchers have suggested that political tolerance in the United States may be part of an official culture learned through the educational system (Weil 1985; Phelan et al. 1995), but no one had explored the application of status culture theories to this problem. By conceptualizing political intolerance as a set of symbolic boundaries, I separate intergroup affect from beliefs about civil rights. Sullivan et al.'s (1979: 792) suggestion that political tolerance is not related to education when tolerance presumes dislike might be better understood if the importance of the negative relationship between *dislike* and education is considered. It is not the sophisticated understandings of democratic liberalism that vary, as Jackman and Muha (1984) suggest, but the dislike of cultural (and presumably political) "otherness."

This study also contributes to our understanding of racism by lending support to Schuman and Bobo's (1988) finding that educated respondents resist racial integration only when it means class integration. The correlation between race and class is an important feature of modern industrialized societies. The relationship creates substantial room for ideological confusion and provides an opportunity to study how two types of symbolic boundaries interact. Therefore, research into strategies of self-definition and symbolic exclusion may be crucial to an understanding of class and ethnic relations as well as of the way these cultural categories interact (Lamont 1997).

I also find that class is not the only important basis of cultural exclusion – musical dislikes parallel racial group conflict as well. This finding challenges Bourdieu's description of taste as rooted in class and caused by varying levels of freedom from necessity. The underlying notion that one's experiences shape cultural taste can be applied more broadly, but the way this process shapes other group boundaries remains to be specified.

Finally, this anlaysis shows how Bourdieu's (1984) theory of high-status cultural exclusiveness may still be useful despite strong evidence that patterns of cultural appreciation in the contemporary United States are inconsistent with his description of cultural capital's *content* (Peterson and Simkus 1992; Halle 1993). Increasing tolerance has undoubtedly made high-status culture more open to racial and ethnic cultural differences. However, tolerance itself may separate high-status culture from other group cultures. This *tolerance line* recreates the pattern of high-status (cosmopolitan) culture in opposition to non-high-status (group-based) culture. Thus, it provides a new criterion of cultural exclusion....

To the extent that symbolic boundaries are used as a basis of social exclusion, study of the politics of taste is essential to our understanding of the subtle forces at work in power relationships and the reproduction of the social structure.

References

Adorno, Theodore W., Else Frenkel-Brunswick, Daniel J. Levinson, and R. Nevit Stanford. 1950. *The Authoritarian Personality*. New York: Harper.

Anderson, Elijah. 1990. *Streetwise: Race, Class and Change in an Urban Community*. Chicago, IL: University of Chicago Press.

Binder, Amy. 1993. "Media Depictions of Harm in Heavy Metal and Rap Music." *American Sociological Review* 58: 753–67.

Bourdieu, Pierre. 1977. *Outline of a Theory of Practice*. Cambridge, England: Cambridge University Press.

—— 1984. *Distinction: A Social Critique of the Stratification of Taste*. Cambridge, MA: Harvard University Press.

Bourdieu, Pierre and Jean-Claude Passeron. 1977. *Reproduction in Education, Society and Culture*. Beverly Hills, CA: Sage.

Bourdieu, Pierre and Loïc J. D. Wacquant. 1992. *An Invitation to Reflexive Sociology*. Chicago, IL: University of Chicago Press.

Cerulo, Karen A. 1995. *Identity Designs: The Sights and Sounds of a Nation*. Rose Book Series of the American Sociological Association. New Brunswick, NJ: Rutgers University Press.

Collins, Randall. 1979. *Credential Society.* New York: Academic Press.

Davis, James A. 1975. "Communism, Conformity, Cohorts, and Categories: American Tolerance in 1954 and 1972–73." *American Journal of Sociology* 82: 491–513.

—— 1982. "Achievement Variables and Class Cultures: Family, Schooling, Job, and Forty-Nine Dependent Variables in the Cumulative GSS." *American Sociological Review* 47: 569–86.

Davis, James and Tom Smith. 1993. *General Social Surveys, 1972–1993: Cumulative Codebook.* Chicago, IL: National Opinion Research Center [producer]. Storrs, CT: Roper Center for Public Opinion Research [distributor].

DeNora, Tia. 1991. "Musical Patronage and Social Change in Beethoven's Vienna." *American Journal of Sociology* 97(2): 310–46.

DiMaggio, Paul. 1982. "Cultural Capital and School Success: The Impact of Status Culture Participation on the Grades of U.S. High School Students." *American Sociological Review* 47: 189–201.

—— 1987. "Classification in Art." *American Sociological Review* 52: 440–55.

—— 1991. "Social Structure, Institutions, and Cultural Goods: The Case of the United States." Pp. 133–55 in *Social Theory for a Changing Society*, edited by P. Bourdieu and J. Coleman. Boulder, CO: Westview Press.

DiMaggio, Paul and Bethany Bryson. 1995. "Americans' Attitudes Towards Cultural Diversity and Cultural Authority: Culture Wars, Social Closure or Multiple Dimensions." General Social Survey Topical Report No. 27. National Opinion Research Center, Chicago, IL.

DiMaggio, Paul, John Evans, and Bethany Bryson. 1996. "Have Americans' Social Attitudes Become More Polarized?" *American Journal of Sociology* 102(3): 690–755.

DiMaggio, Paul and Richard Peterson. 1975. "From Region to Class, the Changing Locus of Country Music: A Test of the Massification Hypothesis." *Social Forces* 53(3): 497–506.

Dowd, Timothy J. 1992. "The Musical Structure and Social Context of Number One Songs, 1955–88: An Exploratory Analysis." Pp. 130–57 in *Vocabularies of Public Life: Empirical Essays in Symbolic Structure*, edited by R. Wuthnow. London, England: Routledge.

Erickson, Bonnie H. 1991. "What is Good Taste Good For?" *Canadian Review of Sociology and Anthropology* 28: 255–78.

Farley, Reynolds, Charlotte Steeh, Maria Krysan, Tara Jackson, and Keith Reeves. 1994. "Stereotypes and Segregation: Neighborhoods in the Detroit Area." *American Journal of Sociology* 100: 750–80.

Feuer, Lewis. 1991. "From Pluralism to Multiculturalism." *Society* (November/December): 19–22.

Gamson, William A. 1995. "Hiroshima, the Holocaust, and the Politics of Exclusion: 1994 Presidential Address." *American Sociological Review* 60: 1–20.

Gieryn, Thomas F. 1983. "Boundary-Work and the Demarcation of Science from Non-Science: Strains and Interests in Professional Ideologies of Scientists." *American Sociological Review* 48: 781–95.

Greeley, Andrew M. and Paul B. Sheatsley. 1971. "Attitudes Toward Racial Integration." *Scientific American* 225: 13–19.

Griswold, Wendy. 1992. "The Writing on the Mud Wall: Nigerian Novels and the Imaginary Village." *American Sociological Review* 57: 709–24.

Halle, David. 1993. *Inside Culture: Art and Class in the American Home.* Chicago, IL: University of Chicago Press.

Hebdige, Dick. 1979. *Subculture: The Meaning of Style.* New York: Methuen.

Holt, Douglas B. 1995. "Class Boundaries Inscribed in Consumption Practices." Paper presented at the 65th Annual Meeting of the Eastern Sociological Society, March, 31, Philadelphia, PA.

Hyman, Herbert and Charles Wright. 1979. *Education's Lasting Influence on Values*. Chicago, IL: Chicago University Press.

Jackman, Mary and Michael Muha. 1984. "Education and Intergroup Attitudes: Moral Enlightenment, Superficial Democratic Commitment, or Ideological Refinement?" *American Sociological Review* 49: 751–69.

Johnson, Sven. 1994. "Gender Differences and Social Change in Cultural Capital Investment: An Investigation of an Elite Population." Paper presented at the annual meeting of the American Sociological Association, August, 6, Los Angeles, CA.

Kalmijn, Matthijs. 1994. "Assortive Mating by Cultural and Economic Occupational Status." *American Journal of Sociology* 100: 422–52.

Kanter, Rosabeth. 1977. *Men and Women of the Corporation*. New York: Harper.

Kinder, Donald R. and David O. Sears. 1981. "Prejudice and Politics: Symbolic Racism versus Racial Threats to the Good Life." *Journal of Personality and Social Psychology* 40: 414–31.

Lamont, Michèle. 1992. *Money, Morals and Manners: The Culture of the French and American Upper-Middle Class*. Chicago, IL: University of Chicago Press.

—— 1997. "Colliding Moralities Between Black and White Workers." Pp. 263–85 in *From Sociology to Cultural Studies: New Perspectives*, edited by E. Long. New York and Oxford: Blackwell.

Lamont, Michèle and Annette Lareau. 1988. "Cultural Capital: Allusions, Gaps, and Glissandos in Recent Theoretical Developments." *Sociological Theory* 6: 153–68.

Lipset, Seymour Martin. 1981. *Political Man*. Baltimore, MD: Johns Hopkins University Press.

Marsden, Peter and Joseph Swingle. 1994. "Conceptualizing and Measuring Culture in Surveys: Values, Strategies, and Symbols." *Poetics* 22(4): 269–89.

Milner, Murray, Jr. 1972. *The Illusion of Equality: The Effect of Education on Opportunity, Inequality, and Social Conflict*. San Francisco, CA: Jossey-Bass.

Nunn, Cyde Z., Harry Crockett, Jr., and J. Allen Williams, Jr. 1978. *Tolerance for Nonconformity*. San Francisco, CA: Josey-Bass.

Parkin, Frank. 1979. *Marxism and Class Theory: A Bourgeois Critique*. New York: Columbia University Press.

Peterson, Richard A. 1990. "Audience and Industry Origins of the Crisis in Classical Music Programming: Toward World Music." Pp. 207–27 in *The Future of the Arts: Public Policy and Arts Research*, edited by D. B. Pankratz and V. B. Morris, New York: Praeger.

—— 1992. "Understanding Audience Segmentation: From Elite and Mass to Omnivore and Univore." *Poetics*. 21: 243–58.

Peterson, Richard A. and Roger M. Kern. 1996. "Changing Highbrow Taste: From Snob to Omnivore." *American Sociological Review* 61: 900–7.

Peterson, Richard A. and Albert Simkus. 1992. "How Musical Tastes Mark Occupational Status Groups." Pp. 152–86 in *Cultivating Differences: Symbolic Boundaries and the Making of Inequality*, edited by M. Lamont and M. Fournier. Chicago, IL: Chicago University Press.

Phelan, Jo, Bruce G. Link, Ann Stueve, and Robert E. Moore. 1995. "Education, Social Liberalism, and Economic Conservativism: Attitudes Towards Homeless People." *American Sociological Review* 60: 126–40.

Rose, Tricia. 1994. *Black Noise: Rap Music and Black Culture in Contemporary America*. Hanover, MA: Wesleyan University Press.

Schuman, Howard and Lawrence Bobo. 1988. "Survey-Based Experiments on White Racial Attitudes Toward Residential Integration." *American Journal of Sociology* 94: 273–99.

Stouffer, Samuel A. 1955. *Communism. Conformity, and Civil Liberties*. New York: Doubleday.

Sullivan, John L., James Piereson, and George E. Marcus. 1979. "An Alternative Conception of Political Tolerance: Illusory Increases 1950s–1970s." *American Political Science Review* 73: 781–94.

Swidler, Ann. 1986. "Culture in Action: Symbols and Strategies." *American Sociological Review* 51: 273–86.

Veblen, Thorstein. [1899] 1953. *The Theory of the Leisure Class: An Economic Study of Institutions.* New York: Mentor.

Weber, Max. [1968] 1978. *Economy and Society.* Translated by G. Roth and C. Wittich. Berkeley, CA: University of California Press.

Weil, Frederick. 1985. "The Variable Effects of Education on Liberal Attitudes: A Comparative-Historical Analysis of Anti-Semitism Using Public Opinion Survey Data." *American Sociological Review* 50: 458–74.

Weinstein, Deena. 1991. *Heavy Metal: A Cultural Sociology.* New York: Lexington.

Willis, Paul. 1977. *Learning to Labor: How Working-Class Kids Get Working-Class Jobs.* Farnborough, England: Saxon House.

Wilson, B. R. 1970. *The Youth Culture and the Universities.* London, England: Faber.

Editor's Notes on Further Reading

Bryson on Symbolic Exclusion and Musical Dislikes

Investigating how social status is related to taste, Bryson asks whether people express social exclusiveness in their musical antipathies, discussing symbolic boundaries marking race and education. Overall, she finds that while racists do dislike music associated with people of color, musical dislikes tend to be influenced more by education than by racial prejudice. More educated people exhibit patterned tolerance: they dislike fewer types of music, but those genres they do dislike are associated with uneducated audiences. Bryson's investigation adds to research responding to Bourdieu's studies of the relation between social position and cultural taste (see Lamont excerpt and editor's note, this volume).

For more on links between music and group identity see, for example, Lauraine LeBlanc, *Pretty in Punk: Girls' Gender Resistance In a Boys' Subculture* (New Brunswick, NJ: Rutgers University Press, 1999); Jon Cruz, *Culture on the Margins: The Black Spiritual and the Rise of American Cultural Interpretation* (Princeton, NJ: Princeton University Press, 1999); Richard Peterson, *Creating Country Music: Fabricating Authenticity* (Chicago: University of Chicago Press, 1997); Karen Cerulo, *Identity Designs: The Sights and Sounds of a Nation*, ASA Rose Book Series (New Brunswick NJ: Rutgers University Press, 1995); Tricia Rose, *Black Noise: Rap Music and Black Culture in Contemporary America* (Hanover, NH and London: University Press of New England and Wesleyan University Press, 1994); George Lipsitz, *Dangerous Crossroads: Popular Music, Postmodernism and the Poetics of Place* (London and New York: Verso, 1994); Richard Peterson and Albert Simkus, "How Musical Tastes Mark Occupational Status Group," pp. 152–86 in Michèle Lamont and Marcel Fournier, *Cultivating Differences: Symbolic Boundaries and the Making of Inequality* (Chicago and London: University of Chicago Press, 1992); Amy Binder, "Media Depictions of Harm in Heavy Metal and Rap Music," *American Sociological Review* 58 (1993): 753–67; Tia De Nora, "Musical Patronage and Cultural Change in Beethoven's Vienna," *American Journal of Sociology* 97 (1991): 310–46; Deena Weinstein, *Heavy Metal: A Cultural Sociology* (New York: Lexington, 1991); Judith Blau, "Music as Social Circumstance," *Social Forces* 66 (1988): 883–902; and Dick Hebdige's classic study of punk subculture in *Subculture: The Meaning of Style* (London and New York: Routledge, 1979). For a sampling of research on music which emphasizes the organization of production more than audiences, see editor's note on excerpt from work by Peterson, this volume. For a classic study of the way formal properties affect response to music see Leonard Meyer, *Emotion and Meaning in Music* (Chicago and London: University of Chicago Press, 1956); other studies which attend to intrinsic properties of music include Albert Bergesen, "Spirituals, Jazz, Blues, and Soul Music: The Role of Elaborated and Restricted Codes," pp. 333–50 in Robert Wuthnow, ed., *The Religious Dimension: New Directions in Quantitative Research* (New York: Academic Press, 1979), and Timothy Jon Dowd, "The Musical Structure and Social Context of Number One Songs, 1955 to 1988: An Exploratory Analysis," pp. 130–57 in Robert Wuthnow, ed., *Vocabularies of Public Life: Empirical Essays in Symbolic Structure* (London and New York: Routledge, 1992).

12 Raced Ways of Seeing

Darnell Hunt

This [chapter] seeks to capture a slippery micro–macro link. It focuses on (1) the role that race-as-representation plays in the micro-level process of meaning negotiation and construction, and (2) the role that the television experience plays in the construction and reproduction of raced subjectivities. Furthermore, it generically conceptualizes the television viewing and discussion environment in terms of the network analytic concept of clique, employing insights from Garfinkel (1967) and small-groups research in order to trace the meaning-making process in action. The case study I employ is the Los Angeles events of 1992 ... ["riots" on "rebellion"] and surrounding news coverage. Should one expect to find important raced differences in how viewers make sense of these texts? If so, what are the implications for debates concerning the power of media to influence versus the ability/tendency of viewers to resist? How is the construction and reproduction of raced subjectivities inscribed in the process? ...

The Use of Pronouns

I defined "race" as "the central axis of social relations" in the United States (Omi and Winant 1986, p. 61: 1994), a "collective representation" that serves to account for (and even legitimate) difference and stratification in society (Prager 1982, p. 102). Because race-as-representation is so pervasive in US culture, it acts as "a fundamental organizing principle of social relationships" (p. 66). At the micro-level, race-as-representation informs the construction and reproduction of identity. As Omi and Winant (1986) put it, "One of the first things we notice about people when we meet them (along with their sex) is their race ... Without a racial identity, one is in danger of having no identity" (p. 62). But as Hall (1988) points out, identity is composed of multiple dimensions including "race," gender, sexual orientation, class, and so on – the salience of each waxing and waning from situation to situation. How, then, are we to isolate an individual's raced identity as the source of his or her attitudes and actions? That is, how do we know whether what we have termed "raced ways of seeing" is really attributable to "race?"

One approach to answering this question involves identifying how social actors understand themselves, the immediate subject position from which they think and act. In respect to the question at hand, this *subjectivity* consists largely of what is often termed *racial consciousness* – "a set of political beliefs and action orientations" arising out of "the awareness of having ideas, feelings and interests similar to others who share the same [raced] characteristics" (Gurin *et al.* 1980, p. 30). Previous studies (e.g., Cramer and Schuman 1975) suggest that pronoun usage may serve as an insightful indicator of the solidarity social actors share with important ingroups and their distance from certain outgroups. When the referents of these pronouns are raced groups, raced solidarity and distance – raced subjectivity – may be established. ...

I divided pronouns into two classes: pronouns of solidarity ("we," "us" and "our") and pronouns of distance ("they," "them" and "their"). The first finding that emerges is that the black-raced groups had a higher average rate of solidarity pronoun use (2.54 per minute) than either Latino-raced (1.77 per minute) or white-raced groups (1.44 per minute). Black-raced groups also had a higher average rate of distance pronoun use (9.79 per minute) than either Latino-raced (5.42 per minute) or white-raced groups (4.01 per minute). The significance of these differences for the raced subjectivity question becomes clear when the referents of the pronouns used are explored. . . .

Three important findings emerge regarding the question of raced subjectivities. First, in their discussion of the events and KTTV text, informants in the Latino-raced groups seemed to understand themselves as members of their immediate study group (60 uses), while informants in the South Central groups also thought of themselves as people who live in South Central Los Angeles (48 uses) and as "Latinos" (11 uses):

> Not all of *us* were thugs. (mumbled something) That has nothing to do with it! But, you know, last year, I mean, they just, everybody in South Central, they're thugs. *We're* gangsters. *We're* . . .   (LATINA group)

> It's about people trying to come up with money, with things, freeloading. Because that's what it's really all about. I mean, *our race*.   (YOUTH group)

At the same time, the Latino-raced groups generally talked about event participants (204 uses) and the media (163 uses) as if they were distant others:

> I understand *they* were very angry and I don't think that justifies anything that *they* did.   (MARIA group)

> *They* [reporters] were scared because *they* thought *they* were going to get hurt too.   (FAMILY group)

Second, informants in the black-raced groups understood themselves first and foremost as "blacks" (101 uses):

> *We* [blacks] cared about Rodney King, man, because that was one of *our* brothers.   (GANG group)

In two of the groups (CORNER and KEISHA) informants also expressed solidarity with event participants (11 uses):

> I mean, but that was some stress that people needed to get off they chest, though. *We* really did.   (CORNER group)

> This is a, umm, white-dominated society and black people have no, no, no – you know, they don't fit in anywhere. And so, I think that, that's why *we* rebel.   (KEISHA group)

In contrast, no such solidarity with event participants was expressed in any of the Latino-raced or white-raced groups. For the most part, however, black-raced groups also tended to discuss event participants as if they were distant others (133 uses):

I really don't know what *they* should have done, but that's just not...I don't have the answer really, but that, that did a lot of damage to the city and everything else.   (NORTH group)

Black-raced groups also tended to treat the media (173 uses), "whites" (35 uses) and the police (30 uses) as distant others:

During the Gulf War, okay. Wasn't *they* [the media] telling us to be strong, stick together, support your family? Okay, so why *they* wasn't doing that...even though it was a riot, but why *they* wasn't giving us moral support? From the media? You know, I mean *they* wasn't saying nothing.   (CORNER group)

We have to do it the white man's way. The only way we can beat, beat the game is to beat *them* [whites] at *their* own game.   (CHURCH group)

They [police] was out there by Fox Hills Mall, protecting it. As soon as you go out there, *they* all around you, waiting for somebody to do something.   (CORNER group)

Third, informants in the white-raced groups seemed to think of themselves primarily as members of their immediate study group (55 uses):

What's interesting about what *we* just watched [the KTTV text] is that it's so detached.

In three of these groups (MATES, DORM2 and DORM3) informants also talked about themselves as "Americans" (5 uses):

...You say, "That, that couldn't happen here." That total anarchy. You know, the country of Democracy that *we* have – just can't imagine that!   (DORM3 group)

But in none of the white-raced groups did informants use solidarity pronouns when speaking of "whites." At the same time, these informants talked about the media (162 uses), event participants (152 uses), and "blacks" (33 uses) as if they were distant others:

That's what happens when *they* [the media] get stories like this, when *they* don't have time for someone to write all of the lines for *them*...   (JILL group)

It [the events] was just an excuse for *them* to go wild – a bunch of, of animals.   (MATES group)

Well, I just never, I...growing up, I. I, always felt that, ah, African Americans were more or less, ah, a whole separate culture. It was like a, ah, you really, you really, *they* wouldn't really interact with you. I think *they* felt, ah, more like a solidarity amongst *themselves*.   (JILL group).

In short, an analysis of pronoun usage suggests that when black-raced informants discussed the events and KTTV text they clearly understood themselves as "black" subjects. White-raced informants, in contrast, generally talked about themselves as members of their immediate study group, while Latino-raced informants seemed to approach the events and KTTV text from a variety of subject positions, "race" being just one....

[A]n individual-level analysis of racial effects supports the group-level findings: black-raced informants left the screening significantly more tolerant of event-related looting and significantly less supportive of event-related arrests than their white-raced and Latino-raced counterparts. Furthermore, socio-economic status and gender, net of raced identification, did *not* seem to be a major determinant of informants' attitudes toward event-related activities. Other studies, of course, highlight the importance of both class and gender in shaping how people make sense of media (see Morley 1980, 1992; Press 1991), in channeling them to specific interpretive communities (Lindlof 1988). But the Los Angeles events were evidently so pregnant with racial meanings that raced subjectivity was the primary identity activated as informants made sense of the KTTV text....

Group Viewing Modes

The most obvious finding is that the white-raced groups tended to be visibly more passive in their reception of the text than either Latino-raced or black-raced groups. Viewers in the white-raced groups sat motionless and quietly throughout the 17-minute screening. I noted no visible reactions in these groups when the KTTV anchor referred to event participants as "thugs," or when the plight of the "Asian" man "drenched in blood" was described. In only one of the groups was there any talk when the KTTV anchors attempted to summarize the events, package them into a coherent, unified narrative. And this talk was *not* critical of KTTV efforts.

In contrast, black-raced groups were quite animated during the screening, with Latino-raced groups not far behind. Several of the black-raced groups and one of the Latino-raced groups promptly reacted with laughter or talk to the labeling of event participants as "thugs." At least two of the black-raced groups and three of the Latino-raced groups responded with talk or body gestures during the report of the "Asian" man "drenched in blood." All of the black-raced and Latino-raced groups engaged in continuous or intermittent episodes of talk during the anchors' summary of the events at the end of the KTTV text.

My failure to note similar visible reactions within white-raced groups during key points in the screening, of course, does not preclude the possibility that invisible reactions were occurring within the heads of white-raced viewers. But when the dearth of *social* activity in white-raced groups is compared to the relative wealth of such activity in black-raced and Latino-raced groups, the case for "race"-based reception differences seems to gain strength. Furthermore, no clear pattern emerged *within* black-raced and Latino-raced groups suggesting that socio-economic status made a difference in reception styles.

Why did black-raced and Latino-raced groups feel it necessary *or* appropriate to be animated during the screenings? Did viewers in the white-raced groups find such activity during the screenings unnecessary or inappropriate? One possible interpretation of the differences in viewing styles between white-raced and non-white-raced informants (black-raced informants, in particular) is that white-raced informants arrived at the screening already in agreement with the textual assumption that "blacks" were the event insiders, feeling somewhat distant from the text and events.

Furthermore, the events had subsided more than eight months prior to the interviews. Perhaps white-raced informants simply were not aroused by the text; maybe they *valued* its meanings differently than black-raced and Latino-raced informants. As one white-raced informant put it:

> I mean, it's [the events] just, just kind of a memory that comes up occasionally. But it's not something that I take time, because I wasn't there and it didn't personally affect me.

In contrast, Latino-raced informants who lived in the areas depicted in the text, and black-raced informants, who were depicted as event insiders, responded as if they had a stake both in the events and the KTTV text. Perhaps the zest with which these informants received the text was emblematic of their attempts to negotiate unresolved issues that were important to them. Moreover, given the nature of the assumptions embedded in the text, maybe these informants were forced to "work harder" than their white-raced counterparts to resolve these issues in a satisfying way (see Condit 1994, p. 432)....

Conclusions

When one surveys intergroup patterns in pronoun use, in attitudes toward event-related activities, in group viewing modes, and in polarization outcomes, evidence begins to mount for what I have referred to as "raced ways of seeing." Black-raced and Latino-raced study groups were quite animated during the screening of the KTTV text, while white-raced study groups watched quietly. For black-raced informants, in particular, raced subjectivity was clearly an important lens through which the events and text were viewed. The relatively low salience of raced subjectivity among Latino-raced and white-raced informants echoed the non-black-raced/black-raced divide observed in informant attitudes toward the events. That is, while white-raced and Latino-raced informants were *less* likely than their black-raced counterparts to talk about themselves in raced terms, they were *more* likely than black-raced informants to condemn the looting and fires and to support the arrests. Moreover, socio-economic status and gender seemed to have very little impact on these raced differences. There was clearly a link between racial subjectivity and how informants made sense of the events.

In many respects, the finding of attitude polarization and/or convergence (44 percent of the possible cases) is emblematic of the role that group pressures and expectations play in individual decoding behaviors. Each informant, of course, brought certain personal experiences and understandings concerning the events to his or her own screening and the discussion that followed. These experiences and understandings were in part the products of previous social interactions, previous discussions between the informant and important others. But these experiences and understandings were also the product of *intertextual* relations, informants' continuous dialogue with other texts stored in memory. The group screenings and discussions analyzed in this study represent the intersection of both sets of relations at a given point in time. To put it another way, they represent yet another cycle in the process of meaning-making for the informants, a process that is ongoing.

   This observation is important for the following reason: because "race" is not some fixed essence (Prager 1982; Omi and Winant 1986, 1994; Hall 1988, 1989), specific category attributes can be quite fluid and ambiguous from one moment to the next. And because category members often have an investment in their category membership (e.g., seeing it as integral part of identity), they must continually work to achieve and re-achieve membership status anew (Garfinkel 1967) – that is, in the eyes of important others (e.g., network members), and as measured by the texts that position them (Hall 1988, Gray 1995). In this sense, the study screenings and group discussions served as a forum for informants to "do-being Latino," "do-being black," or "do-being white" – to negotiate positions from which to make sense of the KTTV text *and* affirm their own raced subjectivities. In other words, informants activated memories of past experiences and other texts to negotiate group expectations about how Latino-raced, black-raced or white-raced subjects *should* discuss the KTTV text. Indeed, these expectations seemed to influence the subsequent performance and understandings of informants in the study.

   For Latino-raced and black-raced informants, in particular, evidence of these expectations at work can be found in several of the arguments that emerged in the group discussions – for example, that people should "stick" to their own "race" (e.g., the FAMILY group) or that "blacks" must unify before they can effectively challenge the system or move ahead (e.g., the CHURCH and KEISHA groups). These prescriptions seem to echo other texts and discourses about key values in "Latino" and "black" culture.

   For example, Marin and Marin (1991) argue that "Latino" culture tends to "emphasize the needs, objectives, and points of view of an ingroup," rather than the personal objectives, attitudes and values typically privileged in more individualistic cultures (p. 11). Among Chicanos, in particular, Blea (1988) notes that "[i]ndividualism is seen as Anglo, and profit is valued to the degree that it does not disrupt social relationships" (pp. 64–5). Most Latino-raced informants discussed the events as if they were *not* in the interest of the ingroup. "Latinos" who participated in the events, they argued, were just taking advantage of the situation. Accordingly, Latino-raced informants found relatively little to criticize in the KTTV text's depiction of the events as "undesirable."

   This was not the case for black-raced informants.

   In his ethnographic study of everyday black-raced Americans, Gwaltney (1980) identifies ethnic solidarity as a key tenet of "black" culture. "White America," he notes, loomed large in his subjects' narratives concerning the history of "black" oppression and resistance. The black-raced informants in this study discussed the events in similar terms, returning again and again to issues of "white" racism and "black" solidarity. It was as if these informants – in accord with classic discourses on black-raced consciousness (see e.g., DuBois 1965; Fanon 1967) – were expected to trace their anxieties back to contact with the "white" world. Indeed, consistent with recent texts highlighting a general "black" suspicion of official knowledge (Gabriel 1988; Turner 1993; Fiske 1994), black-raced informants (unlike their Latino-raced counterparts) seemed predisposed to questioning many of the assumptions embedded in the KTTV text, if not the text's construction itself. As Gray (1993, p. 191) put it,

Various reading strategies and practices produced by black audiences have been, indeed must be, critical, suspicious, and mindful of the dominant and dominating impulses of a racialized social and cultural order, an order that has historically stereotyped, excluded, objectified, and silenced black subjects.

Accordingly, black-raced informants received the KTTV text as a "white text" – one that might provide snippets of useful information, but that ought not be taken at face value.

White-raced informants were much more at ease with the KTTV text, despite their familiarity with and enactment of discourses of media deconstruction. Three of the white-raced groups contained one or more Asian-raced members who agreed with white-raced members that the system was more or less fair, that the events were an undesirable, counterproductive breach of order. Accordingly, these groups sat quietly during the screening of the KTTV text, opting not to talk back to the screen. Furthermore, "race" – with a few exceptions – was not a salient topic in these group discussions. Informants in these groups were generally hesitant to talk about the events in raced terms, despite their frequent references to "blacks" and "African-Americans." Perhaps membership in the dominant "major race" (Hacker 1992) presented white-raced informants with the expectation and luxury to talk about themselves as "Americans" first – *not* as raced subjects (Waters 1990; Feagin and Vera 1995).

In short, while this study's exploration of group discussion and polarization effects treats "race" as a social construct whose reproduction is dependent upon an endless succession of micro-level interactions, the study also acknowledges that raced meanings are reified and reinforced at the macro-level of economics and politics (see Omi and Winant 1986, 1994). In other words, structures situate groups *vis-à-vis* one another in social space, while individuals continually decode the meanings of their unique situations in accordance with normative understandings and expectations (Fine and Kleinman 1983). Over time, this process leads to a patterning of individual–group relationships, thereby establishing an important micro–macro link....

Nonetheless, the relationship at any given moment between raced identification and decoding – what I have termed "raced ways of seeing" – is always a probabilistic one, never a deterministic one (see Fiske 1987). For race-as-representation, as an *immediate* social force, is always experienced by actors through the conduit of concrete situations. In this case study, at least, raced ways of seeing appeared to be a critical factor in informants' decoding of the KTTV text. Moreover, as informants negotiated these ways of seeing, as they replayed intertextual memories and engaged themselves in discussion with network members, they also affirmed (directly or by default) their own raced subjectivities.

References

Blea, Irene I. 1988, *Toward a Chicano Social Science*, New York: Praeger.
Condit, Celeste Michelle 1994, "The Rhetorical Limits of Polysemy," in H. Newcomb (ed.), *Television: The Critical View*, New York: Oxford University Press.
Cramer, M. Richard and Howard Schuman 1975, "We and They: Pronouns as Measures of Political Identification and Estrangement," *Social Science Research* 4, 231–240.

DuBois, William E. B. 1965, *The Souls of Black Folks*, in *Three Negro Classics*, New York: Avon.

Fanon, Frantz 1967, *Black Skin, White Masks*, New York: Grove Press.

Feagin, Joe R. and Hernan Vera 1995, *White Racism*, New York: Routledge.

Fine, Gary Alan and Sherryl Kleinman 1983, "Network and Meaning: An Interactionist Approach to Structure," *Symbolic Interaction* 6: 1, 97–110.

Fiske, John 1987a, *Television Culture*, London: Routledge.

—— 1987b, "British Cultural Studies," in R. Allen (ed.), *Channels of Discourse: Television and Contemporary Criticism*, Chapel Hill NC: University of North Carolina Press.

—— 1989a, *Understanding Popular Culture*, Boston: Unwin Hyman.

—— 1989b, Moments of Television: Neither the Text Nor the Audience in E. Seiter, H. Borchers, G. Kreutzner and E. Warth (eds.), *Remote Control: Television, Audiences, and Cultural Power*, London: Routledge.

—— 1994a, "Ethnosemiotics: Some Personal and Theoretical Reflection," in H. Newcomb (ed.), *Television: The Critical View*, New York: Oxford University Press.

—— 1994b, *Media Matters: Everyday Culture and Political Change*, Minneapolis: University of Minnesota Press.

Gabriel, Teshome H. 1988, "Thoughts on Nomadic Aesthetics and the Black Independent Cinema: Traces of a Journey," in *Blackframes: Critical Perspectives on Black Independent Cinema*, Cambridge MA: The MIT Press.

—— 1993, "Ruin and The Other: Towards a Language Of Memory," in H. Naficy and T. Gabriel (eds.), *Otherness and Media: The Ethnography of the Imagined and the Imaged*, New York: Harwood Academic Publishers.

Garfinkel, Harold 1967, *Studies in Ethnomethodology*, Cambridge: Polity Press.

Gray, Herman 1993, "The Endless Slide of Difference: Critical Television Studies, Television and the Question of Race," *Critical Studies in Mass Communication* 10, 190–7.

—— 1995, *Watching Race: Television and the Struggle for "Blackness,"* Minneapolis: University of Minnesota Press.

Gurin, Patricia, Arthur H. Miller and Gerald Gurin 1980, "Stratum Identification and Consciousness," *Social Psychological Quarterly* 43: 1, 30–47.

Gwaltney, John Langston 1980, *Drylongso. A Self-Portrait of Black America*, New York: Random House.

Hacker, Andrew 1992, *Two Nations: Black and White, Separate, Hostile, and Unequal*, New York: Ballantine Books.

Hall, Stuart 1988, "New Ethnicities," in K. Mercer (ed.), *Black Film, British Cinema*, London: Institute of Contemporary Arts.

—— 1989, "Cultural Identity and Cinematic Representation," *Framework* 36, 68–81.

Lindlof, Thomas R. 1988, "Media Audiences as Interpretive Communities," *Communication Yearbook* 11, 81–107.

Marin, Gerardo and Barbara VanOss Marin 1991, *Research with Hispanic Populations*, Newbury Park: Sage.

Morley, David. 1980, *The 'Nationwide' Audience*, London: BFI.

—— 1992, *Television, Audiences and Cultural Studies*, London: Routledge.

Omi, Michael and Howard Winant 1986, *Racial Formation in the United States From the 1960s to the 1980s*, New York: Routledge and Kegan Paul.

—— 1993, "The Los Angeles 'Race Riot' and Contemporary U.S. Politics," in R. Gooding-Williams (ed.), *Reading Rodney King, Reading Urban Uprising*, New York: Routledge.

—— 1994, *Racial Formation in the United States From the 1960s to the 1990s*, New York: Routledge.

Prager, Jeffrey 1982, "American Racial Ideology as Collective Representation," *Ethnic and Racial Studies* 5, 99–119.

Press, Andrea 1990, "The Active Viewer and the Problem of Interpretation: Reconciling Traditional and Critical Research," *Communication Yearbook* 15, 91–106.

—— 1991, *Women Watching Television: Gender, Class, and Generation in the American Television Experience*, Philadelphia: University of Pennsylvania Press.

Turner, Patricia A. 1993, *I Heard It Through the Grapevine: Rumor in African-American Culture*, Berkeley: University of California Press.

Waters, Mary C. 1990, *Ethnic Options: Choosing Identities in America*, Berkeley: University of California Press.

Editor's Notes on Further Reading

Hunt on Race and the Media

Combining recent scholarship on two of the most influential institutions in contemporary American society, race and media, Darnell Hunt asks how different audiences respond to a news broadcast about an episode of racially-identified civil unrest. The larger study uses focus groups along with textual analysis to explore the assumptions implicit in television news, to compare the ways cliques of Latino-raced, black-raced, and white-raced young people interpret the news, and to improve understanding of the ways media audiences both resist and accept media messages.

"Raced ways of seeing" in the media or in response to the media are also investigated in Jacobs' study excerpted this volume; see also Darnell Hunt, *O.J. Simpson Facts and Fictions: News Rituals in the Construction of Reality* (Cambridge and New York: Cambridge University Press, 1999); Hunt, "(Re)affirming Race: 'Reality,' Negotiation, and the 'Trial of the Century'," *The Sociological Quarterly* 38 (1997): 399–422; S. Craig Watkins, *Representing: Hip Hop Culture and the Production of Black Cinema* (Chicago and London: University of Chicago Press, 1998); Herman Gray, *Watching Race: Television and the Struggle for "Blackness"* (Minneapolis and London: University of Minnesota Press, 1995); Robert Gooding-Williams, ed., *Reading Rodney King, Reading Urban Uprising* (New York: Routledge, 1993); Amy Binder, "Constructing Racial Rhetoric: Media Depictions of Harm in Heavy Metal and Rap Music," *American Sociological Review* 58 (1993): 753–67, and JoEllen Shively, "Cowboys and Indians: Perceptions of Western Films Among American Indians and Anglos," *American Sociological Review* 57 (1992): 725–34.

On race and culture more generally, see for instance Jeffrey Prager, "American Racial Ideology as Collective Representation," *Ethnic and Racial Studies* 5 (1982): 99–119; Michèle Lamont, ed., *The Cultural Territories of Race: Black and White Boundaries* (Chicago: University of Chicago Press and New York: Russell Sage Foundation, 1999); Michèle Lamont, "Colliding Moralities Between Black and White Workers," pp. 265–85 in Elizabeth Long, ed., *From Sociology to Cultural Studies: New Perspectives* (Malden, MA: Blackwell, 1997); and Michael Omi and Howard Winant, *Racial Formation in the United States From the 1960s to the 1990s* (New York: Routledge, 1994).

In contrast to Horkheimer and Adorno (excerpted this volume) and others who emphasize the power of the media over audiences, research like Hunt's investigates the complicated and sometimes critical ways in which audiences negotiate meaning in the mass media. For more on media audiences see, for instance, Ron Lembo, *Thinking Through Television* (Cambridge and New York: Cambridge University Press, 2000); Jon Cruz and Justin Lewis, eds., *Viewing, Reading, Listening: Audiences and Cultural Reception* (Boulder, CO: Westview Press, 1994); David Morley, *Televison, Audiences, and Cultural Studies* (London and New York: Routledge, 1992); Karl Erik Rosengren, ed., Special Issue on Audience Research, *Poetics* 21 (4) August 1992; Andrea Press, *Women Watching Television: Gender, Class, and Generation in the American Television Experience* (Philadelphia: University of Pennsylvania Press, 1991); Ronald Lembo and Kenneth Tucker, Jr., "Culture, Television, and Opposition: Rethinking Cultural Studies," *Critical Studies in Mass Communication* 7 (1990): 97–116; Tamar Liebes and Elihu Katz, *The Export of Meaning: Cross-Cultural Readings of Dallas* (New York: Oxford University Press, 1990); Ann Swidler, Melissa Rapp, and Yasemin Soysal, "Format and Formula in Prime-Time TV," pp. 324–37 in Sandra Ball-Rokeach and Muriel Cantor, eds., *Media, Audience, and Social Structure* (Beverly Hills: Sage, 1986); Todd Gitlin, *The Whole World is Watching* (Berkeley: University of California Press, 1980), and Gitlin, "Media Sociology: The Dominant Paradigm," *Theory and Society* 6 (1978): 205–54. See also the discussion of reception in Ronald Jacobs, "Producing the News, Producing the Crisis: Narrativity, Television, and News Work," *Media, Culture and Society* 18 (1996): 373–97.

For another example of the use of focus group methodology to investigate interpretations of news see William Gamson, *Talking Politics* (Cambridge and New York: Cambridge University Press, 1992); for an experimental study of the agenda-setting effects of television news see in Shanto Iyengar and Donald Kinder, *News that Matters* (Chicago: University of Chicago Press, 1987).

More generally see Pierre Bourdieu, *On Television*, trans. Priscilla Parkhurst Ferguson (New York: The New Press, 1996); Muriel Cantor and Joel Cantor, *Prime Time Television: Content and Control*, 2nd edn. (Newbury Park: Sage: 1992); and Todd Gitlin, *Inside Prime Time* (New York: Pantheon, 1983).

Important in the rich synthesis of theoretical traditions influencing Hunt's work is a line of reflection about domination and resistance drawing on Gramsci and Raymond Williams (see excerpt this volume) and flourishing in the work of the Birmingham School and later cultural studies; some introduction to this work can be found in Stuart Hall "Culture, the Media and the 'Ideological Effect,'" pp. 315–48 in James Curran, Michael Gurevitch, and Janet Woollacott, eds., *Mass Communication and Society* (Beverly Hills and London: Sage, 1977), and Stuart Hall, "Encoding/decoding," pp. 128–38 in Centre for Contemporary Cultural Studies, *Culture, Media, Language* (London: Hutchinson, 1980); for later reflections see Long, ed., *From Sociology to Cultural Studies*.

13 "Close to Home": The Work of Avoiding Politics

Nina Eliasoph

> If it's not something that [pause] effects [pause] my [pause] family. I don't see [pause] me [pause] doing it. [Speeds up] And-I-mean-of-course-nuclear-war-*could*-affect-my [chuckles] family. But I still don't – if it's not local, I mean, I'm more – maybe it's small-minded.
>
> *(Sherry, a schools volunteer, in an interview)*

Was she really as small-minded as she claimed to be? "I care about issues that are close to home," "I care if it affects me personally," "I care if it's for my children": these are the familiar phrases that many Americans use to explain political involvement and apathy. Journalists, activists, and theorists often take these phrases at face value; politicians base social policies on them, trying to play to voters whom they imagine to be self-interested and short-sighted, cutting funds for projects that do not seem "close to home." The phrases are usually interpreted as transparently obvious indications of citizens' self-interest and lack of broad political concern – their "small-mindedness." But these insistant, extravagant expressions of self-interest do not simply indicate clear, straightforward self-interest or parochial thinking. The phrases work hard. Activists, intellectuals, and other concerned citizens often assume that someone like Sherry just doesn't care or is self-interested or ignorant; we try to draw people like her into political participation by impressing upon them that they should care (perhaps by telling them how nuclear war might affect their kids), or telling them not to be so self-interested.

This article shows just how hard someone such as Sherry has to work to avoid expressing political concern. Penetrating this pervasive *culture of political avoidance* requires a new way of understanding this thing that sounds like apathy and self-interest....

It took what I will call "cultural work" for volunteers to transmute feelings of powerlessness into expressions of self-interest. Coming from a range of perspectives, many theorists of public life argue that structural powerlessness, inner feelings, and cultural expressions cannot be distilled out of each other; each layer of experience depends on the others – and the public sphere is vital precisely because these levels of experience never match up perfectly. This article spotlights three moments in the *intellectual, emotional*, and *interactional* process of everyday political meaning-making: citizens' 1. implicit knowledge about their own *structural power*, 2. implicit agreement about what kinds of *feelings* citizens should have, and 3. implicit agreement about what the *very act of speaking about politics* in public means....

The illustrations I use to make this article's theoretical point come from a study that examined how political disengagement was socially produced in interaction, and was not just a by-product of "inner" beliefs or "outer" structural conditions. I spent over two years from 1989 to 1991 as a participant-observer in a range of groups in U.S. civil society: two recreational groups, both at a country-western dance club and fraternal organization; and a network of volunteer groups, including, with most intensive scrutiny, an anti-drugs group and a PTA-style organization; and two activist groups – an anti-toxics group and a disarmament group. I picked these groups because advocates of democracy have long looked to groups that work on small, local issues as potential schools for wider political concern; I wanted to know what happened within these groups that evoked, or curtailed, public concern for the greater good. Of course, I did not expect these groups to devote much time to publicly-minded political discussion (which I define not as a topic but as a style of talking that implies connection to the wider world), but I was interested in whether and how political conversation ever happened, and whether groups seemed actively to avoid political conversation.

In all the groups, I did whatever other regular group members did: go to meetings, hearings, demonstrations, raffles, track meets, fairs, parades, fashion shows, rodeos, theme parks, and parties. I listened to participants' interactions with each other in a wide range of contexts, and to their interactions with the institutions that surrounded their groups – social service agencies that worked with the volunteers, government agencies that dealt with activists, country-western commercial culture that surrounded recreation group members. I was also a participant-observer among local reporters, and I analyzed news stories. The larger study shows how citizens made fine, relentless distinctions between what was sayable in one context and another: citizens sounded more public-minded in casual or intimate contexts than in public contexts; the wider the audience, the narrower were the ideas citizens could express. This article focusses mainly on interviews, but without the understanding that came from fieldwork, the interviews would not have made sense. I heard the "close to home" refrain over and over from volunteers, until I could predict responses to my interview questions: in other words, until the "category was saturated," to use a standard criterion for feeling satisfied, as an observer, that one has indeed found a pattern.

Power, Emotions, and Talk in the Production of Limited Horizons

Clue #1: Intuiting powerlessness: "What am I gonna do – bomb the place?"

The most obvious clue to interpreting these expressions of self-interest is the unmistakable connection between participants' expressions of self-interest and their seemingly realistic assessment of their own power. In the anti-drugs group interview, Pete described the relation between the "problems of the world" and self-interest:

> I know there are things out there that affect me, you know, they, uh, bother me, but I guess I – my first priority is my home and my immediate surroundings and I'm not anxious to go out and solve the problems of the world. I guess it's just my personality, I guess. I knew someone in college who just could not . . . who saw all these problems and took them on as "personal," as her personal responsibility to solve all these things [he describes her briefly, saying it made her miserable to be so overwhelmed]. Of course, everyone would love to, if they had the power themselves, to stop war or end drug abuse or whatever, they'd do it, but obviously there's a *feeling of impotence* [my emphasis] when you're dealing with issues like that. Boils down to just, "find the opportunity in your life to try to make a difference, even if it's a small one."

A moment later in the conversation, he refers to this statement, summarizing it this way: "That gets back to – if I'm gonna actually expend energy to alter my lifestyle to affect one of these things, I'm probably gonna expend it where it's closer to home." The way he himself summarized the long, earlier statement shows his method for actively, imperceptibly translating "a feeling of impotence" into a feeling of empowerment on small issues "close to home." This was to rename that feeling of impotence as a lack of concern. "Close to home" and "for my children" was a package for a cluster of ideas about caring, power, and truth. Animals, like the whales stuck in Alaska, drugs and schools were "close to home." Nuclear war, the local nuclear battleship station, the local protest against U.S. policy in Central America, the local proposed toxic incinerator, and the local oil and chemical spills and explosions were not.

Members of the high school parent group used the same vocabulary, gracefully transmogrifying a feeling of impotence into a feeling of empowerment on issues labelled "close to home," and "in my interest," and "for the children." In the group interview, Danielle said, "really, I'm involved because my kids are here." Elaine said it next:

> All my efforts are geared – I will get involved in anything that involves kids. . . . So I'll join committees like the Just Say No committee in Amargo, that you know, for sure, is the issue of drugs, but, you know, my view, really is it's an issue about kids.

Whenever I mentioned that all the groups I studied said they were involved "for the children," volunteers would reconsider the phrase for just a moment, say that indeed anything could be considered to be "close to home" and "for the children," and then, just moments later, all would revert to the "close to home," "for the children" discourse. This vocabulary of self-interest was so automatic, volunteers could not extricate themselves from it even when they rationally knew that it did not adequately describe their motives.

This gerrymandered engagement might seem easy to explain. In appearing rationally self-interested, volunteers might appear to confirm the idea that people are "rational actors," that is, people who will bestir themselves to community action only when they think that time invested will be worth the personal payoff, and only when they cannot easily hitch a "free ride" to that personal payoff on other people's backs.

But if volunteers were rationally calculating where to invest scarce energy, it was a peculiar kind of calculation: as will become more apparent below, the *goal* was to *feel* empowered; they had to forget that there were wide arenas in which they did feel powerless. If the work they did to divvy up the world into "close to home/do-able" and "not close to home/not do-able" had been conscious, it would not have had the desired effect, of allowing them to feel hopeful, powerful, and free. This is an unusual kind of calculation that works only when actors can forget they did the calculation. Instead of calculating individually, volunteers relied on a culturally standard, automatic second nature that taught them how to translate feelings of impotence into feelings of efficacy. . . .

A second explanation of volunteers' speech would shift volunteers' sense of power and powerlessness onto the level of culture instead of the level of individual conscious calculation, by saying that after years of political domination, volunteers may have created a culture of silence, too hopeless even to voice feelings of outrage, too powerless even to formulate their own interests even to themselves. . . .

The idea of hegemony rightly treats people as members of cultures, who are doing their best to make sense of discouraging circumstances, even if it means turning their backs on politics. It treats political experience as a convoluted, uncalculating, historically specific, inherently cultural, and interactive response to power and powerlessness.

But we can refine the concept of hegemony, here, by asking: how do citizens actively explain their powerlessness? Volunteers' self-interest talk did indeed respond to powerlessness, but calling it simply "a response to powerlessness" is not enough. If there is no exit from the political world, then political silence must be as active and as colorful as a bright summer shadow. Developing a sense of togetherness happened in reference to a sense of powerlessness, but was not just a reaction to it; cultural work acknowledges powerlessness but does not stop there. If the ways of avoiding political engagement are potentially infinite, then why did packaging gloomy feelings inside of professions of "self-interest" feel better to volunteers? Thus, the next clue asks how *this* language in particular made the world seem to make sense, by cheering volunteers up, making a certain emotional tone possible in volunteer groups.

Clue #2: "You can have more of an impact uh . . . at least you feel like you can": Feeling rules in public spaces

Volunteers *wanted* to believe that all people are aware of their own desires, are self-interested, and invest their energies wisely. Volunteers themselves strenuously tried to confirm this rational model of humanity, even if it meant making extraordinary claims about human nature:

Carolyn: I don't think anyone does anything that is not going to benefit them in some form or another, or there'd be no point. . . .

Pete: Whether we admit it or not . . . someone like Gandhi, you know, he may be the pinnacle of altruism, but he was doin his stuff for his own people. [Murmurs of agreement. . . .]

Lisa: And he felt good about what he did [implying that "feeling good" is a self-interested benefit].

This language helped the volunteers to convince themselves of something that they earnestly wanted to believe. When I asked the forced-choice survey question, "How much of the time do you think you can trust the government in Washington to do what is right?" one typical volunteer said,

Most of the time. Well, at least I'd like to *think* it's most of the time. Of course, I'm not so sure it really is. But I hope it *is*. So, I'd say "most of the time." Yes, put "most of the time."

Notice – neither yes nor no nor undecided was the most "real" belief here. The belief *included* an effort at convincing herself. In the interview with Carolyn and her eighteen year old son, the son made less of an effort. Each time he said that people do not get involved because they don't think it will have an effect, his mother gently corrected him, saying that people just did not have enough time. Similarly, typical volunteers responded to the question, "Can a person like you make a difference?" by saying "Yes," with an "at least I hope so" tagged on. . . .

When a volunteer expressed a criticism of the election process on one election day, she sounded extremely apologetic about it. She did not express her worries in the meeting, but whispered them before the meeting, while standing outside with the banquet-sized coffeemaker, waiting for the janitor to unlock the door to the meeting room. During the meeting, a fellow volunteer kept whispering to her, saying, "Don't worry, I'm sure you'll get over it," and asking, "Don't you feel better now?" The problem had to be treated as if it were just "her mood," not a problem with the political system. Volunteers did not want to be too critical, too "cynical"; if the government and corporations suggested that citizens could get involved in solving the drug problem, then volunteers were willing to cooperate, even though drug abuse *could* have been considered a harder issue to solve than some environmental problems. But the volunteers meant only the consensual and non-structural aspects of drug abuse, home, children, and families. They did not want to be discouraged by problems that seemed out of their control, and the vocabulary of "close to home" helped them feel in control of "home." . . .

Being a volunteer meant not only convincing oneself that good citizenship was possible, but convincing other people as well, and creating public contexts in which regular people could get together to work on community projects. It meant convincing people that good citizenship is possible today, right now, in the society as it is, not in some dreamworld. Rather than try to change the institutions that kept them feeling powerless (because that could require too much depressing discussion), volunteers tried to change their feelings. Good citizenship was primarily a matter of *feeling good* about the community and nation, and showing one's neighbors that people care and can be effective; cultivating the feeling of "having an impact" was, in an important way, *the same* for them as "hav(ing) . . . an an impact." As a refrain went, "if everyone cared . . ." Working on feelings was, itself, the goal . . .

There are varied cultural rules for this cultivation and expression of feeling. For the unempowered volunteer trying to feel confident that democracy is working according to its promise – as in Arlie Hochschild's examples of an unhappy bride trying to feel joy, a happy funeral attendee trying to suppress his glee, and a blasé star halfback trying to "psych himself up at a game" – there is "emotion work," that bridges the

> discrepancy, between what ones does feel and what one wants to feel (which is, in turn, affected by what one thinks one ought to feel in such a situation). In response, the individual may try to eliminate the pinch by working on feeling.[1]

Different groups required different emotion work, different relations *to* feelings of powerlessness, different relations to inconsistency, doubt, ambivalence, rough edges in general. And the different groups' demands for emotion work were context-specific. Volunteers required cheer in some situations, and could express doubts in others. The effort at being smoothly upbeat differed from one group to the next, and one context to the next.

The concept of emotion rules throws light on how hard volunteers worked to muster unequivocally upbeat feelings in group contexts. But a question remains: why did volunteers assume that the way to be upbeat was to avoid making the connection between the local and the global, instead of talking about their worries more openly, or complaining or venting outrage? After all, the volunteers were not peasants who could starve if they offended their lords, or victims of direct censorship who had to hide their criticism of the government; they believed that they *were* free to speak their minds. So why did they assume that appearing unequivocal and happy was so urgent? Exposing the rough edges of one's thoughts has often been considered the essence of democratic citizenship; George Herbert Mead, for example, would have said that good, active citizenship is *supposed* to be confusing, that thought itself is argument – that in the public realm, consistency is death.[2] The question is how willing people are to exhibit the rough edges, doubts, and challenges in public. If the need to appear unequivocally upbeat is not just a fact of human nature, and no direct censorship prevented volunteers from voicing doubts, then how did they come to assume that the way to gain a sense of control was to avoid talk, avoid debate, when other groups gained a sense of mastery by talking? What was it about political talk itself that they feared?

Clue #3: "That's rhetoric": The value of talk itself

> Clara (a schools volunteer): [A social problem is close to home] if it affects you personally and your family... You can hold your opinions about what a country can do, or can't do, about a situation, but *that's rhetoric*... I don't really think a person can really make a difference unless they have the *power at hand*.

Volunteers assumed that talking politics would not accomplish anything positive, it would only scare members away and undermine hope. The easy-seeming explanation of "self-interest" made apathy about un-doable problems seem self-evident, not in need of explanation or discussion. The explanation did not just *appeal* to the American tradition of individualism. It *embodied* individualism, as a practice and not just a set of beliefs, by allowing volunteers to assume that their goals were not a product of interaction and could not benefit from group discussion. Everyone was assumed always already to have personal opinions, before discussion or interaction. According to this folk theory of language, if all people are is naturally out for themselves, citizens don't need to talk (they just need to act on their beliefs or interests), and democracy is working just fine.

Volunteers assumed that citizens' talk itself would change neither individuals' opinions nor the political world. With different assumptions about how and where talk matters could come different emotion rules. For example, Patricia Waseliewski[3] shows that a pivotal moment in the life of a feminist group is when women learn to value anger, to talk about the causes of their anger, thus allowing righteous, collective anger to become a lever for critical grassroots action instead of a shameful, private sentiment. Given volunteers' low valuation of talk itself, the best way to maintain faith and hope was to avoid expressing discouraging, critical, "cynical" thoughts and feelings in public.

Thus, in Parent League meetings, volunteers actively avoided talking about the race problems in the high school, the lack of funds for library books, heating, music, and theater supplies, and other potentially troubling topics that newcomers tried to raise. On the one hand, volunteers wanted to encourage these potential new members, but, on the other hand, they did not want to risk the sense of discouragement that wide-ranging discussion could bring. For example, the local NAACP representative came to one meeting of the Parent League to tell the group that a teacher had made racist jokes and that skinheads were recruiting on the schoolgrounds at lunchtime. He suggested getting more parents involved in the Parent League, so they could discuss these problems publicly. The parent volunteers (who were not, incidentally, all white, but who did share the distinctive "volunteer culture" I am describing in this article) barely responded, except to say that the NAACP representative should not underestimate them, because they "made efficient use of small numbers" of people, and they cited a very successful fundraiser the group held. When teachers came to meetings trying to drum up discussion about funding for theater lights, or about limiting senior year expenses for activities like the prom and the class picnic (that all together added up to over a thousand dollars), volunteers, who were usually extremely well-organized in their meetings, would wander in and out, play with their pens, and fall unusually silent. In an anti-drugs group meeting, Julie (a former anti-nuclear activist – her confrontation with feelings of power-lessness was not the only thing that made her unusual – she also sometimes tried to push volunteers to be a little more debate oriented than they were) asked what she could say when people argued against the group's plans; there was total silence following her question, until Julie brought up a logistical question. The consensus was that talking was not the point. Members had not explicitly decided not to talk; it was just part of their practical cultural work in the group context.

The ability to express broad political engagement systematically changed from one context to the next. Behind the scenes, but not in meetings, Danielle could say that it was really a disgrace that a country as rich as ours had homeless people; she said that the school should not make parents pay for kids to play in the school's swing band, and that Republican-sponsored cutbacks had harmed the school, and more. But she never spoke like this in the group context. Behind the scenes, she spoke enthusiastically about her work with the school district to plan ecologically-sound landscaping for a new school, but when she got to the meeting of the parents group, the other parents translated her excitement about the general principle of ecological groundskeeping into "preventing hayfever in local kids." Behind the scenes, another volunteer was a very involved union activist, talked about connections between corporate flight and government policies, and had supported Jesse Jackson for president in an earlier election. But in meetings, he was very quiet and when he did speak, he sounded just like the others. Behind the scenes, Cora, the volunteer who confessed her feelings of cynicism while standing outside waiting for the janitor, offered quite a wide-ranging criticism and self-criticism session before entering the meeting: she said there were too many paid political consultants, too few informed voters, too many non-voters; and to give added bite to her point about her cynicism, she exclaimed with chagrin that, for the first time, she had voted for the Democrat, *only* because he had done her a favor. . . .

Volunteers welcomed public-spirited talk, in its place; free-ranging talk was just out of place in everyday meetings and other public settings. Thus, after each group interview I conducted with volunteers, participants thanked me, saying they had never had the opportunity to talk about these things together, as a group, before. . . .

The point is that there was a *culture of political avoidance*, a common-sense understanding of what the act of talking politics itself means, not just that volunteers obeyed some natural urge to avoid disagreement.

With their taken-for-granted assessment of talk, volunteers did not simply think that talking about an undo-able social problem was a waste of time, either. It was immoral, because it could undermine their bouyant sense of the rightness of the world, by excluding "regular" people who are not always eloquent, do not have equal amounts of cultural capital, as Pierre Bourdieu[4] would put it, and are not always eager to talk politics. As one Parent League member put it, "The way to get a volunteer is to ask, 'Who has a drill bit and can drill eight holes in this board next Saturday?' Someone will come who maybe never volunteered before, and then maybe they'll come again." *Beliefs about talk itself were key here* in setting the emotional tone, and in setting the boundaries of the "do-able" – beliefs about who talks, about what talk accomplishes, about where talk belongs, about when talk is "just rhetoric," or dangerous, or depressing, and beliefs about how regular people talk. The intellectual, emotional, and interactional dimensions of cultural work are inseparable. . . .

[L]inguistic anthropologists investigate the idea that cultural assumptions about talk itself embody implicit understandings of power, politics, and selfhood. But they usually treat these talk-cultures as customary, traditional, time-honored, habitual responses to particular local histories in longstanding communities. How do citizens establish cultures of talk in a multicultural, transient, potentially global polity, in which citizens often do not even think that they know what is going on, who is in charge, how to act in a diverse setting, where the power is, or what kind of power it is? In an area like the one described here, we can more clearly hear how different groups can variously interpret, reproduce, and challenge, the "same" institutional, political field, thus more clearly specifying the work of political culture itself.

And so, we are back to the question of power, that started this round robin of explanations: part of why volunteers assumed they were powerless was that they assumed that citizens' talk was "just rhetoric," not a source of power. With a new reckoning of the value of talk itself would have come a new source of power. . . .

Conclusion: Power, Emotions and Politeness in an Imperfect World

Taking volunteers' professions of "small-mindedness" at face value would be a mistake. Expressions of political disconnection worked hard; people exerted themselves to keep the wider world at bay. Treating these expressions of apathy – and treating beliefs in general – this way helps specify just what it is *about* beliefs that makes them matter for public life. All along the way, I have entertained possible alternate interpretations of volunteers' use of the "close to home" language: interpretations that highlight power (that they were rational actors; or that a cross-contextual hegemonic process prevented volunteers from noticing problems); emotions or other inner psychic processes (that volunteers were avoiding cognitive dissonance or numbing their feelings); and culturally patterned interactional styles (that volunteers feared voicing anxiety, ambivalence, getting angry, or asking questions in public because of their low valuation of public talk itself). These "structural," "psychological," and "cultural" levels of analysis do not correspond to their separate objects of study ("the structure," "the individual," and "the cultural institutions") but rather, are mutually implicated and inextricable. All of these explanations call forth something that the others offer; each fills in what others leave uncharted, each layer is contingent on the others.

Understanding the tortured, twisted use of "close to home" helps show how these explanations are connected; the interconnections could help us interpret other public languages, as well. What if the things we call "beliefs" are always so equivocal? Then hope and hopelessness, apathy and engagement would not seem so far apart; they would always be intertwined, actively making sense of a world that doesn't.

By showing how hard this apparent apathy is to produce, the concept of cultural work reveals the kernel of political hope embedded in volunteers' strenuous expressions of self-interest and political disengagement. At the same time that it leaves more room for hope than other approaches, the idea of cultural work seriously acknowledges people's sense of political powerlessness. While politicians all over the globe extol the virtues of voluntary associations like the ones portrayed here – treating them as a panacea for all social ills, from lack of trust, to crime, to poverty, to economic inefficiency – this article shows how hidden obstructions to citizens' communication can fuel this prevalent language of political disconnection.

In an imperfect world, each of the groups described here responded dexterously and creatively to powerlessness; each groups' response lacked different aspects of the democratic ideal. *But all retained some aspect of it.* I can put this even more strongly: the effort at retaining some aspect of it *included* an implicit recognition of its failings. The effort at retaining a faith that the world makes sense, is just and democratic, included acknowledgement of the ways in which the world does not make sense, is not just, not democratic.

The people portrayed here worked hard to appear politically disconnected and self-interested. They did not want to be apathetic and self-interested, but feared that expressing self-interest was the only way to retain faith in the possibility of democracy. Cynics', activists', and volunteers' cultural work opened up different kinds of spaces for publicly-minded political engagement. The point is to draw these openings out; that is what theorists, politicians, journalists, and activists should be doing, instead of just glumly taking citizens' expressions of apathy at their word.

Notes

1   Arlie Hochschild, "Emotion work, feeling rules, and social structure," *American Journal of Sociology* 85/3 (1979): 551–75. Harry Frankfurt makes a similar point, when he says

that the essence of human desire is that it is not just raw appetite, but culturally, morally determined "desires about desires" [as Albert Hirschman summarizes in *Shifting Involvements: Private Interest and Public Action* (Princeton: Princeton University Press, 1982)]. See also Amartya Sen's "Rational fools: A critique of the behavioural foundations of economic theory" in Jane Mansbridge, editor, *Beyond Self-Interest* (Chicago: University of Chicago Press, 1990), 25–43, 39.

2   George Herbert Mead, *Mind, Self and Society* (Chicago: University of Chicago, 1964); see also John Dewey, *The Public and its Problems* (Denver: Allan Swallow, 1927). Michael Billing calls this "the spirit of contradiction," in *Arguing and Thinking: A Rhetorical Approach to Social Psychology* (Cambridge: Cambridge University Press, 1987).

3   Patricia Wasielewski, "Emotion as a resource" (paper given at American Sociological Association meetings, San Francisco, 1989).

4   Pierre Bourdieu, *Distinction: A Social Critique of the Judgement of Taste*, translated by Richard Nice (Cambridge, Mass.: Harvard University Press, 1984).

Editor's Notes on Further Reading

Eliasoph on Political Avoidance

Many students of political culture and participatory democracy puzzle about the conditions encouraging involvement or apathy, and about explanations for declining political participation. Nina Eliasoph argues that disengagement is actively produced: the appearance of apathy is culturally patterned by norms of what counts as proper feeling and norms about what talking should do. Her extended study, in *Avoiding Politics: How Americans Produce Apathy in Everyday Life* (Cambridge and New York: Cambridge University Press, 1998) compares different ways of talking in the different contexts of volunteer, activist, and recreational groups, providing a deeply grounded sense of both the ideals and the realities of the contemporary public sphere. See also her "Making a Fragile Public: a Talkcentered Study of Citizenship and Power," *Sociological Theory* 14 (1996): 262–89 on the power of creating legitimate interactional styles.

This work builds on a thriving tradition of theory and qualitative investigation into the possibilities and realities of public participation, extending from Tocqueville to Habermas and beyond. Some related studies of cultures of collective action include those of Lichterman, excerpted this volume; Penny Edgell Becker, *Congregations in Conflict: Cultural Models of Local Religious Life* (Cambridge and New York: Cambridge University Press, 1999); Mary Patillo-McCoy, "Church Culture as a Strategy of Action in the Black Community," *American Sociological Review* 63 (1998): 767–84; Steven Hart, *What Does the Lord Require?* (New York: Oxford University Press, 1992); William Gamson, *Talking Politics* (Cambridge and New York: Cambridge University Press, 1992); Rick Fantasia, *Cultures of Solidarity: Consciousness, Action, and Contemporary American Workers* (Berkeley and Los Angeles: University of California Press, 1988); and Robert Bellah, Richard Madsen, William Sullivan, Ann Swidler, and Steven Tipton, *Habits of the Heart* (Berkeley and Los Angeles: University of California Press, 1985). For more on volunteering in American culture see Robert Wuthnow, *Acts of Compassion* (Princeton: Princeton University Press, 1991) and Ann Swidler, "Inequality and American Culture: The Persistence of Voluntarism," pp. 294–314 in Gary Marks and Larry Diamond, eds., *Reexamining Democracy: Essays in Honor of Seymour Martin Lipset* (Newbury Park, CA: Sage, 1992).

Methodologically, Eliasoph demonstrates the importance for cultural sociology of ethnographic research in natural settings (cf. Geertz excerpt, this volume). She argues that surveys cannot generate valid information about aspects of culture which are a matter of interactional context, and since participatory democracy is intrinsically tied to interactional context, studies of political culture are particularly susceptible to validity questions if not conducted in natural settings. See also Nina Eliasoph, "Political Culture and the Presentation of a Political Self: A Study of the Public Sphere in the Spirit of Erving Goffman," *Theory and Society* 19 (1990): 465–94; Pierre Bourdieu, "Public Opinion Does Not Exist," in Armand Mattelart and Seth Siegelaub, eds., *Communication and Class Struggle*, vol. 1 (NY: International General, 1979); and Pierre Bourdieu, "Opinion Polls: A 'Science' Without a Scientist," pp. 168–74 in *In Other Words: Essays Toward a Reflexive Sociology*, trans. Matthew Adamson (Stanford: Stanford University Press, 1990). The work also models the "extended case method," linking micro- and macro-sociological analysis; see Michael Burawoy, "The Extended Case Method," *Sociological Theory* 16 (1998): 4–33, and Nina Eliasoph and Paul Lichterman, "'We Begin With Our Favorite Theory,': Reconstructing the Extended Case Method," *Sociological Theory* 17 (1999): 228–34.

14 How Culture Works: Perspectives from Media Studies on the Efficacy of Symbols

Michael Schudson

How does culture work? That is, what influence do particular symbols have on what people think and how they act?

An anthropologist might find the question bizarre, one that by the asking reveals a fundamental misunderstanding. Culture is not something that works or fails to work. It is not something imposed on or done to a person; it is constitutive of the person. It is the precondition and the condition of human-ness. The meanings people incorporate in their lives are not separate from their activities; activities are made of meanings. Culture, as Clifford Geertz says, "is not a power, something to which social events, behaviors, institutions, or processes can be causally attributed; it is a context, something within which they can be intelligibly – that is, thickly – described."[1] Insofar as this is true, the question of the "impact" of culture is not answerable because culture is not separable from social structure, economics, politics, and other features of human activity.

And yet, even Clifford Geertz and other symbolic anthropologists are far from having given up efforts at causal attribution when it comes to culture. If we think of culture as the symbolic dimension of human activity and if we conceive its study, somewhat arbitrarily, as the study of discrete symbolic objects (art, literature, sermons, ideologies, advertisements, maps, street signs) and how they function in social life, then the question of what work culture does and how it does it is not self-evidently foolish. Indeed, it can then be understood as a key question in sociology, anthropology, and history, closely related to the central question in Western social thought since Marx (as James Fernandez has asserted) – the debate between cultural idealism and historical materialism. It is the problem raised by Max Weber's essay on the Protestant ethic: do systems of ideas or beliefs have causal significance in human affairs over against material forces? It is the problem suggested by the debates in Marxism about the relation of "superstructure" to "base." . . .

In history and the social sciences, answers to the question of the efficacy of cultural symbols or objects cluster around two poles. At one end, cultural objects are seen as enormously powerful in shaping human action – even if the cultural objects themselves are shown to be rather simply derived from the interests of powerful social groups. Ideas or symbols or propaganda successfully manipulate people. "Ideology" (or the somewhat more slippery term "hegemony") is viewed as a potent agent of powerful ruling groups, successfully molding the ideas and expectations and presuppositions of the general population and making people deferent and pliable. This position, which in its Marxist formulation has been dubbed "the dominant ideology thesis," is equally consistent with what David Laitin identifies as a conventional, social-system, rather than social-action, view, or the "first face" of culture.[2]

At the other end, concepts of culture cluster around a more optimistic view of human activity, a voluntaristic sense in which culture is seen not as a program but as a "tool kit" (in Ann Swidler's words, although she is not herself a tool-kit theorist) or "equipment for living" (in Kenneth Burke's).[3] Culture is not a set of ideas imposed but a set of ideas and symbols available for use. Individuals select the meanings they need for particular purposes and occasions from the limited but nonetheless varied cultural menu a given society provides. In this view, culture is a resource for social action more than a structure to limit social action. It serves a variety of purposes because symbols are "polysemic" and can be variously interpreted; because communication is inherently ambiguous and people will read into messages what they please; or because meaning is at the service of individual interest. Symbols, not people, are pliable. This is what Laitin calls the "second face" of culture in which culture is largely an ambiguous set of symbols that are usable as a resource for rational actors in society pursuing their own interests. Taken to its logical extreme, this position assigns culture no efficacy in social action at all. It suggests that while people may need a symbolic object to define, explain, or galvanize a course of action they have already decided on an appropriate object will always be found to clothe the pre-existing intention. . . .

To understand the efficacy of culture, it is essential to recognize simultaneously that (1) human beings make their own history and (2) they do not make it according to circumstances of their own choosing.

It is not surprising that a good many thinkers have sought some kind of middle position that recognizes both the constraining force of culture (thereby supporting the social mold or hegemonic position) and the instrumental and voluntaristic uses of culture by individuals (thus lending weight to the tool-kit position). . . .

I want to pursue a middle position myself here. . . . I focus especially on the influence of the mass media because this is the field I am most familiar with. I am most of all interested in the direct influence of cultural objects. Does TV lead to a more violent society or a more fearful society? Do romance novels buy off potential feminist unrest? Does advertising make people materialistic? Do cockfights in Bali provide an emotional training ground for the Balinese? Did Harriet Beecher Stowe help start the Civil War? Did Wagner give aid and comfort to the rise of Fascism? These are naive questions. They are, nonetheless, recurrent questions, popular questions, and publicly significant ones. (Should advertisements on children's television programs be banned? Should pornography be forbidden? What impact do sex education classes have? Or warning labels on cigarette packages?) There are a variety of more subtle questions concerning the role of culture in social life, but these questions of whether "exposure" to certain symbols or messages in various media actually lead people to change how they think about the world or act in it are powerful and central. . . .

Does culture "work"? Instead of asking whether it does, I ask about the conditions – both of the cultural object and its environment – that are likely to make the culture or cultural object work more or less. I will try to do this without bowdlerizing the concept of culture – but I recognize a tendency in this enterprise to reduce culture to information, to neglect the emotional and psychological dimensions of meaning, to ignore culture that is unconsciously transmitted or received, to focus on the most discrete and propositional forms of culture. The examples I present here draw primarily from media studies and so do not represent all of what one might mean by "culture," but I think they set the general questions clearly.

I want to examine five dimensions of the potency of a cultural object. I call these, for the sake of alliteration, retrievability, rhetorical force, resonance, institutional retention, and resolution.

Retrievability

If culture is to influence a person, it must reach the person. An advertisement is of little use to the manufacturer if a consumer never sees it; it is equally of little use if the person sees the ad but cannot locate the product in a store or find out how to order it by mail. Advertising agencies spend time and energy learning to place ads where they are most likely to be seen by the people most likely to be in the market for the product they announce. Cosmetic ads appear more frequently in *Vogue* than in *Field & Stream* because more cosmetic purchasers read *Vogue* than read *Field & Stream*.

In the language of marketing, we can call this "reach," in the language of cognitive psychology, we can refer to it as "availability," but the general term I will use, to suggest more easily the sociological dimension of the phenomenon, is "retrievability." . . .

From the individual's perspective, some elements of experience are more readily drawn upon as bases for action than other elements. From the perspective of someone who would seek to manipulate cultural objects to advantage, the question is how to make some key elements of culture more available to audiences.

What puts a cultural object in the presence of (and therefore potentially in the mind and memory of) an individual in an audience? Sociologically, there are a variety of dimensions of retrievability. A cultural object or cultural information is more *economically* retrievable if it is cheaper for people to retrieve. Marketers know that price is a barrier to customers' trying out a new product, so they distribute free samples or announce low introductory price offers, reducing the economic barrier to direct, experiential knowledge of the product. Libraries send bookmobiles to neighborhoods to attract readers who would find getting to the nearest library inconvenient or expensive.

Culture can be socially as well as economically retrievable. Books in a library's general collection are socially more retrievable than books in the Rare Book Room where a person must go through a librarian and show some identification or announce a special purpose for examining a book. It is as much the etiquette of the Rare Book Room as its formal constraints that erects a barrier to its use. Working-class parents get more information about their children's public schools from school newsletters than from parent–teacher conferences while middle-class parents make better use of the conferences. The working-class parent often feels socially awkward or inadequate talking with teachers and finds it difficult to breach the social barrier to the school system's personnel directly.[4]

There are other categories of retrievability – ways in which a part of culture becomes more or less accessible to the awareness, mind, or memory of an individual.

All the categories concern the retrievability of culture either in space or in time. The examples of social and economic retrievability I have already mentioned have to do with the availability of culture in space – whether a cultural object or piece of information is geographically in the presence of the individual. There are also ways that cultural retrievability may be expanded or limited temporally. A written message lasts longer than a verbal one, other things being equal (which is not to say it will be as rhetorically potent as the verbal message). If a cultural object is connected to a culturally salient event institutionalized on the cultural calendar, it will be more available – not only more present, that is, but more easily remembered over time. . . .

Rhetorical Force

. . . Different cultural objects have different degrees of rhetorical force or effectiveness. What makes one novel more powerful than another, one advertisement more memorable than another, one ritual more moving than another, is a matter that does not afford easy answers. . . .

If the cultural object is taken to be a communicative act, there may be a rhetorical aspect to each of its analytically distinct features. There may be a rhetorical aspect of the sender (higher-status speakers will be more persuasive to an audience than lower-status speakers); of the receiving audience (messages that flatter the audience without arousing suspicion of the speaker's insinerity will be more persuasive than messages that do not flatter); of the medium (people in a given culture may find one medium, say, television, generally more credible than another, say, radio); of the form or format (a whispered confidence is more persuasive than a public, joking insinuation); of the cultural situation (a painting in a museum more easily wins attention and respect than a painting in an antique store or on a bathroom wall); and of the message itself.

This last factor is the most slippery; indeed, some would be sure to deny that a cultural object or message can ever have such a thing as rhetorical force in its own right, separate from its relationship to the audience and its relationship to the cultural field it is a part of . . . There is something, even if that something is far from being everything, to a concept of art or craft, something to the idea that one person or group may create a cultural object more vivid, funny, appealing, graphic, dramatic, suspenseful, interesting, beautiful, stunning than another. . . .

And yet it is equally true that cultural objects do not exist by themselves. Each new one enters a field already occupied. If it is to gain attention, it must do so by displacing others or by entering into a conversation with others. The power of a cultural object or message exists by virtue of contrastive relationships to other objects in its field. A new painting can be understood only as it follows from or departs from traditions of painting that have gone before, both in the artist's own work and in the history of art to which the artist's efforts are some kind of new response. . . .

Resonance

The importance of the conventions of the subcommunity brings me to the third feature of cultural power: the degree to which the cultural object is resonant with the audience. A rhetorically effective object must be relevant to and resonant with the life of the audience. This is a simple and familiar point. It is made, for instance, by George Mosse when he argues in a study of the power of political ideology and ritual that rulers cannot successfully impose culture on people unless the political symbolism they choose connects to underlying native traditions.[5] So far as this is true, an analysis of cultural power inevitably leans toward the second face of culture, the "tool-kit" sense of culture as a set of resources from which people choose, depending on their "interests." ...

People not only attend to media selectively but perceive selectively from what they attend to. Obviously, then, people normally participate in culture-making; as some literary theorists would say today, readers are co-authors, "writing" the texts they read. This can be taken too far, I think – and does go too far if it falls altogether into the tool-kit view of culture – but there is a great deal of truth in it.

For producers of mass media culture, the issue of "resonance" will be experienced as a central problem. Whether a new television show, book, or record album will be a "hit" is notoriously difficult for the "culture industry" to predict. The broader the audience a message reaches, the less likely the message is to be specifically relevant to a given individual receiving it. . . .

The relevance of a cultural object to its audience, its utility, if you will, is a property not only of the object's content or nature and the audience's interest in it but of the position of the object in the cultural tradition of the society the audience is a part of. That is, the uses to which an audience puts a cultural object are not necessarily personal or idiosyncratic; the needs or interests of an audience are socially and culturally constituted. What is "resonant" is not a matter of how "culture" connects to individual "interests" but a matter of how culture connects to interests that are themselves constituted in a cultural frame . . . .

The "culture" that resonates or fails to resonate is itself no more autonomous than interests: it has as much an interest-driven history as individual interests have a culture-generated constitution. Barbara Herrnstein Smith makes this point with reference to Homer:

> The endurance of a classic canonical author such as Homer... owes not to the alleged transcultural or universal value of his works but, on the contrary, to the continuity of their circulation in a particular culture. Repeatedly cited and recited, translated, taught and imitated, and thoroughly enmeshed in the network of intertextuality that continuously *constitutes* the high culture of the orthodoxly educated population of the West... that highly variable entity we refer to as "Homer" recurrently enters our experience in relation to a large number and variety of our interests and thus can perform a large number of various functions for us and obviously has performed them for many of us over a good bit of the history of our culture.[6]

. . . One of the reasons a symbol becomes powerful is that – sometimes more or less by chance – it has been settled on, it has won out over other symbols as a representation of some valued entity and it comes to have an aura. The aura generates its own power and what might originally have been a very modest advantage (or even lucky coincidence) of a symbol becomes, with the accumulation of the aura of tradition over time, a major feature.

Relevance or resonance, then, is not a private relation between cultural object and individual, not even a social relation between cultural object and audience, but a public and cultural relation among object, tradition, and audience.

Institutional Retention

Culture interpenetrates with institutions as well as with interests. It exists not only as a set of meanings people share but as a set of concrete social relations in which meaning is enacted, in which it is, in a sense, tied down....

A good many cultural objects may be widely available, rhetorically effective, and culturally resonant, but fail of institutionalization. If they never turn up in a school classroom, never become a part of common reference, never enter into the know-ledge formally required for citizenship or job-holding or social acceptability, their power will be limited. A "fad" is the phenomenon that epitomizes this situation: a fad is a cultural object that makes its ways into public awareness and use, is widely adopted, and then fades completely or almost completely from view.

Powerful culture is reinforced in and through social institutions that have carrots and sticks of their own. Some culture – say, popular entertainment – is only modestly institutionalized. For certain social groups – notably, teenagers – familiarity with popular entertainment is a key element in social life and there are serious sanctions for lack of knowledge or lack of caring about it. For most adults, popular entertainment is framed as "this is fun" or, in other words, "this does not matter." That is quite different from the social-cultural framework for "serious" art where the culture – and a whole series of powerful institutions from schools to museums to government funding agencies – tell us "this is relevant." It may be fun but it is fun that bears on the meaning of an individual's life – or, so the frame tells us, it should....

The more thoroughly a cultural object is institutionalized – in the educational system or economic and social system or in the dynamics of family life, the more opportunity there is for it to exercise influence. This is not the same thing as retrievability. If an object is retrievable, it can still be disregarded with impunity; if an object is institutionally retained, there are sanctions, social or economic or legal, for disregard.

Resolution

Some elements in culture are more likely to influence action than others because they are better situated at a point of action or because they are by nature directives for action. An advertisement is a cultural text of high "resolution" in that it normally tells the audience precisely what to do to respond. It says: go out and buy. Books of advice or instruction – Jane Fonda's exercise books, a cookbook, Dr. Spock, the Boy Scout Handbook also give precise directions and can usually be readily enacted. Sacred texts are highly resolved in another sense – they are performative cultural acts, that is, the very act of reading them is itself part of the desired response; reading the book is itself an enactment of the devotional behaviour the text urges. But most cultural texts are not imperatives in so clear a fasion or, indeed, in any fashion. They may be powerful in a variety of ways but their low "resolution" means that they are unlikely to stimulate action in concrete, visible, immediate, and measurable ways. (It may be that culture achieves its end precisely when it keeps action from happening; the aim of art may be to inflict waiting and reflection, and Auden's claim that "poetry makes nothing happen" might be read – though I do not think he intended this – as a strong claim about something poetry does, not a statement that poetry does nothing.)

James Lemert has studied what he calls "mobilizing information" in the news media. Mobilizing information tells the reader how to respond in action to the news story. A news story on a 4th of July parade might include information on the parade route. This is more likely to get someone to the parade than a story that gives no indication of how a person might actually observe the parade. The American news media have an unwritten policy that it is acceptable, even desirable, to print mobilizing information about topics on which there is a cultural consensus – the 4th of July parade or a charity drive at Christmas, but not to print mobilizing information about topics of controversy (the parade route for a political demonstration, for instance). The news media thereby choose a path of low resolution in a way that demobilizes or depoliticizes the public over issues of political controversy. This is another case where a cultural producer – here a news organization – acts to limit the direct cultural power of its own creation.[7] . . .

To say that a cultural object is more powerful the more it is within reach, the more it is rhetorically effective, the more it resonates with existing opinions and structures (without disappearing entirely into them so as to have no independent influence to exert), the more thoroughly it is retained in institutions, and the more highly resolved it is toward action, helps provide a language for discussing the differences in influence of different aspects of culture.

Notes

1   Clifford Geertz. *The Interpretation of Cultures* (New York: Basic Books, 1973), 14.

2   The "dominant ideology thesis" is the phrase of Nicholas Abercrombie, Stephen Hill, and Bryan S. Turner, *The Dominant Ideology Thesis* (London: George Allen and Unwin, 1980). They identify the thesis with the work of Jürgen Habermas, Herbert Marcuse, Ralph Miliband, Nicos Poulantzas, and in some form "in almost all forms of modern Marxism" (1). David Laitin's position is reported in David D. Laitin, *Hegemony and Culture: Politics and Religious Change among the Yoruba* (Chicago: University of Chicago Press, 1986).

3   Ann Swidler, "Culture in Action: Symbols and Strategies," *American Sociological Review* 51 (1986) 273–86. Kenneth Burke, "Literature as Equipment for Living," in Kenneth Burke, *The Philosophy of Literary Form* (Berkeley: University of California Press, 1973), 293–304.

4   Steve Chaffee, "The Public View of the Media as Carriers of Information Between School and Community," *Journalism Quarterly* 44 (Winter, 1967), 732.

5   George Mosse, "Caesarism, Circuses, and Monuments," *Journal of Contemporary History* 6 (1971), 167–82.

6   Barbara Herrnstein Smith, "Contingencies of Value," in Robert von Hallberg, *Canons* (Chicago: University of Chicago Press, 1984), 35.

7   James B. Lemert, "News Context and the Elimination of Mobilizing Information An Experiment" *Journalism Quarterly* (Summer 1984) 243–9, 259. See also James B. Lemert, *Does Mass Communication Change Public Opinion After All? A New Approach to Effects Analysis* (Chicago: Nelson-Hall, 1981), 117–60. News on crime has relatively slight influence on people's actions to keep from becoming crime victims because it so rarely provides concrete information on how to stay clear of crime. This is another example of the problem of resolution. See Tom R. Tylen et al., "Assessing the Risk of Crime Victimization: The Integration of Personal Victimization Experience and Socially Transmitted Information," Journal of Social Issues 40 (1984): 27–38.

Editor's Notes on Further Reading

Schudson on Effective Symbols

Under what conditions can particular elements of culture influence individuals and groups? Answers to this question link studies focusing on individual identities and practices, such as those in Part II, with studies of cultural production, the topic of Part III. Schudson's analysis of influential symbols points both to audience/symbol relations (rhetorical force, resonance, and resolution) and to institutional conditions (retrievability, institutional retention) as creating effectiveness in particular circumstances. In this volume, excerpts from the work of Kunda on organizational rituals, and Wagner-Pacifici and Schwartz on the Vietnam Veterans Memorial, provide additional examples of how these factors might vary.

Different reflections on how elements of culture might affect identities and practices include Steve Derné, "Cultural Conceptions of Human Motivation and Their Significance for Culture Theory," pp. 267–87 in Diana Crane, ed., *The Sociology of Culture* (Oxford and Cambridge, MA: Blackwell, 1994); Gary Alan Fine and Kent Sandstrom, "Ideology in Action: A Pragmatic Approach to a Contested Concept," *Sociological Theory* 11 (1993): 21–37; Bennett Berger, "Structure and Choice in the Sociology of Culture," *Theory and Society* 20 (1991): 1–20; Ann Swidler, "Culture in Action: Symbols and Strategies," *American Sociological Review* 51 (1986): 273–86; Gary Alan Fine, "Small Groups and Culture Creation: The Idioculture of Little League Baseball Teams," *American Sociological Review* 44 (1979): 733–45; Sherry Ortner, "On Key Symbols," *American Anthropologist* 75 (1973): 1338–46; and C. Wright Mills, "Situated Actions and Vocabularies of Motive," *American Sociological Review* 5 (1940): 904–13. More generally, focusing on features of cultural elements is one way of addressing a key issue in cultural theory, the question of whether, when and how culture is powerful. Some of the many other approaches to this question can be seen in excerpts from the work of Raymond Williams, Bourdieu, Swidler, Sewell and Wuthnow in this volume, and associated editor's notes; see also Karen Cerulo, "Identity Construction: New Issues, New Directions," *Annual Review of Sociology* 23 (1997): 385–409.

Schudson's approach is grounded in his research on media and public life: see for instance his *The Power of News* (Cambridge, MA: Harvard University Press, 1995); *Watergate in American Memory: How We Remember, Forget, and Reconstruct the Past* (New York: Basic Books, 1992); and *Advertising, the Uneasy Persuasion: Its Dubious Impact on American Society* (New York: Basic Books, 1984). For further discussion of media effects see the selection by Hunt, and accompanying editor's note in this volume.

Part III

Cultural Production: Institutional Fields

15 Market Structure, the Creative Process, and Popular Culture: Toward an Organizational Reinterpretation of Mass-Culture Theory

Paul DiMaggio

Long-term change in the quality of a society's popular culture is easy to notice, but difficult to characterize. In twentieth-century America, we can note the apparent decline in importance of folk cultures, and the concommitant rise of such commercial "mass" media as cinema, radio, and television; but the ultimate effect of such changes on the cultural landscape of the society itself – their impact on the range and quality of materials available to different publics is not easily assessed. The terms of much of the sociological discourse on this topic have been defined by critics of what have been called "mass culture" and "mass society." Put briefly, these writers have discerned a gradual decline in the quality of American culture from a condition of abundance, diversity, and vitality to one of homogeneity, blandness, and triviality.

Mass-society theorists have argued that urbanization, industrialization, and the rise of national markets and mass communications have caused traditional communities to decline in importance. As more and more of the individual's needs are served by agencies that are national in scope, and fewer and fewer by local primary and secondary groups (for example, the family or the P.T.A.), the importance and vitality of such groups diminishes. They lose their identities, social boundaries break down, and individuals face the world in relative isolation, as part of a mass public described by one commentator as "a huge, inchoate, sociocultural compost in which everything is mixed up together."[1]

Mass society, its critics assert, has its own kind of culture. Whereas, in the past, a people's tastes were formed through intense interaction in family, workplace, and community, in mass society taste is detached from its social moorings. Cultures of class and region vanish and, in their place, stands a single national culture shared by all but, perhaps, a small elite that can appreciate traditional high culture. Conservatives suggest that mass culture's contents are determined solely by the demands of the masses who, estranged from the wholesome influence of traditional communal groups, let their libidinal urges reign. Radicals argue that the disoriented mass accepts with enthusiasm whatever it is served: manipulative elites provide a steady diet of cultural TV dinners to program their ostensibly free subjects into apathy and dull acquiescence. Leisure is "colonized" and creative pursuits succumb to "those passive amusements, entertainments, and spectacles . . . offered as substitutes for life itself."[2] In both the conservative and radical view, taste is first leveled, then homogenized. Significant innovation becomes rare and the thematic range of popular culture narrows as the search for a mass audience forces corporate producers to transcend "the peculiar interests and preoccupations of the special and segmented organized groups and direct their appeal to the mass."[3]

The trouble with mass-culture theory is that, in place of concrete analysis, mass-culture critics have offered one or the other of two vulgar economic suppositions. Conservatives adhere to an implicit theory of pure competition: what the public wants, the public will get. Radicals write from an implicit theory of pure monopoly behavior: the public will lap up whatever it is offered. Both camps fail to take into account the fact that, in western industrial democracies like the United States, most items of popular culture – books, motion pictures, records, television programs – are produced by profit-making firms operating under the contraints of the marketplace.

In fact, the core characteristics of "mass culture" can be seen as attributes of industries, not of societies. On the one hand, the industries that produce trade books, records, movies, and special-interest magazines create materials for specialized audiences and promote and distribute them through separate advertising media and market channels. On the other hand, certain culture producers *do* act as mass-culture theory suggests they should. Industries that create television programs, mass-circulation magazines, and, to a lesser extent, elementary and secondary-school textbooks and the mass-market paperbacks sold on newstands and supermarket racks provide similar materials to all segments of the public, utilizing the techniques of mass production and mass distribution. This coexistence of two very different kinds of popular culture within the same system suggests that changes in the degree of cultural innovation and diversity are not traceable entirely to broad socio-demographic tendencies. Rather, such economic and organizational factors as how a popular-culture form is distributed and how the market for it is segmented may determine in large part the level of independence granted creators and the degree of innovation and diversity in the products themselves.

This observation leads to two sets of questions. First, why do some culture-producing industries fit the mass-culture model, while others diverge? What economic forces and organizational strategies enable certain firms profitably to distribute mass-cultural fare, while others supply diverse goods to smaller markets? Second, will the market structures and patterns of organization that permit homogeneous materials to yield profits spread with time, as mass-culture theorists suggest, or is the current mix a stable one?

A Tentative Model

Let us begin by attempting to apply to a society's culture as a whole the implicit analytic model developed by Peterson and Berger in their seminal articles on the American popular-music industry.[4] Studying popular-music production over a twenty-year span, Peterson and Berger noted that at times the products of the recording industry were mass-cultural and at times they were not. Periods in which only a few companies accounted for a large share of the industry's sales were characterized by homogeneity and stagnation. By contrast, periods of creative ferment – the rise of rock and roll, the psychedelic sound – seemed to follow, rather than precede, increased competition in the popular-music marketplace. What is more, the authors noted that the degree of competition seemed also to affect the roles that producers and artists played in the creative process. During periods of oligopolistic control, creative decision-making was relatively centralized and artists and producers had a minumum of autonomy; during periods of competition, artists played a more important role in the recording process and producers themselves demonstrated increased independence from management.

The Model then goes as follows:

market structure	organization of the creative process	degree of innovation and diversity of popular-culture products

According to this model, the market structure of an industry, in particular the degree of what economists call "seller concentration," determines the degree of control over the market that firms hold and the certainty of corporate managers that their products will be sold. This, in turn, strongly influences the independence granted popular-culture creators which, in turn, affects the degree of innovation and diversity in the products that the industry manufactures. Peterson and Berger have shown that such a model accurately describes one major cultural-production system. Can it be generalized to the cultural economy as a whole?

Three major assumptions are implicit in this model. First, it is assumed that managers of organizations place a high value on predictability. Certainty that the performance of similar tasks in similar ways will lead consistently to a desired outcome – whether it be a working transistor or a best-selling novel – facilitates the establishment of stable procedures, routines, communications channels, and interpersonal relationships that ensure continued performance and minimize risk, administrative overload, and interpersonal and intergroup conflict over goals and means. Research on individual psychology and organizational behavior alike indicates that individuals, including managers of firms, find uncertainty stressful and will go to great lengths to minimize it.

Second, it is assumed that consumers desire a diverse range of cultural products and that the demand for diversity usually exceeds the supply. Peterson and Berger document this for the music industry.[5] The existence of latent demand is also illustrated by public acceptance of independent film-making in the 1960's; the recent financial success of pay television and, increasingly, of cable television more generally; and the survival of small presses and recording companies in the absence of commercially practical marketing and distribution systems.

Finally, it is assumed that creators of culture in contemporary American society have a nearly universal desire to innovate, to generate new cultural forms, and to deal with new areas of content. While there may be instances of innovation being instigated from above, nearly every study of a cultural institution has identified endemic conflict between creators and their patrons over issues of creativity and control.

If these three assumptions are correct, managers in popular-culture industries are faced with two major dilemmas. First, they must control their markets: they must maintain enough economic power to prevent competitors from entering the market and satisfying latent cultural demand. Second, they must control and coordinate their own creative divisions, so that creation remains routine, predictable, and guaranteed to produce materials acceptable to the widest possible range of individuals in the controlled market. To the extent that managers in an industry succeed on both counts, the popular culture produced by that industry will be mass cultural. To the extent that they are unable both to inhibit competition and to control creators, the industry will provide varied cultural offerings. During the last twenty years, for example, the television industry has successfully controlled both its own creative personnel and the market for its goods. Three networks, dominant throughout this period, now account for 90 percent of viewing time; as they have tightened their control, the blandness and homogeneity of their fare has become an intellectual *cause célèbre*. The recording industry has controlled its market and personnel with varying success. Between 1953 and 1973 the number of major pop labels rose from twenty-three to ninety then fell to sixty-one, and musical styles ranged from placid and repetitive to wildly innovative. Finally, publishers have, in general, been unable to control either markets or authors, instead developing strategies to deal with uncertainty by limiting expenses and providing a wide variety of materials. At the beginning of this decade between one thousand and six thousand book publishers competed for the book buyer's dollar. By the criteria set out above – abundance and thematic range – television programming is the most mass cultural, book publishing the least, and recorded music somewhere in between. A society with a mass culture would be one in which firms in industries that produced popular culture had all solved both these problems of control.

Having set out this tentative model, I should like now to explore some of its more problematic elements, particularly the notions of innovation and uncertainty as they apply to the creation of popular culture. To do this let us draw on some of the work of economists who have studied the relationship between market structure and innovation.

Innovation and Uncertainty in the Production of Popular Culture

Economists who study market structure and economic concentration have noted that the conduct of oligopolistic firms – those in industries dominated by a few sellers – can have a major impact on the market as a whole. Degree of oligopoly, or market control, is represented by what are called "concentration ratios" – the percentage of all domestic shipments of a good provided by the leading four or eight manufacturers. Where concentration is high (over 50 percent), oligopolists may erect significant barriers to entry for would-be competitors, control prices, maintain a high level of corporate productivity and profits, and pursue technological innovation.[6]

What does this have to do with popular culture? Remember our first assumption, that managers place a premium on predictability, routine, and control. To the extent that significant innovation incurs a risk, managers of firms in highly concentrated industries may successfully use their market power to avoid providing significantly innovative (and thus disruptive and chancy) materials to their publics. In fact, economists have studied the relationship between concentration or firm size and innovativeness since Schumpeter first asserted that only giant corporations had the resources necessary to innovate. Their findings have been mixed but, in sum, it appears that, while large firms possess the means to *develop* and *exploit* expensive new technologies, most significant inventions have *originated* with individuals, or smaller organizations. As Scherer puts it:

> In a small firm, the decision to go ahead with an ambitious project typically involves a very few people who know one another well. In a large corporation, the decision must filter through a whole chain of command – the person with the idea, his section chief, the laboratory manager, the vice-president for research, and if substantial financial commitments are required, several members of top management. Each participant is risking his reputation, if not his money, in backing the project. (p. 354)

In the book publishing, recording, and movie industries, where fashions change rapidly and new styles are frequently introduced, many of the most important cultural innovations have come from small firms and independent producers. For example, the best-selling manual *Women: Our Bodies, Our Selves* was first published by a Boston-area women's collective; Elvis Presley and Jerry Lee Lewis first recorded their unique brand of rockabilly for the lilliputian *Sun* label. By contrast, in television change comes more slowly. Gaining approval for a new program concept is exceedingly difficult, precisely because of the number of individuals involved. An ABC programming vice-president has written:

> Usually, anyone from the program executive level up is empowered to receive a program submission, though at the lower levels, this power is strictly negative – they can say no if they are cool to an idea. They cannot say yes. Instead, if they like an idea, they pass it up the chain of command in the form of a recommendation. Many yeses can begin at the director level and yes power increases as you move up. Still, there are all kinds of yeses. Even a president is circumscribed in his power to say a really big yes – putting a program into the prime-time schedule, for instance. This is usually legislated in committee by a group that may be called the Program Board which consists of one or more presidents, the chairman of the Board of the company, and the highest layer of program vice-presidents – plus vice-presidents of Sales, Research, Affiliates, Business Affairs, Standards and Practices.[7]

The work of economists is suggestive, but we must extrapolate from it with caution. For one thing, their research on the effects of market structure has been somewhat inconclusive. For another, much of their work compares the roster of giant firms (e.g., the top two hundred), from which culture suppliers are nearly all absent, to smaller firms, some of which would dwarf even medium-sized publishers or record companies. Furthermore, except for certain kinds of publishers, no concentration ratios are available for industries producing popular culture.

The major problem, however, concerns the definition of innovation used by economists and by many organizational sociologists as well. Innovation is usually taken to mean major changes in technology, product design, or product specifications. Such changes would include 45-RPM records, 32-track studies, dolbies, and quadrophonic sound in the recording industry; CRT-typesetting and high-speed printing for publishers: and satellite video transmission or large-screen receivers in television. The innovation we are concerned with here – significant change in themes, values, modes of presentation, or concerns in popular culture – is of a very different sort.

There is a *third* kind of innovation, as well, which is critical to this argument: I will call it *product generation*. This kind of innovation is not variable; rather it constitutes the very mission of culture-producing organizations, to generate a constant stream of unique (if often similar) products with severely limited life spans. Product generation is important because it represents an inherent source of instability in even those organizations that exercise the greatest control over their markets.

Since all culture-producing firms must generate new products, the question is not who can afford to innovate, as it is for large-scale technical research and development, but who can afford not to. Here we may begin to develop an analogy between control of creativity and control of price. Just as other oligopolists are unwilling to engage in price competition, lest the equilibrium of their profitable market structure be upset, oligopolistic culture producers may attempt to refrain from unnecessary product competition through significant innovation. They may do this because the aesthetic preferences of consumers are in many ways unknowable and major changes in theme, style, or content may meet with commercial resistance or disrupt sales-division routines; and, perhaps more importantly, significant innovation must be carried out by personnel in creative divisions who, because of the difficulty of defining their work, present persistent challenges to management control. Thus any sort of product competition that requires the deroutinization of creative work may be both an economic and an organizational threat to the oligopolistic firm.

With this in mind, let us turn our attention to the creative process itself, to the relationship between the environment of organizations – the conditions under which a firm pursues its goals – and their structures, with particular attention to the nature of uncertainty in the creation of popular culture. Uncertainty is intimately related to the exigencies of product generation. Supplying goods to markets based not on need but on taste, with few standards of creative competence or expertise, the management of culture-producing firms, no matter how powerful, must constantly negotiate and renegotiate the norms and rules governing the creation of new products with writers, artists, and other creative personnel. The need for constant review of new materials, the absence of a priori standards or marketability, and the restiveness of creators, requires that managers employ brokers to link the creative process with the other functions of the firm, to represent the goals of management to popular-culture creators, and sometimes to champion the creators themselves. Such brokers include book and magazine editors, television and record producers, and motion picture directors.

Brokerage Systems of Administration

I shall refer to the negotiated administration of production common to all the cultural-production industries as *brokerage administration*. Brokerage administration is, I believe, a distinct form of administration differing significantly from bureaucratic and craft administration. If bureaucratic administration of production is based on close supervision, repetition of routine, and compliance with orders, and craft administration based on professional competence, market relations, and separation of employer and employee by contract, brokerage administration is characterized by ambiguity, informality, and negotiation. Unlike bureaucratic and craft forms, brokerage administration is not defined by a legal relationship: it can operate whether the artist is an employee or a contractee of the culture-producing firm. Contractual labor is drawn towards the firm, employed labor is separated from it, and control over production is continuously negotiated among individuals with competing priorities and interests. This conflict must be institutionalized in the broker's role because brokerage systems lack precisely that which makes a craft system practicable – standards for evaluating the acceptability of the final product. Like craft administrators, brokerage administrators lack professional competence to build a finished product and must defer to specialists beneath them on the organizational charts; but unlike craft administrators, they can never be certain exactly what professional competence is or who may be expected to possess it. Artists, and often brokers themselves, can only be evaluated post hoc on the basis of success, or on the basis of reputation and track record.

Virtually all culture-producing organizations include brokers who mediate between the aspirations of artists for creative expression and the desires of management to be able to predict and control. Differences among culture-producers in the amount of control maintained over the product is reflected in differences in the roles these brokers play. Let us consider, briefly, three ideal types of brokerage system – one pure form of brokerage administration and two extreme variants, entrepreneurial and centralized.

In a *pure brokerage system*, the broker serves both management and creators, acting as mediator, double-agent, and advocate for both, with ultimate loyalty to the former. The pure brokerage role is best described by Herbert S. Bailey, Jr. in his volume on book publishing:

> The editor represents the publisher to the author, but he is *not* the publisher. After talking to the author, he must return to his office and represent the author to the publisher – in terms of the interests of the publisher... The editor becomes the author's ally in developing a project that the publisher will approve, just as he is the publisher's ally in seeking authors and developing projects that will further the publisher's goals. He is not exactly in the middle, however; he is part of the publishing house and he is not likely to forget that he is on the publisher's payroll.[8]

The pure broker is subject to regular communication with management and must observe a set of norms and traditions prescribing loosely the attributes of a marketable product; at the same time, the pure broker has considerable discretion in contracting and dealing with creative personnel. M. Lincoln Schuster, who founded the company that bears his name, described the roles of publishers and editors nicely: "an editor selects manuscripts; a publisher selects editors."

In *entrepreneurial brokerage* systems, similar to those described by Peterson and Berger and Hirsch as characteristic of the most turbulent and competitive sectors of popular-culture production, managers abdicate control over acquisitions and production decisions to the broker, who, depending on his personality and expertise, may or may not abdicate it to creative workers themselves. The attitude of management in entrepreneurial brokerage systems is typified by a comment from the vice president for talent of EMI, a large and conservative British record company that had just signed a "punk-rock" band called The Sex Pistols: "The fact that many of us are now over thirty means we don't have our fingers on the pulse."

Centralized brokerage systems exist in industries dominated by a few producers, often with high unit costs and government regulations. In such a system, management exerts strong pressures upon creators and innovation and diversity are, in most cases, successfully minimized. Brokers represent management's views to creators; they themselves are subject to vertical communication through multiple hierarchies of control; decisions to fund products are made by committee; and management personnel are involved in the creative process itself. As Muriel Cantor describes the process of creating television dramas:

> The network controls operate in several ways. In the case of new shows a network liason man often sits in on the story conference where ideas for shows are developed. All scripts (whether the show is new or not) must be submitted to the network censor for approval; in some cases the story idea or story presentation must also be submitted. No show goes on the air without final approval from the network.[9]

Perhaps the most extreme example of centralized brokerage administration of culture production is the textbook, which is often produced almost entirely by committee. An idea originates with editors or marketing personnel, who develop budgets and send the idea to a publications committee, which includes top company officials. If an idea is accepted in committee and approved by the company's president, conceptualization and goal-setting are performed in-house by editors in consultation with outside specialists. An outline is developed and an author team, headed by two or three individuals with marketable credentials who frequently lend little but their names, is appointed and tasks assigned to as many as thirty writers. As their material comes in, it is inspected and often rewritten by editors, sent out to the sales division for comments and review, and reworked by production editors. The broker, here an acquisitions editor responsible for the text's subject area, coordinates all these activities, making sure that schedules are met and that the sales force is impressed with the book's market potential. The creative and conceptual role of authors is often insubstantial.

The centralized brokerage system, characteristic of the more economically concentrated, less innovative, popular-culture industries, may be seen as an administrative form well adapted to the production of mass culture. Television producers and textbook editors operate under more constant attention, communicate more with individuals in management and other divisions, and have less autonomy in initiating projects than do their counterparts in trade publishing, special interest magazines, or record companies. Even in the relatively concentrated mass market paperback industry which, in contrast to television or textbook publishing, operates in an unregulated consumer market with low per-project costs, decision-making involves "seemingly endless rounds of meetings and conferences attended by key... personnel."[10] Such extensive communication among individuals from different divisions and administrative levels ensures that editors are exposed to the positions and subject to the control of their colleagues and superiors.

A number of qualifications should be put forth at this point. First, although I have followed Peterson and Berger,[11] Blair, and others in treating economic concentration as the principle determinant of market control, it should be noted that horizontal concentration is only one element of market structure. A more complete model would have to take into account the effects of regulation, oligopsony (the control of the market by a few large buyers), vertical concentration, and, most important, conglomerate concentration (the prominence of large corporations, such as MCA or Warner Communications, with divisions and subsidiaries competing in a wide range of different culture-producing industries).

In addition, I have said little about the impact of technology, through size of investment per project, on degree of control over creative personnel. It may be argued that high-investment media materials can only be manufactured by highly capitalized and oligopolistic firms who, because the expense of each item is so high, will maintain close control over creators. In the long run, I believe, this argument is simply incorrect. Cultural media are technologically malleable; those that now require large investments do so principally because they are controlled by large firms that can afford it. For example, Williams and Barnouw demonstrate that the current network structure of television was neither historically nor technologically inevitable. What is more, the decentralization (and substantial decrease in cost) of radio programming after the onset of television, and current developments in public television, videocassettes, and cable and satellite transmission, indicate that cost and technical-quality considerations are hardly irreversible. In the short run, however, production cost may well be an element of the market structure that independently affects the organization of creative work.

Moreover, little work exists on the determinants of market segmentation, that is, the division of a consumer market into smaller markets defined by age, social-class, or life-style criteria, for which separate products are manufactured and often marketed through different media and channels. The degree of market segmentation in an industry is intimately related to the amount of diversity in the products it produces. Finally, little is known concretely about what we might call the quality-elasticity (in contrast to price-elasticity) of the market for popular culture. Cross-national studies indicate that consumer demand for television programming is high and relatively inelastic. In contrast, Peterson and Berger's work indicates that the market for popular music has been quality-elastic.

Conclusions

The model developed here is a highly tentative one, in need of considerable testing and elaboration. To consider where a more sophisticated version of this model might lead us, let us reconsider the debate over mass culture and the fate of cultural innovation and diversity in society as a whole. Imagine three ideal types of cultural-production systems, each with its own form of organization and each generating a different form of predominant culture. The first, mass culture, has already been discussed.

	Mass Culture	*Class Culture*	*Pluralistic Culture*
Market structure	Strict oligopoly	Multiple oligopolies or multidivisional oligopoly	Competition
Form of organization	Centralized brokerage	Centralized brokerage	Pure or entrepreneurial brokerage
Market segmentation	No market segmentation	Strict market segmentation	Loose market segmentation
Innovation	Low innovation	Low innovation	High innovation
Diversity	Low diversity	High diversity	High diversity

By class culture I refer to a system in which varying materials are produced for strictly segmented markets based on class or status groupings. Since strict segmentation might reduce uncertainty regarding the range of acceptable materials, such markets would probably be dominated by a few firms, or divisions of firms, and staffed by creators who restricted their output to materials for the market addressed. The major principle of such a system would be separation – separation of creators, of materials, and of market outlets.

By pluralistic culture I mean a system in which varying materials are created in a range of organizational settings, distributed through mass-market channels, and consumed by markets segmented loosely by differences in taste or interest. In such a system, individuals would have the greatest degree of cultural choice and producers would face the greatest amount of competition.

Contemporary American culture represents a mix of these three ideal types. Television, textbooks, and, to a lesser extent, mass-market paperback fiction are mass-cultural, presenting similar materials to a wide range of audiences. Ethnic magazines and recording companies, the foreign-language press, pulp magazines, and high-culture producers are class-cultural, providing specialized materials to relatively solidary groups through specialized market channels. Trade publishers, most record companies, and much of the magazine industry are pluralistic in that they supply diverse materials to overlapping and shifting special-interest audiences through common market channels.

Can we expect this mix to continue? Or, translating the mass-culture argument into organizational terms, can we expect cultural-production industries to become increasingly concentrated, to control their markets and their creative employees with increasing efficacy? Barring a radical change in the role of the state in cultural affairs, the answer to this question is probably no. For one thing, economists have noted no major trend toward greater horizontal concentration in manufacturing industries between 1954 and 1966. Bain found that industries starting with low four-firm concentration ratios became somewhat more concentrated, while those with higher concentration ratios became somewhat less so. Similarly, Blair found no major trends between 1947 and 1963. He suggests that the development of decentralizing technologies and the impact of diseconomies of size will, over time, counteract the effects of merger, acquisitions, nonprice competition, and predation.

Within culture-producing industries, no trend towards decreased competition can be observed. Since the late 1940's, radio programming has become less concentrated; film and recording have fluctuated with a probable downward trend; and mass-market magazines have declined. Magazine publishing as a whole has become less concentrated; book publishing as a whole has remained stable; and general book publishing (including trade) has become less concentrated.

Furthermore, a trend towards diversification within large culture-producing firms may further contribute to an increase in cultural choice. Peterson and Berger[12] note that adoption of the multidivisional form, whereby divisions of the same firm compete against one another, has to some extent counteracted the effects of reconcentration in the recording industry. Similarly, the sales manager of Bantam Books, a leader in the relatively concentrated mass-market paperback industry, has cited a trend towards organization along product lines in that field as well.

Finally, television, the mass medium par excellence, has remained highly concentrated, but new technologies may even fragment that bastion of mass culture. Videocassettes that can be used on regular receivers, the availability of inexpensive transmission by satellite and cable, and the rise of independent syndication and advertiser networks, could result in a significant decline in network contribution to total viewing time and, perhaps, a tendency toward demographic television programing within the next fifteen years.

This is not to say that mass-culture theorists have been completely wrong. Over the past fifty years, folk cultures and class cultures have most probably declined. And it may be argued that certain significant kinds of innovation are blocked throughout popular-culture media by informal norms regarding permissible content. Furthermore, competition does not guarantee diversity. As the case of the oil industry demonstrates, efficiently integrated firms in industries with relatively low concentration ratios can exercise considerable control over their markets.

Nonetheless, the history of American popular culture indicates that the extent of diversity and innovation available to the public – and, conversely, the degree of massification of culture – has more to do with the market structures and organizational environment of specific industries than with strongly felt demands of either the masses or their masters for certain kinds of homogeneous cultural materials. What we know about these industries suggests that, in the short run at least, the nightmares of mass-culture theory show little prospect of becoming real.

Notes

1   R. Clausse, "The Mass Public at Grips with Mass Communications," *International Social Science Journal* 20 (1968), p. 627.
2   Harry Braverman, *Labor and Monopoly Capital: The Degradation of Work in the Twentieth Century*, N.Y.: Monthly Review Press, 1974, p. 278.
3   Louis Wirth, "Consensus and Mass Communications," *American Sociological Review* 13 (1948), p. 10.
4   Richard A. Peterson and David Berger, "Entrepreneurship in Organizations: Evidence From the Popular Music Industry," *Administrative Science Quarterly* 16 (1971), pp. 97–106; "Cycles in Symbol Production: The Case of Popular Music," *American Sociological Review* 40 (1975), pp. 158–73.
5   Peterson and Berger, "Cycles in Symbol Production."

6 Richard Caves, *American Industry: Structure, Conduct, Performance*, 2nd edition, Englewood Cliffs, N.J.: Prentice-Hall, 1967; Frederick M. Scherer, *Industrial Market Structure and Economic Performance*, Chicago: Rand McNally, 1970; John M. Blair, *Economic Concentration: Structure, Behavior, and Public Policy*, N.Y.: Harcourt Brace Jovanovich, 1972.

7 Bob Shanks, *The Cool Fire: How to Make it in Television*, N.Y.: Vintage Books, 1977, pp. 75–6.

8 Herbert S. Bailey, Jr., *The Art and Science of Book Publishing* (N.Y.: Harper & Rowe, 1970), pp. 29–30.

9 Muriel C. Canton, *The Hollywood TV Producer* (N.Y.: Basic Books, 1971), p. 122.

10 Clarence Petersen, *The Bantam Story: Thirty Years of Paperback Publishing*, revised edition, N.Y.: Bantam Books, 1975.

11 Peterson and Berger, "Cycles in Symbol Production."

12 Petersen and Berger, "Cycles in Symbol Production."

Editor's Notes on Further Reading

DiMaggio on Mass Culture Organization

Whereas many observers of modern culture have feared a remorseless trend to homogenization and mass production (see Horkheimer and Adorno excerpt, this volume) Paul DiMaggio argues that such fears are exaggerated, because culture industries take a variety of organizational forms, and the extent to which diversity and innovation are encouraged varies according to organizational form and industry structure. Thus, homogenized mass culture is only one of several possible outcomes of culture industries.

DiMaggio's argument is an early example of increased attention to midrange organizational explanation of cultural outcomes, characteristic of the "production of culture" perspective which developed from the mid-1970s onwards. For more on this development in cultural sociology, see for example Paul Hirsch, "Processing Fads and Fashions: An Organization-Set Analysis of Cultural Industry Systems," *American Journal of Sociology* 77 (1972): 639–59; Richard Peterson, ed., *The Production of Culture* (Beverley Hills: Sage, 1976); Peterson, "Revitalizing the Culture Concept," *Annual Review of Sociology* 5 (1979): 137–66; Diana Crane, "Reward Systems in Art, Science, and Religion," pp. 57–72 in Richard Peterson, *The Production of Culture*; Crane, *The Production of Culture: Media and the Urban Arts* (Newbury Park, CA: Sage, 1992); and Lewis Coser, Issue Editor, The Production of Culture, *Social Research* 45 (2) 1978. For an updated overview with discussion of numerous examples see Richard Peterson, "Cultural Studies Through the Production Perspective: Progress and Prospects," pp. 163–90 in Diana Crane, ed., *The Sociology of Culture: Emerging Theoretical Perspectives* (Cambridge, MA and Oxford: Blackwell, 1994).

For more on cultural production of television, music, visual art, and literature, see selections from the work of Hunt, Peterson, Becker, and Griswold and accompanying editors note's this volume. On media institutions see John Ryan and William Wentworth, *Media and Society: The Production of Culture in the Mass Media* (Needham Heights, MA: Allyn and Bacon, 1999); Rodney Benson, "Field Theory in Comparative Context: A New Paradigm for Media Studies," *Theory and Society* 28 (1998): 463–98; Joseph Turow, *Media Systems in Society*, 2nd edn. (New York: Longman, 1997); and Gaye Tuchman, "Mass Media Institutions," pp. 601–26 in Neil Smelser, ed., *Handbook of Sociology* (Newbury Park, CA: Sage, 1988).

For cultural sociologists, the issue of how and why "high" culture comes to be distinguished from "mass" and "popular" culture is closely related to the investigation of "mass" culture itself: does something intrinsic to the product, or something in the social organization of production, make something "high" culture? Some of the many important discussions of this issue include Diana Crane, "High Culture versus Popular Culture Revisited: A Reconceptualization of Recorded Cultures," pp. 58–74, and Paul DiMaggio, "Cultural Boundaries and Structural Change: The Extension of the High Culture Model to Theater, Opera, and the Dance, 1900–1940," pp. 21–57, both in Michèle Lamont and Marcel Fournier, *Cultivating Differences: Symbolic Boundaries and the Making of Inequality* (Chicago and London: University of Chicago Press, 1992); Judith Blau, *The Shape of Culture: A Study of Contemporary Cultural Patterns in the United States* (Cambridge and New York: Cambridge University Press, 1989); Paul DiMaggio, "Social Structure, Institutions, and Cultural Goods: The Case of the United States," pp. 133–55 in Pierre Bourdieu and James Coleman, eds., *Social Theory for a Changing Society* (Boulder and New York: Westview Press and Russell Sage Foundation, 1991); DiMaggio, "Classification in Art," *American Sociological Review* 52 (1987): 440–55; DiMaggio, "Cultural Entrepreneurship in Late Nineteenth Century Boston," *Media Culture, and Society* 4 (1982): 33–50, 303–21; Lawrence Levine, *Highbrow/Lowbrow: The Emergence of Cultural Hierarchy in America* (Cambridge, MA: Harvard University Press, 1988); Herbert Gans, *Popular Culture and High Culture* (New York: Basic Books, 1974), and Leo Lowenthal, "Historic Perspectives on Popular Culture," *American Journal of Sociology* 55 (1950): 323–32 and *Literature, Popular Culture, and Society* (Palo Alto, CA: Pacific Books, 1961).

16 Why 1955? Explaining the Advent of Rock Music

Richard A. Peterson

At the time, 1929, 1939, 1945 and 1968 all seemed important turning points in the track of our civilisation. By contrast, as anyone alive at the time will attest, 1955 seemed like an unexceptional year in the United States at least. Right in the middle of the 'middle-of-the-road' years of the Eisenhower presidency, 1955 hardly seemed like the year for a major aesthetic revolution. Yet it was in the brief span between 1954 and 1956 that the rock[1] aesthetic displaced the jazz-based aesthetic in American popular music. Frank Sinatra, Tommy Dorsey, Patty Page, Perry Como, Nat King Cole, Tony Bennett, Kay Starr, Les Paul, Eddie Fisher, Jo Stafford, Frankie Lane, Johnnie Ray and Doris Day gave way on the popular music charts to Elvis Presley, Chuck Berry, The Platters, Bill Haley, Buddy Holly, Little Richard, Carl Perkins and the growing legion of rockers.[2] ...

Employing the 'production of culture' perspective (Peterson 1976, 1979), we will show the essential contributions of the culture industry to the emergence of rock music and its associated aesthetic and culture. Before beginning this central task, however, we will briefly explore the roles of creators and audiences in the process.

It is easy to characterise eras in terms of the leaders of the time. The 'Napoleonic' era is an obvious case in point. It is no less tempting to identify an aesthetic revolution with its most celebrated exponents – Vivaldi, Shakespeare, Beethoven, Picasso. In this vein, it is possible to point to specific individuals like Chuck Berry, Little Richard, Elvis Presley and Jerry Lee Lewis and say that rock emerged in the late 1950s because, like other creative circles of artists (Kadushin 1976), they began their creative efforts at this specific moment. In bringing into question this 'supply side' explanation, I do not, for a moment belittle their accomplishments. Rather, I suggest that in any era there is a much larger number of creative individuals than ever reach notoriety, and if some specific periods of time see the emergence of more notables, it is because these are times when the usual routinising inhibitions to innovation do not operate as systematically, allowing opportunities for innovators to emerge. ...

What of the 'demand-side' explanation of the emergence of rock music? As applied to this instance, it says the remarkably large cohort of newly-affluent young people, the vanguard of the 'baby-boom' could not relate to the jazz-based sensuous slow dance music created for twenty-year-olds approaching the age of first marriage. Characteristically, songs in this vein featured a male who abstractly promises marriage if the female is willing to share her sexual favours.

The baby-boomers demanded music that spoke to their own condition. The appropriate themes included a mix of the excruciating joys of first love, fights with parents, and frustrations with high school and the older generation generally. Although it can be argued that the uniquely large baby-boom cohort has been responsible for a number of changes in the US, it did not cause the emergence of rock in the mid-

1950s. In fact, it could not have done so. After all, in 1954 the oldest of the baby-boomers were only nine years old and half had not even been born yet!

Although the emergence of rock was not caused by the baby-boom, we are not arguing that audience preferences had nothing to do with the rise of rock. Quite to the contrary, the newly affluent teens and pre-teens comprised the heart of the market exploited in the rise of rock music. The point is that this market demand had been growing gradually for over a decade and remained largely unsatiated because the decision-makers in the culture industry simply did not recognise that it was there (Peterson and Berger 1975).

It is, indeed, ironic that the commercial culture industry, which is consecrated to making money by providing the mass of people with the kinds of entertainment that they want, was systematically blind to the unsatiated demand for cultural products that spoke more directly to the condition of young people. In unravelling this irony, we will argue that it was the structure of arrangements, habits, and assumptions of the commercial culture industry itself that caused the blindness. Likewise, we will argue that it was the systematic change in these factors that created the opportunity for rock to emerge....

Law and Regulation

Copyright law, patent law and Federal Government regulation of radio station broadcasting licenses importantly influenced the advent of rock music though in ways completely unintended and unanticipated as well. To begin to understand why rock became a mass success in 1955 we have to go right back to the beginning of the twentieth century.

Copyright

The US Copyright Law of 1909 for the first time gave protection to the owners of musical compositions. Heretofore, American sheet music printer–publishers had subsisted primarily by reprinting standard favourite songs and appropriating con-temporary works by European composers who received no royalties for their use. Writer–publishers of new songs had lobbied aggressively for the copyright protection the new law would provide because it clearly made a song into a piece of property that could be bought, sold and developed by its owner. With copyright protection, the aggressive New York sheet-music writer–publishers could afford to spend a great deal of money promoting a new song because other printers could not pirate the valuable properties thus created. Their activity fostered a quick succession of innovations in music and popular dancing, most notably ragtime and jazz.

Unlike the European laws of the time (Ploman and Hamilton 1980; Frith 1981, 1988), the new American law also mandated that song-owners should be compen-sated for the use of their music in all public places such as concert halls, dance halls, and restaurants. Though wide-sweeping in its coverage, the law provided no mechan-ism for collecting these royalties from the thousands of places where music was publicly performed. In 1914 a number of the new music writer–publishers banded together and formed ASCAP, a private membership company, to collect the royalties for public performance. As Ryan (1985) and Sanjek (1988) show in detail, ASCAP was not very successful in its early years, but by the 1930s it effectively controlled access to exposing new music to the public. It did this by, in effect, mandating that only ASCAP licenced music could be played in Broadway musicals, performed on the radio, and incorporated into movies. As late as 1950 an oligopoly of just eighteen publishers determined which songs could reach the public ear (Ryan 1985, p. 104).

These oligopolists shared an aesthetic which accented well-crafted, abstract love themes, strong melodies and muted jazz rhythms and harmonies. 'Tea For Two', 'Stardust' and 'Always' come to mind as exemplars of this aesthetic. But the point for our story is not whether they were good or bad, but that they and the innumerable less memorable songs like them were the only songs that Americans could hear through the dominant media of dissemination. The work of black musicians in the blues, jazz, r&b, and what later came to be called soul genres was systematically excluded, as were the songs in the developing Latin and country music traditions, as Ryan (1985) shows with numerous specific examples. The effect was that these forms could not reach a wide audience.

In 1939 the radio networks, in a dispute with ASCAP over the increased licencing fees ASCAP wanted to charge, formed a rival licencing agency, BMI. BMI offered inducements to ASCAP publishers and songwriters to defect. Few did, and so BMI signed numerous publishers and writers that had been excluded from membership in ASCAP. Many of these worked in the jazz, Latin, r&b and country music traditions. When in 1940 ASCAP failed to come to terms with the networks over the use-fees to be paid for music, all ASCAP-licenced songs were excluded from radio airplay, and BMI songs, and the genres that they represented, for the first time gained widespread public exposure (Ryan 1985). Even after ASCAP came to terms with the radio networks, the latter still welcomed BMI-licenced songs. Now for the first time it became possible to make a living as a songwriter or publisher in these alternative genera[3] that in fusing formed the foundations of the rock aesthetic. But rock did not break out in 1942. ASCAP came to terms with the networks, and all those with a vested interest in the older swing and crooner pop music worked hard to keep that aesthetic ascendant in the marketplace (Ryan 1985; Sanjek 1988). A number of other factors described below needed to change before rock could break out.

Patent Law

The application of patent law is another of those factors that influenced the timing of rock's emergence. From the inception of the industry before the turn of the twentieth century, the major phonograph record companies battled over alternative music recording and reproducing technologies in hopes of garnering the lion's share of the consumer market. By 1930 the 10-inch 78 rpm shellac disc had become the standard, but CBS and RCA laboratories experimented with the size of the disc, the distance between grooves, and the speed of the record in hopes of greatly increasing the amount of music that could be put on a record. While numerous advances were made, and patents registered, the long-playing record was not introduced in the 1930s because, it is said, the record industry was so depressed due to the Great Depression that consumers would not have paid the price for the new players and records (Metz 1975; Sanjek 1988).

Following the Second World War, Columbia records began intensive experimentation to develop a long-playing high-fidelity record. A newly-developed vinyl material was used for the discs because it held the musical fidelity better than the older shellac. In 1948 Columbia was ready to release its 12-inch, 33 1/3 rpm LP. Demonstrating its invention to arch-rival RCA, Columbia offered to share all information so an industry standard could be established. According to Metz (1975), General Sarnoff, long-time head of RCA was appalled that the much smaller firm had bested his research department. He refused the offer and ordered his engineers to quickly bring to market an alternative system for the high fidelity play of classical music. Their response was the 7-inch vinyl record with the large hole in the middle that played at 45 rpm.

The 'battle of the record speeds' went on for several years, by which time there were millions of record players on the market that were capable of playing both speeds, and 78s as well. The battle of the speeds was finally resolved when, through government mediation, the rivals agreed to pool their patents and produce records in both new formats. By 1952, the LP had become the medium for classical music and the 45 the format for popular single records for radio airplay, jukeboxes and retail sales (Sanjek 1988).

The 45 was important to the advent of rock primarily because it was (virtually) unbreakable. One of the great expenses of 78s was the extreme care that had to be taken in handling and shipping them, and each of the major record companies developed a national distribution system that was geared to handling its own delicate 78s. The small record companies could not afford the costs of the national distribution of 78s, and there being no independent distribution companies, it was virtually impossible for a small company in 1948 to have a national hit record. The smaller, lighter, virtually indestructible 45s made it much cheaper to ship records in bulk, making feasible the development of independent national distribution companies. As importantly for the promotion of new songs, it also made it practical for small record companies to use the mail service to send promotional copies to radio stations.

FCC Regulation

A number of local, state and federal government regulatory agencies arguably influenced the advent of rock, but the Federal Communications Commission (FCC) played a vital role. Among other things, the FCC regulates the number and allocation of broadcasting stations throughout the US. During the 1930s, when the interest in radios was growing rapidly and virtually every American home had a set, the FCC restricted the number of stations licenced to each market to three to five. This meant that each of the established networks, NBC (with its Red and Blue Networks), CBS and Mutual had an outlet, and there might be one independent station. A large number of applications for new stations were submitted, but these were denied or deferred 'in the public interest' because the networks lobbied successfully to maintain this small number of stations. When the War came, all requests were deferred. It was reasoned that scarce electronic material could not be spared from the war effort to build transmitters.

All this changed in 1947 when the FCC began to approve most of the backlog of applications, and, in a matter of just four years, the number of radio stations authorised to most markets doubled in number (Sterling and Haight 1978). Most of the new licences went to poorly capitalised independent stations. What did these stations use as programming? Most relied heavily on phonograph records. What kinds of records did they play? Ah, that gets us ahead of our story. What is the answer to the prior question, why did the networks withdraw their opposition to the granting of new broadcast licenses? To answer this question, it is useful to introduce the second major class of contraints, technology.

Technology

The development of the vinyl 45 rpm record, just discussed, was a major technological innovation important to the advent of rock music. Here we will note the importance of the advent of television and the development of the transistor radio receiver.

Television

Television, more than any other technological development, shaped the advent of rock music even though its influence was primarily indirect. Television began to be popular in the US in 1949. By 1955 65 per cent of all American households had a TV set (Sterling and Haight 1978) and the network programmes that had been the staple of network radio programming were transferred to television. Many experts, reasoning that no one would listen to a box when they could listen to a box that also showed moving pictures, thought that TV would completely replace radio. For this reason, the networks removed their objection to the licencing of many additional radio stations. For the same reason, radio network affiliates were put on the market in great numbers. A glut on the market, their price was further depressed by the fact that a spate of newly licenced AM radio stations were going on the air just at that time.[4] TV *programming* did have some direct effect on the advent of rock music in the 1954–6 period. . . .

The Transistor

Until the mid-1950s, radio receivers used a set of large, power-consuming, heat-generating, vacuum tubes. Their use dictated that sets would be large, heavy and expensive pieces of furniture. While most American homes had a radio, few had more than two. Auto radios were the exception, and portable radios were not common. These so-called 'portables' were relatively large, fragile and, because of the large batteries required, quite heavy.

American radio manufacturers intended to introduce transistors, a Bell Laboratories invention, as a prestige item in their top-of-the-line TV and phonograph consoles and put them into cheaper TVs, phonographs and radios only gradually in succeeding years. The Japanese upset this strategy by shipping to the US hundreds of thousands of cheap, lightweight, compact transistor radios that operated on small flashlight batteries. Quickly young Americans learned to take these extremely inexpensive sets to school, to the beach, to parties, to work – everywhere they went (Eisenberg 1986).

Industry Structure

To understand industry structure, one must consider both words: industry and structure. Defining the boundaries of the industry under consideration sounds simple but the process often raises issues of inclusion and exclusion that help reveal the structure. Our concern here is the popular music industry in the 1950s, but for present purposes the manufacture of musical instruments is not included. Live performance in bars, dance halls, concert halls and arenas while vital to building careers and promoting new records, is also peripheral to our concern. The empirical focus here is the popular music conveyed via the electronic media and via phonograph records. This brings into focus two sets of corporations that are conventionally identified as quite distinct industries, the manufacturers of phonograph records on the one hand and commercial radio stations on the other. The growing symbiotic relationship between phonograph record makers and commercial radio station owners was centrally important in the advent of rock music in the mid-1950s.

Industry structure can vary in several important ways: the degree of oligopoly, vertical integration and horizontal integration. Empirically, these three tend to go together but they can vary independently. Industry structure is oligopolistic when a few firms effectively control the style, amount and price of products produced. Perfect competition is when the actions of no firms significantly influence any of these factors. While an industry may vary from perfect competition to perfect oligopoly (that is monopoly), another structure is possible as well. This is an industry field in which there are a few firms that interact like an oligoply, but in which there is also a large number of small firms that survive and prosper by serving small special segments of the total potential market not served by the oligopolists. Such a dual industry structure became well established in the music industry in the years between 1948 and 1958 (Gillett 1983). Second, industry structure involves vertical integration, the degree to which all production processes from securing raw materials to retail sales are performed by single firms. Third, industry structure has to do with the degree to which firms in an industry produce products only for that industry, or alternatively are conglomerates linked financially and functionally to other industries, that is, the degree of horizontal integration (Hirsch 1972; Peterson 1985).

Radio Broadcasting, 1948

In the discussion that follows, and for much of the rest of the article, we will contrast the state of affairs in 1948, that is the time clearly before the advent of rock, with the state of affairs in 1958 after rock music had become well established. In 1948 the American radio industry consisted of four national networks and their affiliated stations in each of the radio markets around the country. In addition, there was a number of newly licensed independent commercial stations.

The networks competed with each other using what I call a 'slice strategy' which is characteristic in such conditions of oligopolistic competition. In such conditions, each network tried to increase the size of its slice of the total American radio audience. Programmes which drew large audiences to one of the networks stimulated the other networks to create similar programmes to capture back the lost 'market share'. In just a few seasons this strategy made for a daily and weekly cycle of programmes that was virtually the same from network to network. Thus, the weekly radio schedule of programmes on the air in 1948 looked not unlike the cycle of television broadcasting a decade or two later.

There was, however, more popular music played on radio in 1948 than on network television in 1958. On weekend evenings, each of the radio networks featured the major dance bands of the era broadcast *live* from one of the many large dance halls or elegant hotels around the country. The popular hits of the day were also played on the air by studio orchestras as part of the mix of the comedy and variety shows hosted by the likes of Bob Hope and Jack Benny. There was a programme called 'Your Hit Parade', that featured the top ten selling records of the week. But the *records* were not played! Rather, the studio band and its male or female singer, as appropriate, performed each of the songs in turn. Since the hit songs of 1948 were written, arranged and recorded by professionals to fit widely understood swing era conventions, it was easy for the studio band to faithfully reproduce the sound of the record. The early morning network 'wake-up' shows also had studio bands as did the homemaker shows that played around lunch time.

As far as I have been able to ascertain, there never was a national network programme in the 1940s that played phonograph records on the air. There were, however, several music programmes broadcast locally by network affiliates that *did* use phonograph records. Their form tells a great deal about the radio-programming aesthetic of the time. The most famous and most often copied was Martin Block's 'Make Believe Ballroom' that was first broadcast over New York's WNEW on 3 February 1935 (Sanjek 1988, p. 128). Through his introductions, sequencing of songs and even pseudo-interviews with band leaders, Block gave the programme the semblance of being broadcast live from a hotel ballroom.

The numerous independent radio stations that were being licensed at the time varied widely in their programming. We will focus here only on their music content. The better financed stations aired transcriptions which consisted of studio band concerts recorded on 16-inch metal-backed disks recorded and played back at 33 1/3 rpm. Again, they simulated live music performance. Many country music bands played live on independent radio stations in all parts of the country (Peterson and Gowan 1973, pp. 1–27). No blues or r&b bands, however, received this kind of exposure via live performance on the air. There were in 1948, however, several innovative radio programmes that played records intended for black buyers. At several radio stations in the South and Mid-West, small independent record companies simply bought thirty-minute segments of airtime and used it to play and promote their own records. Innovative record stores also bought airtime to play and promote such records on sale in their stores.[5]

The Record Industry, 1948

In 1948 (and the year following) the record industry was as concentrated as it had ever been and more concentrated than it has been at any time since. Four firms –

RCA, Columbia (CBS), Capitol and American Decca (MCA) – had released 81 per cent of all the records that reached the weekly top-ten hit list any time during the year. The top eight firms together released 95 per cent of all the hits and only three other firms had any hits at all! These figures, and the discussion that follows, are drawn from Peterson and Berger (1975) which presents a detailed analysis of how, in the late 1940s and early 1950s so few firms were able to control the market for recorded music so effectively, even though the basic product, a phonograph record, was cheap to record and manufacture.

Suffice it to say here that the leading firms maintained their predominance through combining both vertical integration in the record industry and horizontal integration with the film, radio, Broadway musical and film industries. The major record companies were able to maintain a dominant position by controlling three key points in the hit-making process. First, they garnered the services of creative people including songwriters and performers under long-term contracts investing a good deal of money promoting their name recognition. Second, they monopolised the channels of record distribution. As we have already noted, this was facilitated by the breakability of the 78 rpm shellac records of the time. Third, the major record companies maintained close ties with the people in network radio who decided what songs would be heard over the air. They were equally successful in controlling the songs that reached the public ear via Broadway musicals and movies.

Radio Broadcasting, 1958

Radio did not die with the advent of TV as the pessimists had predicted. In the years between 1948 and 1958, however, the radio broadcasting industry was totally transformed. In 1948 the radio industry had been a national medium broadcasting a small number of expensively produced nationally distributed programmes over four networks that vied with each other for a larger slice of the total national radio audience. By 1958 there were a large number of locally programmed radio stations in each city across the US. Thus, in effect, what had been one single national market with four contending networks, became upwards of one hundred autonomous local markets each with eight to a dozen or more radio stations competing with each other (Sterling and Haight 1978, p. 45).

Financed by national advertisers, the old radio networks had been able to afford expensive forms of programming: dramatic programmes, comedy shows and live music. Depending primarily on local advertisers in each city, however, radio stations could not afford such expensive programming (Sterling and Haight 1978, p. 124). In the search for an inexpensive yet appealing form of entertainment, and this is crucial for our story, stations in increasing numbers between 1950 and 1956 turned to playing phonograph records on the air.

Thus, in the span of just six years, the relationship between the radio and record industries was transformed. The two industries had been, or at least were thought to be, in direct competition. Ever since the 1920s when the two technologies emerged, it was reasoned that if people heard records played on the air, they would not purchase them for themselves. As he reached the height of his popularity, for example, Bing Crosby required Decca to stamp on each of his records, 'Not licenced for radio air play'. For their part, radio executives had disdained playing 'canned music'. Now, the two were inexorably bound together. Radio depended on the music industry for programming material, and record-makers, finding that radio airplay increased rather than depressed the demand for a record, quickly came to depend on radio to, in effect, advertise and promote their new releases.

As the numerous local stations competed with each other for listeners, they began to differentiate themselves by playing different kinds of records. Thus, the aesthetic range of records played on the air increased dramatically by the mid-1950s. We will examine this process in greater detail below.

The Record Industry, 1958

The greatly increased play of records on the air profoundly changed the record industry in the 1950s. Statistics show the picture very clearly. Record sales which had been in decline in 1948 and 1949 increased gradually from 1950 through 1954. Then every year for the rest of the decade sales grew rapidly so that the total value of records sold in 1959 was well over double what it had been in 1954.[6]

The major record companies, committed to the swing and crooner aesthetic, were slow to adapt to the changes that were taking place in radio and a large number of recently founded small record companies like Sun Records, Atlantic Records, Stax, King, Chess, Vee Jay, Dot, Coral, and Imperial provided the sorts of music that proved more popular. Thus they were able to successfully compete in the national popular music market (Gillett 1983). Again, the statistical figures show this in stark detail.

The four firms that had 81 per cent of the popular music hits in 1948 gradually lost market share until it reached 74 per cent in 1955. Then things changed rapidly. Their market share was down to 66 per cent in 1956 and sank rapidly over the next few years reaching just 34 per cent by 1959! In 1948 just fifty-seven songs were hits, these were produced by eleven firms, and five of these firms had just one hit. In 1949, there were ninety-two hits that were produced by forty-two record companies, and of these, twenty-nine of these firms had just one hit. In a word, an industry that had been dominated by an oligopoly of four firms rapidly became an industry in which a large number of small firms were able to compete on even terms with the majors. The crucial reason was that, to attract larger numbers of listeners, radio stations sought out attention-catching records irrespective of their source.

The two other factors that had helped ensure the hegemony of the major companies changed as well. The majors no longer had a corner on the creative talent. On the contrary, it was the small companies that developed the rock performers and writers while the majors resisted the changing aesthetic or, as in the case of Elvis Presley, bought the contracts of rock performers only after they had proven successful on one of the new small record labels (Gillett 1983). In addition, the majors no longer controlled the national distribution of records. While only a few of the new companies had their own systems of distribution, several national independent distribution companies were formed who were willing to distribute records for anyone willing to pay the fee.

Organisation Structure

Organisation structure has three dimensions. The first is the number of decision levels in the organisation. The more levels there are, the greater is the bureaucracy, and the lower the ability to adapt to changes coming from the environment. Large organisations tend to have more levels but not necessarily (Peterson and Berger 1971). The second dimension of organisation structure is functional differentiation, the degree to which tasks are performed by specialised departments. A record company, for example, might have separate departments for songwriters, performers, producers, studio technicians and promotion. RCA and Columbia were organised this way in 1948. Alternatively, a firm might have several independent divisions each with its own groups of such specialists working together on related musical projects that are released under a distinctive divisional label. Warner Brothers Records in the 1970s and 1980s exemplified this pattern. The third dimension of organisation structure mirrors vertical integration for industry structure. At the firm level, the question is to what degree all stages in the production, promotion and distribution process are performed 'in-house' by divisions of the company or, alternatively, are performed by a series of firms that specialise in just one aspect or stage of the process. Such specialty firms are called 'job-shops' because they contract with a number of different clients on a job-to-job basis. In the 1950s another form of organisation emerged which I call 'solo production'. Here all the creative stages are performed in-house but they are performed by or under the direct supervision of a single individual. A number of the most innovative producers of the early rock era worked in this way, but perhaps the best contemporary exemplar of solo production is Prince and his Paisley Park production company. In 1948 all of the major record companies had their own recording studios and contractually required their artists to record in-house. By 1980 the majors had sold almost all of their own studios allowing their artists to record in independent job-shop studios or as solo producers.

Radio Stations

In 1948 there were two quite different sorts of network-affiliated stations. There were the three or four stations of each network where the dramatic, comedy, variety, and soap opera programmes were created. Virtually all the network programming was created at these production stations located in New York, Chicago, Los Angeles and Nashville. Each major programme had its own staff of actors, singers, script writers, joke-writers, and other creative personnel. A staff band would play on several different programmes. Technicians were organised by function and jealously protected their job rights from each other. For example, by labour union contract it was illegal for anyone but a union engineer to touch the studio control board or phonograph record turntables. Finance, sales and promotion, as well as transmission engineering, were separate departments. The total staff at each of these production stations numbered well over a hundred and in New York approached a thousand.

The rest of the network-affiliated stations in 1948 were organised quite differently. They acted primarily as the local transmitters of network-fed programming. There was some local news, agricultural reports and sports broadcasting, but to keep their network status, stations had to air virtually all the programming that was supplied. The staff consisted of several engineers, several announcers and a small advertising staff that worked to get local advertisers for the locally generated programmes and for the local advertising spots built into some of the network programming. Dependent as they were on network programming, there was little scope for creativity by the local affiliate stations.

In 1958 radio station structure was totally different. The network production stations simply did not exist. Most of their creative and technical personnel had not been fired; rather, they were transferred to the network's television affiliate and continued to do their work, much as before. By 1948, radio stations had few levels of authority and many fewer specialised departments and jobs. Typically, the staff consisted of several engineers who kept the equipment running, a small marketing staff that worked to get local merchants to buy advertisements, and a group of djs. The djs (except at the biggest and most traditional stations) cued and played records themselves while keeping up a banter that included comments about community and school events, forthcoming rock concerts, advertisements and brief segments of news and weather. Network affiliates and independent stations were much alike except that at the former the national news was fed from New York as were several Programmes including major sports events, and the New York Metropolitan Opera Programmes on Saturday afternoons (Roult *et al.* 1978).

Phonograph Record Firms

The oligopolistic record companies of 1948 were bureaucratically organised with both a large number of levels in the hierarchy of authority and numerous function-ally differentiated and vertically integrated departments. This is a form of organisa-tion well suited to efficiently producing a large number of standard products. Given their collective control of entry into the popular music market, the major record firms were able to operate profitably by crafting the kind of music that could be produced by such a bureaucratic machine.

By 1958 a large number of small companies operating on a mix of job-shop and solo-production had successfully entered the market. They survived by using every means, legal and illegal, to get their records played on the air and then get copies of the records distributed to record stores quickly and in sufficient numbers. Most of the independents that survived more than two or three years and moved up in the ranks of record firms did so by crafting a sound that could be identified with the company. Motown, Stax and A&M are good examples of companies that grew in market share rivalling for a time the major companies by creating a distinctive sound.

The established major companies lost three-quarters of the market share, as noted above, but did not disappear. Rather they adapted to the new conditions. By the 1970s the majors had regained much of their prior market share, by, in effect, becoming financing and distribution companies for a series of divisions that were allowed to operate as independent small firms (Peterson and Berger 1971; Denisoff 1973). By 1958, however, this major structural reorganisation had not yet begun. Instead, the majors were attacking rock and its creators in the press, and in the courts, believing that it was an artificially induced fad that would soon fade away if they could just gain control, once more, of the music played on the radio (Chapple and Garofalo 1977)....

This article has focused on a unique event, the advent of rock at a particular historical moment. Nonetheless, as I have shown elsewhere (Peterson 1967; 1972), the advent of jazz following the First World War was sudden, and like the great change in country music in the 1970s (Peterson and DiMaggio 1975) involved many of the same processes found to be important here. This suggests that an analysis of the role of ... 'constraints' on the production of culture together with the influence of creators and audiences might be useful in understanding the dynamics of other facets of music and the culture industry more generally.

Notes

1 The word 'rock' or 'rock music' will be used to refer to all forms of the music including its 1950s pre-Beatles forms that are often designated 'rock'n'roll' and 'rockabilly'.
2 There is disagreement among the historians of rock over dating its nascence, but all agree that it emerged as a major force on the commercial popular culture scene in 1954. See Gillett 1983; Denisoff 1973; Chapple and Garofalo 1977; Marcus 1976; Hendler 1983; Curtis 1987; Shaw 1987.
3 For an exquisite case study of how the advent of BMI fostered country music song writing, see Rumble (1980).
4 Large numbers of FM-band radios stations were also being licenced in this period further adding to the confusion over the future of radio broadcasting. FM did not influence the development of rock music, however, until the latter part of the 1960s when FM gave impetus to the development of 'underground rock' (Denisoff 1973; Chapple and Garofalo 1977).
5 Personal interviews with Randy Wood, John R. and R. Murphy Nash.
6 These figures, and all the others cited in this section, unless otherwise noted, are drawn from Peterson and Berger (1975).

References

Chapple, Steve and Garofalo, Reebee. 1997. *Rock'n' Roll is Here to Pay: the History and Politics of the Music Industry* (Chicago).
Curtis, Jim. 1987. *Rock Eras: Interpretations of Music and Society* (Bowling Green, OH).
Denisoff, R. 1973. *Solid Gold: The Popular Record Industry* (New Brunswick, NJ).
Eisenberg. Evan. 1986. *The Recording Angel: the Experience of Music from Aristotle to Zappa* (New York).
Frith, Simon. 1981. *Sound Effects: Youth, Leisure and the Politics of Rock'n' Roll (New York).*
——. 1984. *The Sociology of Youth* (Bodmin Cornwall).
——. 1988. 'Copyright and the music business', *Popular Music*, 7, pp. 57–76.
Gillett, Charlie. 1983. *The Sound of the City*. Rev. edn. (London).
Hendler, Herb. 1983. *Year by Year in the Rock Era: Events and Conditions Shaping the Rock Generations that Reshaped America* (Westport, CT).
Hirsch, Paul H. 1972. 'Processing fads and fashions: an organization-set analysis of cultural industry systems', *American Journal of Sociology*, 77, pp. 639–59.

Kadushin, Charles. 1976 'Networks and circles in the production of culture' in *The Production of Culture*, ed, Richard A. Peterson (Beverly Hills, CA), pp. 107–22.

Marcus, Greil. 1976. *Mystery Train: Images of America in Rock'n'Roll Music* (New York).

Metz, Robert. 1975. *CBS: Reflections in a Bloodshot Eye* (New York).

Peterson, Richard A. 1967. 'Market and moralist censors of a rising art form: jazz', *Arts in Society*, 4, pp. 253–64.

——. 1972. 'A process model of the folk, pop, and fine art phases of jazz', in *American Music: From Storyville to Woodstock*, ed. Charles Nanry (New Brunswick, NJ), pp. 135–51.

——. 1976. 'The production of culture: prolegomenon', *American Behavioral Scientist*, 19, pp. 669–84.

——. 1979. 'Revitalizing the culture concept', *Annual Review of Sociology*, 5, pp. 137–66.

——. 1985. 'Six constraints on the production of literary works', *Poetics: International Review for the Theory of Literature*, 14, pp. 45–67.

Peterson, Richard A. and Berger, David C. 1971. 'Entrepreneurship in organizations: evidence from the popular music industry', *Administrative Science Quarterly*, 16, pp. 97–107.

——. 1975. 'Cycles in symbol production: the case of popular music', *American Sociological Review*, 40, pp. 158–73.

Peterson, Richard A. and Davis Jr, Russell B. 1974. 'The contemporary American radio audience', *Journal of Popular Music and Society*, 3, pp. 299–313.

Peterson, Richard A. and DiMaggio, Paul. 1975. 'From region to class, the changing locus of country music: a test of the massification hypothesis'. *Social Forces*, 53, pp. 497–506.

Peterson, Richard A. and Gowan, Mark. 1973. 'The unnatural history of rock festivals: an instance of media facilitation', *Journal of Popular Music and Society*, 2, pp. 1–27.

Ploman, E. W. and Hamilton, L. Clark. 1980. *Copyright: Intellectual Property in the Information Age* (London).

Roult, Edd., McGrath, James B. and Weiss, Fredric A. 1978. *The Radio Format Conundrum* (New York).

Rumble, John. 1980. 'Fred Rose and the Development of Publishing in Nashville', unpublished PhD dissertation, Vanderbilt University.

Ryan, John. 1985. *The Production of Culture in the Music Industry: the ASCAP-BMI Controversy* (Lanham, MD).

Sanjek, Russell. 1988. *American Popular Music and its Business*. Vol. 3. *From 1900 to 1984* (New York).

Shaw, Arnold. 1987. *The Rockin' 50s* (New York).

Sterling, Christopher H. and Haight, Timothy R. 1978. *The Mass Media: Aspen Institute Guide to Communication Industry Trends* (New York).

Wright, John W. 1986. 'Radio and the foundation of American broadcasting' in *American Mass Media: Industries and Issues*, ed. Robert Atwan (New York), pp. 236–46.

Editor's Notes on Further Reading

Peterson on Musical Change and the Culture Industry

Explanations of changes in popular music styles usually focus on changes in the audience, affecting demand, or on changes among creators and performers themselves. Peterson challenges such explanations of musical change from a "production-of-culture" perspective in his carefully focused analysis of how and why rock music attained its sudden popularity in the 1950s. Important but unrecognized "supply-side" factors like regulations, technology, industry structure, organization structure, and (not included here) types of occupational careers prompted the emergence of rock and roll as the new basis of pop music.

For related work on this topic see for example Simon Frith, "The Industrialization of Popular Music," pp. 49–74 in James Lull, ed., *Popular Music and Communication*, 2nd edn. (Newbury Park, CA: Sage, 1992); Richard Peterson and David Berger, "Cycles in Symbol Production: The Case of Popular Music," *American Sociological Review* 40 (1975): 158–73; John Ryan and Richard Peterson, "The Product Image: the Fate of Creativity in Country Music Songwriting," *Annual Reviews of Communication Research* 10 (1982): 11–32; John Ryan, *The Production of Culture in the Music Industry: The ASCAP–BMI Controversy* (New York: University Press of America, 1985); Samuel Gilmore, "Coordination and Convention: The Organization of the Concert World," *Symbolic Interaction* 10 (1987): 209–28; Timothy Jon Dowd, "The Musical Structure and Social Context of Number One Songs, 1955 to 1988: An Exploratory Analysis," pp. 130–57 in Robert Wuthnow, ed., *Vocabularies of Public Life: Empirical Essays in Symbolic Structure* (London and New York: Routledge, 1992); Paul Lopes, "Innovation and Diversity in the Popular Music Industry, 1969–1990," *American Sociological Review* 57 (1992): 56–71; and Richard Peterson, *Creating Country Music: Fabricating Authenticity* (Chicago: University of Chicago Press, 1997). See also the articles collected in *Poetics* 28 (2–3) 2000, "The Production and Consumption of Culture: Essays on Richard A. Peterson's Contributions to Cultural Sociology," John Ryan and Michael Hughes, eds. For a different application of the same framework see Richard Peterson, "Six Constraints on the Production of Literary Works," *Poetics* 14 (1985): 45–67. For more on these factors and other discussions of cultural production see the notes to the preceding selection by Paul DiMaggio and the other editor's notes in Part III. For studies of music and group identity see the editor's note to the excerpt from work by Bryson.

Peterson's article shows that the production-of-culture perspective provides a framework for understanding social change and cultural innovation. For general discussion of larger-scale cultural innovation see Part V, this volume.

17 Art Worlds

Howard S. Becker

It was my practice to be at my table every morning at 5:30 a.m.; and it was also my practice to allow myself no mercy. An old groom, whose business it was to call me, and to whom I paid £5 a year extra for the duty, allowed himself no mercy. During all those years at Waltham Cross he was never once late with the coffee which it was his duty to bring me. I do not know that I ought not to feel that I owe more to him than to any one else for the success I have had. By beginning at that hour I could complete my literary work before I dressed for breakfast.

Anthony Trollope, 1947 [1883], p. 227

The English novelist may have told the story facetiously, but being awakened and given coffee was nevertheless integral to the way he worked. No doubt he could have done without the coffee if he had to; but he didn't have to. No doubt anyone could have performed that service; but, given the way Trollope worked, it had to be performed.

All artistic work, like all human activity, involves the joint activity of a number, often a large number, of people. Through their cooperation, the art work we eventually see or hear comes to be and continues to be. The work always shows signs of that cooperation. The forms of cooperation may be ephemeral, but often become more or less routine, producing patterns of collective activity we can call an art world. The existence of art worlds, as well as the way their existence affects both the production and consumption of art works, suggests a sociological approach to the arts. It is not an approach that produces aesthetic judgments, although that is a task many sociologists of art have set for themselves. It produces, instead, an understanding of the complexity of the cooperative networks through which art happens, of the way the activities of both Trollope and his groom meshed with those of printers, publishers, critics, librarians, and readers in the world of Victorian literature, and of the similar networks and results involved in all the arts....

Cooperative Links

Whatever the artist, defined as the person who performs the core activity without which the work would not be art, does not do must be done by someone else. The artist thus works in the center of a network of cooperating people, all of whose work is essential to the final outcome. Wherever he depends on others, a cooperative link exists. The people with whom he cooperates may share in every particular his idea of how their work is to be done. This consensus is likely when everyone involved can perform any of the necessary activities so that, while a division of labor exists, no specialized functional groups develop. This might occur in simple communally shared art forms like the square dance or in segments of a society whose ordinary members are trained in artistic activities. Well-bred nineteenth-century Americans, for instance, knew enough music to perform the parlor songs of Stephen Foster, just as their Renaissance counterparts could perform madrigals. In such cases, cooperation occurs simply and readily.

When specialized professional groups take over the performance of the activities necessary to an art work's production, however, their members develop specialized aesthetic, financial, and career interests which differ substantially from the artist's. . . .

Aesthetic conflicts between support personnel and the artist also occur. A sculptor I know was invited to use the services of a group of master lithographic printers. Knowing little of the technique of lithography, he was glad to have these master craftsmen do the actual printing, this division of labor being customary and having generated a highly specialized craft of printing. He drew designs containing large areas of solid colors, thinking to simplify the printer's job. Instead, he made it more difficult. When the printer rolls ink onto the stone, a large area will require more than one rolling to be fully inked and may thus exhibit roller marks. The printers, who prided themselves on their craft, explained that they could print his designs, but the areas of solid color might cause difficulty with roller marks. He had not known about roller marks and talked of using them as part of his design. The printers said no, he could not do that, because roller marks were an obvious sign (to other printers) of poor craftsmanship and they would not allow a print exhibiting roller marks to leave their shop. His artistic curiosity fell victim to the printers' craft standards, a neat example of how specialized support groups develop their own standards and interests (see Kase, 1973).

The artist was at the printers' mercy because he did not know how to print lithographs himself. His experience exemplified the choice that faces the artist at every cooperative link. He can do things as established groups of support personnel are prepared to do them; he can try to make those people do it his way; he can train others to do it his way; or he can do it himself. Any choice but the first requires an additional investment of time and energy to do what could be done less expensively if done the standard way. The artist's involvement with and dependence on cooperative links thus constrains the kind of art he can produce. . . .

Artists often create work which existing production or exhibition facilities cannot accommodate. Try this thought experiment. Imagine that, as curator of sculpture of an art museum, you have invited a distinguished sculptor to exhibit a new work. He arrives driving a flatbed truck, on which rests a giant construction combining several pieces of large, heavy, industrial machinery into an interesting and pleasing shape. You find it moving, exciting. You ask him to take it around to the museum loading dock where the two of you discover that the door on the dock will not admit anything taller than fifteen feet; the sculpture is much larger than that. The sculptor suggests removing the wall, but by now you have realized that, even if you got it into the museum, it would fall through the floor into the basement; it is a museum, not a factory, and the building will not support so much weight. Finally, disgruntled, he takes it away. . . .

How do nonstandard works ever get exhibited, performed, or distributed? . . . [T]here often exist subsidiary, nonstandard distribution channels and adventurous entrepreneurs and audiences. The former provide methods of distribution, the latter take a chance on the result. Schools often provide such an opportunity. They have space and more-or-less free personnel in their students, and thus can muster forces more commercial presentations could not afford: real crowds for crowd scenes, outlandish assortments of instrumentalists and vocalists for musical experiments.

More artists adapt to what existing institutions can handle. By accommodating their conceptions to available resources, conventional artists accept the constraints arising from their dependence on the cooperation of members of the existing cooperative network. Wherever artists depend on others for some necessary component, they must either accept the constraints they impose or expend the time and energy necessary to provide it some other way.

Conventions

Producing art works requires elaborate cooperation among specialized personnel. How do they arrive at the terms on which they cooperate? They could, of course, decide everything afresh on each occasion. A group of musicians could discuss and agree on which sounds would be used as tonal resources, what instruments might be constructed to make those sounds, how those sounds would be combined to create a musical language, how the language would be used to create works of a particular length requiring a given number of instruments and playable for audiences of a certain size recruited in a certain way. Something like that sometimes happens, for instance, in the creation of a new theatrical group, although in most cases only a small number of the questions to be decided are actually considered anew.

People who cooperate to produce a work of art usually do not decide things afresh. Instead, they rely on earlier agreements now become customary, agreements that have become part of the conventional way of doing things in that art. Artistic conventions cover all the decisions that must be made with respect to works produced, even though a particular convention may be revised for a given work. Conventions dictate the materials to be used, as when musicians agree to base their music on the notes contained in a set of modes, or on the diatonic, pentatonic, or chromatic scales, with their associated harmonies. Conventions dictate the abstractions to be used to convey particular ideas or experiences, as when painters use the laws of perspective to convey the illusion of three dimensions or photographers use black, white, and shades of gray to convey the interplay of light and mass. Conventions dictate the form in which materials and abstractions will be combined, as in music's sonata form or poetry's sonnet. Conventions suggest the appropriate dimensions of a work, the proper length of a performance, the proper size and shape of a painting or sculpture. Conventions regulate the relations between artists and audience, specifying the rights and obligations of both.

Humanistic scholars – art historians, musicologists, and literary critics – have found the concept of the artistic convention useful in explaining artists' ability to make art works which evoke an emotional response in audiences. By using such a conventional organization of tones as a scale, composers can create and manipulate listeners' expectations as to what sounds will follow. They can then delay and frustrate the satisfaction of those expectations, generating tension and release as the expectation is ultimately satisfied (Meyer, 1956, 1973; Cooper and Meyer, 1960). Only because artist and audience share knowledge of and experience with the conventions invoked does the art work produce an emotional effect. Barbara H. Smith (1968) has shown how poets manipulate conventional means embodied in poetic forms and diction to bring poems to a clear and satisfying conclusion, in which the expectations produced early in the lyric are simultaneously and satisfactorily resolved. E. H. Gombrich (1960) has analyzed the visual conventions artists use to create for viewers the illusion that they are seeing a realistic depiction of some aspect of the world. In all these cases (and in others like stage design, dance, and film), the possibility of artistic experience arises from the existence of a body of conventions that artists and audiences can refer to in making sense of the work.

Conventions make art possible in another sense. Because decisions can be made quickly, plans made simply by referring to a conventional way of doing things, artists can devote more time to actual work. Conventions make possible the easy and efficient coordination of activity among artists and support personnel. William Ivins (1953), for instance, shows how, by using a conventionalized scheme for rendering shadows, modeling, and other effects, several graphic artists could collaborate to produce a single plate. The same conventions make it possible for viewers to read essentially arbitrary marks as shadows and modeling. Seen this way, the concept of convention provides a point of contact between humanists and sociologists, being interchangeable with such familiar sociological ideas as norm, rule, shared understanding, custom, or folkway, all referring to the ideas and understandings people hold in common and through which they effect cooperative activity. Burlesque comedians could stage elaborate three-man skits without rehearsal because they had only to refer to a conventional body of skits they all knew, pick one, and assign the parts. Dance musicians who are total strangers can play all night with no more prearrangement than to mention a title ("Sunny Side of the Street," in C) and count off four beats to give the tempo; the title indicates a melody, its accompanying harmony, and perhaps even customary background figures. The conventions of character and dramatic structure, in the one case, and of melody, harmony, and tempo, in the other, are familiar enough that audiences have no difficulty responding appropriately.

Though standardized, conventions are seldom rigid and unchanging. They do not specify an inviolate set of rules everyone must refer to in settling questions of what to do. Even where the directions seem quite specific, they leave much to be resolved by reference to customary modes of interpretation on the one hand and by negotiation on the other. A tradition of performance practice, often codified in book form, tells performers how to interpret the musical scores or dramatic scripts they perform. Seventeenth century scores, for instance, contained relatively little information; but contemporary books explained how to deal with questions, unanswered in the score, of instrumentation, note values, extemporization, and the realization of embellishments and ornaments. Performers read their music in the light of all these customary styles of interpretation and could thus coordinate their activities (Dart, 1967). The same thing occurs in the visual arts. Much of the content, symbolism, and coloring of Italian Renaissance religious painting was conventionally given; but a multitude of decisions remained for the artist, so that even within those strict conventions different works could be produced. Adhering to the conventional materials, however, allowed viewers to read much emotion and meaning into the picture. Even where customary interpretations of conventions exist, having become conventions themselves, artists can agree to do things differently, negotiation making change possible.

Conventions place strong constraints on the artist. They are particularly constraining because they do not exist in isolation, but come in complexly interdependent systems, so that one small change may require a variety of other changes. A system of conventions gets embodied in equipment, materials, training, available facilities and sites, systems of notation, and the like, all of which must be changed if any one component is (cf. Danto, 1980).

Consider what changing from the conventional Western chromatic musical scale of twelve tones to one including forty-two tones between the octaves entails. Such a change characterizes the compositions of Harry Partch (1949). Western musical instruments cannot produce these microtones easily, and some cannot produce them at all, so conventional instruments must be reconstructed or new instruments must be invented and built. Since the instruments are new, no one knows how to play them, and players must train themselves. Conventional Western notation is inadequate to score forty-two-tone music, so a new notation must be devised, and players must learn to read it. (Comparable resources can be taken for granted by anyone who writes for the conventional twelve chromatic tones.) Consequently, while music scored for twelve tones can be performed adequately after relatively few hours of rehearsal, forty-two-tone music requires much more work, time, effort, and resources. Partch's music was often performed in the following way: a university would invite him to spend a year. In the fall, he would recruit a group of interested students, who would build the instruments (which he had already invented) under his direction. In the winter, they would learn to play the instruments and read the notation he had devised. In the spring, they would rehearse several works and finally would give a performance. Seven or eight months of work finally would result in two hours of music, hours which could have been filled with more conventional music after eight or ten hours of rehearsal by trained symphonic musicians playing the standard repertoire. The difference in the resources required measures the strength of the constraint imposed by the conventional system.

Similarly, conventions specifying what a good photograph should look like embody not only an aesthetic more or less accepted among the people involved in the making of art photographs (Rosenblum, 1978), but also the constraints built into the standardized equipment and materials made by major manufacturers. Available lenses, camera bodies, shutter speeds, apertures, films, and printing paper all constitute a tiny fraction of the things that could be made, a selection that can be used together to produce acceptable prints; with ingenuity they can also be used to produce effects their purveyors did not have in mind. The obverse of the constraint is the standardization and dependability of mass-produced materials that photographers prize; a roll of Kodak Tri-X film purchased anywhere in the world has approximately the same characteristics and will produce the same results as any other roll.

The limitations of conventional practice are not total. You can always do things differently if you are prepared to pay the price in increased effort or decreased circulation of your work. The experience of composer Charles Ives exemplifies the latter possibility. He experimented with polytonality and polyrhythms early in the 1900s before they became part of the ordinary performer's competence. The New

York players who tried to play his chamber and orchestral music told him that it was unplayable, that their instruments could not make those sounds, that the scores could not be played in any practical way. Ives finally accepted their judgment, but continued to compose such music. What makes his case interesting is that, though he was also bitter about it, he experienced this as a great liberation (Cowell and Cowell, 1954). If no one could play his music, then he no longer had to write what musicians could play, no longer had to accept the constraints imposed by the conventions that regulated cooperation between contemporary composer and player. Since his music would not be played, he never needed to finish it; he was unwilling to confirm John Kirkpatrick's pioneer reading of the *Concord Sonata* as a correct one because that would mean he could no longer change it. Nor did he have to accommodate his writing to the practical constraints of what could be financed by conventional means, and so wrote his *Fourth Symphony* for three orchestras. (That impracticality lessened with time; Leonard Bernstein premiered the work in 1958, and it has been played many times since.)

In general, breaking with existing conventions and their manifestations in social structure and material artifacts increases artists' trouble and decreases the circulation of their work, but at the same time increases their freedom to choose unconventional alternatives and to depart substantially from customary practice. If that is true, we can understand any work as the product of a choice between conventional ease and success and unconventional trouble and lack of recognition.

Art Worlds

Art worlds consist of all the people whose activities are necessary to the production of the characteristic works which that world, and perhaps others as well, define as art. Members of art worlds coordinate the activities by which work is produced by referring to a body of conventional understandings embodied in common practice and in frequently used artifacts. The same people often cooperate repeatedly, even routinely, in similar ways to produce similar works, so that we can think of an art world as an established network of cooperative links among participants. If the same people do not actually act together in every instance, their replacements are also familiar with and proficient in the use of those conventions, so that cooperation can proceed without difficulty. Conventions make collective activity simpler and less costly in time, energy, and other resources; but they do not make unconventional work impossible, only more costly and difficult. Change can and does occur whenever someone devises a way to gather the greater resources required or reconceptualizes the work so it does not require what is not available.

Works of art, from this point of view, are not the products of individual makers, "artists" who possess a rare and special gift. They are, rather, joint products of all the people who cooperate via an art world's characteristic conventions to bring works like that into existence. Artists are some subgroup of the world's participants who, by common agreement, possess a special gift, therefore make a unique and indispensable contribution to the work, and thereby make it art.

Art worlds do not have boundaries around them, so that we can say that these people belong to a particular art world while those people do not. I am not concerned with drawing a line separating an art world from other parts of a society. Instead, we look for groups of people who cooperate to produce things that they, at least, call art; having found them, we look for other people who are also necessary to that production, gradually building up as complete a picture as we can of the entire cooperating network that radiates out from the work in question. The world exists in the cooperative activity of those people, not as a structure or organization, and we use words like those only as shorthand for the notion of networks of people cooperating. For practical purposes, we usually recognize that many people's cooperation is so peripheral and relatively unimportant that we need not consider it, keeping in mind that such things change and what was unimportant today may be crucial tomorrow when events suddenly have made that kind of cooperation difficult to obtain.

Art worlds do not have clear boundaries in another sense. To the sociologist studying art worlds, it is as clear as, but no clearer than, it is to the participants in them whether particular objects or events are "really art" or whether they are craft or commercial work, or perhaps the expression of folk culture, or maybe just the embodied symptoms of a lunatic. Sociologists, however, can solve this problem more easily than art world participants. One important facet of a sociological analysis of any social world is to see when, where, and how participants draw the lines that distinguish what they want to be taken as characteristic from what is not to be so taken. Art worlds typically devote considerable attention to trying to decide what is and isn't art, what is and isn't their kind of art, and who is and isn't an artist; by observing how an art world makes those distinctions rather than trying to make them ourselves we can understand much of what goes on in that world. (See Christopherson, 1974a and b, for an example of this process in art photography.)

In addition, art worlds typically have intimate and extensive relations with the worlds from which they try to distinguish themselves. They share sources of supply with those other worlds, recruit personnel from them, adopt ideas that originate in them, and compete with them for audiences and financial support. In some sense, art worlds and worlds of commercial, craft, and folk art are parts of a larger social organization. So, even though everyone involved understands and respects the distinctions which keep them separate, a sociological analysis should take account of how they are not so separate after all.

Furthermore, art worlds provoke some of their members to create innovations they then will not accept. Some of these innovations develop small worlds of their own; some remain dormant and then find acceptance from a larger art world years or generations later; some remain magnificent curiosities of little more than antiquarian interest. These fates reflect both the judgments of artistic quality made by contemporary art worlds and the perhaps chance operations of a variety of other factors.

The basic unit of analysis, then, is an art world. Both the "artness" and the "worldness" are problematic, because the work that furnishes the starting point for the investigation may be produced in a variety of cooperating networks and under a variety of definitions. Some networks are large, complicated, and specifically devoted to the production of works of the kind we are investigating as their main activity. Smaller ones may have only a few of the specialized personnel characteristic of the larger, more elaborate ones. In the limiting case, the world consists only of the person making the work, who relies on materials and other resources provided by others who neither intend to cooperate in the production of that work nor know they are doing so. Typewriter manufacturers participate in the small worlds of many would-be novelists who have no connection with the more conventionally defined literary world.

In the same way, the cooperative activity may be carried on either in the name of art or under some other definition, even though in the latter case the products might seem to us to resemble those made as art. Because "art" is an honorific title and being able to call what you do by that name has some advantages, people often want what they do to be so labeled. Just as often, people do not care whether what they do is art or not (as in the case of many household or folk arts – cake decorating, embroidery, or folk dancing, for instance) and find it neither demeaning nor inter-esting that their activities are not recognized as art by people who do care about such things. Some members of a society can control the application of the honorific term *art*, so not everyone is in a position to have the advantages associated with it, if he wants them.

For all these reasons, it is not clear what to include in an analysis of art worlds and what to leave out. To limit the analysis to what a society currently defines as art leaves out too much that is interesting: all the marginal cases in which people seek but are denied the name, as well as those in which people do work that outside observers can see might meet the definition but whose makers are not interested in that possibility. That would allow the process of definition by members of the society, which ought properly to be the subject of our study, to set its terms. On the other hand, to study everything that might meet a society's definition of art includes too much. Almost anything might meet such a definition, if we applied it ingeniously enough. . . .

Though art worlds do not have sharp boundaries, they do vary in the degree to which they are independent, operating in relative freedom from interference by other organized groups in their society. Put another way, the people who cooperate in the work being studied may be free to organize their activity in the name of art, as is the case in many contemporary Western societies, whether they make use of that possibility or not. They may, however, find that they must take into account other interests represented by groups organized around other definitions. The state may exercise such control over other areas of society that major participants in the making of art works orient themselves primarily to the concerns of the state apparatus rather than to the concerns of people who define themselves as interested in art. Theocratic societies may organize the making of what we, from the perspec-tive of our society, would recognize as works of art as an adjunct of activity defined in religious terms. In frontier societies subsistence may be so problematic that activities which do not contribute directly to the production of food or other necessities may be seen as unaffordable luxuries, so that work we might define, from a contemporary vantage point, as art gets done in the name of household necessity. What cannot be justified that way is not done. Before people can organize themselves as a world explicitly justified by making objects or events defined as art, they need sufficient political and economic freedom to do that, and not all societies provide it.

This point needs emphasis, because so many writers on what is ordinarily described as the sociology of art treat art as relatively autonomous, free from the kinds of organizational constraints that surround other forms of collective activity. I have not considered those theories here because they deal essentially with philosophical questions quite different from the mundane social organizational problems with which I have concerned myself (see Donow, 1979). Insofar as what I have to say questions the assumption of freedom from economic, political, and organizational constraint, it necessarily implies a criticism of analytic styles based on it.

Art worlds produce works and also give them aesthetic value.... [T]he interaction of all the involved parties produces a shared sense of the worth of what they collectively produce. Their mutual appreciation of the conventions they share, and the support they mutually afford one another, convince them that what they are doing is worth doing. If they act under the definition of "art," their interaction convinces them that what they produce are valid works of art.

References

Bucher, Rue. "Pathology: A Study of Social Movements within a Profession." *Social Problems* 10 (Summer 1962): 40–51.

Christopherson, Richard. "Making Art with Machines: Photography's Institutional Inadequacies." *Urban Life and Culture* 3 (1974a): 3–34.

——. "From Folk Art to Fine Art: A Transformation in the Meaning of Photographic Work." *Urban Life and Culture* 3 (1974b): 123–57.

Cooper, Grosvenor, and Meyer, Leonard B. *The Rhythmic Structure of Music*. Chicago: University of Chicago Press, 1960.

Cowell, Henry, and Cowell, Sidney. *Charles Ives and His Music*. New York: Oxford University Press, 1954.

Danto, Arthur C. "Munakata in New York: A Memory of the '50s." *The Print Collector's Newsletter* 10 (January–February, 1980): 184–9.

Dart, Thurston. *The Interpretation of Music*. 4th ed. London: Hutchinson, 1967.

Donow, Kenneth. "The Structure of Art: A Sociological Analysis." Ph.D. dissertation, University of California, San Diego, 1979.

Gombrich, E. H. *Art and Illusion: A Study in the Psychology of Pictorial Representation*. Princeton: Princeton University Press, 1960.

Ivins, William, Jr. *Prints and Visual Communication*. Cambridge: MIT Press, 1953.

Kase, Thelma. "The Artist, the Printer and the Publisher." M.A. thesis, University of Missouri, Kansas City, 1973.

Mead, George Herbert. *Mind, Self and Society*. Chicago: University of Chicago Press, 1934.

Meyer, Leonard B. *Emotion and Meaning in Music*. Chicago: University of Chicago Press, 1956.

——. *Explaining Music: Essays and Explorations*. Berkeley and Los Angeles: University of California Press, 1973.

Partch, Harry. *Genesis of a Music*. Madison: University of Wisconsin Press, 1949.

Rosenblum, Barbara. *Photographers at Work*. New York: Holmes and Meiers, Publishers, Inc., 1978.

Smith, Barbara. *Poetic Closure: A Study of How Poems End*. Chicago: University of Chicago Press, 1968.

Trollope, Anthony. *An Autobiography*. Berkeley and Los Angeles: University of California Press, 1947 [1883].

Editor's Notes on Further Reading

Becker on Art Worlds

Howard Becker's simple but illuminating observation that producing art is a collective enterprise depending on an extensive division of labor and on shared conventions challenges the commonsense emphasis on individual artistic creativity and absolute aesthetic criteria (compare Peterson on rock and roll, excerpted this volume). His book elaborates on the many ways art worlds enable and constrain artistic production – mobilizing resources, distributing products, assigning critical assessments, and influencing editing processes and artistic reputations – as well on the ways the state may influence art worlds, how different artistic roles are defined in relation to art worlds, and how art worlds change. Becker demonstrates that the "production of culture" perspective is not limited to understanding the outcomes of culture industries involving mass production for the market but also helps understand other sorts of social organization of artistic production.

For a related overview of studies of the arts see Samuel Gilmore, "Art Worlds: Developing the Interactionist Approach to Social Organization," pp. 148–78 in Howard Becker and Michal McCall, eds., *Symbolic Interaction and Cultural Studies* (Chicago and London: University of Chicago Press, 1990), and for other approaches to arts institutions see Judith Blau, "Study of the Arts: A Reappraisal," *Annual Review of Sociology* 14 (1988): 269–92; Blau, *The Shape of Culture: A Study of Contemporary Cultural Patterns in the United States* (Cambridge and New York: Cambridge University Press, 1989); and Pierre-Michel Menger, "Artistic Labor Markets and Careers," *Annual Review of Sociology* 25 (1999): 541–74. For an example of cultural production which combines both market and aesthetic determinants see Larson on architecture, this volume. For development of similar ideas from perspectives which stress more explicitly longer-term historical and broader structural forces than does Becker, see for example Vera Zolberg, *Constructing a Sociology of the Arts* (Cambridge: Cambridge University Press, 1990); Janet Wolff, *The Social Production of Art* 2nd edn. (New York: New York University Press, 1993); and Raymond Williams, *The Sociology of Culture*, with a new foreword by Bruce Robbins (Chicago: University of Chicago Press, 1995 [1981]).

While Becker's examples are drawn from work in many media, including various musical and literary forms and genre (see notes to excerpts from Peterson and Griswold, this volume), studies of visual art probably provide the richest lode of exemplars, extensions and critiques of the perspective Becker articulates here. On the visual arts see for example Harrison White and Cynthia White, *Canvases and Careers* (New York: John Wiley, 1965); Michael Baxandall, *Patterns of Intention: On the Historical Explanation of Pictures* (New Haven: Yale University Press, 1985); Diana Crane, *The Transformation of the Avant-Garde: The New York Art World, 1940–1985* (Chicago and London: University of Chicago Press, 1987); Liah Greenfeld, *Different Worlds: A Sociological Study of Taste, Choice, and Success in Art* (Cambridge and New York: Cambridge University Press, 1989); Rosanne Martorella, *Corporate Art* (New Brunswick NJ: Rutgers University Press, 1990); Gladys Engel Lang and Kurt Lang, *Etched in Memory: the Building and Survival of Artistic Reputation* (Chapel Hill and London: University of North Carolina Press, 1990); Albert Bergesen, "A Theory of Pictorial Discourse," pp. 158–68 in Robert Wuthnow, ed., *Vocabularies of Public Life: Empirical Essays in Symbolic Structure* (London and New York: Routledge, 1992); Judith Huggins Balfe, ed., *Paying the Piper: Causes and Consequences of Art Patronage* (Champaign, IL: University of Illinois Press, 1993); Anne Bowler, "Methodological Dilemmas in the

Sociology of Art," in Diana Crane, ed., *The Sociology of Culture* (Oxford and Cambridge, MA: Blackwell, 1994) 247–66; Victoria Alexander, "From Philanthropy to Funding: The Effects of Corporate and Public Support on American Art Museums," *Poetics* 24 (1996): 87–129; Alexander, "Pictures at an Exhibition: Conflicting Pressures in Museums and the Display of Art," *American Journal of Sociology* 101 (1996): 797–839; and Vera Zolberg and Joni Maya Cherbo, eds., *Outsider Art: Contesting Boundaries in Contemporary Culture* (Cambridge and New York: Cambridge University Press, 1997). In "The Culture of Production: Aesthetic Choices and Constraints in Culinary Work," *American Journal of Sociology* 97 (1999): 1268–94, Gary Alan Fine extends the production-of-culture perspective to apply to accounts of aesthetic and expressive dimensions of the work of restaurant cooks.

18 American Character and the American Novel: An Expansion of Reflection Theory in the Sociology of Literature

Wendy Griswold

Is the American novel unique, as it is often said to be? If so, do its peculiar properties reflect some American character or experience? I have examined the relationship between American novels and the society that produced them by analyzing a random sample of 130 novels published in the United States between 1876 and 1910. The analysis shows that seemingly mundane things such as copyright laws have had considerable influence on the content of American novels. My findings demonstrate that the concept of literature as reflection must be expanded to include reflection of production circumstances, author characteristics, and formal problems, as well as the preoccupations of any particular society.

To begin, consider the background of the production and consumption of novels in the late 19th century. Americans during this period were highly literate and interested in reading (Cipolla 1969, table 21). Following the Civil War there had been an unprecedented growth of the reading habit in the United States (Tebbel 1975).... Within 10 years of Appomattox, books, magazines, and newspapers were proliferating, and the publishing industry was expanding rapidly, with some 200 houses operating by the early 1880s.

Fiction led in sheer quantity of titles published. The fiction flood began in the 1870s and continued until 1908, the first year when novels did not lead all other categories of books published.... In view of the vast number of novels being written and read in late 19th-century America, it seems reasonable to examine these novels to see if they reveal anything about the society that produced them. The first question that must be asked is whether there was anything peculiarly American about the American novel.

I

The rise of the novel has been well charted, particularly by Ian Watt ([1957] 1974). Watt shows that the 18th-century novel in England was the product of an age in which the human personality was believed to be essentially knowable, knowledge of it coming from the accumulation of evidence drawn from the detailed observation of behavior. This interest coincided with two other 18th-century developments. One was the rapid expansion of a new audience for literature, the literate middle class, especially the leisured middle-class women. Lacking the education and inclination to read Latin or serious verse, yet wanting diversion, these women offered a ready market for a not-too-demanding literary form. The second development was the decline of patronage and the appearance of its economic equivalent for writers, the bookseller, who encompassed the activities of publisher and printer as well as merchant. The booksellers knew that their customers wanted hours of entertainment, not moments of exquisite feeling. Therefore, they paid authors by the page. For the author, in consequence, "Speed and copiousness tended to become the supreme economic virtues" (Watt [1957] 1974, p. 56).

This confluence of interest in the human personality, audience, and economic institutions gave rise to a genre that was easy to read, long, written in prose, fictitious, devoted to subjects of interest to middle-class women and to an analysis of character through detailed description of behavior – the genre we know as the novel. Eighteenth-century novelists explored the subjects of particular interest to their readership: love and marriage, economic individualism, the complexities of modern life, the possibility of personal morality in a corrupting world.

It has often been held that although "the novel" looks like what I have just described, "the American novel" does not. One version of this argument is that classic American fiction is about men removing themselves from society, especially from women who seem to represent the constraints of social and domestic life. Often with a dark-skinned male companion, these men, or boys, flee to the ocean, the forest, the unknown lands down river and there test their individual strength (Marx 1964). Leslie Fiedler (1966), basing his case on classic works which fit the man-fleeing-society pattern, has asked,

> Where is our *Madame Bovary*, our *Anna Karenina*, our *Pride and Prejudice* or *Vanity Fair?* Among our classical novels...the best attempt at dealing with love is *The Scarlet Letter*, in which the physical consummation of adultery has occurred and all passion burned away before the novel proper begins. For the rest, there are *Moby Dick* and *Huckleberry Finn, The Last of the Mohicans, The Red Badge of Courage*, the stories of Edgar Allan Poe – books that turn from society to nature or nightmare out of a desperate need to avoid the facts of wooing, marriage, and child-bearing. (Fiedler 1966, pp. 24–5)

Fiedler attributes this theme of flight from society to an American pathology, a social and sexual immaturity, tinged with racial guilt, that manifests itself in the American novelist's inability to write about adult subjects such as heterosexual love and the reconciliation of individual freedom with social life....

Any attempt to read American character from American novels should begin with a more systematic attempt to determine just what Americans were writing and reading. Then, one must ask whether these American novels were different from European novels, and how they compared with our conception of the "standard novel" as the genre was formulated in the 18th century. To the extent that the peculiar character of American novels is substantiated, one should look for some possible causes for these distinctive American traits other than simply some uniqueness of the national psyche. Reflection theory is not necessarily wrong, but it can be used to encompass more complex societal/literary relationships than most of its proponents have thus far demonstrated.

II

My search for links between American society and American novels entailed taking a random sample from all novels published in the United States between 1876 and 1910. The source of the sample was the *American Catalogue*, a series begun in 1876 that recorded every book published in this country. A sample of 130 novels was divided into time periods. Period I covered novels published from 1876 to 1884, Period II from 1884 to 1895, Period III from 1895 to 1905, and Period IV from 1905 through 1910. About half of the novels were written by American authors, and the other half were American reprints of foreign works. Analysis focused on a number of variables pertaining to plot, author characteristics, and bibliographic information . . .

The study began with two propositions. First, the overall differences between American and foreign novels might be less impressive than has often been supposed. The search for "the American novel" may in part have been self-fulfilling. For in seeking some quintessentially American literature, scholars must pass by *The House of Mirth* and seize upon *Huckleberry Finn* because of the latter's very uniqueness; novels like *The House of Mirth*, dealing with marriage, money, and the social world, are too indistinguishable from their European counterparts to lay claim to being representative of "the American novel." . . . A comparison of a broad sample of American and foreign novels, keeping in mind the norm set by 18th-century English novelists, should reveal fewer differences of content and treatment than the reflection-of-national-character theories would suggest.

My second proposition was that, to the extent that 19th-century American novels did contain a unique set of themes and subjects, it was neither because American readers were not interested in novels about love and marriage nor because American authors lacked the capacity to write such novels. Instead, American authors had economic incentives to deviate from the standard subjects of the genre. This hypothesis derives from the history of American copyright legislation.

During most of the 19th century, American copyright laws protected citizens or permanent residents of the United States but not foreign authors (Clark 1960). The result was that British and other foreign works could be reprinted and sold in the United States without royalties being paid to their authors, while American authors did receive royalty payments. Many interests in the United States benefited from this literary piracy and lobbied to maintain the status quo. (Actually, piracy is something of a misnomer, for the practice was perfectly legal.) The nascent printing industry was kept busy. Publishers made huge profits from reprinting foreign books. Readers had available the best foreign literature at low prices; for example, in 1843 *A Christmas Carol* sold for 6 ¢ in the United States and the equivalent of $2.50 in England. . . .

After almost a century of ineffective pressure from American authors for legal relief from this competition, in 1891 the Platt-Simmonds Act extended copyright to foreign authors. Ironically, the turnabout in Congress was the consequence of the American publishers themselves being undercut by printers of "cheap books," those immensely popular, flimsy reprints of classics and best-sellers, which flourished in the 1880s (Shove 1937)....

I contend that the choices American novelists made regarding the subjects and themes of their novels, insofar as these choices differed from those made by their foreign counterparts, were due less to the differences in American character or experience than to different market constraints....

Platt-Simmonds erased the different market positions of the two groups of authors, and the incentive for American authors to select nontraditional subjects disappeared. Therefore, I hypothesized considerable thematic divergence between the American novels and the foreign novels published in the United States prior to 1891, and convergence after that year.

I looked at the differences between the American and foreign novels of the sample during the four time periods, the first two falling largely before Platt-Simmonds, the second two after....

Overall, there should be more consistency than variation between the American and foreign authors' novels, and both groups should resemble the standard novel that deals with love, marriage, and money.... [and some] plot variations between the foreign and American novels in the earlier two periods should decrease or disappear during the later two. This decreased variation represents the hypothesized convergence following 1891....

III

...Love, marriage, and seduction were the subjects of the 18th-century novels. I was interested in seeing whether these original preoccupations had persisted, and what forms they had taken by the time under consideration.

Adult heterosexual love continued to be of overwhelming importance, being the key to the plot in 55% of the sample novels and of considerable importance in an additional 33%. The love complications usually revolved around the question of marriage, important in 64% of the novels. Matters of love and marriage generally worked out in satisfying, unsurprising ways. Most often, the marriage took place as anticipated, though occasionally one or both of the expected partners married someone else.

Other forms of love were given less, though considerable, attention. Love between adult members of the same sex was seldom the center of the novel's action but was of some importance in over 40% of the novels, and a similar proportion of them dealt with the love between an adult and a child. And although love and marriage were nearly omnipresent, seduction, the keystone of Richardson's novels and many to follow, was not a standard feature of the sample novels, figuring in about one-fifth of the plots.

American and foreign authors did not differ in their emphases on love and marriage, and both groups wrote about these subjects in the majority of their novels. Nor was there any evidence of an increase or decrease of stress on these subjects over time... There were no differences between American and foreign authors about the likelihood of the anticipated marriage occurring, the emphasis on love between adult members of the same sex, or the importance of love between adults and children.

These last two findings cast doubt on Fiedler's stress on the homoeroticism of American novels....

Young adults constituted 60% of the protagonists, somewhat over 10% were middle-aged, and an additional 10% were followed through several stages of their lives. This emphasis on young adulthood, roughly defined as 18–30, held true for both American and foreign novels and did not change over time. The vast majority of our protagonists were single at the beginning of their respective novels. By the end of the novels, most were married or about to marry....

The novel is traditionally regarded as the genre read by, and concerned with, the middle class. Surprisingly, though, the majority of the sample novels did not feature middle-class protagonists. The American authors were significantly more apt to have protagonists begin in and, especially, end up in the middle class; the foreign authors favored upper-class protagonists. Both groups of authors seemed to feel that working-class characters were not likely to be interesting protagonists. The difference between American and foreign authors regarding the protagonist's class at the beginning of the novel was greatest in Period I and diminished thereafter. The difference in outcomes was more persistent, Americans being significantly more apt to have the hero or heroine end up in the middle class during all periods except the third.

Sample protagonists rose in social ranking in about one-quarter of the novels, occasionally descended, but usually (68%) stayed put. Again, a breakdown by period is revealing. In the first period, American authors were significantly more inclined to depict social mobility; 53% of the American novels presented socially mobile protagonists, compared with 19% of the foreign novels. *Eirene* (Ames 1870) is typical: the heroine starts out as the daughter of a poor but loving farm family, goes through hardships as a hand in a New England textile mill, and ends up in a New York mansion, married to the scion of one of the city's old Dutch families. But in the later three periods, the American and foreign authors are nearly identical on this variable, treating social mobility in about one-third of their novels....

Prison conditions, temperance, the treatment of women, the plight of the poor, and cruelty to animals were subject to the reforming zeal of the sample authors. Social reform was an important theme in 39% of the American novels and 29% of the foreign ones. The difference between the two groups of authors was greatest in the first period, when American authors dealt with social reform in 69% of their novels, foreign authors in 40% of theirs. Thereafter, the two groups converged, with about one-quarter of their novels dealing with reform.

About one-third of both American and foreign novels were set in large cities. Americans favored small towns as well, locating 30% of their novels in small towns, a setting less popular with foreign authors (15%). The American preference for small towns was strongest in Period I, in which 53% of their novels had small town settings. Few novels were set in the wilderness and, contrary to the Fiedler argument, Europeans were slightly more likely to utilize wilderness settings (15%) than were Americans (7%)....

The action generally took place in the present or the immediate past. Foreign authors showed somewhat more interest in exploring the remote past, especially in the first two periods, in which about one-quarter of the foreign novels took place before the 19th century. The difference disappeared in the last two periods.

Money, the necessity of having it, its acquisition, and occasionally its loss, was a central element in 57% of the plots. During the first three periods there was a considerable difference between American and foreign authors, with the latter writing about money in three-quarters of their novels, Americans in about half. Period IV shows an unexplained drop in the importance of money in foreign novels (27%), so while convergence may be taking place, the trend is by no means clear.

About one-third of the sample novels dealt with religion, and there seems to have been an uneven decline in its importance over the 35 years. The American and foreign authors were equally likely to write about religion. Supernatural elements, the ghosts and gothic devices that Fiedler argued Americans substituted for the excitements of passionate adult love, played a role in only 15% of the novels. Foreign authors were somewhat more likely to include supernatural elements during the first two periods than were Americans; during the last two periods, the two groups converged.

Humor is often cited as a characteristic of American literature. Although only 11% of the sample novels contained significant humor, the American novels were slightly more apt to be humorous (16%) than the foreign ones (6%). This difference between the two groups of authors was most pronounced in the first two periods, during which no humorous novels by foreign authors appeared in the sample....

IV

A sociological approach to literature assumes that literary works are in some way linked to the society that creates and/or reads them (Escarpit 1971). Reflection has been a popular metaphor in the attempt to explain recalcitrant literary phenomena. This study demonstrates the need for an expanded conception of how literature reflects the social world.

What have the sample novels reflected? The most consistent finding is the mutual resemblance among the novels, both between those by American and by foreign authors and among those of all four periods. And, lest this be regarded as an artifact introduced by American publishers seeking any novels, native or foreign, that catered to some unique American reading tastes, one should remember that the characteristics shared by the sample novels are much the same as the 18th-century archetypal features of the genre. Like their forerunners, the sample novels are about love and marriage, money and social life. Their protagonists start out single and end up married. They operate in a complex social world familiar to their readers, they are basically virtuous, they encounter a sequence of emotional and moral dilemmas, they often improve their lot.

This resistance to changes of subject matter that novels seem to possess is especially striking when one considers the self-imposed limits of the genre, the many things about which novelists do not write. Missing most conspicuously is material related to work, such as career histories or the depiction of on-the-job working relationships. Also missing is an intensive examination of married life, posthoneymoon, especially as it involves the rearing of children; this may be the feminine counterpart to the absence of novelistic treatment of male work... Much of this continuity of subject matter can be explained by considering what I shall call the imperatives of the genre. . . .

[T]he fact that novels are long means that they are normally not consumed in one sitting. Novels require a considerable investment of time, and several decisions to sit down and read rather than do something else. This poses a formal problem for the novelist: he needs not only to attract the initial interest of his reader but also to influence a subsequent series of decisions. Working within such a genre, the novelist cannot orchestrate an emotional tension and release, such as that of tragic catharsis; he cannot set the stage and structure the emotional experience to provide his audience a brief transportation to another world. The novelist's problem is to interest the reader enough so that he keeps deciding to pick up the novel again and to enable the reader to slip easily back into the novel's world at almost any point. . . .

The novelist must write about some aspect of common life that is emotionally engaging, that arouses his reader's feelings and curiosity. And this curiosity must ultimately be satisfied, so the novelist needs a subject that lends itself to dramatic shaping by having a distinct climax and resolution.

Love, especially love associated with the selection and winning of a marriage partner, is the perfect solution. It is familiar to most readers, it is full of intense feeling and emotional conflict, and – unlike working life or child rearing, which share those two features – it reaches a definite resolution. When recounting a love affair or possible marriage, one can always say "how it turned out." Love and marriage solve the novelist's formal problem by offering both connection points and dramatic structure. The imperatives of the genre compel many novelists to give love and marriage an inordinate amount of attention, disproportionate to the amount of time they occupy in most people's actual experience. The sample novels reflect this. Many of the resemblances among novels stem from these formal imperatives.

But although the sample novels share a preoccupation with love and marriage, they also exhibit some differences between the works of American and foreign authors. Most of these differences – social reform themes, the class of the protagonist, the concentration on small towns, the depiction of the remote past, the treatment of money, the presence of humor – follow a common pattern: the difference between the American and the foreign authors is most marked during the first one or two periods, and during the later periods the two groups converge. In many cases of early divergence, it was the American authors who deviated from what we regard as the standard subjects and treatments of the novel, writing more about social reform and less about money, using more humor, and so forth.

If these differences had persisted over all four periods, they might have constituted a reflection of some peculiarities of the American character or experience. But the pattern of differences in the 1870s, which then converge sometime in the 1890s, supports the proposition that what was being reflected in the initial differences were the different market positions occupied by the American and the foreign authors. Both were subject to the imperatives of the genre and the traditions of the novel. But the American authors had greater incentive to deviate from the norm, to write on nontraditional themes that the European authors had not effectively monopolized. After 1891, there was no longer the same incentive for deviation, the novelistic imperatives took over, and the American authors swung into line with everyone else. So in addition to reflecting imperatives of the genre, the novels reflected differential market positions brought about by the state of American copyright laws. . . .

References

Albrecht, Milton. 1954. "The Relationship of Literature and Society." *American Journal of Sociology* 59:425–36.

Ames, Mary Clemmer. 1870. *Eirene*. New York: Putnam.

Brown, Helen Dawes. 1889. *Two College Girls*. Boston: Ticknor.

Cipolla, Carolo M. 1969. *Literacy and Development in the West*. Harmondsworth, Middlesex: Penguin.

Clark, Priscilla P. 1977. "Stratégies d'auteur au XIXe siècle." *Romantisme* 17–18:92–102.

———. 1979. "Literary Culture in France and the United States." *American Journal of Sociology* 84: 1057–77.

Clark, Robert J. 1960. *The Movement for International Copyright in Nineteenth Century America*. Washington, D.C.: Catholic University Press.

Cornwallis, Kinahan. 1886. "International Copyright: A Copyright Law Wanted to Stimulate American Literature." *Publishers Weekly* 29:106.

Dorius, R. J. 1965. "Comedy." Pp. 143–47 in *Princeton Encyclopedia of Poetry and Poetics*. Princeton, N.J.: Princeton University Press.

Douglas, Ann. 1978. *The Feminization of American Culture*. New York: Avon.

Ennis, Philip H. 1965. *Adult Book Reading in the United States*. Chicago: National Opinion Research Center.

Escarpit, Robert, 1971. *Sociology of Literature*. 2d ed. Translated by Ernest Pick. London: Cass.

Fiedler, Leslie. 1966. *Love and Death in the American Novel*. Rev. ed. New York: Dell.

Gallup, George. 1972. *The Gallup Poll: Public Opinion 1935–1971*. New York: Random House.

Goldman, Lucien. 1967. "The Sociology of Literature: Status and Problems of Method." *International Social Science Journal* 19:493–516.

Hackett, Alice Payne, and James Henry Burke. 1977. *80 Years of Best Sellers: 1895–1975*. New York: Bowker.

Hart, James D. (1950) 1963. *The Popular Book: A History of America's Literary Taste*. Berkeley and Los Angeles: University of California Press.

Hirsch, Paul M. 1972. "Processing Fads and Fashions: An Organization-Set Analysis of Cultural Industry Systems." *American Journal of Sociology* 77:639–59.

Hopper, James, and Fred Bechdolt. 1909. "*9009*." New York: Moffat.

Huizinga, Johan. (1950) 1955. *Homo Ludens*. Boston: Beacon.

Ingraham, J. H. 1876. *Frank Rivers, or The Dangers of the Town*. New York: DeWitt.

Knight, Douglas M., and E. Shepley Nourse. 1969. *Libraries at Large*. New York: Bowker.

Lawrence, D. H. (1923) 1977. *Studies in Classic American Literature*. New York: Penguin.

Lowenthal, Leo. 1961. *Literature, Popular Culture, and Society*. Englewood Cliffs, N.J.: Prentice-Hall.

Marx, Leo. 1964. *The Machine in the Garden*. New York: Oxford University Press.

Mathews, Virginia H. 1973. "Adult Reading Studies: Their Implications for Private, Professional, and Public Policy." *Library Trends* 22:149–76.

Mott, Frank Luther. 1947. *Golden Multitudes*. New York: Macmillan.

Peterson, Richard A. 1979. "Revitalizing the Culture Concept." *Annual Review of Sociology* 5:137–66.

Publishers Weekly. 1876–1910.

Sharon, Amiel T. 1973–74. "What Do Adults Read?" *Reading Research Quarterly* 9:148–69.

Shove, Raymond Howard. 1937. *Cheap Book Production in the United States, 1870 to 1891.* Urbana: University of Illinois Library.

Smith, Henry Nash. 1978. *Democracy and the Novel.* New York: Oxford University Press.

Steinberg, S. H. (1974) 1977. *Five Hundred Years of Printing.* 3d ed. Harmondsworth, Middlesex: Penguin.

Tebbel, John. 1975. *A History of Book Publishing in the United States.* Vol. 2, *The Expansion of an Industry, 1865–1919.* New York: Bowker.

Watt, Ian. (1957) 1974. *The Rise of the Novel.* Berkeley and Los Angeles: University of California Press.

White, H. C., and C. A. White. 1965. *Canvases and Careers.* New York: Wiley.

Williams, Raymond. 1966. *Culture and Society, 1780–1950.* New York: Harper & Row.

Wright, Will. 1975. *Six Guns and Society.* Berkeley and Los Angeles: University of California Press.

Yankelovich, Skelly, and White. 1978. Study prepared for the Book Industry Consulting Group, summarized in *Publishers Weekly* 214:16.

Editor's Notes on Further Reading

Griswold on Literature and Society

How is literature related to the society within which it is produced? Griswold undermines overgeneralized claims that literatures reflect societies by showing the surprising impact of a simple change in copyright law on literary themes, and more broadly by drawing attention to the formal demands of novels as a genre, the context of the publishing industry, and the nature of the audience for fiction. Her content analysis of a large sample of late nineteenth-century novels by authors from different countries compares many aspects of their plots, protagonists, settings and themes, finding, against "reflection theory," overwhelming similarities and increasing convergence between novels by American and by non-American authors. (For a more general challenge to reflection theory, see the excerpt by Raymond Williams, this volume; for another example of the impact of the law on cultural products, see excerpt from Peterson, this volume.)

Other studies demonstrating the way specific aspects of art world or production context influence literature and its interpretation include Richard Peterson, "Six Constraints on the Production of Literary Works," *Poetics* 14 (1985): 45–67; Griswold, "The Writing on the Mud Wall: Nigerian Novels and the Imaginary Village," *American Sociological Review* 57 (1992): 709–24; Sarah M. Corse, *Nationalism and Literature: The Politics of Culture in Canada and the United States* (Cambridge and New York: Cambridge University Press, 1997); Janice Radway, *A Feeling For Books: The Book-of-the-Month Club, Literary Taste and Middle-Class Desire* (Chapel Hill: University of North Carolina Press, 1997); Wendy Griswold and Fredrik Engelstad, "Does the Center Imagine the Periphery? State Support and Literary Regionalism in Norway and the United States," *Comparative Social Research* 17 (1998): 129–75; and Wendy Griswold, *Bearing Witness: Writers, Readers, and the Novel in Nigeria* (Princeton: Princeton University Press, 2000). Some related studies emphasizing literary themes or readers' interpretation include Gaye Tuchman and Nina Fortin, "Fame and Misfortune: Edging Women Out of the Great Literary Tradition," *American Journal of*

Sociology 90 (1984): 72–96; Janice Radway, *Reading the Romance: Women, Patriarchy and Popular Literature* (Chapel Hill: University of North Carolina Press, 1984); Elizabeth Long, *The American Dream and the Popular Novel* (Boston: Routledge and Kegan Paul, 1985); Griswold, "The Fabrication of Meaning: Literary Interpretation in the United States, Great Britain, and the West Indies," *American Journal of Sociology* 92 (1987): 1077–117; Marjorie DeVault, "Novel Readings: The Social Organization of Interpretation," *American Journal of Sociology* 95 (1990): 887–921; and Elizabeth Long, "Textual Interpretation as Collective Action," pp. 181–211 in John Cruz and Justin Lewis, eds., *Viewing, Reading, Listening: Audiences and Cultural Reception* (Boulder, CO: Westview Press, 1994).

Among the many classic examinations of literature and society are Milton Albrecht, "The Relation Between Literature and Society," *American Journal of Sociology* 59 (1954): 425–36; Ian Watt, *The Rise of the Novel* (Berkeley: University of California Press, 1957); Eric Auerbach, *Mimesis: The Representation of Reality in Western Literature*, trans. W. R. Trask (Princeton: Princeton University Press, 1968 [1953]); Raymond Williams, *Culture and Society: 1780–1950* (New York: Columbia University Press, 1983 [1958]); Leo Lowenthal, *Literature, Popular Culture, and Society* (Palo Alto: Pacific Books, 1961); Georg Lukács, *Studies in European Realism* (New York: Grosset and Dunlap, 1964); Lucien Goldmann, "The Sociology of Literature: Status and Problems of Method," *International Social Science Journal* 19 (1967): 493–516; Raymond Williams, "Literature and Sociology: In Memory of Lucien Goldmann," *New Left Review* 67 (1971) 3–18; John Cawelti, *Adventure, Mystery, and Romance: Formula Stories in Art and Popular Culture* (Chicago: University of Chicago Press, 1976); Raymond Williams, *Marxism and Literature* (Oxford: Oxford University Press, 1977); Lewis Coser, Charles Kadushin, and Walter W. Powell, *Books: The Culture and Commerce of Publishing* (New York: Basic Books, 1982); and Pierre Bourdieu, *The Field of Cultural Production: Essays on Art and Literature* (New York: Columbia University Press, 1983). See also Wendy Griswold, "Recent Moves in the Sociology of Literature," *Annual Review of Sociology* 19 (1993): 455–67, and the useful collection of essays assembled in Philippe Desan, Priscilla Ferguson, and Wendy Griswold, eds., *Literature and Social Practice* (Chicago: University of Chicago Press, 1989).

19 Behind the Postmodern Façade: Architectural Change in Late Twentieth-Century America

Magali Sarfatti Larson

From a sociological point of view, discourse includes all that a particular category of agents say (or write) in a specific capacity and in a definable thematic area. Discourse commonly invites dialogue. However, in architecture (as in all professions), discourse is not open to everyone but based on social appropriation and a principle of exclusion. Laypersons are not entitled to participate in the production of the profession as a discipline.[1]

The discourse of architecture is based on a contested premise that it must always seek to prove. Critics, historians, and practitioners of architecture operate on the assumption that only what legitimate architects do deserves to be treated as art and included in architectural discourse. I call this basic exclusionary principle the ideological syllogism of architecture: "Only architects produce architecture. Architecture is an art. Architects are necessary to produce art."

Although the syllogism is necessary to found the discipline's discourse, it is compromised by a contradiction characteristic of this profession. The discourse of architecture is constructed autonomously, by experts who are accountable only to other experts. However, in order to continue "formulating fresh propositions," disciplines need to show how their rules become embodied in a canon, and the canon of architecture consists of beautiful or innovative *built exemplars*. These buildings are not and cannot be exemplars of the architect's autonomous application of knowledge and talent alone. They are also striking manifestations of the architect's dependence on clients and the other specialists of building, be they rival professionals or humbler executants. I call this dependence *heteronomy*, because it contrasts radically with the autonomy that is always considered a defining attribute of professional work.

In sum, because the discourse of architecture is ultimately based on its practice, and because this practice points to a fundamental heteronomy, the basic syllogism is as much an ideological position as a functioning principle of exclusion. The dialectics of discourse and practice (or of autonomy and heteronomy) are salient in architecture. They are particularly significant in the analysis of its discursive shifts.

Twice in our century, Western architecture has gone through significant changes in both discourse and realizations. In the orthodox historiographic accounts, submerged currents of stylistic change seem to have produced both times the architectural conceptions of elite designers. Indeed, despite architecture's characteristic dependence on patrons or clients for its work, the histories of architecture locate the origins of change within the discursive field itself, in the theories and ideas of architects.

The first and most radical shift in the discourse of architecture culminated in the Modern Movement of the 1920s in Europe. An adapted European modernism became *the* architectural style of international capitalism after World War II. The second shift originated in reaction to the debased architecture that, however unwanted, derived from modernism. Arising against the latter's universalistic claims, the postmodern revision refuses formal and ideological unity (and indeed does not appear to have any)....

On the one hand, postmodernism is undeniably connected to architectural discourse: What became of European modernism in the United States (and spread from here to the whole world) was both the target of postmodern attacks and the antithesis that gave postmodernism much of its substance....

On the other hand, I hold the general hypothesis that changes in ideas and styles correspond to (and attempt to make sense of) structural changes lived through and perceived by strategically located groups of people. In ways that should not be prejudged but always explored empirically, cultural change may also correspond to broad changes in social structure. Given this hypothesis, I take changes in aesthetic preference and taste among architects not as signs of whim or trendiness, nor as indications of idealist reorientation, but as symptoms of changes in architects' conceptions of their professional role and in the conditions of their practice. In postmodern discourse, the model of European modernism is related as much to practical conceptions of the architect's role and to changes in the way architects must make a living as to their formal imagination....

The Relevance of Discursive Battles

Architectural schools and distinctive pedagogies, professional organizations and journals, market-induced specialization and associations, the public interest piqued by the general press, all serve as channels for the circulation and the reproduction of architectural ideas, inducing imitation and promoting stylistic trends. But this is not all. The occupational identity formed and nourished by these means can include a deeper attention to the idea of architecture as art.

Normal architectural practice is oriented to service and commercial interests, inevitably heteronomous, and often subordinate and alienating. To compensate for these disadvantages, it may prompt broad attention among architects to the discourse that exalts the artistic dimension of their trade. It does not have to be conscious attention: it may well be only distracted, or nostalgic, or resentful. Appropriately, a Philadelphia architect with a "normal" practice quips that the annual design awards of the journal *Progressive Architecture* are "*True Confessions* for architects." Awards for "pure" design (and "pure" design itself) are pipe dreams, this architect thinks; nonetheless, these dreams engage deep and unspoken yearnings and thus offer architects a fantasy, one that supports their ideological claim to be artists, not mere crafts-people. Technological advances, after all, are the province of engineers and manufacturers; and being a commercial hack or a good employee is nothing to fantasize about. Art and celebrity are the stuff of which individual dreams are made in this profession.

Two kinds of struggle in the discursive field of architecture are able to elicit at least the unconscious attention of ordinary professionals. Neither is unique to architecture, but they both appear repeatedly in the modern politics of culture.

The first kind of struggle is framed in specialized terms, even though it may implicate several art media in an aesthetic movement and exceed the boundaries of a delimited "art world." Specialized cultural debates matter most of all to the producers and other specialists of the field rather than to clients. The reason, as Pierre Bourdieu has argued for scientific fields, is not purely intellectual and disinterested. Rather, there are special interests at stake: The outcomes of disputes among experts affect each field's internal hierarchy, rankings, networks of influence, and personal standing – all the strategic positions by means of which symbolic capital is formed and resources of wealth and power claimed.[2]

When "purely" aesthetic challenges reverberate through the medium of discourse in the professional field of architecture, they can evoke support or opposition from heterogeneous sources. Debates that originate among different factions of the design elite can thus become (as in other specialized fields) the occasion for conflicts and alliances of another sort. What is distinctive in architecture is the role that clients' choices can play in the resolution of the debate. Controversy is fierce, but where a project reaches the stage of realization, controversy must normally be tempered at least enough to assuage the clients' fears (if not quite to accommodate their wishes).

The second kind of cultural struggle draws the first into a broader (and hazier) frame, but it is a different phenomenon analytically. The impulse for the first kind of struggle comes from within the field, picking up steam from possible coalitions with insiders or related outsiders as it unfolds. The second kind of struggle has its own specific language and objectives, but the impulse comes from the outside: In specific historical circumstances, the modern politics of culture are played out against the background of larger social conflicts, from which delimited fields borrow intensity and substance. These are the distinctive moments of the Western art avant-gardes. On the one hand, formal aesthetic challenges are infused with the resonance of political and moral struggle. On the other hand, debates that are still couched in esoteric language and concerned with specialized issues may come to move along with larger movements: The dissenters, not content with challenging discourse alone, may attempt to renegotiate the power relationships within and around their special field of practice and may, in fact, attack its established protective boundaries.

The modernist phase of twentieth-century architecture, distinguished by an ideological moment of birth, clearly illustrates the struggle of a political-aesthetic avant-garde. In the 1920s, new visions of architecture inflamed the profession's discourse by seeking to transcend the internal divisions and to forge anew the institutions of practice. My study will show that political fervor was not characteristic of the postmodern transformation yet not entirely absent from its early phases.

Battles in the discursive field of architecture are as narrow and specialized as in any other field. However, the utility, the visibility, and the public character of architecture tend to give to its battles a metaphorical significance greater than in other arts and even other professions. Indeed, I believe that the ideas of architectural innovators have shaped the distinctive public face of our modernity....

In the late 1960s and early 1970s the revision of architectural discourse coincided with challenges waged from inside the profession against the architect's subservience to power. The coincidence came from different groups of architect-activists taking dogmatic modernism (which had made architecture part and parcel of the relentless modernization of cities) as a common enemy.[3]

In the United States, modernism-as-modernization primarily referred to the large-scale urban renewal that started in the 1950s. In the late 1970s, an extraordinary wave of real estate speculation succeeded the momentous economic crisis and spurred on architectural revisionism (at least of one kind). Clients with more credit than capital wanted their buildings to look rich, playful, and different. Developers' much-vaunted discovery of design contributed to the fame of a few "signature architects," but their main criterion in selecting design was and continues to be product differentiation. Postmodernism was bound to become tainted by its alliance with invidious status distinction, "image-making," and mere visual variety.

Architects' commissions and the glamor associated with the profession in the 1980s registered the effects of financial deregulation and the redistribution of income from poor and middle strata to the wealthiest. When architects and critics scoff at traditional postmodernism as an architecture "for the age of Reagan," they refer mainly to *style*. Few architects identify an age by the types of commissions that became prevalent or extinct. Yet the architectural sign of the period was less a style than the overabundance of office and retail space, luxury hotels, rich men's homes, and cultural institutions for the elite.

During the revision of the modern, divergent ideals clustered around the conflict between "image" and the "reality" of architecture. These terms can be read as transpositions of the basic disjunction between conception and execution in architects' work, for architects always design images (plans and working drawings are technical images of the building to be) while others do the building. That image and reality occupied a central place in the postmodern contest suggests that something was perceived to be changing (by will or by chance) in the architect's basic social identity.

The problematic relations of architectural image and reality call into question the place of aesthetic conception in the economy of building. If, indeed, architects are increasingly and primarily hired to embellish buildings and attract customers with images and symbols, their social function has changed. In Scott Lash's words, symbols have "a purchase on meaning but not on reality"; unlike signs, symbols have no referents. Buildings (or cities) do not refer to anything, they are. They can function as symbols, but their reality is overwhelmingly material and utilitarian. They are not circulating goods (cultural or material) but the primary stage of life and commerce on which goods are exchanged and consumed.[4]

If the best architectural work becomes the projection of symbolic and cultural significance, then architects are resigned to abandon to others the material design of the environment. It may, of course, be argued that they have never designed but a very small part of it. At issue, however, is their collective intention to provide the keynote.

Architectural supremacism, a professional ideology that extolled design for design's sake, rose in the mid-1970s on a contested and insecure professional scene. In the beginning, it had attempted a return to the imperious and autonomous self-definition of modernism, but it was too late. Not only did supremacism abandon earlier efforts to rethink cities gutted by modernism-as-modernization; its proponents did not have the professional power to restore modernism by a "working through" of partially developed aesthetic possibilities. Yet tacitly admitting all building types to the legitimacy of architecture in reality functioned as a reconstructive strategy.

At the same time, an ideal of environmental "nondisturbance" was inspiring a powerful middle-class movement, risen to preserve what was left of the ravaged urban fabric. This movement was also in part too late. The precedent of massive urban displacement and the explosive protest of poor residents cast a different retrospective light on the preservation movement.

Its goals transposed the urgency of urban protest into an aesthetic and nostalgic ideological key, dear to cultivated and politically empowered professionals. In turn, the historicist or populist styles of architectural revisionism transposed the concerns of preservation – care for the old, the meaningful, the picturesque, the layered diversity of the urban fabric – into eclectic allusions to the remote or recent past of architecture. The resulting pastiches often collate fragments that never had a historical existence together, with disturbing effect. Perhaps more disturbing is the dim sense that pastiche harbors a double reversal of collective concerns: First, pastiche reverses the concern with security and a decent life into concern for the old neighborhoods in which these people live; second, it reverses the concern for preservation into a preoccupation with cute historical allusions.

Rejecting traditional postmodernism became *de rigueur* among professionals in the second part of the 1980s, but this should not conceal other facts. First, any style can be impressed in the service of speculative profit. Second, the urban working class and the poor suffered more from renewal than from remodeling and restoration. Third, the emphasis on context, the respect for the labyrinthine streets and motley construction of living cities is one of traditional postmodernism's most positive and significant contributions. Fourth, the proponents of contextualism can help invest even preservation with oppositional force. Last, at the level of the architectural objects themselves, the essence of postmodernism is not one style but the tolerance of multiple languages.

If "a thousand flowers bloomed," it is because the growing numbers of architects found (with difficulty) increasingly diverse clients for a great variety of projects. Either these diverse clients wanted stylistic novelty and excitement, or they could be convinced to accept new and momentarily different architectural idioms. A recession that aggravated the perennial structural problems of the profession pressed all but the most recalcitrant dogmatists to accept, even to encourage, the blooming. When postmodern pluralism is expressed in these terms, the situation after 1980 becomes clearer.

Architecture emerged from its double crisis with a restorative professional ideology – the formalist emphasis on pure design – and a pluralism that applied both to styles and building types. Having reconstructed the traditional identity of the architect-as-artist, formalism helped designers to effect a strategic retreat toward the individualism of one-of-a-kind commissions.

In the United States of the 1980s, social commissions and democratically oriented public architecture had all but vanished. The ideological comfort that formalism tendered to architects was excellence for excellence's sake, in either the playful or the rigorous delights of an eclectic discourse. The profession of architecture thus entered the speculative boom of the 1980s with new gatekeepers and a varied design elite but neither a common style nor a common vision. No group had enough power or enough influence to propose a direction, much less enforce common standards for the disparate professional enterprise. Yet the adoption of traditional postmodernism as favored style of the real estate boom made it easy to take it for a dominant style and blame it for what was happening to architecture.

Denying legitimacy to the use of architects as scenographers or stylists and of architecture as "packaging" matches the revaluation of craftmanship and service, which architects emphasized when aesthetic standards became uncertain. But despite their importance, constructional and pragmatic standards cannot define what architecture will look like (except multiple in form).

In sum, in our century architectural modernism went from technocratic social engineering to the service of corporate power. With the loss of social impetus, the aesthetic vision became routine. Strains and revisions multiplied at the level of discourse, quickening aesthetic disintegration. When an activist generation ignited political dissent and criticism inside the profession, the primacy of practice forced the symbolic gatekeepers to admit the ineradicable de facto diversity of architects' work.

Viewed from this angle, postmodern pluralism is a legacy of the anti-authoritarian politics of the 1960s, but the transformative impulses were contained within the specialized limits of a still weak and basically untransformed profession. The most substantial change was therefore in architecture's official discourse. The oppositional content of postmodernism (its emphasis on urban community, its advocacy of accessible design and authentic symbolism) struggles on within practices perforce devoted to the places of work, life, and leisure of the new urban middle class.

Architecture and Cultural Transitions

I have shown throughout this study that architecture is special, both as an intellectual discipline and as a professional practice. Despite this overdetermined specificity, its recent evolution suggests that transitions in the production of culture may have some common traits. I submit them as tentative hypotheses.

First of all, the study of architecture indicates that change in specific cultural discourses has local origins. This goes further than the well-established notion that modern cultural practices are "self-legislating."[5] Identifiable impulses toward change start within the specialized practices of identifiable agents and within specific circles of producers. Thus, what I was able to show about postmodern revisionism concerns the specialized discourse of architecture in the United States in a specific period. The postmodern accent on relativism and particularism agrees with the localism of architecture, the practice of which begins in a concrete locality, even if it can go international after that.

Second, discontinuities within specialist discourses do not *necessarily* respond to much more vast external discontinuities. World War II's awesome sequence of stasis, destruction, and reconstruction brought the Modern Movement from a minority position (already past its prime in the mid-1930s) to a universal and totalizing style. In turn, the global triumph of a banal and impoverished modernism compelled architects to react. The monotony and dreary sameness they call "exhaustion of forms" set in early, crying for aesthetic innovation and theoretical rearticulation. Not the catastrophic discontinuity of war but a later movement of young and educated people meant that a younger generation did both tasks.

Third, youth and education would not have been as significant without large numbers. The pressure of numbers within a delimited field deserves special attention for it is likely to engender competition for finite rewards. Competition, in turn, has been related to cultural innovation in settings as diverse as Islamic religion, nineteenth-century French painting, and twentieth-century American science.[6]

The booming economy probably absorbed most of the fast-growing numbers of architects produced by American schools in the 1950s and 1960s. Nevertheless, pressure for elite standing was bound to increase in the narrow and self-contained circles that make up the "scene" in major art centers, the "circuit" of elite graduate schools, the boards of major journals, and the juries of major contests. Moreover, the strongest push for aesthetic innovation and typological diversity coincided with the mounting pressure of "overproduced" architects on a field beset by the economic crisis of the 1970s. Without prejudging in any way the form or the content of cultural innovation, I expect that a larger number of players makes it more likely to emerge. Architectural postmodernism thus reinforces the rough correlations between numbers, competition, and innovation in the narrow ranks of specialized producers of culture.

Fourth, the partial overlap of personnel creates concrete connections between specialized cultural fields and larger political and social movements. The latter inspire and sustain within the former homologous actions of dissent, the objective of which is to redefine dominant intellectual paradigms and prescriptions about the specialists' roles.

Postmodernism could not have replicated the deliberate and fiery merger of artistic and political avant-gardism of the 1920s, for the revolutionary conditions of 1918 were not present in the 1960s in countries rich enough to afford an architecture. Yet what oppositional content there is in architectural postmodernism derives from the phase when, on both sides of the Atlantic, the New Left was raising its antitechnocratic banner.

Implicit in the above points is a fifth one, the most important corollary of cultural specialization: The interaction between producers of culture and their potential audiences (and even, if one so wishes, the expression of the *Zeitgeist*) is always mediated by conditions of the producers' practices and by the historical circumstances that surround them. From this sociological position, it follows that bypassing the specific and localized analysis of cultural practice is unsound. Rushing to determine what cultural objects "say," one risks ignoring the experience of those by whom culture is "spoken" and of those to whom it "speaks."

Two things stand out in the practice of the American design elite during the postmodern transition. One is the sheer complexity of the architectural task, a good part of which is the economic and organizational difficulty of keeping the business of architecture going. To paraphrase Joseph Esherick, there is no time at all to think of the *Zeitgeist*.

Besides, even if an architect conveys a personal vision of the times, polysemic objects are always open to multiple and conflicting interpretations. Yet in architecture one interpretation clearly prevails upon any designer's message. Although building type is understood through and by means of stylistic conventions, the social function that type denotes is more broadly and immediately accessible than style or aesthetics. The idea that significance can be exhaustively explained by the author's intention is thus conspicuously doubtful in architecture.

The second thing that stands out is the convergence of parts of architectural work with parts of the culture industries. The material base of this convergence is clearer than its moral and social implications, and I will limit myself to sketching the former.[7]

Postmodernism has marked the ascendancy of small- and medium-sized idea firms within the discourse, not the business, of American architecture. Their relations with organizational clients recall those of the creative technical producers with the organizational and managerial core of the culture industries. Like musicians for record companies or independent producers for television, architectural firms have no tenure beyond their project contracts. Because the smaller firms organize production in an almost artisanal way, overhead costs tend to be relatively low. If costs are reliably controlled, the firms enjoy full autonomy: The high level of professional competence (for which architects are presumably hired) makes it too costly for the sponsor to deny them responsibility.

Product selection occurs in architecture, as in the culture industries, at the "input boundary." Architects propose a range of alternatives (much expanded by postmodernism) to clients; like managers in the culture industries, large clients sponsor a selected sample for realization. In the large developers' offices, there is increasing professionalization of both "talent scouts" and marketing personnel, charged with co-opting the "mass media gatekeepers" (although in a minor way, compared to the culture industries). In the culture industries, book, music, film, or TV critics can strategically block or facilitate the "diffusion of particular fads and fashions."[8] In architecture, media critics have probably less power.

Elite designers do their own marketing to find clients, but big commercial clients market the architects, their names, and their personas as part of the commercial packaging of a new project. However, star architects' access to reputedly autonomous critics (and, for some exceptional designers like Robert Stern, access to their own television programs) does not sell more products. It can "sell" a project to users and the architect's ideas to the vast ranks of followers in schools and offices across the land. Therefore, in architecture, the "diffusion of fads and fashions" does not depend as much on the general media as on the organized profession, the specialist press, and especially the system of training institutions. The design process is still too complex and too highly professionalized, and, above all, building is still too expensive for clients and banks to permit momentary fads.

These caveats suggest that elite architects see image-making as a qualitative jump, more than just a further loss of control over the construction process. The decrease in the fiscal life of buildings, the multiplication of images from which clients can choose, and the increase in the media's emphasis on the architect as "culture hero," all conspire to subject stylistic conventions (the most noticeable sign of a building's architectural aspiration) to rapidly exhausted trends. Architects have not only moved closer to providing images instead of buildings; the life cycles of the images themselves have moved closer to those of the fashion and culture industries. The providers of these images can run after newness or imitation, for the decisive factor is what each can add to rental or resale values.

As an activity, postmodern architecture epitomizes material forces that tend to erase the differences between "high" and "mass" cultural production. Hired for their creativity and granted freedom to innovate, specialized cultural producers constrict their creative autonomy in anticipation of the client's choice. A subtler and more pervasive heteronomy channels cultural practices in the general direction of what sponsors can accept. This is in marked contrast with the autonomy of discourse.

Indeed, in most cultural fields, academic expansion and the continued growth of educated audiences allow increasing theoretical sophistication to develop in discourse. Architecture reveals a dialectic that appears with variations in many cultural fields: The autonomy of discourse encourages technical producers to take risks in cultural practice, while the costs of realization (a good indicator of producers' dependence on markets and funding) hold them back. This general condition helps us understand why theorists and philosophers take architecture as a pivotal allegory of postmodernism. . . .

Notes

1   I adopt Michel Foucault's concept of discipline as a "system of control in the production of discourse" ("The Discourse on Language," trans. Rupert Swyer, appendix to *The Archaeology of Knowledge* [New York: Pantheon, 1972]). . . .

2   The concept of "art world" and the complex networks that permit production, circulation, and social appreciation of art works is elaborated by Howard Becker in *Art Worlds* (Berkeley: University of California Press, 1982), Chap. 1. On the concept of "field" see Pierre Bourdieu, "Le Champ scientifique," *Actes de la recherche en sciences sociales* 2–3 (June 1976): 88–104.

3   My empirical study supports Andreas Huyssen's argument: "A crucial question . . . concerns the extent to which modernism and the avant-garde as forms of an adversary culture were nevertheless conceptually and practically bound up with capitalist modernization and/or with communist vanguardism, modernization's twin brother . . . Postmodernism's critical dimension lies precisely in the radical questioning which linked modernism and the avant-garde to the mindset of modernization" ("Mapping the Postmodern," in *After the Great Divide* [Bloomington: University of Indiana Press, 1986], 183). See also Kenneth Frampton's similar approach in "Towards a Critical Regionalism: Six Points for an Architecture of Resistance," in Hal Foster, ed., *The Anti- Aesthetic: Essays on Postmodern Culture* (Port Townsend, Wash.: Bay Press, 1983), 20.

4   Scott Lash's sociological approach to modernism/postmodernism in both architecture and cities admits that it is confusing and ambiguous to take the latter as cultural objects (*Sociology of Postmodernism* [London and New York: Routledge, 1990], 31; see in particular 31–6 and Chap. 8).

5   Lash takes as a criterion of modernity Weber's central concept about the "self-legislation" of each sphere of culture (the attempt by social actors within each sphere to develop their own conventions and mode of valuation; *Sociology of Postmodernism*, 9). See Max Weber, "Religious Rejections of the World and Their Directions," in Hans Gerth and C. W. Mills, eds. *From Max Weber* (New York: Oxford University Press, 1958).

6   M. J. Mulkay and B. S. Turner, "Over-production of Personnel and Innovation in Three Social Settings," *Sociology* 5 (1971): 47–61.
7   This sketch is based on Paul M. Hirsch's work "Processing Fads and Fashions: An Organization-Set Analysis of Cultural Industry Systems," *American Journal of Sociology* 77 (1972): 639–59. For a full indictment, see the classic text by Theodor Adorno and Max Horkheimer, "The Culture Industry: Enlightenment as Mass Deception," in *Dialectic of Enlightenment*, trans. John Cumming (New York: Continuum, 1989).
8   Hirsch, "Processing Fads," 649.

Editor's Notes on Further Reading

Sarfatti Larson on Architecture

Magali Sarfatti Larson examines architecture as a professional context for cultural production to account for the change from modernist to postmodernist architecture at the beginning of the last quarter of the twentieth century. Her research interweaves questions of discourse and practice, aesthetics, organization, and economic context, and she shows how the profession combines aspects of both "art world" and "culture industry" (see excerpts from Becker, Peterson, and DiMaggio, this volume). The larger study uses in-depth interviews to analyze how architects think of the practical context of their work (firms, clients, commissions, and careers) and the ways they articulate aesthetic criteria and aesthetic conflicts: this analysis is backed up with an analysis of design awards. While Larson argues for attention to specific production context, she also fills in the background to her study with the larger story of twentieth-century architecture and the political economy of cities.

Other sociological works on architecture include Larson, "Reading Architecture in the Holocaust Memorial Museum: A Method and an Empirical Illustration," pp. 62–91 in Elizabeth Long, ed., *From Sociology to Cultural Studies: New Perspectives* (Malden, MA and Oxford: Blackwell, 1997); David Brain, "Cultural Production as "Society in the Making": Architecture as an Exemplar of the Social Construction of Cultural Artifacts," pp. 192–220, in Diana Crane, ed., *The Sociology of Culture* (Malden, MA and Oxford: Blackwell, 1994); Brain, "Practical Knowledge and Occupational Control: The Professionalization of Architecture in the United States," *Sociological Forum* 6 (1991): 239–68; Brain, "Discipline and Style: The Ecole des Beaux-arts and the Social Production of an American Architecture," *Theory and Society* 18 (1989): 807–68, and Judith Blau, *Architects and Firms* (Cambridge, MA: MIT Press, 1984).

On the broader topic of material culture, see for example Mihaly Csikszentmihalyi and Eugene Rochberg-Halton, *The Meaning of Things: Domestic Symbols and the Self* (Cambridge and New York: Cambridge University Press, 1981); the overview in Chandra Mukerji "Towards a Sociology of Material Culture: Science Studies, Cultural Studies, and the Meanings of Things," pp. 143–62 in Crane, ed., *Sociology of Culture*, and Mukerji, *Territorial Ambitions and the Gardens of Versailles* (Cambridge and New York: Cambridge University Press, 1997). On professions see for example Magali Sarfatti Larson, *The Rise of Professionalism: A Sociological Analysis* (Berkeley: University of California Press, 1977) and Andrew Abbott, *The System of Professions: An Essay on the Division of Expert Labor* (Chicago: University of Chicago Press, 1988).

The analysis is also informed with wider theoretical concerns. For instance, an important strand of postmodern social theory often takes architecture as metonym for broader social changes, but Larson shows the more specific professional context in which postmodern architecture emerged. Compare the excerpt from Jameson, and accompanying editor's note, this volume, and on architecture see especially also for example Andreas Huyssen, "Mapping the Postmodern," *New German Critique* 33 (1984): 5–52; David Harvey, *The Condition of Postmodernity* (Oxford and Cambridge, MA: Blackwell, 1989), 66–98; Scott Lash, *Sociology of Postmodernism* (London and New York: Routledge, 1990), 201–36; Jürgen Habermas, "Modern and Postmodern Architecture," pp. 317–329 in John Forester, ed., *Critical Theory and Public Life* (Cambridge, MA and London: MIT Press, 1987); and M. Gottdiener *Postmodern Semiotics: Material Culture and the Forms of Postmodern Life* (Oxford and Cambridge, MA: Blackwell, 1995) chs. 4–7.

Notably, Sarfatti Larson concludes her book observing that "the most beloved and visited architectural work of the profligate 1980s was not a hotel nor a museum but the Vietnam Veternas Memorial in Washington . . ." (253), the subject of the following excerpt by Wagner-Pacifici and Schwartz.

20 The Vietnam Veterans Memorial: Commemorating a Difficult Past

Robin Wagner-Pacifici and Barry Schwartz

In this article, we address two problems, one general and one particular, and claim that they are best approached by referring each to the other. The first, general, problem is that of discovering the processes by which culture and cultural meaning are produced. Collective memory, moral and political entrepreneurship, dominant ideologies, and representational genres are all refracted through these processes and must all be sociologically identified and gauged. The second, particular, problem is the Vietnam Veterans Memorial. This unusual monument grew out of a delayed realization that some public symbol was needed to recognize the men and women who died in the Vietnam War. But its makers faced a task for which American history furnished no precedent – the task of commemorating a divisive defeat.

By dealing with the problem of commemoration in this case study of the Vietnam Veterans Memorial, we can address general concerns in the sociology of culture. Our concentration on the details of a particular case follows Clifford Geertz's maxim that "the essential task of theory building... is not to codify abstract regularities but to make thick description possible, not to generalize across cases but to generalize within them" (1973, p. 26). However, we are also concerned to locate commemorative formulas as they are repeated across cases. Thus we will be moving from the case of the Vietnam Veterans Memorial to monuments that have similarly vexed commemorative missions, seeking to bring together the resemblances and differences under a single analytic framework....

Dilemmas of Commemoration

The memory of the Vietnam War and its epoch takes place within a culture of commemoration. Current analytic approaches to culture define commemorative objects, and cultural objects in general, as "shared significance embodied in form" (Griswold 1987a, p. 13). However, our concern is in formulating an approach to those kinds of commemoration for which significance is not shared....

The Vietnam Veterans Memorial provides a good case to use in thinking about these issues. The succession of events that led to the Memorial's creation and public reception was a culture-producing process. In that process, contrasting moral evaluations of the Vietnam War and its participants were affirmed. The process itself consisted of seven stages, each defined by the activity of different individuals and different institutions: (1) the Pentagon's decision to mark the way by an inconspicuous plaque in Arlington Cemetery; (2) congressional activity culminating in a Vietnam Veterans Week and a series of Veterans' support programs; (3) a former Vietnam soldier's conception and promotion of a tangible monument; (4) intense controversy over the nontraditional monument design selected by the United States Commission of Fine Arts; (5) modification of this original design by the incorporation of traditional symbols; (6) the public's extraordinary and unexpected reaction to the Memorial; and (7) the ongoing controversy over its further modification. Our analysis will pass through these stages as we chart the Vietnam Veterans Memorial's development.

From a comparative perspective, the moral evaluations reflected in the Vietnam Memorial derive from a formula common to all societies that seek to commemorate controversial military ventures. When the cause of a lost war is widely held to be immoral or at best needless, then, in James Mayo's (1988, p. 170) words, "defeat...cannot be forgotten and a nation's people must find ways to redeem those who died for their country to make defeat honorable. This can be done by honoring the individuals who fought rather than the country's lost cause."...

Commemoration as a Genre Problem

Controversies over the merits of a war are expressed at some point in debates over measures taken to commemorate it. The stages in the Vietnam Memorial's construction reveal, on the one hand, the desire for a design that reflects the uniqueness of the Vietnam War and, on the other, the desire for a design that recognizes the sense in which the Vietnam War was similar to previous wars. The Vietnam War differed from other wars because it was controversial, morally questionable, and unsuccessful. It resembled other wars because it called forth in its participants the traditional virtues of self-sacrifice, courage, loyalty, and honor. Tension between alternative commemorative designs centers on the problem of incorporating these contrasting features into a single monument.

Distinctions among war monuments are, like all generic distinctions, produced by "sorting, seeing the similarities in different...objects, abstracting the common elements from a welter of particular variations" (Grisworld 1987a, p. 17). Genre, in Wendy Griswold's view, is a kind of schema that organizes perception. Griswold asserts, however, that literary and artistic genres are impermanent and express the changing character of their creators, audiences, and contexts. This conception of genre is relevant to our present problem: What kind of monument can be built in the context of changes in traditional beliefs about what war monuments should look like and represent?...

Attitudes and interests are translated into commemorative forms through enterprise. Before any event can be regarded as worth remembering, and before any class of people can be recognized for having participated in that event, some individual, and eventually some group, must deem both event and participants commemorable and must have the influence to get others to agree. Memorial devices are not self-created; they are conceived and built by those who wish to bring to consciousness the events and people that others are more inclined to forget. To understand memorial making in this way is to understand it as a construction process wherein competing "moral entrepreneurs" seek public arenas and support for their interpretations of the past. These interpretations are embodied in the memorial's symbolic structure.. . .

A Nation's Gratitude: Search for a Genre

The first official recognition of the Vietnam veteran was not bestowed until 1978, three years after the last American was flown out of Saigon. The recognition itself was hesitant and uncertain. A Vietnam War crypt had already been prepared in the Tomb of the Unknown Soldier, but the Army determined that neither of its two unidentified bodies (only 30% of the remains in either case) made for a decent corpse. Instead of honoring its Vietnam battle dead by symbolically joining them, through entombment of unknown soldiers' remains, with men fallen in earlier wars, the army recommended that a plaque and display of medals be set apart behind the tomb, along with the following inscription: "Let all know that the United States of America pays tribute to the members of the Armed Forces who answered their country's call." This strange declaration bears no reference at all to the Vietnam War, and it required an act of the Veterans Affairs subcommittee to make it more specific: "Let all people know that the United States pays tribute to those members of the Armed Forces who served honorably in Southeast Asia during the Vietnam era" (*The Nation*, April 8, 1978, p. 389). In even this second, stronger statement, three things are noteworthy: (1) although revised in Congress, the statement was initiated by the military; (2) it received little publicity; and (3) it designated the conflict in Vietnam by the word "era" rather than "war." Thus the recognition came from only a small part of the society for whose interests and values the war was fought; it was communicated to that society without conspicuous ceremony; and it betrayed confusion about the meaning of the war by its failure to find a word to describe it. This last point is the most noteworthy of all. Although a war had not been officially declared, many congressional resolutions during the 1980s referred to the hostilities in Vietnam as "the Vietnam war." Touchiness during the late 1970s about what to call the conflict stemmed from social, not legal, concerns. To name an event is to categorize it morally and to provide an identity for its participants. Anomalous names betray ambiguity about an event's nature and uncertainty about how to react to the men who take part in it.

The first solution to the war's commemorative genre problem was thus halting and uncertain. The fighters were honored but not by an imposing monument. They were honored by a plaque, inconspicuously placed, whose inscription was, itself, indirect and muted. Undeclared wars are usually fought with restraint, however violent they might be. The Vietnam War's first official commemoration mirrored this restraint, marking the cause without really drawing attention to it.

Official ambivalence toward the Vietnam War showed up next in the activities of Congress. It was in Congress, in fall 1978, that the work culminating in the Veterans Memorial began. The plan then discussed, however, was not to commemorate those who had died in the war, but to set aside a special "Vietnam Veterans Week" for its survivors. Thus evolved a second solution to the problem of finding a genre to commemorate the Vietnam War. Time, rather than granite, the dedication of a week rather than the dedication of a tangible monument, sufficed to honor the Vietnam fighting man. This plan's principal entrepreneurs were the members of the Vietnam-Era Caucus, 19 U.S. representatives and senators who had served in the military during the Vietnam War years. They meant to achieve two goals: to unify a nation divided by war and to induce Congress to recognize that many war veterans were suffering from unmet needs. Before anything could actually be accomplished, however, certain obstacles had to be overcome, obstacles inherent in the object of commemoration itself.

To promote unity by separating the event from its men was Congress's first concern. In Congressman Grisham's words, "We may still have differing opinions about our involvement in the Vietnam War, but we are no longer divided in our attitudes toward those who served in Vietnam" (U.S. House of Representatives 1979, p. 12588). At one time, however, the division was deep. Grisham himself acknowledged that the veterans were stigmatized or, at best, ignored on their return from the battlefront. No ceremony dramatized and ennobled their sacrifices. Most of the other congressmen knew this, and they wanted to upgrade the veterans' status. Transforming the Vietnam soldier from an Ugly American into a patriot who innocently carried out the policy of elected leaders, Congress tried to create a positive image that all Americans could accept.

However, the very attempt to improve the veterans' status raised unsettling questions. Congressmen openly recognized that America's lower-income minorities were disproportionately represented in the armed forces and that the trauma of war bore more heavily on them, economically and psychologically, than it would have on a middle-class army. An uncomplimentary view of the returning soldier accompanied this recognition. The congressmen made no mention of the crimes allegedly committed by American soldiers in Vietnam; however, they did recognize publicly "statistics such as the fact that 25 percent of the persons incarcerated in correctional institutions in America are veterans of the Vietnam War," along with the veterans' need for "an expanded drug and alcohol abuse treatment and rehabilitation program." Family counseling needs were also described: "Of those veterans married before going to Vietnam almost 40 percent were divorced within six months of their return" (U.S. House of Representatives 1979, pp. 12589, 12593, 12584; for details, see Johnson [1976, 1980]; U.S. House Committee on Veterans' Affairs 1981). Congresswoman Mikulski recognized the veterans' social marginality by pleading for the government to "be responsive to the unique problems which they face . . . so that they will be better able to fill their roles in society." Congressman Mikva spoke to the same point. Existing veterans' programs, he explained, are not enough for this group. "We must back up this symbolic recognition of their efforts for our country with . . . educational and rehabilitative programs geared to their special needs" (U.S. House of Representatives 1979, pp. 12583, 12588). Here, as elsewhere, the emphasis is on the veterans' shortcomings, and this emphasis reflects society's desire to reconstitute them morally. . . .

Entrepreneurs and Sponsors

Negative characterizations of the Vietnam veteran might have eventually undermined his positive recognition were it not for a new development, one that was oriented less to the living than to the dead. During the time that the Vietnam-Era Caucus worked on its legislation, a former army corporal from a working-class family, Jan Scruggs, had independently decided on a plan of his own. As noted above, one of the premises of Vietnam Veterans Week was that the soldier must be separated from the cause. This separation is precisely what Scruggs aimed to cele-brate publicly. At first, his idea attracted little notice, but it eventually overshadowed Vietnam Veterans Week in commemorative significance. He would build a memorial to the men who served in Vietnam and would inscribe on it the names of all the war dead. The plan represented a different solution to the commemorative genre prob-lem than those previously proposed. It was different in that it combined the traditional idea of a stone monument to the war dead with the radical idea of excluding from it any prominent symbol of national honor and glory. In place of such a symbol would appear a list of the dead soliders' names – 58,000 of them. On May 28, 1979, Scruggs announced the formation of the Vietnam Veterans Memorial Fund to raise money to build the monument.

The accumulation of money to build the Veterans Memorial did not automatically follow from the desire to build it. What needed to be overcome was not only opposition from the still vocal critics of the war, but more important, a sense of uncertainty in the public at large as to what the monument would look like and what it would represent. These suspicions and uncertainties were relieved when the Memorial's original framing rule – "Honor the soldier, not the cause" – was reiter-ated in the very selection of its sponsors. Chosen were men and women who differed visibly and widely on many political questions but shared the desire to honor the Vietnam veterans. The sponsoring leaders and celebrities included Vernon Jordan, president of the National Urban League; Ruben Bonilla, national president of the League of United Latin American Citizens; Carol Burnett, the actress who played the mother of a soldier killed in the war in the television drama, *Friendly Fire;* First Lady Rosalynn Carter and former First Lady Betty Ford; Father Theodore Hesburgh, president of the University of Notre Dame; Bob Hope; Rocky Bleir, described as a "wounded Vietnam veteran who came back to star with the Pittsburgh Steelers"; and Admiral James B. Stockdale, formerly a prisoner of war and now president of The Citadel. These individuals represented many sectors of society: blacks, Hispanics, women, religious and academic figures, entertainment and sports celebrities, and military men. With the support of this noncontroversial coalition of sponsors, funds were quickly raised to pay for design and construction costs and, by July 4, 1980, a few days after the proclamation of Vietnam Veterans' Week, President Carter signed a joint resolution that reserved a two-acre site in Constitution Gardens, between the Washington Monument and Lincoln Memorial, for the Veterans Memorial's place-ment....

It was the redemptive qualities of Scruggs's project – precisely, its embodiment of gratitude, the only currency for paying off a moral debt – that congressional supporters emphasized. As President Carter approved Congress's resolution, he expressed his belief that the formal honoring of the veteran would also promote the healing of a nation divided by war. To this end, the Memorial fund's directors continued to avoid political statements in both fund-raising efforts and in contem-plation of the Memorial design. The universal support of the Senate and strong support of the House were based on this same requirement: that the Memorial make no reference to the war, only to the men who fought it. Political neutrality was the condition for the support of other sponsoring organizations, including the Reserve Officers Association, Veterans of Foreign Wars, Marine Corps League, Retired Officers Association, and American Gold Star Mothers. These organizations had been assured by Scruggs that the Memorial "will stand as a symbol of our unity as a nation and as a focal point of all Americans regardless of their views on Vietnam" (U.S. House of Representatives 1980, p. 4805). Indeed, its very name would be noncontroversial: it would be a "Veterans Memorial" rather than a "War Memorial." The federal agencies responsible for approving the final design and placement of the Memorial, particularly the Commission of Fine Arts and the Department of Interior, were guided by this same principle.

An apolitical monument was thus supported by the apolitical makeup of its sponsoring agencies.... The memorial chosen by the Commission of Fine Arts from the more than 1,400 designs submitted was, indeed, the simplest and least imposing: two unadorned black walls, each about 250 feet in length, composed of 70 granite panels increasing in height from several inches at the end of each wall to 10 feet where they come together at a 125 degree angle. Although this angle aligns the two walls with the Lincoln Memorial and Washington Monument, the walls themselves are placed below ground level, invisible from most vantage points on or near the Mall. The Vietnam War is thus defined as a national event, but in a spatial context that brackets off that event from those commemorated by neighboring monuments. The walls add to this sense of detachment by their internal format, which draws the viewer into a separate warp of time and space. As one moves from the edge of one wall to the point where it joins the other, one experiences a descending movement in space and a circular movement in time, for the 57,939 soldiers' names appear in the chronological order of the dates of their deaths, such that the war's first and last fatalities are joined at the walls' conjunction.

The commission's preference for this design was unanimous. However, for every layman who approved that choice, another seemed to be enraged by it. Those who shared the designer's goals were inclined to believe she had achieved them. Maya Ying Lin declared that her design was not meant to convey a particular political message but to evoke "feelings, thoughts, and emotions" of a variant and private nature: "What people see or don't see is their own projection." Jan Scruggs concurred: "The Memorial says exactly what we wanted to say about Vietnam – absolutely nothing." Indeed, on the original design the word, Vietnam, did not even appear (a statement indicating that the names on the wall belong to dead soldiers, and identifying the war in which they fought, was added later)....

Opposition to the memorial wall was expressed by attacks on details like color, shape, and location, but underlying all specific objections was a disdain for the style itself. Many believed that that style violated the limits of the war-memorial genre. Designed to be apolitical, this memorial struck critics as nonpatriotic and nonheroic. It conveyed a conception of the war and a conception of the soldier that ran counter to those of many Americans. These Americans, responded Jan Scruggs, "wanted the Memorial to make Vietnam what it had never been in reality: a good, clean glorious war seen as necessary and supported by the united country." One leading opponent of the design conceded that the nation had not looked back favorably on the Vietnam War; however, he believed that "history can be re-evaluated" and "a piece of art remains, as a testimony to a particular moment in history, and we are under a solemn obligation to get that moment down as correctly as possible" (quoted in Scruggs and Swerdlow 1985, p. 94).

Most critics believed that only a "real" memorial could correctly represent the Vietnam War, but since that was politically impossible, they sought an addition to the present design in order to offset the "national humiliation" it perpetuated. At length, a compromise was conceived. An American flag, and next to that, a realistic statue of three soldiers, identifiable as white, black, and Hispanic, portrayed returning from patrol and gazing toward the names on the wall, would bring the original design closer to the traditional genre – would make it look more like a real war memorial. . . .

Considering the memorial complex as a whole, we find an even broader pattern of assertion and qualification. The wall embodied a controversial assertion: that individuals should be remembered and their cause ignored; the qualifications came with the flag and statue. These, in turn, were beset by their own internal tensions. The statue was conceived as a reactive assertion of pride, heroism, and masculinity, but, through the particular form it took, it emerged as a tempering of all these things. The flag seems to be unconditionally assertive because it is the only part of the memorial site that draws our eyes upward, but we notice in the peculiar dedication inscribed on its base a kind of backing off: "This flag affirms the principles of freedom for which [the Vietnam veterans] fought and their pride in having served under difficult circumstances." The euphemism is transparent enough. By "difficult circumstances" we are to understand not the power of our enemy but the feebleness of our cause. In this light, the similarities among the three parts of the Memorial become more salient than their differences, despite the realism of the statue's figures and the vertical prominence of the flag. Whether we look down, across, or up, we find ambivalence about the meaning of this war and its protagonists refracted throughout. . . .

Uses of Genre: The Enshrinement Process

The meaning of the Vietnam Veterans Memorial is defined by the way people behave in reference to it. Some monuments are rarely talked about or visited and never put to ceremonial use. Other monuments, like the Tomb of the Unknown Soldier, are used often as formal ceremonial sites and visited year after year by large numbers of people. Between the Vietnam Veterans Memorial and its visitors, a very different relationship obtains. Not only is the Memorial an object of frequent ceremony and frequent visitation (more than 2.5 million visitors and 1,100–1,500 reunions per year), it is also an object with which visitors enter into active and affective relationships. These relationships have thwarted all original intentions as to what the Memorial should be and represent.

Conceived as something to be passively looked at and contemplated, the Vietnam Memorial has become an object of emotion. This is not the case for the Memorial site as a whole, just the wall and its names. The names on the wall are touched, their letters traced by the moving finger. The names are caressed. The names are reproduced on paper by pencil rubbing and taken home. And something is left from home itself – a material object bearing special significance to the deceased or a written statement by the visitor or mourner.

The dedications of the aggrieved are a spectacle that to many is more moving than the Memorial wall itself. More goes into spectators' reactions, however, than morbid curiosity, for the scenes of mourning are not altogether private affairs. These scenes make palpable a collective loss known to all. Not only, therefore, do friends and family bring their personal grief to the Memorial wall, but society exercises a moral pressure over those not directly affected by loss to add their presence to the situation and to align their sentiments with it. . . .

When profusely decorated with patriotic emblems, the wall alone may enhance our idea of the traditional war monument, but it cannot embody that idea. This is because patriotism is not the only response that the wall excites. The Memorial wall has in fact become a kind of debating forum – a repository of diverse opinions about the very war that occasioned its construction. Traditional war monuments serve no such reflexive function. . . .

[L]etters and poems, no less than the other items brought to the wall, reveal that many people are unable to look back on the war in a politically neutral way. Notwithstanding the claims of its official sponsors, the Vietnam Veterans Memorial elicits the same tensions as those that divided the nation during the war itself. As time passes, this capacity to evoke affirmative and critical sentiments endures. The volume of objects deposited at the Memorial is as great or greater today as when the Memorial was dedicated, and the range, if not the exact proportion of the different objects, is the same. Flags, although no longer stored and inventoried, continue to appear in profusion. Military objects are still deposited by Vietnam veterans, and these are supplemented by military objects deposited by post-Vietnam soldiers. Personal items and letters, too, appear as frequently as ever. And many of the recent letters bear criticism of American policy in different parts of the world, particularly Central America, comparing it to the policy that led to war in Vietnam.

In the Veterans Memorial, then, we see none of the hegemonic influence that forms the basis for Gusfield and Michalowicz's "manipulative theories" of secular symbolism (1984, pp. 424–7). If the Memorial were in fact a tool of state power, if it were adopted by the state in order to maintain allegiance to an elite and to promote authoritative ways of seeing society (as Haines [1986] suggests), then that tool has not been used very effectively. . . .

[T]he least prestigious war in American history, the war fought and remembered with the most controversy, is precisely the one whose monument is most revered and most often visited. This essential fact must be incorporated into any effort to theorize our understanding of the Vietnam Memorial. As we outlined it in our introduction, the development of a thick description of the Vietnam Memorial involved the disclosure of relevant social, political, and cultural processes. These processes were, in their substance, interactive: moral enterpreneurs interacting with their constituencies and with political and cultural authorities; politicians interacting with their colleagues and within a conservative social climate, veterans interacting with their memories and their current situations; artists interacting with politically forged competition guidelines, with denizens of the art world and with lay audiences; visitors interacting with the wall. The key to the Memorial's multifold meaning lies in this interaction web. The Memorial's ability to bring off commemoration of a dark and controversial part of the past comes to rest on the surrounding society's interaction with the Memorial itself. Whatever processes brought this cultural object into being in the first place, it is the use made of it that brings it into the life of the society. Wendy Griswold, in her outline of a model for analyzing cultural objects, notes that meaning is produced by the interaction between "the symbolic capacities of the object itself and the perceptual apparatus of those who experience the object" (1987*b*, p. 1079). We have come to understand the complex evolution of the Vietnam Veterans Memorial in the same way: as a succession of interacting producers, sponsors, and audiences.

References

Geertz, Clifford, 1973. *The Interpretation of Cultures*. New York: Basic.

Griswold, Wendy, 1987*a*. "A Methodological Framework for the Sociology of Culture." Pp. 1–35 in *Sociological Methodology*, vol. 17. Edited by Clifford Clogg. Washington, D.C.: American Sociological Association.

—— 1987*b*. "The Fabrication of Literary Meaning." *American Journal of Sociology* 92: 1077–117.

Gusfield, Joseph, and Jerzy Michalowicz. 1984. "Secular Symbolism: Studies of Ritual, Ceremony, and the Symbolic Order in Modern Life" Pp. 417–35 in *Annual Review of Sociology*, edited by Ralph Turner. Palo Alto, Calf.: Annual Reviews.

Haines, Harry W. 1986. "What Kind of War: An Analysis of the Vietnam Veterans Memorial." *Critical Studies in Mass Communication* 3: 1–20.

Johnson, Loch, 1976. "Political Alienation among Vietnam Veterans." *Western Political Quarterly* 29: 398–410.

—— 1980. "Scars of War: Alienation and Estrangement among Wounded Vietnam Veterans." Pp. 213–27 in *Strangers at Home*, edited by Charles R. Figley and Seymour Leventman. New York: Praeger.

Mayo, James M. 1988. *War Memorials as Political Landscape: The American Experience and Beyond*. New York: Praeger.

Scruggs, Jan C., and Joel L. Swerdlow, 1985. *To Heal a Nation: The Vietnam Veterans Memorial*. New York: Harper & Row.

U.S. House Committee on Veterans' Affairs. 1981. *Legacies of Vietnam: Comparative Adjustment of Veterans and Their Peers*. Report no. 14. March 9. Washington, D.C.: Government Printing Office.

U.S. House of Representatives. (1979). *Congressional Record*. May 24. Washington, D.C.: Government Printing Office.

U.S. Senate. 1980. *Congressional Record*. April 30 Washington, D.C.: Government Printing Office.

Editor's Notes on Further Reading

Wagner-Pacifici and Schwartz on Commemoration

As Wagner-Pacifici and Schwartz demonstrate in their account of the Vietnam Veteran's Memorial in Washington, DC, looking closely at processes of production can help explain national public culture. Examining the memorial's creation, revision, and reception, they show how conflict and ambivalence about the events to be commemorated ultimately influenced the very form of the memorial itself, a combination of an innovative design with more traditional commemorative elements.

For more on war memorials, see for instance Barry Schwartz and Todd Bayma, "Commemoration and the Politics of Recognition: The Korean War Veterans Memorial," *American Behavioral Scientist* 42 (1999): 946–77; K. S. Inglis assisted by Jan Brazier, *Sacred Places: War Memorials in the Australian Landscape* (Melbourne: The Miegunyah Press at Melbourne University Press, 1998); Martin Evans and Ken Lunn, eds., *War and Memory in the Twentieth Century* (Oxford and New York: Berg, 1997); Jay Winter, *Sites of Memory, Sites of Mourning: The Great War in European Cultural History* (Cambridge and New York: Cambridge University Press, 1995); George Mosse, *Fallen Soldiers: Reshaping the Memory of the World Wars* (New York and Oxford: Oxford University Press, 1990); and James Mayo, *War Memorials as Political Landscape: The American Experience and Beyond* (New York: Praeger, 1988). For a nuanced account of conflict over a city seen as sacred symbol, see Roger Friedland and Richard Hecht, *To Rule Jerusalem* (Cambridge and New York: Cambridge University Press, 1996).

Some classic works on collective memory include Maurice Halbwachs, "The Social Frameworks of Memory," in Lewis Coser, ed., *On Collective Memory* (Chicago and London: University of Chicago Press, 1992); Eric Hobsbawm, and Terence Ranger, eds., *The Invention of Tradition* (Cambridge and New York: Cambridge University Press, 1984); and Edward Shils, *Tradition* (Chicago: University of Chicago Press, 1981). For introductions to the rapidly growing contemporary literature on collective memory see Howard Schuman and Amy D. Corning, "Collective Knowledge of Public Events: The Soviet Era from the Great Purge to Glasnost," *American Journal of Sociology* 105 (2000): 913–56; Jeffrey Olick, "Collective Memory: The Two Cultures," *Sociological Theory* 17 (1999): 333–48; Olick, "Genre Memories and Memory Genres: A Dialogical Analysis of May 8, 1945 Commemorations in the F. D. R.," *American Sociological Review* 64 (1999): 381–402; Barry Schwartz, "Postmodernity and Historical Reputation: Abraham Lincoln in Late Twentieth-Century American Memory," *Social Forces* 77 (1998): 63–103; Jeffrey Olick and Joyce Robbins, "Social Memory Studies: From 'Collective Memory' to the Historical Sociology of Mnemonic Practices," *Annual Review of Sociology* 24 (1998): 105–40; Jeffrey Olick and Daniel Levy, "Collective Memory and Cultural Constraint: Holocaust Myth and Rationality in German Politics," *American Sociological Review* 62 (1997): 921–36; the articles collected in *Qualitative Sociology* 19 (3), Fall 1996, Special Issue on Collective Memory, guest ed. Barry Schwartz; and in *Social Science History* 22 (4) 1998, special issue on collective memory, ed. Jeffrey Olick.

For more by cultural sociologists on national symbol and ritual in the United States, see the excerpt from work by Alexander and Smith, this volume, and accompanying editor's notes as, well as Barry Schwartz, *Abraham Lincoln and the Forge of National Memory* (Chicago and London: University of Chicago Press, 2000); Sarah Corse, *Nationalism and Literature: The Politics of Culture in Canada and the United States* (Cambridge and New York: Cambridge University Press, 1997); Lyn Spillman, *Nation and Commemoration: Creating National Identities in the United States and Australia* (Cambridge and New York: Cambridge University Press, 1997); Karen Cerulo, *Identity Designs: The Sights and Sounds of a Nation*, ASA Rose Book Series (New Brunswick, NJ: Rutgers University Press, 1995); and Schwartz, *George Washington: The Making of an American Symbol* (Ithaca and London: Cornell University Press, 1987). Good portals to the large body of work by historians of American collective memory and national identity can be found in John Bodnar, *Remaking America: Public Memory, Commemoration, and Patriotism in the Twentieth Century* (Princeton: Princeton University Press, 1992), and Michael Kammen, *Mystic Chords of Memory: The Transformation of Tradition in American Culture* (New York: Knopf, 1991).

In addition to influences from public debate surrounding the making of the memorial, Wagner-Pacific and Schwartz note that norms associated with memorial genres also influenced debate and design in this case. On conventions or normative expectations associated with genre, see also excerpts from studies by Becker, Berezin, Jacobs and Griswold, this volume.

Part IV

Cultural Frameworks: Categories, Genre, and Narrative

21 The Fine Line: Making Distinctions in Everyday Life

Eviatar Zerubavel

Reality is not made up of insular chunks unambiguously separated from one another by sharp divides, but, rather, of vague, blurred-edge essences that often "spill over" into one another. It normally presents itself not in black and white, but, rather, in subtle shades of gray, with mental twilight zones as well as intermediate essences connecting entities. Segmenting it into discrete islands of meaning usually rests on some social convention, and most boundaries are, therefore, mere social artifacts. As such, they often vary from one society to another as well as across historical periods within each society. Moreover, the precise location – not to mention the very existence – of such mental partitions is often disputed even within any given society.

Culture and Classification

There is more than one way to carve discrete chunks out of a given continuum, and different cultures indeed mold out of the same reality quite different archipelagos of meaning. While all cultures, for example, distinguish the edible from the inedible or the young from the old, they usually differ from one another in where they draw the lines between them. The distinction between the sexually accessible and inaccessible is likewise universal (all cultures, for example, have an incest taboo), yet the specific delineation of those who are considered off limits often varies from one culture to another. Surrounding oneself with a bubble of "personal space," too, is a universal practice, yet, in marked contrast to other species, humans exhibit substantial sub-specific cultural variations in where they draw its boundaries. (Along similar lines, the precise delineation of one's "personal" circle of intimates also varies from one culture to another.) By the same token, not everyone who is considered "black" in America would necessarily be classified as such in the West Indies or Brazil....

Languages likewise differ from one another in the way they generate distinct lexical particles, and it is not unusual that a single word in one language would cover the semantic range of several separate words in another. Thus, for example, while there is a single word for both rats and mice in Latin, insects and airplanes in Hopi, and brothers-in-law and grandnephews in the Algonquian language of the Fox, there are separate words for blankets that are folded and spread out, for water in buckets and in lakes, and for dogs that stand and sit in Navajo. Such differences have considerable cognitive implications. After all, it is much easier to isolate a distinct mental entity from its surroundings when one has a word to denote it. That explains why the Navajo, who use different verbs to denote the handling of objects with different shapes, indeed tend to classify objects according to shape much more than English speakers. By the same token, lacking the necessary lexical tools for differentiating, it took me, a native speaker of Hebrew, a long time before I could actually notice the mental gaps – so obvious to English-speakers – that separate jelly from jam or preserves....

Any notion of logic is valid only within a particular cultural milieu, and our own classifications are no more logical than those of "savages." We must therefore resist the ethnocentric tendency to regard our own way of classifying reality as the only reasonable way to do it. That entails giving up the idea that some ways of classifying are more correct and "logical" than others and, therefore, also reconsidering the standard tests through which we usually measure intelligence. Thus, for example, "a person, asked in what way wood and alcohol are alike [should not be] given a zero score if he answers: 'Both knock you out' [just] because the examiner prefers logical categories of scientific classification."[1] By the same token, nor should we penalize someone who maintains (as did my daughter, when she was five) that the difference between a bus and an airplane lies in the fact that we need not pay the pilot on boarding a plane.

Ways of classifying reality vary not only across cultures but also across historical periods within the same culture. The last couple of centuries, for example, saw substantial shifts in the location of the lines we draw between the sexes, the "races," public and private, family and community. Along similar lines, our calendar year did not always begin on January 1, opiates were still legal in America only eighty years ago, and lungs and gills did not become "similar" until comparative anatomists began classifying organisms according to functional rather than morphological features. Even the location of the line separating art from life changes over time – the Romans, for example, would often execute real-life convicts on stage as part of theatrical shows. A few decades ago, Americans were taught to regard the color of one's skin (and Germans the color of one's hair) as most salient for social exclusion. Today they learn to ignore it as socially irrelevant....

The lines we draw vary not only across cultures and historical periods but also within cultures at a given point in history, as one can tell from the joke about the Orthodox Jew from New York who asks a Southerner who is obviously intrigued by his traditional garb and heavy accent, "What's the matter, you've never seen a Yankee before?" At the same time that one needed seven-eighths "white blood" to avoid being considered a "person of color" in Florida, a mere three-quarters would suffice in Nebraska, and in universities that rarely tenure their young faculty, the line normally separating faculty from students may not be as pronounced as the one separating tenured faculty from both students and nontenured faculty. The lines believed by residents of fancy neighborhoods to separate them from those who live in less prestigious neighborhoods nearby are likewise often blurred by the latter. (When I asked the man from whom I bought my house about the nearest train station, he mentioned a station located six minutes away in a fancier neighborhood, yet "forgot" to mention a station located only two minutes away in a much less prestigious one.) Likewise, within the same culture, meat eaters draw the line between what is edible and inedible quite differently than do vegetarians. (Whereas Bertrand Russell would claim that this line ought to be drawn "at the level of the species," vegetarians may not find ordinary meat eaters that different from canni-bals.) Similarly, though "*inter*marriage" normally denotes unions between blacks and whites or Jews and Christians, Ashkenazic Jews also use it to refer to marrying Sephardic Jews.

Of course, from the proverbial Martian's standpoint, since we only marry other humans, we are all "boringly endogamous"[2] and any cross-racial or interfaith "intermarriage" is embarrassingly trivial, yet even within the same culture, lines that seem obvious to some groups may be totally ignored by others. Thus, for example, despite their obvious ubiquity to their own members, the boundaries of communes are usually ignored by the state. And the wide mental gaps that nine-year-olds believe separate them from eight-year-olds, or that rat breeders perceive as separating their own "refined" show animals from ordinary rats, are not appreciated by anyone but them. Along similar lines, whereas no radical bookstore would place a book on the women's movement alongside books on beauty or homemaking, bookstores less sensitive to the distinction between feminist and traditional notions of womanhood might well do so. The distinction some current college students make between "stylish radical-chic" and "granola" lesbians is likewise lost on many alumni, "to whom the shadings of lesbian politics are as irrelevant as the difference between Sodom and Gomorrah."[3]

Such diversity also generates discord. As we carve mental entities out of reality, the location as well as the very existence of the lines separating them from one another is quite often disputed.

The prototypical border dispute is a battle over the location of some critical line in actual space, as manifested in disputes ranging from local turf feuds between neighbors or street gangs to full-scale international wars. It is the original on which numerous battles over the location of various partitions in mental space are modeled. Controversies regarding the location of group divisions (the eighteenth-century debate over whether blacks are "closer" to whites or to apes, family fights over who should be invited to a wedding) or moral boundaries (the line separating legal from illegal drugs, the ethical limits of euthanasia) are perfect examples of such border disputes. So are the battles over the fine line between politicians' private and public lives, the definition of work (the distinction between mere "chores" and actual "labor," the status of housework), and whether phrenology or chiropractic are part of science. Just as disputable is the delineation of frames, as evident from heated arguments between comedians and their audience over whether personal insults are within the limits of the comedy show frame....

Even when we do not dispute its location, we often still disagree with one another on how impenetrable we expect a given boundary to be. Such disagreement is at the bottom of disputes over the walls of prisons (whether prisoners may take weekend leaves, how often they may be visited, the conditions for paroling them) and nation-states (immigrant quotas, the status of guest workers, the right to travel abroad), battles over the extent to which groups ought to allow their languages to be "contaminated" by foreign words, and family fights over whether children may close the doors to their rooms. Moreover, we often wage battles over the very existence of a given boundary. States, for example, usually ignore boundaries drawn by separatists, while conservatives and liberals fight over the necessity of drawing a line between "X" and "R" rated films and evolutionists and creationists debate the distinction between science and ideology. Along similar lines, animal rights activists defy the "experiment" frame that allows the killing of animals, whereas feminists question the distinction between erotic art and pornography and object to sexism even in fiction or jokes. Governments and dissidents likewise often debate the legitimacy of the frames that distinguish "religious" sermons, "satirical" plays, and "academic" discourse from explicit political protest.

Such battles are basically about whether what may look like several separate entities are indeed just different variants of a single entity. The entire debate over the reunification of East and West Germany or North and South Korea, for example, was basically over whether there should be one or two of each. Such disagreements also led some people to reproach those who found John Poindexter's and Oliver North's reasoning at the Iran-Contra hearings, for example, evocative of the Nuremberg trials, as well as those who compared the secession of Lithuania from the Soviet Union in 1990 to that of South Carolina from the Union in 1860, with "How can you even compare?" The current battle between Israeli liberals and ultranationalists over whether or not to prosecute Jewish vigilantes in the West Bank is, likewise, basically about whether they and others who break the law constitute one moral entity or two separate ones ("lawbreakers" and "overzealous patriots").

Language certainly plays a major role in such disputes. That is why Israel has traditionally refused to recognize Palestinians as a distinct entity and why a seceding East Pakistan immediately renamed itself Bangladesh. When sociology conference organizers debate whether to include a single "Race and Ethnicity" session or two separate ("Race" and "Ethnicity") ones, they are actually fighting over whether or not being black or Oriental is different from being Irish or Italian, and when Czechs and Slovaks debate whether to name their union "Czechoslovakia" or "Czecho-Slovakia," the separatist overtones of the latter name are quite obvious. The label "*para*psychological" clearly excludes phenomena from the realm of science, whereas the label "nonhuman animals" clearly defies the conventional distinction between human and animal. Moving away from the discrete labels "homosexual" and "heterosexual" to a continuous homosexuality–heterosexuality scale likewise helps rid the gay of their "specialness" stigma, whereas using "Ms." as the counterpart of "Mr." clearly helps feminists downplay the distinction between married ("Mrs.") and unmarried ("Miss") women (which, since it does not apply to men, implies that marriage transforms women more than it does men).

Such labeling politics reveal how attitudes toward (protecting or defying) boundaries and distinctions betray deep sentiments (conservative or progressive) toward the social order in general. Like the heated battles over drugs, censorship, and abortion, they show that not only does the way we cut up the world underlie the way we think, it clearly also touches the deepest emotional as well as moral nerves of the human condition.

The Color Gray

That the location as well as the very existence of boundaries is often disputed is even more understandable given the pervasive presence of ambiguity in our life. To the rigid mind, the world is a set of discrete entities separated from one another by gaps. Crossing these gaps entails sharp, dramatic breaks. Movement between islands of meaning therefore has a jerky, staccato nature characterized by abrupt transitions.

That is why we gain or lose a full hour as we cross time-zone boundaries or experience some shock upon waking up from a daydream. Such experience of reality obviously allows no room for ambiguity. Yet "things," noted Anaxagoras, are rarely "cut off with an axe."[4] In reality, there are no discrete entities literally detached from their surroundings by actual gaps. Nature "refuses to conform to our craving for clear lines of demarcation; she loves twilight zones."[5] Our neat and orderly classifications notwithstanding, the world presents itself not in pure black and white but, rather, in ambiguous shades of gray, with mental twilight zones and intermediate essences. Despite the stubborn efforts of the rigid mind to deny it, at least some element of ambiguity in our life is inevitable....

In short, instead of well-defined islands unequivocally separated from each other by substantial gaps, the world normally presents itself in the form of blurred-edge essences distinguished from one another only by "insensible gradations."[6] Analytic thinking, therefore, is clearly not the only mode by which we process reality. In fact, even most of the concepts we use to organize our experience are not clear-cut and sharply delineated but, rather, vague[7] and often modified by such "hedges" as "largely," "sort of," "quite," "almost," or "more or less."[8] (Until recently, such an ability to process fuzzy categories and negotiate subtle nuances actually distinguished our thinking from that of machines.)...

The Social Construction of Discontinuity

Breaking up reality into discrete islands of meaning is, thus, an inevitably arbitrary act. The very existence of dividing lines (not to mention their location) is a matter of convention. It is by pure convention, for example, that we regard Danish and Norwegian as two separate languages yet Galician as a mere dialect of Portuguese. It is likewise by sheer convention that we draw a line between heroin and other lethal substances such as alcohol and tobacco (not to mention its own chemical cousins, which we use as pain-killers or as controlled substitutes for heroin itself). It is mere convention that similarly leads us to regard cooking or laundering as "service" occupations and fishermen or raftsmen as less skilled than assembly-line workers or parking-lot attendants. Just as arbitrary is the way in which we carve supposedly discrete species out of the continuum of living forms, separate the masculine from the feminine, cut up continuous stretches of land into separate continents (Europe and Asia, North and Central America), or divide the world into time zones. Nor are there any natural divides separating childhood from adulthood, winter from spring, or one day from the next (both my children, indeed, used to refer to the morning before their last afternoon nap as "yesterday"), and if we attribute distinctive qualities to decades ("the Roaring Twenties") or centuries ("nineteenth-century architecture"), it is only because we happen to count by tens. Had we used nine, instead, as the basis of our counting system, we would have undoubtedly discovered the historical significance of 9-, 81-, and 729-year cycles and generated fin-de-siècle and millenary frenzy around the years 1944 and 2187. We probably would also have experienced our midlife crisis at the age of thirty-six! It is we ourselves who create categories and force reality into supposedly insular compartments. Mental divides as well as the "things" they delineate are pure artifacts that have no basis whatsoever in reality. A category, after all, is "a group of things [yet] things do not present themselves...grouped in such a way.... [Nor is their resemblance] enough to explain how we are led to group...them together in a sort of ideal sphere, enclosed by definite limits."[9] Classification is an artificial process of concept formation rather than of discovering clusters that already exist. Entities such as "vitamins," "politicians," "art," and "crime" certainly do not exist "out there." The way we construct them resembles the way painters and photographers create pictures by mentally isolating supposedly discrete slices of reality from their immediate surroundings. In the real world, there are no divides separating one insular "thing" from another. The "introduction of closure into the real" is a purely mental act.

And yet, while boundaries and mental fields may not exist "out there," neither are they generated solely by our own mind. The discontinuities we experience are neither natural nor universal, yet they are not entirely personal either. We may not all classify reality in a precisely identical manner, yet we certainly do cut it up into rather similar mental chunks with pretty similar outlines. It is indeed a mind that organizes reality in accordance with a specific logic, yet it is usually a group mind using an unmistakably social logic (and therefore also producing an unmistakably social order). When we cut up the world, we usually do it not as humans or as individuals, but rather as members of societies.

The logic of classification is something we must learn. Socialization involves learning not only society's norms but also its distinctive classificatory schemas. Being socialized or acculturated entails knowing not only how to behave, but also how to perceive reality in a socially appropriate way. An anthropologist who studies another culture, for example, must learn "to see the world as it is constituted for the people themselves, to assimilate their distinctive categories.... [H]e may have to abandon the distinction between the natural and the supernatural, relocate the line between life and death, accept a common nature in mankind and animals."[10] Along similar lines, by the time she is three, a child has already internalized the conventional outlines of the category "birthday present" enough to know that, if someone suggests that she bring lima beans as a present, he must be kidding.

Whenever we classify things, we always attend some of their distinctive features in order to note similarities and contrasts among them while ignoring all the rest as irrelevant. The length of a film, for example, or whether it is in color or in black and white is quite irrelevant to the way it is rated, whereas the color of a dress is totally irrelevant to where it is displayed in a department store. What to stress among what is typically a "plethora of viable alternatives" is largely a social decision,[11] and being socialized entails knowing which features are salient for differentiating items from one another and which ones ought to be ignored as irrelevant. It involves learning, for example, that, whereas adding cheese makes a hamburger a "cheeseburger," adding lettuce does not make it a "lettuceburger," and that it is the kind of meat and not the condiment that goes with it that gives a sandwich its distinctive identity. It likewise involves learning that the sex of the person for whom they are designed is probably the most distinctive feature of clothes (in department stores men's shirts are more likely to be displayed alongside men's pajamas than alongside women's blouses), and that the way it is spelled may help us locate an eggplant in a dictionary but not in a supermarket. Similarly, we learn that in order to find a book in a bookstore we must attend its substantive focus and the first letters of its author's last name (and ignore, for example, the color of its cover), yet that in order to find it in a book exhibit we must first know who published it. (We also learn that bookstores regard readers' ages as a critical feature of books, thus displaying children's books on dogs alongside children's books on boats rather than alongside general books on dogs.) We likewise learn that, in supermarkets, low-sodium soup is located near the low-sugar pineapple slices ("diet food"), marzipan near the anchovy paste ("gourmet food"), and canned corn near the canned pears (rather than by the fresh or frozen corn). And so we learn that, for the purpose of applying the incest taboo, brother-hood "counts" as a measure of proximity to oneself, whereas having the same blood type is irrelevant.

Separating the relevant (figure) from the irrelevant (ground) is not a spontaneous act. Classifying is a normative process, and it is society that leads us to perceive things as similar to or different from one another through unmistakably social *"rules of irrelevance"*[12] that specify which differences are salient for differentiating entities from one another and which ones are only negligible differences among variants of a single entity. Ignoring differences which "make no difference" involves some social pressure to disregard them. Though we often notice them, we learn to ignore them as irrelevant, just as we inhibit our perception of its ground in order to perceive the figure. Along the same lines, ignoring the stutter or deformity of another is not a spontaneous act but rather a social display of tact. It is rules of irrelevance that likewise lead judges, professors, and doctors to display "affective neutrality" and acquit innocent defendants, reward good students, and do their best to save patients' lives even when they personally despise them. They also lead bureaucrats who screen applications to exclude applicants' sex or race from their official considerations even if they are personally attentive to it.

The social construction of discontinuity is accomplished largely through language:

> We dissect nature along lines laid down by our native languages. The categories ... we isolate from the world of phenomena we do not find there because they stare every observer in the face. . . . [T]he world is presented in a kaleidoscopic flux of impressions which has to be organized by our minds – and this means largely by the linguistic systems in our minds. We cut nature up ... as we do, largely because we are parties to an agreement to organize it in this way – an agreement that . . . is codified in the patterns of our language. . . . [W]e cannot talk at all except by subscribing to the organization and classification of data which the agreement decrees.[13]

Not only does language allow us to detach mental entities from their surroundings and assign them fixed, decontextualized meanings, it also enables us to transform experiential continuums into discontinuous categories ("long" and "short," "hot" and "cold"). As we assign them separate labels, we come to perceive mental essences such as "professionals," "criminals," or "the poor" as if they were indeed discrete. It is language that allows us to carve out of a continuous voice range the discrete categories "alto" and "soprano," distinguish "herbs" (basil, dill) from leaves we would never allow on our table, define vague discomfort in seemingly sharp cat-egories such as "headache" or "nausea," and perceive after-shave lotion as actually different from eau de toilette or cologne. At the same time, it is our ability to assign them a common label that also allows us to lump things together in our mind. Only the concept "classical," for example, makes Ravel's music similar to Vivaldi's, and only the concept "alcoholic" makes wine seem "closer" to vodka than to grape juice.

Since it is the very basis of social reality, we often forget that language rests on mere convention and regard such mental entities, which are our own creation, as if they were real. "The trouble," the Eleatic Stranger reminds Young Socrates,

> began at the moment when you [said] that there are two classes of living creature, one of them being mankind, and the other the rest of the animals lumped together.... [B]e-cause you were able to give the common name "animals" to what was left, namely to all creatures other than man, you thought that these creatures do in actual fact make up one class.... [Yet cranes too might] classify the race of cranes as being distinct from all other creatures: the rest they might well lump together, men included, giving them the common appellation of "the beasts." So let us try to be on the watch against mistakes of that kind.[14]

By the same token, as we divide a single continuous process into several conceptual parts ("cause" and "effect," "life" and "death"), we often commit the fallacy of misplaced concreteness and regard such purely mental constructs as if they were actually separate. We likewise reify the mental divide separating "white-collar" from "manual" labor as well as the purely mental outlines of such entities as races, classes, families, and nations. Like the dwellers of Plato's proverbial cave, we are prisoners of our own minds, mistaking mere social conceptions for actual experiential perceptions.

It is society that helps us carve discrete islands of meaning out of our experience. Only English speakers, for example, can "hear" the gaps between the separate words in "perhapstheyshouldhavetriediteearlier," which everyone else hears as a single chain of sound. Along similar lines, while people who hear jazz for thé first time can never understand why a seemingly continuous stretch of music is occasionally interrupted by bursts of applause, jazz connoisseurs can actually "hear" the purely mental divides separating piano, bass, or drum "solos" from mere "accompaniment." Being a member of society entails "seeing" the world through special mental lenses. It is these lenses, which we acquire only through socialization, that allow us to perceive "things." The proverbial Martian cannot see the mental partitions separating Catholics from Protestants, classical from popular music, or the funny from the crude. Like the contours of constellations, we "see" such fine lines only when we learn that we should expect them there. As real as they may feel to us, boundaries are mere figments of our minds. Only the socialized can "see" them. To all cultural outsiders they are totally invisible.

Only through such "glasses" can entities be "seen." As soon as we remove them, boundaries practically disappear and the "things" they delineate fade away. What we then experience is as continuous as is Europe or the Middle East when seen from space or in ancient maps, or our own neighborhood when fog or heavy snow covers curbs and property lines, practically transforming familiar milieus into a visually undifferentiated flux. This is the way reality must appear to the unsocialized – a boundless, unbroken world with no lines. That is the world we would have in-habited were it not for society.

Notes

1   Rudolf Arnheim, *Visual Thinking* (Berkeley: University of California Press, 1969), p. 200.
2   Werner Sollors, *Beyond Ethnicity* (New York: Oxford University Press, 1986), pp. 71–2.
3   "Have Gays Taken over Yale?" *Newsweek*, October 12, 1987, p. 96.
4   Sven-Tage Teodorsson, *Anaxagoras' Theory of Matter* (Goteborg, Sweden: Universitatis Gothoburgensis, 1982), p. 99.
5   Arthur O. Lovejoy, *The Great Chain of Being* (Cambridge: Harvard University Press, 1964 [1936]), p. 56.
6   Henri Bergson, *Matter and Memory* (London: George Allen & Unwin, 1911 [1908]), p. 278.
7   Ludwig Wittgenstein, *Philosophical Investigations* (New York: Macmillan, 1958 [1953]), part I. 68–71.
8   George Lakoff, "Hedges: A Study in Meaning Criteria and the Logic of Fuzzy Concepts," *Journal of Philosophical Logic* 2 (1973): 458–508; George Lakoff, *Women, Fire, and Dangerous Things* (Chicago: University of Chicago Press, 1987), pp. 122–5.
9   Emile Durkheim and Marcel Mauss, *Primitive Classification* (Chicago: University of Chicago Press, 1973), pp. 7–8.
10 Rodney Needham, "Introduction" to Durkheim and Mauss, *Primitive Classification*, p. viii.
11 Stephen J. Gould, "Taxonomy as Politics: The Harm of False Classification," *Dissent*, Winter 1990, p. 73.
12 Erving Goffman, *Encounters* (Indianapolis: Bobbs-Merrill, 1961), pp. 19–26.
13 Benjamin L., Whorf, "Science and Linguistics," in *Language, Thought, and Reality* (Cambridge: MIT Press, 1956 [1942]), pp. 213–14.
14 Plato, *Statesman* (New Haven: Yale University Press, 1952), 263c–263d.

Editor's Notes on Further Reading

Zerubavel on Cognitive Categories

One of the fundamental tools for analyzing culture is the concept of cognitive categories. As Zerubavel demonstrates here by synthesizing many examples, cognitive categories create meaning from a potentially undifferentiated flux of experience. Further, they vary according to time, place, and social context, and frequently generate dissent and debate. Zerubavel's book suggests that while categorical distinction is essential, people may classify in either rigid, fuzzy, or flexible ways, creating or blurring gaps between mental entities to different degrees.

For other examples of variation in categorization see, for instance, excerpts from Benedict on adolescence, Lamont on status, and Nippert-Eng on home and work, this volume; and Eviatar Zerubavel, *Hidden Rhythms: Schedules and Calendars in Social Life* (Chicago: University of Chicago Press, 1981). For more general overviews and theorizing about categorization, see Barry Schwartz, *Vertical Classification: A Study in Structuralism and the Sociology of Knowledge* (Chicago and London: The University of Chicago Press, 1981); Paul DiMaggio, "Classification in Art," *American Sociological Review* 52 (1987): 440–55; Mary Douglas and David Hull, eds., *How Classification Works: Nelson Goodman Among the Social Scientists* (Edinburgh: Edinburgh University Press, 1992); John Mohr, "Soldiers, Mothers, Tramps and Others: Discourse Roles in the 1907 New York City Charity Directory," *Poetics* 22 (1994): 327–57; Kathleen Carley, "Extracting Culture Through Textual Analysis," *Poetics*

22 (1994); 291–312; Christena Nippert-Eng, "Beyond Home and Work: Boundary Theory," pp. 277–92 in *Home and Work: Negotiating Boundaries in Everyday Life* (Chicago and London: University of Chicago Press, 1996); Kristen Purcell, "In a League of Their Own: Mental Leveling and the Creation of Social Comparability in Sport," *Sociological Forum* 11 (1996): 435–56; Eviatar Zerubavel, *Social Mindscapes: An Invitation to Cognitive Sociology* (Cambridge, MA: Harvard University Press, 1997); Paul DiMaggio, "Culture and Cognition," *Annual Review of Sociology* 23 (1997): 263–87; Wayne Brekhus, "A Sociology of the Unmarked: Redirecting Our Focus," *Sociological Theory* 16 (1998): 34–51, and Karen Cerulo, ed., *Culture in Mind: Toward a Sociology of Culture and Cognition* (New York: Routledge, forthcoming). For a guide to related literatures on cognition in social psychology, see Norbert Schwarz, "Warmer and More Social: Recent Developments in Cognitive Social Psychology," *Annual Review of Sociology* 24 (1998): 239–64.

22 The Discourse of American Civil Society: A New Proposal for Cultural Studies

Jeffrey C. Alexander and Philip Smith

Value Analysis and its Critics

From the 1940s to the 1960s, "culture" played a fundamental part in social science theory and research. Primarily by employing the concept of "values," sociologists, political scientists, anthropologists, and even psychologists continued a modified version of the hermeneutic tradition that Max Weber had introduced into social science.

In the period that followed those early postwar decades, it is fair to say that value analysis, and what was taken to be the "cultural approach" more generally, was forcefully rejected. It was convicted, sometimes more and sometimes less justifiably, of idealism. There were two main dimensions to the accusation. On the one hand it was argued that, in both theoretical and empirical work, values had been accorded an illegitimate primacy over other types of social structures. On the other, it was asserted that value analysis was idealistic in that it failed to heed the complexity and contingency of human action.

These critiques, however, merely led to one-sided approaches in turn. Idealism was defeated at the cost of reductionism, and this time it was culture itself that played the subordinate role. Those sensitive to the failure of value analysis to record the significance of social structure recast culture as an adaptive, if creative and expressive response, to ecological and organizational demands. Meanwhile, those concerned with the problem of action reduced culture to the product of action and interaction or aggregate individual behavior. Social structural and actor-centered understandings of culture remain today the dominant trends in mainstream social science.

We take this movement from culture to social structure and action to be premature: It has solved the problems of value analysis at the expense of a consideration of meaning itself. While the careful correlation of culture with social structure represents a real advance over the more idealistic versions of value analysis, the "new institutionalist" focus on practical action and objectification at the expense of representation and internalization and, more importantly, at the expense of internal symbolic logic and cultural process. While we sometimes find in this work the formal language of codes, myths, narratives, and symbols, we do not find the referents of these terms in a substantive sense. Too often, cultural forms are presented as empty boxes to be filled in by structural needs, with the result that the internal content of representations exercises little explanatory power....

Bringing contingency and institutional effects back into our understanding of how culture works is a vital task. In achieving this micro–macro link, however, one must not overlook the reality of emergent properties, which demands that the integrity of different levels of analysis be maintained. Neither the importance of attitudes and actions, nor the significance of organization and environment, negates the existence at still another level of a cultural system. The recent approaches to culture have not provided a satisfactory alternative to the value analysis that was discredited decades ago. They have provided for more subjectivity, more organizational responsiveness, more contingency, and sometimes more empirical pay-off in a traditional causal or predictive sense. They have not, however, provided a model that achieves these advances while allowing for a continuing, formative reference to the cultural order....

An Alternative Model

We would like to propose that culture be thought of as a structure composed of symbolic sets. Symbols are signs that have a generalized status and provide categories for understanding the elements of social, individual and organic life. Although symbols take as referents elements of these other systems, they define and interrelate them in an "arbitrary" manner, that is, in a manner that cannot be deduced from exigencies at these other levels. This is to say that, when they are interrelated, symbols provide a nonmaterial structure. They represent a level of organization that patterns action as surely as structures of a more visible, material kind. They do so by creating patterned order, lines of consistency in human actions. The action of an individual does not create this pattern; at the same time, as we will see, cultural structures do not create the action itself.

We may think of a cultural system as composed of these structures and may think of these structures themselves as being of several different kinds. One important kind of "cultural structure" is the narrative.... As Lévi-Strauss and Barthes have suggested, however, beneath narrative there lie structures of a more basic kind which organize concepts and objects into symbolic patterns and convert them into signs.[1] Complex cultural logics of analogy and metaphor, feeding on differences, enable extended codes to be built up from simple binary structures. Because meaning is produced by the internal play of signifiers, the formal autonomy of culture from social structural determination is assured. To paraphrase Saussure in a sociological way, the arbitrary status of a sign means that its meaning is derived not from its social referent – the signified – but from its relation to other symbols, or signifiers within a discursive code. It is only difference that defines meaning, not an ontological or verifiable linkage to extra-symbolic reality. Symbols, then, are located in sets of binary relations. When meaningful action is considered as a text, the cultural life of society can be visualized as a web of intertwining sets of binary relations.

Taking our leave from Foucault, on the one hand, and from Parsons and Durkheim on the other, we assert that signs sets are organized into discourses.[2] These discourses not only communicate information, structuring reality in a cognitive way, but also perform a forceful evaluative task. Binary sets do so when they are charged by the "religious" symbology of the sacred and profane. In this situation, analogies are not simply relations of sterile signs; they set off the good from the bad, the desirable from the detested, the sainted from the demonic. Sacred symbols provide images of purity and they charge those who are committed to them with protecting their referents from harm. Profane symbols embody this harm; they provide images of pollution, identifying actions, groups, and processes that must be defended against. . . .

The Discourse of American Civil Society

Civil society, at the social structural level, consists of actors, relationships between actors, and institutions. At the very heart of the culture of American civil society is a set of binary codes which discuss and interrelate these three dimensions of social-structural reality in a patterned and coherent way. In the United States, there is a "democratic code" that creates the discourse of liberty. It specifies the characteristics of actors, social relationships and institutions that are appropriate in a democratic-ally functioning society. Its antithesis is a "counter-democratic code" that specifies the same features for an authoritarian society. The presence of two such contrasting codes is no accident: the elements that create the discourse of liberty can signify democracy only by virtue of the presence of antonymic "partners" in an accompany-ing discourse of repression.

Democratic and counter-democratic codes provide radically divergent models of actors and their motivations. Democratically minded persons are symbolically con-structed as rational, reasonable, calm and realistic in their decision making, and are thought to be motivated by conscience and a sense of honor. In contrast, the repressive code posits that anti-democratically minded persons are motivated by pathological greed and self-interest. They are deemed incapable of rational decision making, and conceived of as exhibiting a tendency towards hysterical behavior by virtue of an excitable personality from which unrealistic plans are often born. Whereas the democratic person is characterized by action and autonomy, the coun-ter-democratic person is perceived of as having little free-will, and, if not a leader, as a passive figure who follows the dictates of others.

The discursive structure of actors

Democratic code	Counter-democratic code
Active	Passive
Autonomous	Dependent
Rational	Irrational
Reasonable	Hysterical
Calm	Excitable
Controlled	Passionate
Realistic	Unrealistic
Sane	Mad

Accompanying this discourse on actors and their motivations is another directed to the social relationships that are presumed to follow from such personal needs. The qualities of the democratic personality are constructed as those which permit open, trusting, and straightforward relationships. They encourage critical and reflective, rather than deferential, relations among people. In contrast, counter-democratic persons are associated with secretive, conspirational dealings in which deceit and Machiavellian calculation play a key role. The irrational and essentially dependent character of such persons, however, means that they still tend to be deferential toward authority.

The discursive structure of social relationships

Democratic code	Counter-democratic code
Open	Secret
Trusting	Suspicious
Critical	Deferential
Truthful	Deceitful
Straightforward	Calculating
Citizen	Enemy

Given the discursive structure of motives and civil relationships, it should not be surprising that the implied homologies and antinomies extend to social, political and economic institutions. Where members of the community are irrational in motivation and distrusting in their social relationships, they will "naturally" create institutions that are arbitrary rather than rule governed, that use brute power rather than law, and that exercise hierarchy over equality. Such institutions will tend to be exclusive rather than inclusive and to promote personal loyalty over impersonal and contractual obligations. They will tend to favor the interests of small factions rather than the needs of the community as a whole.

The discursive structure of social institutions

Democratic code	Counter-democratic code
Rule regulated	Arbitrary
Law	Power
Equality	Hierarchy
Inclusive	Exclusive
Impersonal	Personal
Contractual	Ascriptive
Groups	Factions
Office	Personality

The elements in the civil discourses on motives, relationships, and institutions are tied closely together. "Common sense" seems to dictate that certain kinds of motivations are associated with certain kinds of institutions and relationships. After all, it is hard to conceive of a dictator who trusts his minions, is open and honest, and who rigorously follows the law in an attempt to extend equality to all his subjects. The semiologics of the codes, then, associate and bind individual elements on each side of a particular code to the other elements on the same side of the discourse as a whole. "Rule regulated," for example, is considered homologous with "truthful" and "open," terms that define social relationships, and with "reasonable" and "autonomous," elements from the symbolic set that stipulate democratic motives. In the same manner, any element from any set on one side is taken to be antithetical to any element from any set on the other side. Thus, hierarchy is thought to be inimical to "critical" and "open" and also to "active" and "self-controlled."

The formal logic of homology and opposition through which meaning is created, and which we have outlined above, is the guarantor of the autonomy of the cultural codes – despite the fact that they are associated with a particular social-structural domain. However, despite the formal grammars at work in the codes, which turn the arbitrary relationships between the elements into a set of relationships characterized by what Lévi-Strauss has termed an "a posteriori necessity,"[3] it would be a mistake to conceive of the discourse of civil society as merely an abstract cognitive system of quasi-mathematical relationships. To the contrary, the codes have an evaluative dimension that enables them to play a key role in the determination of political outcomes. In American civil society, the democratic code has a sacred status, whereas the counter-democratic code is considered profane. The elements of the counter-democratic code are dangerous and polluting, held to threaten the sacred center of civil society, which is identified with the democratic code. To protect the center, and the sacred discourse that embodies its symbolic aspirations, the persons, institutions, and objects identified with the profane have to be isolated and marginalized at the boundaries of civil society, and sometimes even destroyed.

It is because of this evaluative dimension that the codes of civil society become critical in determining the outcomes of political processes. Actors are obsessed with sorting out empirical reality and, typifying from code to event, with attributing moral qualities to concrete "facts." Persons, groups, institutions, and communities who consider themselves worthy members of the national community identify themselves with the symbolic elements associated with the sacred side of the divide. Their membership in civil society is morally assured by the homology that they are able to draw between their motives and actions and the sacred elements of the semiotic structure. Indeed, if called upon, members who identify themselves as in good standing in civil society must make all their actions "accountable" in terms of the discourse of liberty. They must also be competent to account for those who are thought to be unworthy of civic membership – who are or should be excluded from it – in terms of the alternative discourse of repression. It is through the concept of accountability that the strategic aspects of action come back into the picture, for differing accounts of actors, relationships and institutions can, if successfully disseminated, have powerful consequences in terms of the allocation of resources and power. Strategically, this dual capacity will typically result in efforts by competing actors to tar each other with the brush of the counter-democratic code, while attempting to shield themselves behind the discourse of democracy. This process is clearest in the courts, where lawyers attempt to sway the opinion of the jury by providing differing accounts of the plaintiffs and defendants in terms of the discourses of civil society....

A Modern President Under Attack: Richard Nixon and Watergate

The discourse involved in the push for the impeachment of President Nixon in 1974 is remarkably similar to that of the impeachment of President Johnson some hundred years before. Although the particular issues in hand (in the Watergate break-in and cover-up, the misuse of surveillance powers of the F.B.I., C.I.A., and the I.R.S., the President's failure to obey various subpoenas to hand over documents and tapes, and the secret bombing of Cambodia) contrast with those of Johnson's impeachment (the Tenure of Office Act, the Stanton Removal and various statements opposing Congress), the generalized understandings made by the impeachers were shaped by the logic of the same symbolic structure. As was the case with Johnson, Nixon's motivations were perceived by many in terms of the counter-democratic discourse. As deliberations by the Congressional committee on the impeachment of Nixon made clear, central to this perception was an image of the President as a selfish and fractious person who was interested in gaining wealth and power at the expense of the civil community.

> The evidence is overwhelming that Richard Nixon has used the Office of President to gain political advantage, to retaliate against those who disagreed with him, and to acquire personal wealth.[4]

> He created a moral vacuum in the Office of the Presidency and turned that great office away from the service of the people toward the service of his own narrow, selfish interests.[5]

True to the codes, this self-centered attitude was understood to have arisen from an irrational, unrealistic, slightly paranoid motivational structure. Because of these personality needs, it was argued, Nixon evaluated others, without reasonable cause, in terms of the counter-democratic rhetoric of social relationships.

> Once in the White House, Mr. Nixon turned on his critics with a vengeance, apparently not appreciating that others could strenuously disagree with him without being either subversive or revolutionary.[6]

Irrational, selfish, and narrow motives are connected to sectarian rather than cooperative and communal relations. They cannot form the basis for an inclusive, conflict-containing, civil society. Time and again, Nixon was described as deceitful, calculating, suspicious, and secretive – unacceptable characteristics in a democracy. These perversities, it was believed, led him to resort to counter-democratic and illegal political practices. Nixon had covered up his dark deeds by making false excuses for himself. He had acted in a calculating rather than honorable manner to maximize his own advantage regardless of morality and legality.

> To defend both the bombing [of Cambodia] and the wire-tapping, he invoked the concept of national security.... The imperial presidency of Richard Nixon came to rely on this claim as a cloak for clandestine activity, and as an excuse for consciously and repeatedly deceiving the Congress and the people.[7]

We have seen that the President authorized a series of illegal wire-taps for his own political advantage, and not only did he thereby violate the fundamental constitutional rights of the people of this country but he tried to cover up those illegal acts in the very same way that he tried to cover up Watergate. He lied to the prosecutors. He tried to stop investigations. He tried to buy silence, and he failed to report criminal conduct.[8]

These procedures and relationships were viewed by Nixon's accusers as a dangerous source of pollution, a disease that had to be stopped before it could infect the rest of the civil society, destroying the very tissues of social solidarity.

Mr. Nixon's actions and attitudes and those of his subordinates have brought us to verge of collapse as a Nation of people who believe in its institutions and themselves. Our people have become cynical instead of skeptical. They are beginning to believe in greater numbers that one must look out only for himself and not worry about others.[9]

The President's motivations and relationships were seen as subversive of democracy. His administration had developed into an arbitrary, personalistic organization bent on concentrating power. The institutional aim was, as the *New York Times* argued, dictatorship, and an authoritarian coup d'etat.

One coherent picture emerges from the evidence.... It is the picture of a White House entirely on its own, operating on the assumption that it was accountable to no higher authority than the wishes of and the steady accretion of power by the President. It is the picture of a Presidency growing steadily more sure that it was above and beyond the reaches of the law.[10]

Yet, despite the mounting tide of evidence against Nixon in the early summer of 1974, he still had significant support. Those who continued to support him did not counter the discourse of repression with the picture of a flawless, pristine paragon of democratic morality; they tended to argue, rather, that in the messy world of political reality, Nixon's personal behavior and political achievements were not inconsistent with that discourse broadly conceived.

The President's major contribution to international peace must be recognized to compensate for other matters, to a substantial degree.[11]

As has been written to many representatives on the Judiciary Committee, President Nixon's lengthy list of accomplishments rules out impeachment. Let us be grateful we have such a fine leader, doing his utmost to establish world peace.[12]

As in the case of the evidence relating to the Plumbers' operation they show a specific Presidential response to a specific and serious problem: namely, the public disclosure by leaks of highly sensitive information bearing upon the conduct of American foreign policy during that very turbulent period both domestically and internationally.[13]

These statements suggested that in a world characterized by realpolitik, it would be unwise to punish Nixon's peccadillos when, on balance, he had supported and advanced the cause of the good. Especially important in this equation were Nixon's foreign policy initiatives with the Soviets and Chinese, as well as his ending the Vietnam War, all of which were presented as having advanced the cause of "peace," a state of affairs analogous with inclusive social relationships. Related to this argument was another that focussed not on the impact of the President, but on the consequences of impeachment itself. These consequences, it is suggested, militate against a prolonged period of distracting, generalized discourse.

> Certain members of Congress and the Senate urge the President's removal from office despite the impact such a disastrous decision would have on America's political image and the economy.[14]

> We would do better to retain the President we in our judgement elected to office, for the balance of his term, and in the meantime place our energies and spend our time on such pressing matters as a real campaign reform, a sound financial policy to control inflation, energy and the environment, war and peace, honesty throughout Government, and the personal and economic rights and liberties of the individual citizen against private agglomerations of power in the monolithic state.[15]

The message is that, because of political realities, both mundane political and wider moral goals can be effectively attained only by avoiding impeachment.

The use of these arguments, however, did not preclude Nixon's supporters in Congress from also understanding events in a more generalized manner. They held the impeachment inquiry and its committee members strictly accountable in terms of the two antithetical moral discourses. They linked the lack of hard, irrefutable evidence of the commission to their concern that the inquiry measure up to the highest ethical standards. In principle, therefore, they were compelled to refuse to consider Nixon guilty of an impeachable offense until his accusers could produce a "smoking gun" proof of his direct, personal, and wilful involvement in an indictable crime.

> To impeach there must be direct Presidential involvement, and the evidence thus far has failed to produce it.[16]

> Now many wrongs have been committed, no question about it, but were those wrongs directed by the President? Is there direct evidence that said he had anything to do with it? Of course there is not.[17]

Nixon's supporters pointedly contrasted their hard line on the issue of proof with that of his detractors. They described these opponents in terms of the discourse of repression: Nixon's critics were willing to support impeachment on the basis of evidence that a rational and independent thinker would not accept. Indeed, the critics' motive was greed, their social relationships manipulative. They were the very paradigm of a counter-democratic group: a bloodthirsty and suggestible mob unable to sustain the dispassionate attitude upon which civility depends.

> I join in no political lynching where hard proof fails as to this President or any other President.[18]

> I know that the critics of the President want their pound of flesh. Certainly they have achieved that in all the convictions that have taken place. However, they now want the whole body, and it is self-evident that it is Mr. Nixon who must supply the carcass.[19]

> Yes, the cries of impeachment, impeachment, impeachment are getting louder.... For the past year allegation after allegation has been hurled at the President. Some of them have been stated so often many people have come to accept them as facts, without need of proof.[20]

This evaluation of the impeachers' motives and social relationships was accompanied by a negative evaluation of the institution involved in the impeachment process. They were described as performing in an arbitrary manner, treating Nixon as an enemy rather than as a fellow citizen, and as trying to maximize their own power rather than the power of right. This disregard for the law endangered the democratic foundations of society; it could, indeed, create an antidemocratic revolution.

> [We are] each convinced of the serious threat to our country, caused by the bias and hate pumped out daily by the media.[21]

> The Supreme Court decision that President Nixon must turn over Watergate-related tapes...can make any President virtually a figurehead whose actions can be overturned by any arbitrary high court order.... The Court has, in effect, ignored the Constitution, written its own law, and demanded it be considered the law of the land.[22]

> Five members of the committee have made public statements that Mr. Nixon should be impeached and they have not been disqualified from voting. Leaks detrimental to the President appear almost daily in the media.... When public hearings begin, I fully expect women to appear with their knitting, each a modern Madame Defarge, clicking their needles as they wait for Richard Nixon's head to roll.[23]

Conclusion

... We argue that culture should be conceived as a system of symbolic codes which specify the good and the evil. Conceptualizing culture in this way allows it causal autonomy – by virtue of its internal semiologics – and also affords the possibility for generalizing from and between specific localities and historical contexts. Yet, at the same time, our formulation allows for individual action and social-structural factors to be included in the analytical frame. The codes, we have argued, inform action in two ways. Firstly, they are internalized, and hence provide the foundations for a strong moral imperative. Secondly, they constitute publicly available resources against which the actions of particular individual actors are typified and held morally accountable. By acknowledging the importance of phenomenological processes in channeling symbolic inputs, our model shows that it is precisely these contingent processes that allow codes to make sense in specific situations for specific actors and their interests.

In addition to this claim about action, our model takes account of social structure. We have argued, in theoretical terms, that autonomous cultural codes may be specified to sub-systems and institutions. Their content, we have suggested, reflects and refracts upon the empirical dimensions in which institutions are embedded. Our studies, indeed, provide crucial empirical insights into the relationship between culture and social structure, and more specifically, into the relationship between civil society and the state in American society. They demonstrate that conflicts at the social-structural level need not necessarily be accompanied by divergent values, or "ideologies," at the ideational level. To the contrary, in the American context at least, conflicting parties within the civil society have drawn upon the same symbolic code to formulate their particular understandings and to advance their competing claims.

The very structured quality of this civil culture, and its impressive scope and breadth, help to underscore a paradoxical fact: differences of opinion between contending groups cannot be explained simply as the automatic product of divergent sub-cultures and value sets. In many cases, especially those which respond to new historical conditions, divergent cultural understandings are in part an emergent property of individual and group-level typifications from code to event. This is not to posit a radically individualist theory, but rather to suggest a more interactive conception of the link between cultural and social structures, on the one hand, and the actors, groups, and movements who have to improvise understandings always for "another first time," on the other. Because worthiness can be achieved only by association to the discourse of liberty or by active opposition to the discourse of repression, political legitimacy and political action in the "real world" are critically dependent upon the processes by which contingent events and persons are arrayed in relation to the "imagined" one. In light of these relations among culture, structure, and typification, we can credit the role of political tactics and strategies without falling into the instrumentalist reductions of "institutionalism," on the one hand, or elusive concepts like "structuration" or "habitus" on the other. . . .

Notes

1   Claude Lévi-Strauss, *The Savage Mind* (Chicago: University of Chicago Press, 1966); Roland Barthes, "Introduction to the Structural Analysis of Narratives" in Barthes, *Image/Music/Text* (London: Fontana, 1977).
2   Michel Foucault, *The Archaeology of Knowledge* (New York: Pantheon, 1972); Talcott Parsons and Edward Shils, *Towards a General Theory of Action* (Cambridge, MA: Harvard University Press, 1951); Emile Durkheim, *The Elementary Forms of Religious Life* (New York: Free Press, 1965 [1912]).
3   Lévi-Strauss, *The Savage Mind*.
4   Messrs. Brooks et al., "Report on the Impeachment of Richard M. Nixon, President of the United States," in *Congressional Record*, Vol. 120 [22]: 29–293.
5   Mr. Rangel, ibid., 29302.
6   Mr. Conyers, ibid., 29295.
7   Ibid., 29295.
8   Ms. Holtzman, in *Debate on Articles of Impeachment* (Washington: U.S. Government Printing Office, 1974): 124.
9   Mr. Eilberg, ibid., 44.
10   *New York Times*, Editorial, 7/31/74.
11   *New York Times*, Letter, 8/1/74.
12   Letter, ibid., 7/31/74.
13   Mr. Hutchinson, in *Debate on Articles of Impeachment*: 340.
14   *New York Times*, Letter, 8/1/74.

15   Mr. Dennis, *Debate on Articles of Impeachment*: 43–4.
16   Mr. Latta, *Debate on Articles of Impeachment*: 116.
17   Mr. Sandman, ibid., 19.
18   Mr. Dennis, ibid., 43.
19   *New York Times*, Letter, 7/17/74.
20   Mr. Latta, *Debate on Articles of Impeachment*: 115.
21   *New York Times*, Letter, 7/31/74.
22   *New York Times*, Letter, 7/29/74.
23   *New York Times*, Letter, 7/2/74.

Editor's Notes on Further Reading

Alexander and Smith on Binary Codes in Public Discourse

Alexander and Smith uncover an underlying structure in American public discourse, a formula which consists of a binary code contrasting democratic and counterdemocratic actions, relationships, and institutions. The full study examines the use of this same discursive structure in very different controversies and scandals over two hundred years.

For an earlier cross-national study along related lines see Albert Bergesen, "Political Witch Hunts: The Sacred and the Subversive in Cross-National Perspective," *American Sociological Review* 42 (1977): 220–33. Other studies which investigate the deep structure of American public discourse in different ways include work by Ron Jacobs and Rhys Williams, excerpted this volume; Jeffrey Alexander, "Culture and Political Crisis: 'Watergate' and Durkheimian Sociology," pp. 187–224 in Alexander, ed., *Durkheimian Sociology: Cultural Studies* (Cambridge and New York: Cambridge University Press, 1988); Robert Wuthnow, ed., *Vocabularies of Public Life: Empirical Essays in Symbolic Structure* (London and New York: Routledge, 1992); Philip Smith, "The Semiotic Foundations of Media Narratives: Saddam and Nasser in American Mass Media," *Journal of Narrative and Life History* 4 (1994): 89–118; Robin Wagner-Pacifici, *Discourse and Destruction: The City of Philadelphia versus MOVE* (Chicago and London: University of Chicago Press, 1994); Lyn Spillman, *Nation and Commemoration: Creating National Identities in the United States and Australia* (Cambridge and New York: Cambridge University Press, 1997); the articles by Alexander, Smith, and Jacobs in Jeffrey Alexander, ed., *Real Civil Societies: Dilemmas of Institutionalization* (London and Thousand Oaks, CA: Sage, 1998), and Barry Schwartz, "Frame Images: Towards a Semiotics of Collective Memory," *Semiotica* 121 (1998): 1–40. Influential classics on American public discourse include Louis Hartz, *The Liberal Tradition in America* (New York: Harcourt Brace and Co., 1955), Seymour Martin Lipset, *The First New Nation: The United States in Comparative and Historical Perspective* (New York: W. W. Norton and Co., 1979 [1973]) and Robert Bellah, "Civil Religion in America," pp. 3–23 in W. G. McLoughlin and R. Bellah, eds., *Religion in America* (Boston: Beacon Press, 1968).

Alexander and Smith build on their case studies to make the theoretical point that understanding culture means understanding the internal, emergent patterns of cultural categories which are used in meaning-making. This argument implies that cultural explanation should do more than examine the way categories are used in action (cf. Part II, this volume), or processes of cultural production (cf. Part III, this volume). Indeed, Alexander and Smith criticize work across the spectrum from Shils to Bourdieu for insufficient attention to internal symbolic logic. Excerpts from work by Eliasoph, and Lichterman, with accompanying notes this volume, illustrate a different approach to public culture which emphasizes norms of action rather than discursive structure. For more discussion of the autonomy of "culture-structures" see for instance Jeffrey Alexander, "Analytic Debates: Understanding the Relative

Autonomy of Culture," pp. 1–27 in Alexander and Steven Seidman, eds., *Culture and Society: Contemporary Debates* (Cambridge and New York: Cambridge University Press, 1990); Alexander, *Structure and Meaning: Relinking Classical Sociology* (New York: Columbia University Press, 1989); "The Promise of a Cultural Sociology: Technological Discourse and the Sacred and Profane Information Machine," in Richard Münch and Neil Smelser, eds., *Theory of Culture* (Berkeley and Los Angeles: University of California Press, 1992); Anne Kane, "Cultural Analysis in Historical Sociology: The Analytic and Concrete Forms of the Autonomy of Culture," *Sociological Theory* 9 (1991): 53–69; and Lyn Spillman, "Culture, Social Structure, and Discursive Fields," *Current Perspectives in Social Theory* 15 (1995): 129–54. Alexander and Smith's argument is challenged in Marshall Battani, David Hall, and Rosemary Powers, "Cultures' Structures: Making Meaning in the Public Sphere," *Theory and Society* 26 (1997): 781–812; see also the reply in Jeffrey Alexander and Philip Smith, "Cultural Structures, Social Action, and the Discourses of American Civil Society: A Reply to Battani, Hall, and Powers," *Theory and Society* 28 (1999): 455–61. In *Symbol and Ritual in the New Spain: The Transition to Democracy After Franco* (Cambridge and New York: Cambridge University Press, 1998) Laura Desfor Edles shows the deep cultural structure which conditioned an important political change in the direction of democratization.

23 Cultural Form and Political Meaning: State-subsidized Theater, Ideology, and the Language of Style in Fascist Italy

Mabel Berezin

Social scientists of various theoretical orientations view meaning as located in the content of particular art objects. Their first analytic question is narrative: What story does this picture, film, play, novel tell? The social science paradigm that links meaning to content suggests that a political organization, such as a totalitarian state, that sought to disseminate ideology through art would seek to affect the content of art objects. To invoke George Orwell, an analysis of Newspeak would enable one to understand the political ideology of *1984*.

The theater under Italian fascism presents a puzzle that challenges the social science assumption that meaning resides principally in narrative content. Political ideology is a special case of public meaning – collectively shared understandings of social order. The history of cultural production in the 20th century offers numerous instances of art in the service of politics. Descriptive terms such as "socialist realism" or "Nazi architecture" suggest a straightforward relation between artistic content and political ideology. The relative infrequency of plays [with fascist content] in fascist Italy suggests that the process by which art incorporates political ideology is less direct and raises my central question: How does art express political ideology? . . .

In this article, I reconceptualize the relation between political meaning and ideological content. The Italian fascist regime, like all regimes that institutionalize political ideologies, did not paint pictures, design buildings, or create theater; it did give money in support of various cultural projects. I analyze the theatrical projects that received regime subsidies from 1927 to 1940. The defining characteristics of these projects suggest how a theater without fascist content could plausibly convey fascist ideology.

I argue . . . that the Italian fascist regime affected the form and not the content of theater. . . The pattern of state theatrical funding, analyzed in conjunction with the rhetorical strategy of appropriation and reappropriation that emerged between regime cultural bureaucrats and theatrical cultural entrepreneurs, suggests that it was theatrical form, the performative dimensions of theater staging and acting style, that contained fascist meaning. . . .

Vehicles of Meaning: Theater as Cultural Object

Griswold defines a "cultural object" as "shared significance embodied in form, i.e., ... an expression of meanings that is tangible or can be put into words. Thus, a religious doctrine, a belief about the racial characteristics of blacks, a sonnet, a hairstyle, and a quilt could all be analyzed as cultural objects" (1987b, pp. 4–5). ...

Theater as an artistic genre is vulnerable to misinterpretation if one neglects its formal dimension. The narrative content, or script, of a play is only part of theater. *How* theater is performed is as central to its meaning as *what* is performed. With rare exceptions (e.g., Goldfarb 1980; Levine 1984), the tendency to treat theater as literary text in social analysis (e.g., Griswold 1986; Williams 1979) is quite old (Carlson 1984). A tradition of social analysis dating back to Artistotle's *Poetics* suggests that the meaning of theater lies in its content. Aristotle views plot, character, diction, and thought – the ideational aspects of theater – as primary aspects of theater; he sees spectacle and song – the performative aspects of theater – as secondary (Aristotle 1992, pp. 63–4). Yet, it is precisely theater's experiential dimension, its theatricality, the "grammar of rhetorical and authenticating conventions" (Burns 1972, p. 33), which includes staging and acting style, that makes it adaptable to political ends. Anthropological theories of theater (Turner 1982, 1990) recognize that, to borrow from Aristotle, "spectacle" and "song" are the characteristics of theater upon which its ritual value, and political potential, depends.

Performance is to theater as the play of light and shadow is to painting. The particular blend of light and shadow in a painting, once created, remains whereas a performance is continually recreated (Becker 1982, p. 302). The formal dimension of theater is experiential and based on collective social action both among the actors and between the actors and audience. Theories that focus upon the meaning of social behavior, rather than theories of aesthetics, are germane to an analysis of theater. Georg Simmel's (1971) classical social theory underscores the salience of form in social life and his essay "Sociability" suggests a way to incorporate the disjuncture between form and content into cultural analysis. ...

Between 1934 and 1940, 354 new plays appeared on the Italian stage. I have developed four broad categories based on a reading of the plot summaries of these plays: (1) fascist; (2) possibly political; (3) private life; and (4) detective/mystery. The majority of the new plays (72%) focused on the dilemmas and absurdities of private life. Love stories and drawing-room farces that imitated French boulevard theater represented continuity in the Italian theatrical repertory (Grassi and Strehler 1964). My sample reading of the leading Italian theater magazines *Comedia* and *Scenario* for this period confirmed the prevalence of this "white telephone" genre, as the 1930s variant came to be known. Of the remaining plays, 15% had themes that could be characterized as possibly political in intent. Only 5% had themes that could be characterized as explicitly fascist. Detective/mystery plays of the Sherlock Holmes type exceeded the proportion of fascist plays (8% vs. 5%). ...

The state system of market incentives and regulation may have created company heads who were loyal fascists but it did not create a fascist theater. The "rules" focused upon stimulating production and not upon what was produced. Institutional arrangements within the Italian theater created market rigidities that continued to militate against aesthetic and political innovation. The regime and theatrical reformers recognized that forces external to the market, such as state subsidies, and outside of the company system would have to support innovation, either fascist or aesthetic, on the Italian stage.

A system, which I have elsewhere labeled "state paternalism" (Berezin 1991), developed that gave financial support to a number of theatrical projects, artistic structures with coherent visions, that the market could not sustain. Given corporativism's public rhetoric, which demanded private initiative in the arts, we can assume that, with private financial initiative lacking, the state stepped in because it somehow perceived that these theater projects would promote its interests.

I argue that we may reconstruct how theater became a vehicle of fascist meanings – meanings that were not dependent on content – by shifting our unit of analysis from plays to theatrical projects and by analyzing the pattern of state theatrical subsidy. Projects are more useful for attempting to understand meaning because it is easy to read ideology into isolated performances. The point is not that there were no plays with explicitly identifiable fascist themes, but that they were few and far between. . . .

The Pattern of Subsidy: Performing Fascism

The theatrical projects that continued to receive regime support, in contrast to the ones that lost support, are suggestive of the regime's ideological intentions.

Acting Italian, acting fascist: Personal discipline and national incorporation. – Acting schools and the amateur theater groups attached to them were 19th-century Italian theatrical institutions that the regime turned to its ideological advantage. These schools were only nominally about training for the theater, as Italian actors were frequently "children of art" (*figli d'arte*) who followed their parents into the craft. Diverse dialects divided the Italian populace, and acting schools combined popular amusement and training in standard spoken Italian. The schools flourished after the unification, when the nationalist need for linguistic consolidation became critical (Anderson 1983, pp. 41–9). In 19th-century Italian theater schools, learning to act meant learning to speak, and become, Italian. In fascist Italy, learning to act meant learning to become fascist, as the qualities of a good actor – discipline and subordination within an organization – were the qualities of a good fascist. In the amateur theater, one acted citizenship and national incorporation, whether that be fascist or Italian.

The Dopolavoro's [Fascist Party leisure organization] amateur theater wed the 19th-century emphasis upon language training to the fascist interest in personal discipline and organizational behavior (OND 1929, p. 150). In an English-language propaganda pamphlet intended for international diffusion, an anonymous regime publicist noted: "The dramatic theaters of today have no improvised actors, anxious only to show off, but intelligent, cultivated performers who study with zest. . . . Apart from the artistic merit attained by the amateur theater through its discipline and training, mention should be made of the importance accruing to the wider diffusion of good Italian" (OND 1938, pp. 29–31).

"Discipline" and "training" were antithetical to the acting style of the "improvised actor" or *mattatore* and the system of standardized roles. A Dopolavoro guidebook

(OND 1929) on how to organize and conduct an amateur theater linked theatrical reform to fascist socialization: "The abolition of roles responds to a precise fascist concept to subordinate every personal desire to the success of the whole" (p. 28). According to the guidebook, the theatrical individualism that the *mattatore* represented was aesthetically and politically out of step: "Men are united in groups, in masses. Heroes, solitary giants, the protagonists who gesture and shout for themselves and of themselves, absorbing the attention of others, egotistical and egocentric, that shout: I am! I do! I say! I think! I feel! such a figure is dead" (pp. 100–1)....

Silvio D'Amico's Royal Academy equated personal discipline and professionalism. D'Amico aimed to create professional actors and directors – disciplined craftspersons who subordinated parts to the whole. That professionalism in the theater coincided with fascist values of discipline and hierarchy was a felicitous coincidence for both the regime and the theatrical world. D'Amico's new Italian actor would create "a life always new, and fresh and lively" and his director would "create spectacle" (D'Amico 1941, pp. 14, 15). D'Amico's academy did not eschew the goals of national incorporation inherited from the earlier theater schools. The academy was located in Rome and used scholarships to recruit a national student body (D'Amico 1941). Language training was foremost on its agenda. Dialect and improperly spoken Italian militated against the formation of a national theater as the *mattatore*'s individualism militated against professionalism. According to D'Amico, "recitation" was the "fundamental instruction" required for a young actor in order to "correct with patient reeducation the bad habits originating in dialect" (D'Amico 1941, pp. 23–4).

Emotion and spectacle: Feeling fascist incorporation. – The amateur theater and *filodrammatiche* [theater schools] used acting style, a performative aspect of theater, to suggest a fascist ideological discourse of discipline and hierarchy. The open air theaters created spectacles in public spaces that revived the ritualistic dimensions of theater. Staging that focused upon the appropriation of public space sought to generate emotions that would make all participants feel incorporated into a fascist collectivity. The audience would transfer the feeling of collectivity that the aesthetic community created to a feeling of political community residing in the fascist state. In this regard, the open air theater was similar to the numerous rallies and public events that the fascists staged for purely political reasons.

Of the open air theaters, the National Institute of Ancient Drama and the Thespian Cars received continuous regime support... Given the regime's desire to equate the fascist empire with the Roman empire, an organization that tried to revive classical dramas in their original locale was in its interests (Visser 1992). The statute of the National Institute of Ancient Drama explicitly linked fascist Italy to past imperial glories. The institute viewed itself as in the "avant-garde" of a movement to use the "glorious classical tradition" and to "recover the imperial heights of Greece and Rome" that had "its roots, not in vacant intellectualism, but in the history and in the future of Italy" (Unsigned 1929, p. 215). The emotion or feeling of national incorporation that the institute would promote contrasted sharply with the "vacant intellectualism" of "bourgeois" theater and liberal Italy. The economic requirements of the tourist trade supplemented the institute's ideological and aesthetic dimension. The institute's president noted that "in addition to its artistic and educational ends classical dramas contribute to tourist facilities in our country" (Pace 1937, p. 378).

The Thespian Cars aimed to educate the aesthetic sensibility of the masses. Starace (1938) claimed that the project would "make it possible for persons to become acquainted with the best theatrical productions who in other times would have been constrained to ignore them for lack of means" (p. 48). The content of what was performed did not affect the aesthetic thrust of the performance. Over the nine years for which there is evidence, the Thespian Cars performed 44 different plays representing 37 Italian authors (Corsi 1939, pp. 263–88). The repertory consisted exclusively of Italian dramas and favored historical and canonical works that were "comic and sentimental in a very plain form and easily accessible to the simple creatures of the masses" (Corsi 1939, p. 279). Despite the reliance upon Italian classical authors such as Carlo Goldoni and Vittorio Alfieri – authors whose works demanded period costumes – the contemporary repertory of the Thespian Cars did not differ from what was staged in the company-based city theaters.[1]

Fascist aesthetic education aimed to arouse the emotions, not stimulate the intellect. Rather than drawing intellectual distinctions based upon content, it used the theater's power of spectacle to engender feelings of community. Going to the theater became more important than what one saw at the theater. One fascist publicist drew a connection between the Thespian Cars and religious experience: "Like the faithful have in churches, seats adapted to collect themselves and raise their souls and thoughts to God; likewise a knowing, mature people have in theater seats adapted to raise their spirit to the beauty of art, and in it to find a surging force of life" (OND, n.d., p. 15). A critic writing in the theatrical review *Comedia* argued that in order to have a "theater worthy of Fascism and Rome," it would be necessary to "reach the brain [of the masses] by passing through its heart" (Cantini 1933, p. 12).

Spectacle was the vehicle of feeling, religious or fascist, which educated the heart. The Thespian Cars' productions packed the central town piazzas with throngs of people and employed costumes and lighting to command the attention of the audience. According to fascist sources, popular response was enthusiastic. The Thespian Cars "seemed like a gift of the regime; and a greatly effective gift it was. The public, coarse but intelligent, compressed and strained their astonished eyes in front of the spectacle" (Corsi 1939, p. 268). An American observer reported on the impressive scenic effects and noted that an audience watching a performance "shed tears of joy" (Di Robilant 1931, p. 599)....

Comparing theatrical projects. – Projects that continued to receive funding displayed three characteristics: (1) they did not originate with the regime; (2) ideology was not a salient dimension of theatrical repertory; (3) they emphasized performance and not text – theatrical form and not content – and this emphasis crossed class boundaries.

First, the regime did not design theatrical projects. The Thespian Cars revived the prerailroad method of traveling theater as well as adopting pre-World War I socialist concepts of popular theater. The theater schools were straightforward appropriations of preexisting theatrical institutions. In the prefascist period, experimental theater projects had failed to raise, or to adequately sustain themselves with, private money.

Second, the content of the subsidized theater's repertory was not ideologically distinctive. Publicity brochures for subsidized theater projects and descriptions of them in official regime publications and theatrical reviews conspicuously failed to report or glossed over repertory. For example, fascist propaganda pamphlets on the Thespian Cars focused on production details and emphasized the technological complexity of the stage and the efficiency with which the group moved from town to town. An English edition of a Dopolavoro propaganda book noted that "in the eight years that it has been operating, it has never been necessary to postpone or even delay a performance, nor has it ever been necessary to make emergency arrange-ments on account of the failure of the trucks to arrive" (OND 1938, p. 41). Copious photographs of theatrical machinery and crowd-filled piazzas documented these points (OND 1931).

Third, fascist cultural policy was not uniform across social class boundaries. Fascism's ability to endow the lower middle classes with the cultural capital that they lacked was a large part of its appeal among these classes (Berezin 1990; De Grazia 1981, pp. 127–50). The subsidized theater projects were aimed at different types of audiences with different degrees of cultural sophistication and knowledge. What is striking about these projects is that the capacity to make theatrical distinc-tions within class categories was the same across class boundaries. For example, whether one was an upper-middle-class person attending a performance of classical drama or a lower-middle-class person enthralled by the pageantry of the Thespian Cars, one still had to understand given the general context that the regime had appropriated public space to create a new kind of aesthetic and political community. Similarly, an upper-middle-class audience accustomed to bourgeois theater would take the same message from experimental theater as a lower-middle-class or working-class person would take from a Dopolavoro *filodrammatiche*. Theater was now about order, discipline, and hierarchy.

The absence of the reporting of repertories, not the absence of a repertory, suggests that *how* a play was performed, not *what* was performed, constituted the focus of the regime's theatrical concerns. The secondary position ascribed to the repertory and the primary position ascribed to performance is central to under-standing the meaning of the subsidized theater. Spectacle, emotion, and discipline, qualities of theater in general and not fascism in particular, dominated regime and theatrical discourse on the subsidized theater. Successful projects emphasized the collective and ritualistic aspects of theater that were reflected in the location and staging of performances and the professionalism – the hierarchy and coordination – reflected in the acting style. The performative, or formal properties of theater, dramatized political meanings without resorting to overt political content.[2] The prerequisites of theater as artistic genre merged with the requirements of fascism as political genre to create a fascist theater.

The projects that did not continue to receive funding were playwright centered; that is, they emphasized the primacy of the author and his text. Playwright-centered theater was characteristic of 19th-century theater. The tradition of the *mattatore* hindered its diffusion in Italy, and Italian playwrights and *mattatore* frequently vied with each other for theatrical dominance. The regime came to identify the 19th century with liberalism and words – the polar opposites of fascism and action. Theatrical projects that supported the playwright, the emblem of 19th-century theatrical style, were less likely to receive continuing support. At the same time, the regime could not ignore playwrights such as Pirandello and D'Annunzio, who were internationally known theatrical figures. The regime found it expedient to provide them with funding and to permit their projects to fail in the marketplace.

The regime did not expect subsidized projects to be profitable, but projects did have to generate popular interest if they were to be of any political use. Eliminating emphasis on the author and the text did not guarantee success if the project completely lacked popular support. Content made a difference to the audience, and the regime bowed to popular taste. The *18BL*, the only subsidized project that its producers designed as explicitly fascist, was a popular failure and not repeated. In 1934, several prominent Italian movie directors, theatrical personnel, and elite members of the PNF explicitly decided to create a "fascist" spectacle. The creators of the *18BL* modeled it on Soviet mass propaganda spectacles (Salvini 1934, pp. 251–2). The hero was a huge truck – the *18BL*. The play represented three events in Italian fascist history – World War I, the fascist revolution, and subsequent state reconstruction (Bontempelli [1934] 1974, p. 264). Staged in Florence, the audience sat on one bank of the Arno River (about 200 yards from the stage) and watched shapes and shadows on the other bank of the river. The technological complexity of the staging took precedence over dialogue. Collectivism governed the production. Eight "directors" planned the staging, and although it had one star who played the truck, the rest of the cast consisted of a chorus (D'Amico [1934] 1964, pp. 283–9).

The failure of the *18BL* elicited widespread discussion in regime publications. A theatrical critic in the fascist theater review, *Scenario*, commented, "The Latin temperament that fortunately guides our spirit and our taste, prevents us from conceptualizing a spectacle of this character" (Salvini 1934, p. 253). Another reviewer in *Gerarchia*, a regime review of politics, argued that the *18BL* failed because its creators (all committed fascist intellectuals) had misconceived the true nature of fascist theater: "The theater problem is a problem of the nation, which ought to have a theater of extremely Italian spirit and forms as it has a very Italian political constitution. To do this, it is not enough to construct an edifice but it is necessary to let gush from the subsoil those vital forces that want to ascend toward the sun" (Giani 1934, p. 1052). Critics spoke about the failure of the *18BL* as a failure of style or form, and not content or substance...

The experience of theater from the point of view of both its creators and its audience is an inherently social process – one never stages or sees the same play twice. But theater is not perfectly akin to social life; it is play or, as Turner (1982, pp. 20–59) has noted, the space between structures – the formally mediated aspects of social life. The playfulness of theater bring us back to Simmel's (1971) conception of sociability and points us in the direction of unraveling the meaning of the fascist theater. Sociability is based on an implicit knowledge of formal rules of behavior that participants in particular cultural and social contexts share. Simmel juxtaposes sociability, or form, against values, or content: "Where a connection, begun on the sociable level... finally comes to center about personal values, it loses the essential quality of sociability and becomes an association determined by a content – not unlike a business or religious relation, for which contact, exchange, and speech are but instruments for ulterior ends, while for sociability they are the whole meaning and content of the social processes" (p. 131).

Sociability is an end in itself – it is "the *play-form of association*" (Simmel 1971, p. 130; emphasis in original). The transgression of sociability lies in the violation of the form, or genre, of social behavior, and all participants in a "sociable" connection recognize the transgression. The performance dimension of theater suggests a translation of Simmel – theater is the *play-form of art*. Drawing upon the link between theater and ritual, Turner (1982) argues that "'ludic' recombination" is the "essence of liminality" or theatricality and that in "liminality people 'play' with the elements of the familiar and defamiliarize them" (pp. 27–8). Form in social life and in art is so familiar as to be taken for granted; content is variable. For example, a theater audience expects different plays to be about different subjects; guests at a party expect diverse conversation. A contemporary Broadway theater audience would recognize a shift in form if they found a *mattatore* on the New York stage; party participants would be disconcerted if a fellow guest began to discuss personal problems. As Susanne Langer has stated, "*Familiarity* is nothing but the quality of fitting very neatly into the form of previous experience" (1951, p. 83; emphasis in original). Form, theatrical or social, has the capacity to communicate what is "familiar," and what is not, what is acceptable, and what is not.

The "subsidized" Italian theater, the fascist theater, used formal properties, spatial arrangement, and behavior or, translated into theatrical language, the "performance modes" of theater to convey political meaning by transgressing the boundaries of familiarity. The regime's pattern of subsidy "played" with theatrical form. This playing with form was likely to have resonated more with Italian theater audiences than could overt fascist content, which they could easily ignore. The evidence in this article suggests that theater audiences were resistant to fascist content. In addition, there is much anecdotal evidence, and some empirical evidence, that Italians viewed fascist content as a joke (see, e.g., Passerini 1984, pp. 84–153).

The form of a social, or theatrical, action is arguably a more cogent communicative practice than the specific content of an action. The fascist theater transgressed the boundaries of theatrical expectations. Each type of subsidized theater did this in a different way depending upon the demands of its own format, but the end results were the same.

Expectations of theatrical communication were to go to an urban indoor theater and watch a *mattatore* perform a familiar play. By shifting theater from private to public space, open air theater broadened the conception of theater and emphasized its ritual, or collective, value. Italian theater began in public space and had only moved into private space with the development of modern society (Toschi [1955] 1976). The Thespian Cars sought to instill the spirit of community in adults who were too old for the schools that the fascists were redesigning and too poor to partake of other cultural products (Koon 1985). Assembling the masses in the piazza to watch the spectacle created a temporary aesthetic community that, it was hoped, would evoke the feeling of the political community of the fascist state. This public setting for the Thespian Cars contained cultural and political meaning that would not escape the ordinary Italian citizen, for the piazza was a secular and civil space – a market, a public meeting place, and a scene of sociability (Carandini 1986, p. 47), and this held true across class boundaries. In the early years of the fascist movement, the piazza became a politically charged locale. Fascists and socialists fought for control of the piazza to assert political dominance (Lyttelton 1987, pp. 2, 23). The fascist Thespian Cars in the piazza were an enduring reminder that the fascists had conquered the piazza and Italy. The location of the performance was so charged with meaning it rendered a repertory superfluous.

Although amateur theater and acting schools appear to be unrelated to experimental theaters from the perspective of fascist ideology, the . . . formal properties of these theatrical projects – professional acting and corporativist organization of theatrical production embodied in the prominence of the director – conveyed more strongly than any play a central message of the fascist regime. Just as a populace familiar with the nontheatrical uses of public spaces would have noticed when the regime appropriated those spaces, audiences familiar with the middle-class theater and its tradition of the *mattatore* would have attached some meaning to the move to a professional theater that was director based.

The evidence that I have discussed suggests a more general conclusion. I argue that the regime's support of the performance aspects of theater, rather than theater's content, was not simply utilitarian; there was a deeper connection between fascism and form. The translation of corporativism for the masses was Believe, Fight, and Obey – a call to action without an object, to a style of behavior without a goal – as opposed to Liberty, Equality, and Fraternity – a call to values and content. In liberal democratic societies, understanding the ideas and principles of a nation are central to political participation. In Italian fascist society, the content was secondary because the fascists wished to create a feeling of participation, not actual participation, in the community. Assembling a mass of people in a public square to watch a theatrical performance, or to listen to a speech of Mussolini, represented emotional participation in the community. Corporativism, whose only concrete injunction was to belong to a fascist corporation or union, created a large bureaucratic space in which any content was possible and formality itself became the dominant value. Style and feeling articulated in the language of community and discipline characterized not only fascism but the fascist theater. Individuals subordinated themselves to the "organism" of the state, felt the spirit of community, and assumed their proper productive tasks whatever they might have been.

Conclusion

What are the implications of this case for the problems with which we began – the transmission of ideology and the regime's construction of political meaning? When we shift our unit of analysis from the text of an individual play to a theatrical project, the regime's apparent lack of interest in content does not appear as puzzling as it did at the outset of this article. Theatrical projects included staging and style of acting as well as repertory or text. They contained whole visions of how to do theater and as such are a better index of what the fascists wished their theater to convey than the content of individual plays. Regime subsidies determined that spectacle – the quality that Aristotle in the *Poetics* characterized as the least important dimension of theater – eclipsed the content of theater.

While all case studies are by their nature limited, their value comes from their ability to generate hypotheses for future research. The Italian case suggests that studies of political meaning that restrict their analyses to the content of ideological doctrines and cultural products are potentially misleading. It finds that the formal properties of a cultural product – the performance dimension of theater – convey meaning, in this instance fascist ideology, even when the content of a cultural product – text of a play – does not . . .

Notes

1   The Thespian Cars staged 10 of the plays that appeared in the *Annuario*'s listing of new plays. Of these plays, two fell into the fascist category and three fell into the possibly political category. The Thespian Cars' repertory appears in Corsi (1939, pp. 277–82).
2   Goldfarb (1980, pp. 111–12) reports a similar finding in his study of Polish student theater.

References

Anderson, Benedict. 1983. *Imagined Communities*. London: Verso.

Angelini, Franca. 1988. *Teatro e spettacolo nel primo novecento*. Rome: Laterza.

Aristotle. 1992. *Poetics*, translated by S. H. Butcher. New York: Hill & Wang.

Baldacci, Luigi. 1990. "Forzano drammaturgo." Pp. 109–12 in *Il Piccolo Marat: Storia e rivoluzione nel melodramma verista*, edited by Piero e Nandi Ostali. Milan: Casa Musicale Sonzogno.

Becker, Howard. 1982. *Art Worlds*. Berkeley and Los Angeles: University of California Press.

Berezin, Mabel. 1987. *Public Spectacles and Private Enterprises: Theater and Politics in Italy under Fascism, 1919–1940*. Doctoral dissertation. Harvard University.

——. 1990. "Created Constituencies: The Italian Middle Classes and Fascism." Pp. 142–63 in *Splintered Classes*, edited by Rudy Koshar. New York: Holmes & Meier.

——. 1991. "The Organization of Political Ideology: Culture, State and Theater in Fascist Italy." *American Sociological Review* 56: 639–51.

Bontempelli, Massimo (1934) 1974. *L'Avventura novecentista*, edited by Ruggero Jacobbi. Florence: Valecehi.

Burns, Elizabeth. 1972. *Theatricality*. London: Longman.

Cantini, Guido. 1933. "Teatri all'aperto." *Comedia* 15: 9–12.

Carandini, Silvia. 1986. "Teatro e spettacolo nel medioevo." 6: 169–225 in *Letteratura italiana*, edited by Alberto Asor Rosa. Turin: Einaudi.

Carlson, Marvin. 1981. *The Italian Stage: From Goldoni to D'Annunzio*. London: McFarland.

——. 1984. *Theories of the Theater: A Historical and Critical Survey from the Greeks to the Present*. Ithaca, N.Y.: Cornell University Press.

Corsi, Mario. 1939. *Il Teatro all'aperto in Italia*. Milan: Rizzoli.

D'Amico, Silvio. 1922. "Cenerentola a Palazzo Venezia." *Comedia* 4:433–38.

——. 1929. *Tramonto del grande attore*. Milan: Mondadori.

——. 1931. *Crisi del teatro*. Rome: Arte della Stampa.

——. 1932. *Il Teatro italiano*. Milan: Treves.

——. 1933. "Per una regia italiana." *Scenario* 2: 505–11.

——. (1934) 1964. "Teatro di masse: '18 BL.'" Pp. 283–89 in *Cronache del teatro*, edited by E. Ferdinando Palmieri and Sandro D'Amico. Bari: Laterza.

——. 1941. *La Regia Accademia d'Arte Drammatica di Roma*. Florence: N.p.

——. 1945. *Il Teatro non deve morire*. Rome: Eden Edizioni dell'Era Nuova.

De Grazia, Victoria. 1981. *The Culture of Consent: Mass Organization of Leisure in Fascist Italy*. Cambridge: Cambridge University Press.

Di Robilant, Irene. 1931. "The Chariot of Thespis." *Theater Arts Monthly* 15: 597–601.

Giani, Giampiero. 1934. "Dal Teatro di masse allo sperimentale dei GUF." *Gerarchia* 12: 1052–53.

Goldfarb, Jeffrey C. 1980. *The Persistence of Freedom: The Sociological Implications of Polish Student Theater*. Boulder, Colo.: Westview.

Grassi, Paolo, and George Strehler. 1964. "Sixteen Years of the Piccolo Teatro." *Tulane Drama Review* 8: 28–40.

Griswold, Wendy. 1986. *Renaissance Revivals*. Chicago: University of Chicago Press.

——. 1987a. "The Fabrication of Literary Meaning." *American Journal of Sociology* 92: 1077–1117.

——. 1987b. "A Methodological Framework for the Sociology of Culture." *Sociological Methodology* 14: 1–35.

——. 1990. "Provisional, Provincial Positivism: A Reply to Denzen." *American Journal of Sociology* 95: 1580–83.

Koon, Tracy H. 1985. *Believe Obey Fight: Political Socialization of Youth in Fascist Italy, 1922–43*. Chapel Hill: University of North Carolina Press.

Langer, Susanne K. 1951. *Philosophy in a New Key*. New York: New American Library.

Levine, Lawrence W. 1984. "William Shakespeare and the American People: A Study in Cultural Transformation." *American Historical Review* 89: 34–66.

Lyttelton, Adrian. 1987. *The Seizure of Power: Fascism in Italy, 1919–1929*, 2nd ed. Princeton, N.J.: Princeton University Press.

Opera Nazionale Dopolavoro (OND). 1929. *Il Teatro filodrammatico*. Rome: Opera Nazionale Dopolavoro.

——. 1931. *I Primi cinque anni di attivita dell'Opera Nazionale Dopolavoro, 1926–30*. Rome: Opera Nazionale Dopolavoro.

——. 1938. *The "Opera Nazionale Dopolavoro" (National Leisure Hours Organization in Italy)*. Rome: Novissima.

——. n.d. *Carro di tespi*. Rome: Opera Nazionale Dopolavoro.

Pace, Biagio. 1937. "Degli spettacoli classici in Italia." *Scenario* 6: 377–80.

Passerini, Luisa. 1984. *Torino operaia e fascismo*. Rome: Laterza.

Salvini, Guido. 1934. "Spettacoli di masse e '18BL.'" *Scenario* 3(3): 251–54.

Simmel, Georg. [1911] 1971. "Sociability." Pp. 127–40 in *On Individuality and Social Forms*, edited by Donald N. Levine. Chicago: University of Chicago Press.

Starace, Achille. 1938. *Opera Nazionale Dopolavoro*. Milan: Mondadori.

Toschi, Paolo. [1955] 1976. *Le Origini del teatro italiano*. Turin: Boringhieri.

Turner, Victor. 1982. *From Ritual to Theater: The Human Seriousness of Play*. New York: Performing Arts Journal Publications.

——. 1990. "Are There Universals of Performance in Myth, Ritual, and Drama?" Pp. 8–18 in *By Means of Performance: Intercultural Studies of Theater and Ritual*, edited by Richard Schechner and Willa Appel. New York: Cambridge University Press.

Unsigned. 1927. "600 comparse nella 'Figlia di Iorio'..." *Corriere della sera* (September 7).

——. 1929. "Il nuovo statuto dell'istituto e la nomina a presidenza dell'On. Prof. Biagio Pace." *Bollettino del Istituto Nazionale del Dramma Antico Siracusa* 2 (5): 214.

——. 1930. "Notiziario dell'istituto." *Bollettino del Istituto Nazionale del Dramma Antico Siracusa* 3 (1–2): 66–72.

——. 1931. "Elenco delle compagnie drammatiche italiane." P. 365 in *Almanacco del teatro italiano*, edited by Benvenuto Benvenuti. Arezzo: Contemporanea.

——. 1932. "Giro delle compagnie drammatiche (gennaio-febbraio)." *Bollettino della Societa Italiana degli Autori ed Editori* 7 (January–March): 18–26.

Unsigned. 1935. "Entusiastiche dimonstrazioni al capo." *Il Popolo d'italia* (October 30).

——. 1936. "Quadro delle compagnie drammatiche." *Bollettino di Segnalazioni: Elenco delle Opere Teatrali Approvate Ministero per la Stampa e la Propaganda, Isperatto del Teatro,* vol. 1.

——. 1937. "Le Compagnie primarie di prosa." *Scenario* 3 (10): 478–82.

Visser, Romke. 1992. "Fascist Doctrine and the Cult of *Romanita*." *Journal of Contemporary History* 27: 5–22.

Williams, Raymond. 1979. *Modern Tragedy*. London: Verso.

——. 1982. *Sociology of Culture*. New York: Schocken Books.

Editor's Notes on Further Reading

Berezin on Theatrical Form

Although many students of art and politics would expect state-supported theater during Italian Fascism to promote Fascist themes and messages, Berezin finds that plays were mostly apolitical, and shows how theatrical form, not dramatic content, conveyed Fascist ideology. The case reminds cultural analysts to attend to the effects of formal properties of cultural objects, not just their explicit content. In the extended study Berezin also shows a cultural production process in which cultural entrepreneurs obtained state subsidies by linking theatrical innovations to Fascist rhetoric (thus combining analysis of genre and analysis of cultural production, as do Wagner-Pacifici and Schwartz, this volume).

For more on theater in social context, see for instance Wendy Griswold, *Renaissance Revivals: City Comedy and Revenge Tragedy in the London Theater 1576–1980* (Chicago: University of Chicago Press, 1986); Lawrence Levine, *Highbrow/Lowbrow: The Emergence of Cultural Hierarchy in America* (Cambridge, MA: Harvard University Press, 1988); Raymond Williams, "Forms," in *The Sociology of Culture* (Chicago: University of Chicago Press, 1995 [1981]); and Jeffrey Goldfarb, *The Persistence of Freedom: The Sociological Implications of Polish Student Theater* (Boulder, CO: Westview Press, 1980).

For other work on Fascist political culture in Italy see Mabel Berezin, *Making the Fascist Self: The Political Culture of Interwar Italy* (Ithaca, NY: Cornell University Press, 1997); Berezin, "The Organization of Political Ideology: Culture, State, and Theater in Fascist Italy," *American Sociological Review* 56 (1991): 639–51; Simonetta Falasca Zamponi, *Fascist Spectacle: The Aesthetics of Power in Mussolini's Italy* (Berkeley: University of California Press, 1997); Falasca Zamponi, "Of Storytellers and Master Narratives: Modernity, Memory, and History in Fascist Italy," *Social Science History* 22 (1998): 415–44; and Anne Bowler, "Politics as Art: Italian Futurism and Fascism," *Theory and Society* 20 (1991): 763–94. Related studies in political culture include Laura Desfors Edles, *Symbol and Ritual in the New Spain: The Transition to Democracy After Franco* (Cambridge and New York: Cambridge University Press, 1998); Philip Smith, "Barbarism and Civility in the Discourses of Fascism, Communism, and Democracy: Variations on a Set of Themes," pp. 115–37 in Jeffrey Alexander, *Real Civil Societies: Dilemmas of Institutionalization* (London and Thousand Oaks: Sage, 1998); David Kertzer, *Politics and Symbols: The Italian Communist Party and the Fall of Communism* (New Haven: Yale University Press, 1996); and the overviews provided in Mabel Berezin, "Politics and Culture: A Less Fissured Terrain," *Annual Review of Sociology* 23 (1997): 361–83, and George Steinmetz, ed., *State/Culture* (Ithaca: Cornell University Press, 1999).

24 Deciphering Violence: The Cognitive Structure of Right and Wrong

Karen Cerulo

On March 13, 1996, newspapers and TV stations around the world reported one of the most riveting stories of the decade: the massacre of 16 children and their teacher in a Dunblane, Scotland, classroom. Blazing headlines spread news of the tragedy. The *New York Times* declared: "16 CHILDREN ARE SLAIN IN SCOTLAND AS GUNMAN STORMS INTO A SCHOOL."[1] The *Guardian* announced: "MASSACRE OF THE INFANTS."[2] The *Chicago Tribune* reported the story, saying:

> The pipers who are a fixture at every important Highland funeral will play the laments as 16 1st graders and their teacher are laid to rest.... They were shot to death Wednesday by Thomas Hamilton, a strange and troubled man who took his motive with him when he killed himself after emptying four pistols into a gym full of 5 and 6 year olds.[3]

USA Today recounted the event in a similar way:

> Residents of Dunblane, Scotland held a candlelight vigil on March 13, 1996, mourning 16 kindergartners and a teacher slain by lone gunman Thomas Hamilton, a disgraced boys' club leader.[4]

For days, jarring sights and sounds invaded TV screens across the world: tiny corpses, wounded and traumatized survivors, the painful cries of victims' family members. Such images were played and replayed for months to come.[5]

The headlines and reports surrounding the Dunblane tragedy share a striking resemblance. Readers will soon note that these narratives ordered the facts of the event in a remarkably similar way. In this chapter, I dissect the sequence used to present the Dunblane shootings. In so doing, I explore several more general questions: First, are the sequences that characterize stories on the Scotland massacre indicative of a broader storytelling formula? Do all stories of heinous or *deviant violence* unfold in a similar way? Is the sequencing of deviant violence substantially different from that of justifiable or *normal violence*? And what formats characterize narratives describing *ambiguous violence* – acts too difficult to classify?

In answer to these questions, the pages to follow present a specified set of informational sequences – formats that differentiate stories of deviant, normal, and ambiguous violence. Initially, I rely on journalistic and media accounts to demonstrate these patterns. But as the chapter unfolds, I complement news reports with editorials, short stories, novels, photographs, films, and paintings. In this way, the chapter identifies generalizable formulae for signifying various forms of violence – formulae that denote right, wrong, and ambivalent in both factual and fictional, both verbal and visual accounts of violent activity.

Sequencing Right and Wrong

I have noted that the headlines and reports surrounding the Dunblane tragedy share a striking resemblance. In these accounts, information and images unfold in a remarkably parallel fashion. Specifically, the components of these narratives follow a format I call a *victim sequence*.

Victim sequences prioritize the characteristics of those whom violence strikes. Via such sequences, storytellers can establish an early link between victims of violence and the heinous nature of the acts that befall them. In the victim design, facts and observations concerning perpetrators appear much later in the information chain. Contextual qualifications are reserved for the format's conclusion. As such, readers and viewers become acquainted with a violent event through the "eyes" of the injured. The victim serves as the audience's point of reference.

In analyzing hundreds of journalistic and media reports, I find that victim sequences represent the prototype for deviant violence narratives. For example, storytellers liberally adopted the format in recounting the ultimate deviance of the Scotland massacre. Indeed, we can revisit the headlines and stories earlier introduced, using them to highlight this narrative pattern. Note the *New York Times* headline:

TEXT	IDENTITY QUALIFIER
16 CHILDREN	*Victim*
ARE SLAIN IN SCOTLAND	*Act*
AS GUNMAN	*Performer*
STORMS INTO A SCHOOL	*Context*

The same order characterizes the *Chicago Tribune* story:

TEXT	IDENTITY QUALIFIER
They (16 1st graders and their teacher)	*Victim*
were shot to death Wednesday	*Act*
by Thomas Hamilton, a strange and troubled man	*Performer*
who took his motive with him when he killed himself after emptying four pistols into a gym full of 5 and 6 year olds.	*Context*

A victim sequence organizes the *USA Today* report as well:

TEXT	IDENTITY QUALIFIER
Residents of Dunblane, Scotland held a candlelight vigil on March 13, 1996, mourning	*(Intro)*
16 kindergartners and a teacher	*Victim*
slain	*Act*
by lone gunman Thomas Hamilton, a disgraced boys' club leader.	*Performer*

Victim sequences are not restricted to momentous atrocities. This sequence proves equally prevalent in reports of "everyday" deviant violence. Consider, for example, the following newspaper account of a routine homicide in Queens, NY.[6] In describing the deviant murder, the journalist favored a victim sequence:

TEXT	IDENTITY QUALIFIER
A Queens store owner	*Victim*
was shot to death	*Act/Consequence*
by two robbers	*Performer*
Friday night as he drew a 9 millimeter pistol in an attempt to foil the robbery, the police said.[7]	*Context*

Similarly, a victim sequence frames this account of a child's brutal, deviant murder:

TEXT	IDENTITY QUALIFIER
A 4-year old girl who was hospitalized	*Victim*
after being found stuffed under a waterbed mattress as punishment died on Saturday night, the Broward County Sheriff's office said, adding that	*Act/Consequence*
her mother's boyfriend would be charged with murder. The man, Carlos Schenk,	*Performer*
had been charged with aggravated child abuse and jailed under $50,000 bond.[8]	*Context*

In each of these stories, victims and their fate become the signature of the event. The victim provides the porthole through which readers enter the story. In this way, victim formats can create a special milieu. The directing voice of each report prioritizes the dark side of violence. Violent actors along with their motives and circumstances are met from the vantage point of the offended. Via a victim sequence, readers are encouraged to inhabit the victim; they are urged to process the violence through the lens of the "target."

Normal violence narratives stand in contrast to their deviant counterparts; such stories exhibit their own unique structure. Storytellers generally unfold reports of normal violence using a format I call a *performer sequence*.

Performer sequences prioritize information about the violent actor. Facts regarding her/his intentions, feelings, and behaviors appear early in the information chain; information on victims and context is delayed. In this way, performer sequences direct audience members to step "into the shoes" of the violent actor: Readers and viewers observe violence through the movements of the perpetrator.

In reviewing accounts of normal violence – here, violent acts acceptable under the law – the prevalence of performer sequences becomes clear. Consider, for example, this description of force exacted by the Washington D.C. police against two suspects in the attack:

TEXT	IDENTITY QUALIFIER
D.C. police officers	*Performer*
shot and wounded	*Act/Consequence*
two suspects	*Victim*
Thursday night, both after they allegedly tried to run over officers who were trying to stop them in unrelated incidents.[9]	*Context*

This text references all violent action from the perpetrators' vantage point. The structure of the narrative imposes the violent actor's perspective on the telling of the event. The same can be said of the following account describing a self-defense shooting. (Note that contextual information contained in the story makes clear that the gunman faced life-threatening conditions.) In this account, the performer sequence forces readers to enter the action at the side of the "good guy":

TEXT	IDENTITY QUALIFIER
A truck driver	*Performer*
shot and killed	*Act*
a 15-year-old boy	*Victim*
who was attempting to rob him late Tuesday at a Buckner Terrace gas station, police said. The driver was shot in the chest during the 11 p.m. robbery attempt outside a closed Texaco station.[10]	*Context*

Journalists and reporters also use performer sequences in narrating violence that is normalized by context. For example, a performer sequence unfolds this incident of football-related violence:

TEXT	IDENTITY QUALIFIER
The Steelers	*Performer*
beat up	*Act*
Los Angeles	*Victim*
21–3 yesterday.	*Context*

The story continues:

"We (the Steelers)	*Performer*
are hitting people hard.	*Act*
Go in and look at that Raider locker room, you'll see people beat up."[11]	*Victim*

Similarly, storytellers typically choose performer sequences when reporting the normal violence involved in natural disasters:

TEXT	IDENTITY QUALIFIER
A powerful earthquake	*Performer*
devastated	*Act*
200 villages in the remote mountains of northeastern Iran yesterday, killing at least 1000 people and injuring at least 5000.[12]	*Victim/Context*

And performer sequences are typically used to frame accounts of "figurative" violence. Note the lead on a story addressing the "victims" of medical laboratory "violence":

TEXT	IDENTITY QUALIFIER
David Lynch	*Performer*
likes to kill	*Act*
cells	*Victim*
just to watch them die.[13]	*Context*

These examples illustrate a clear pattern. When violence occurs in culturally acceptable ways, storytellers stress actors and their motives over the consequences of an act. Narrators use performer sequences to facilitate the bonding of audience and perpetrator.

One can observe a dramatic counterpoint – a stark contrast of victim and performer designs – by focusing on stories that simultaneously address both deviant and normal violence. The following Associated Press report offers one such opportunity. This story appeared upon the death of Pat Garret, the law enforcement officer responsible for the justifiable homicide of the infamous killer, Billy the Kid. In describing Garret's normal violence, note that the journalist constructs a performer sequence:

TEXT	IDENTITY QUALIFIER
Garret	*Performer*
hunted down	*Act*
William II. Bonney Jr. a.k.a. Billy the Kid.	*Victim*
He	*Performer*
shot	*Act*
him to death	*Victim/Consequence*
at Old Fort Sumner in Lincoln County on Jul. 14, 1881.	*Context*

In contrast, the journalist reports the deviant murder of Garret via a victim sequence:

TEXT	IDENTITY QUALIFIER
Garret	*Victim*
was slain in 1908.	*Act*
His killer	*Performer*
was never brought to justice.[14]	*Context*

Similarly, consider the following story addressing the war in the former Yugoslavia. When the American journalist reports on Croatian violence – violence inflicted by a nation with whom the U.S. sympathizes – a performer sequence directs the narrative:

TEXT	IDENTITY QUALIFIER
Croation Government Forces	*Performer*
routed	*Act*
rebel Serbs today from Knin.[15]	*Victim*

However, when the story turns to violence perpetrated by Serbian enemies, the reporter adopts a victim sequence:

TEXT	IDENTITY QUALIFIER
Many Croatians who lived in the area	*Victim*
were forced to flee	*Act*
by the Serbs.[16]	*Performer*

The anecdotal data presented heretofore illustrate a broader, more general pattern of reporting. Indeed, in analyzing a sample of 130 newspaper leads,[17] I found that victim sequences were favored overwhelmingly in stories of deviant violence. In contrast, journalists typically structured normal violence accounts using perpetrator formats.... According to the data, 71% of the leads devoted to deviant violence display victim sequences. In contrast, none of the leads reporting normal violence prioritize the victim. Rather, the large majority of these stories – 96% of the leads – favor the performer sequence. . . .

Sequencing Ambiguous Violence

Violence is not always easily identified as deviant or normal. In some cases, violent acts can be ambiguous in nature. *Ambiguous violence* contains both deplorable and moralistic elements; such acts may be distasteful and unpleasant, but nevertheless defined as justifiable. As such, ambiguous violence can elicit great ambivalence from those exposed to it. Individuals can experience mixed feelings in reacting to such events.

The ways in which storytellers recount ambiguous violence speaks to the complex nature of such events. Journalists typically rely on two special sequences when unfolding ambiguous acts of violence: *contextual sequences* and *doublecasting sequences*.

Contextual sequences prioritize data on an act's setting or circumstance. Such information encases the central players in a story. In so doing, contextual sequences offer reasons and explanations for otherwise unacceptable violence. Indeed, such formats provide potential justifications for violent acts, justifications that appear before readers and viewers actually learn of the act itself.

Suicide stories offer one good venue in which to explore the telling of ambiguous violence. While many view suicide as unacceptable violence against the self, others view the act as an acceptable exercise of choice. Recent debates on physician-assisted suicide have further intensified the ambiguity of the act.[18] For those reporting on suicide cases, contextual sequences prove the format of choice. The stories that follow illustrate the style; both reports concern a suicide assisted by Dr. Jack Kevorkian. A contextual sequence directs the *Detroit News* account of the event:

TEXT	IDENTITY QUALIFIER
Janet Atkins, a 54-year-old Portland Oregon woman	*Performer*
suffering from Alzheimer's disease,	*Context*
took her own life June 4, 1990 by using a suicide device.	*Act*
Retired Royal Oak MI pathologist, Dr. Jack Kevorkian, the machine's inventor assisted the woman.[19]	*Context*

The *San Francisco Chronicle* reported the story in a similar way:

TEXT	IDENTITY QUALIFIER
An Oregon woman	*Performer*
suffering from Alzheimer's disease has	*Context*
become the first person to commit suicide	*Act*
using a device created by Dr. Jack Kevorkian, a Michigan Pathologist.[20]	*Context*

By qualifying this suicide with data on the perpetrator's medical condition, storytellers direct readers to consider Atkins' act "in context." The sequence prioritizes the details surrounding the event, presenting the audience with the full complexity of the issue.

Contextual sequences frequently frame other forms of ambiguous violence. Accidental violence provides a case in point. Note this description of an unexpected Japanese attack on a U.S. plane:

TEXT	IDENTITY QUALIFIER
A mechanical problem may have caused	*Context*
a Japanese destroyer	*Performer*
aiming at a target being towed by a U.S. attack bomber	*Context*
to shoot	*Act*
the plane out of the sky.[21]	*Victim*

In this report, qualifications and justifications become the primary point of reference; via contextual sequencing, the violence itself is relegated to the horizon.

Doublecasting sequences represent another popular method by which storytellers unfold accounts of ambiguous violence. In such sequences, contextual information simultaneously casts the central "subject" of the story as both victim and perpetrator. In this way, doublecasting complicates the flow of information; the sequence imposes a point/counterpoint format on an account. In choosing doublecasting sequences to frame a story, narrators encourage their audience to consider multiple dimensions of the violence in question.

The narratives that follow, detailing the murder of serial killer Jeffrey Dahmer, illustrate the links between ambiguous violence and doublecasting formats. Dahmer's death represents a highly ambiguous case. On the one hand, his murder was an act of gruesome, heinous violence. Yet, the murder targeted a brutal serial killer, leading many to view the violence as an acceptable act of justice. The ambiguity of this issue is reflected in the sequencing of the following newspaper excerpts. Note, for example, the *New York Times* headline that announced the story to readers:

JEFFREY DAHMER	MULTIPLE KILLER	IS BLUDGEONED TO DEATH IN PRISON
(*Victim*)	(*Perpetrator*)	(*Act/Context*)

Doublecasting characterizes both the eye-catching banner and the story lead that accompanies it:

TEXT	IDENTITY QUALIFIER
Jeffrey L. Dahmer,	*Victim*
whose gruesome exploits of murder, necrophilia, and dismemberment shocked the world in 1991,	*Context/Perpetrator*
was attacked and killed today	*Act/Consequence*
in a Wisconsin prison where he was serving 15 consecutive life terms.	*Context*[22]

The *Guardian*'s description of Dahmer's murder adopts the same strategy. Doublecasting drives the story's headline:

JEFFREY DAHMER	CANNIBAL AND SERIAL KILLER	MURDERED IN JAIL
(*Victim*)	(*Perpetrator*)	(*Act/Context*)

Doublecasting unfolds the text as well:

TEXT	IDENTITY QUALIFIER
Jeffrey Dahmer,	*Victim*
the serial killer and cannibal,	*Context/Perpetrator*
was found dead	*Act/Consequence*
on November 28, 1994 in the Columbia Correctional Facility in Portage, WI.[23]	*Context*

The doublecasting formats displayed in these examples bar the connection of victim and act. Before allowing readers to fully sympathize with Dahmer's fate, the sequence presents readers with his sins. In this way, doublecasting disrupts the typical subject-predicate structure of the text. The sequence frames a dual status for Dahmer, the focus of the report. Dahmer is the victim acted upon as well as the violent performer. This strategy can problematize the violence at hand. . . .

[T]he data confirm the connection between contextual sequences, doublecasting formats, and the presentation of ambiguous violence. . . . 85% of ambiguous violence narratives display contextual or doublecasting sequences; only 14% of such stories reflect an alternate design. When one reviews ambiguous violence stories with reference to theme . . . the same pattern emerges.

Beyond the News

The signature sequences of deviant, normal, and ambiguous violence reach beyond news reports; they are evident across a wide variety of storytelling genres. Distinct structures of right, wrong, and undecided pattern both factual and fictional works, both verbal and visual images.

Commentary

The formats heretofore reviewed are regularly found in messages of commentary and persuasion. Note, for example, the structural counterpoint that delineates "right" from "wrong" in this letter to the editor of *USA Today*. A citizen writes to contrast the April 19, 1995, bombing of the A. P. Murrah building with the 1993 ATF action against the Branch Davidians in Waco, Texas. Note the victim sequence that embodies the author's discussion of the Oklahoma affair, an event the writer specifically identifies as deviant violence:

TEXT	IDENTITY QUALIFIER
On April 19	*(Time Frame)*
a building of innocent people	*Victim*
was targeted by	*Act*
a lunatic.	*Performer*

In contrast, the citizen adopts a performer sequence in describing what he views to be the normal violence of Waco:

TEXT	IDENTITY QUALIFIER
In Waco,	*(Place Frame)*
the federal government	*Performer*
was pursuing a legitimate, legal process.[24]	*Act*

In this letter, structure as well as content convey the author's assessments. One derives meaning not only from what the author writes, but also from how he frames the message.

In a similar vein, consider two historical examples of persuasive communication on violence: President Roosevelt's address to the U.S. Congress following Japan's attack on Pearl Harbor, and President Truman's address to the nation following the U.S. bombing of Hiroshima. These texts make apparent the sequence formats that differentiate deviance from normalcy. Note that a victim sequence frames Roosevelt's description of Japan's deviant attack:

TEXT	IDENTITY QUALIFIER
Yesterday, December 7, 1941, a date that will live in infamy	*(Temporal Frame)*
the United States of America	*Victim*
was suddenly and deliberately attacked	*Act*
by naval and air forces of the Empire of Japan.[25]	*Performer*

Contrast this approach with President Truman's method in reporting the "necessary" bombing of Hiroshima. A performer sequence structures his opening words:

TEXT	IDENTITY QUALIFIER
Sixteen hours ago	*(Temporal Frame)*
an American airplane	*Performer*
dropped one bomb	*Act*
on Hiroshima, an important Japanese Army base.	*Victim*

Indeed, he uses the performer sequence throughout the speech:

TEXT	IDENTITY QUALIFIER
We	*Performer*
are now prepared to obliterate more rapidly and completely	*Act*
every productive enterprise the Japanese have above ground in any city.	*Victim*
We	*Performer*
shall destroy	*Act*
their docks, their factories and their communications.	*Victim*
We	*Performer*
shall completely destroy	*Act*
Japan's power to make war.[26]	*Victim*

These examples suggest that subjective commentary on violence mirrors the structural formats so common to factual accounts. From "straight" reporting to well-crafted rhetoric, the sequencing of right and wrong remains constant.

Turning to ambiguous violence, one finds that such commentary follows contextual or doublecasting sequences. These patterns parallel the ordering of factual accounts on the subject. Note, for example, this commentary addressing the violent aspects of "outing":

TEXT	IDENTITY QUALIFIER
In an effort to battle stigma against homosexuals,	*Context*
a faction among American gay people	*Performer*
has adopted a tactic that many find an alarming invasion of privacy: unmasking	*Act/Consequence*
prominent people who it says are secretly gay.[27]	*Victim*

The act of outing is fraught with ambiguity. The practice involves an "attack" on individual privacy. Yet, those who perpetrate the attack justify the action as a sacrifice necessary for the "greater good." The sequencing of the outing editorial reflects this dilemma. By couching the perpetrators within the context of their intentions, the writer problematizes the violent nature of the act. Contextual information directs audience members to the multifaceted nature of the event.

In another arena, recall Singapore's controversial caning of U.S. citizen Michael Fay. Editorials in the *Atlanta Constitution*, the *New York Times*, the *San Francisco Chronicle*, the *Times-Picayune*, *USA Today*, the *Wall Street Journal*, and the *Washington Post* were riddled with ambivalence on the caning. Many writers supported some punishment of Fay, yet they also questioned the severity of the Singapore government's response. Commentators regularly invoked doublecasting sequences to express these mixed feelings. Each ambivalent communicator used the same succinct phrase to frame descriptions of Michael Fay: an American teenager who will be caned (victim role) for vandalism (perpetrator role). Fay's *leitmotif* simultaneously referenced him as both victim and performer. This concurrent presentation of Fay's "sins" and sentence was designed to locate readers inside the writers' ambivalence.[28] ...

Notes

1 March 14, 1996: A:1.
2 March 14, 1996: A:1.
3 March 14, 1996: A:1.
4 March 14, 1996: A:1.
5 *Newsweek* magazine published perhaps the most enduring image of the event: seventeen individual portraits and names identifying each of Hamilton's victims. See Pederson (1996: 24).
6 In presenting this anecdotal evidence, I chose accounts describing criminal acts; this strategy allowed me to focus on indisputably deviant violence.
7 "Queens Store Owner Is Shot To Death." *New York Times* (February 26, 1995) A:33. Note that in all newspaper examples, I present the story *leads*. Leads represent the opening sentences of a factual account, those designed to provide a concise, definitive statement of the action. Story leads occupy my primary analytic attention as such segments are typically identified as the guiding frames of factual narratives. Indeed

most journalists argue that the lead "steers the rest of the narrative" (Harrington and Harrington 1929: 68).

8   "Girl Stuffed Into Bed Dies." An Associated Press report appearing in the *New York Times* (November 28, 1994) A:15.

9   "D.C. Police Shoot, Wound Two." *Washington Post* (May 17, 1997) C:5.

10 "Truck Driver Kills Teen Trying to Rob Him, Police Say." *Dallas Morning News* (July 17, 1996) A:21.

11 "Steelers Pound Raiders." *New York Times* (November 11, 1994) C:1.

12 "Iran Earthquake Kills At Least 1000." An Associated Press report appearing in the *Star Ledger* (May 12, 1997) A:1.

13 Lim, Paul J. 1995. "Scientists Seek to Kill Killer Cells." The *Seattle Times* (February 26, 1995) A:1.

14 An Associated Press report appearing in The *Star Ledger* (August 13, 1995) A:9.

15 Bonner, Raymond. 1995. "Croat Army Takes Rebel Stronghold in Rapid Advance." *New York Times* (August 6) A:1.

16 Bonner, Raymond. 1995. "Croat Army Takes Rebel Stronghold in Rapid Advance." *New York Times* (August 6) A:8.

17 The sample was drawn from twelve U.S. newspapers, newspapers selected with an eye toward both regional variation and variation in readerships: the *Atlanta Constitution*, the *Boston Globe*, the *Chicago Tribune*, the *Dallas Morning News*, the *Denver Post*, the *Los Angeles Times*, the *Miami Herald*, the *Philadelphia Inquirer*, Reuter's News Service (online news reports), the *St. Louis Dispatch*, the *Star Ledger*, and *USA Today*. During the period of December 1, 1995, to November 30, 1996, I randomly selected 4 issues of each newspaper for a total of 48 issues. Within each of the 48 issues, I coded all stories pertaining to violent action. This strategy resulted in a sample of 136 stories. These stories were coded for theme, the sequence used to construct the headline, and the sequence used to present the lead.

18 Results from the *General Social Survey* (1996) indicate a good deal of public ambivalence toward suicide and euthanasia. For example, when asked, "Do you think a person has the right to end his or her own life if this person has an incurable disease?" 61% of those sampled answered yes, 34% answered no, and 5% were either unsure or unable to answer. A 1994 Gallup poll directly addressing the Kevorkian situation indicates similar levels of public ambivalence. In response to the question, "Do you approve or disapprove of the actions taken by Dr. Kevorkian?" 43% approved, 47% disapproved, and 10% had no opinion.

19 "Doctor Assists Woman's Suicide." *Detroit News* (June 5, 1990) A:1.

20 "Suicide Machine Used for First Time." *San Francisco Chronicle* (June 6, 1990) A:1.

21 "Japan Accidentally Shoots Down U.S. Plane," an Associated Press report appearing in the *Boston Globe* (June 5, 1996) A:4.

22 Terry, D. T. "Jeffrey Dahmer, Multiple Killer, Is Bludgeoned to Death." *New York Times* (November 29, 1994) A:1.

23 *Guardian* (November 29, 1994) 1:13.

24 Nieman, O. 1995. "Innocent Targeted." *USA Today* (May 1) A:10.

25 As quoted in Commager (1968: 451–452).

26 As quoted in Truman (1961: 197–199).

27 Johnson, D. 1990. "Privacy Versus the Pursuit of Gay Rights." *New York Times* (March 27) A:23.

28 Doublecasting also framed editorials addressing the controversial castration of Texas prisoner Larry Don McQuay. The *Houston Chronicle*, the *San Francisco Chronicle*, and *USA Today* all characterized McQuay as the convicted "child molester" (perpetrator role) awaiting castration (victim role). These double modifiers maintained McQuay's

dual status as perpetrator and victim. Doing so placed the violence of the castration in gray, uncertain territory.

References

Commager, H. S. (ed.). 1968. *Documents of American History*, 8th ed. New York: Appleton-Century-Crofts.

General Social Survey: Data Information and Retrieval System. 1996. www.icpsr.umich.edu/gss/

Harrington, H. F. and Harrington, E. 1929. *Writing for Print*. Boston: D. C. Heath and Co.

Pederson, D. 1996. "Death In Dunblane." *Newsweek*, pp. 24–9 (March 25).

Truman, H. S. 1961. *Public Papers of the Presidents of the United States, April 12–December 31, 1945*. Washington, DC: United States Government Printing Office.

Editor's Notes on Further Reading

Cerulo on Narrative Sequences

Analyzing a random sample of reports from twelve US newspapers during 1995–6, Cerulo demonstrates that the meaning of violent events varies according to the sequencing conventions with which they are presented, demonstrating how the structure of messages influences their meaning. Thus, Cerulo challenges cultural analysts to go beyond a superficial focus on cultural content to examine the way symbolic structure produces meaning. In her book, she also discusses at length how sequencing conventions are learned and institutionalized (that is, the cultural production of these conventions) and the ways interpretations by audience focus groups differed when the same stories were differently configured (cf. Hunt, this volume).

For other analyses of discourse about violence see for instance Robin Wagner-Pacifici, *Discourse and Destruction: the City of Philadelphia versus MOVE* (Chicago: University of Chicago Press, 1994); Philip Smith, "Executing Executions: Aesthetics, Identity, and the Problematic Narratives of Capital Punishment Ritual," *Theory and Society* 25 (1996): 235–61, and Smith, "Codes and Conflict: Toward a Theory of War as Ritual," *Theory and Society* 20 (1991): 103–38. For further research on news media see excerpts from studies by Hunt and Jacobs, and accompanying editor's notes.

Examples of other studies analyzing the impact of symbolic structure on meaning include Karen Cerulo, *Identity Designs: The Sights and Sounds of a Nation*, ASA Rose Book Series (New Brunswick, NJ: Rutgers University Press, 1995); John Mohr, "Soldiers, Mothers, Tramps, and Others: Discourse Roles in the 1907 New York Charity Directory," *Poetics* 22 (1994): 327–57; and Robert Wuthnow, ed., *Vocabularies of Public Life: Empirical Essays in Symbolic Structure* (London and New York: Routledge, 1992), especially chapters by Cerulo, Dowd, Bergesen, and Bergesen and Jones. See also the excerpt on narrative by Jacobs, this volume.

The basic insight about the importance of underlying symbolic structure for producing meaning, common to all excerpts in Part IV, is commonly traced to semiotics. The classic text is Ferdinand de Saussure, "Nature of the Linguistic Sign," pp. 65–70 in *Course in General Linguistics*, trans. W. Baskin (New York: Philosophical Library: 1959 [1915]). See also Marcel Darnesi, *Of Cigarettes, High Heels, and Other Interesting Things: An Introduction to Semiotics* (New York: St Martin's Press, 1999); Mark Gottdiener, "Hegemony and Mass

Culture: A Semiotic Approach," *American Journal of Sociology* 90 (1985): 979–1001; Terence Hawkes, *Structuralism and Semiotics* (Berkeley: University of California Press, 1977); and Roland Barthes, "Myth Today," pp. 109–59, in *Mythologies* (New York: Hill and Wang, 1972). For a critique and alternative formulation of semiotics see Eugene Rochberg-Halton, *Meaning and Modernity: Social Theory in the Pragmatic Attitude*, Part 2 (Chicago and London: University of Chicago Press, 1986).

25 Civil Society and Crisis: Culture, Discourse, and the Rodney King Beating

Ronald N. Jacobs

On March 3, 1991, an African-American motorist, Rodney King, was pursued for speeding. After a brief chase, King was met by 21 police officers, including members of the California Highway Patrol and the Los Angeles Police Department (LAPD). In full view of all present, King was severely beaten by three white LAPD officers as a sergeant and the remaining 17 officers looked on. Unknown to the police officers, the event was videotaped by an amateur cameraman, George Holliday, and sold to a local television station. The videotape, which was broadcast thousands of times, provoked a public crisis over police brutality and racism in Los Angeles. Interest in the crisis died down about a month after the release of the Christopher Commission report on July 9, 1991, but exploded again in April 1992 with the return of not-guilty verdicts for the four police officers who had been indicted for the beating. By the end of the crisis Police Chief Daryl Gates had resigned, Mayor Tom Bradley had decided not to run for reelection (for the first time in 23 years), and the city had experienced the most costly civil disturbance in the nation's history. Given that the city of Los Angeles had paid more than $20 million between 1986 and 1990 as a result of judgments, settlements, and jury verdicts against LAPD officers in over 300 lawsuits dealing with the excessive use of force, how is it that the Rodney King crisis came to be seen as defining racial tensions in Los Angeles? How did the events surrounding the crisis affect political elites and other public actors in civil society? How did they affect social understandings about race relations? Answering these questions, I argue, requires an examination of the cultural dynamics of civil society.

Narratives, Events, and Civil Society

In recent years social scientists have adopted the concept of civil society and modified it by trying to make it more frankly sociological. They have argued that civil society is composed of not one but many public spheres and communities (Calhoun 1994, 1991; Taylor 1995), that the study of civil society should supplement its focus on institutions with a consideration of overarching symbolic codes and narratives (Alexander 1992; Alexander and Smith 1993; Jacobs and Smith 1995), that theories of civil society should dispense with the idea of a "presocial self" in favor of a community-situated self (Etzioni 1995; Walzer 1995), and that events in civil society should be seen as having a cultural significance of their own (Kane 1994; Sewell 1992b). Yet important questions remain for these theoretical revisions if they are to have an empirical payoff. How are the different public spheres related to one another and to the putative "national" sphere of civil society?

How do different communities use the overarching codes and narratives of civil society to construct social identities? How do events influence these narrative constructions?

I argue that a more sociological explanation of the dynamics of civil society can be organized around the central concept of narrative. As Abbott (1992) and Sewell (1992a) have noted, narrative analysis has become an increasingly important tool for social scientists interested in explaining social process and social change. There are two main reasons for this. The first has to do with the role narrative plays in constructing identities and enabling social action. Narratives help individuals, groups, and communities to "understand their progress through time in terms of stories, plots which have beginnings, middles, and ends, heroes and antiheroes, epiphanies and denouements, dramatic, comic, and tragic forms" (Alexander and Smith 1993, p. 156). As studies of class formation (Somers 1992; Steinmetz 1992), collective mobilization (Hart 1992; Kane 1994), and mass communication (Darnton 1975; Jacobs 1996; Schudson 1982) have demonstrated, social actions and identities are guided by narrative understandings. Furthermore, by connecting their self-narratives to collective narratives, individuals can identify with such "imagined communities" as class, gender, race, ethnicity, and nation.[1] As Steinmetz (1992, p. 505) has noted, these collective narratives can be extremely important for how individuals evaluate their lives, even if they did not participate in the key historical events of the collective narrative.

A second useful feature of narrative for studying the dynamics of civil society is that it enables the analyst to consider the significance of events. As Somers (1995, p. 127) has noted, theories of civil society too often fail to consider how events have cultural significance "on their own terms." Depending on how they are defined, how they are linked together in a story or plot, and what determines their selection or exclusion into a particular narrative, events can have important consequences for social identities and social actions (Steinmetz 1992, pp. 497–8). Some events "demand" narration and therefore have the power to disrupt prevailing systems of belief and to change understandings about other events in the past, present, and future (Kane 1994, pp. 504–6; Sewell 1992b, pp. 438–9). Other events get called up from the past, pointing to a foundational point of origin for a newly mobilizing community (A. Smith 1991, pp. 125–45; Hobsbawm and Ranger 1983). The point is that events do not have a unitary causal meaning: they contain multiple plot structures, multiple narrative antecedents, and multiple narrative consequences (Abbott 1992, pp. 438–9). The same event can be narrated in a number of different ways and within a number of different public spheres and communities. These competing narratives influence not only how individuals will understand an event, but also how they will evaluate different communities, including the idealized "societal community" described by Parsons (1971).

Of those types of events that "demand narration," crisis is one of the most important. Crisis develops when a particular event gets narratively linked to a central cleavage in society and demands the attention of citizens as well as political elites (Turner 1974, p. 39). In the modern media age, a crisis becomes a "media event," announced through an interruption of normal broadcast schedules, repeated analysis by "experts," and opinion polling about the central characters involved in the crisis (Scannell 1995; Dayan and Katz 1992). The outcome of a crisis is far from determined, but depends instead on the interaction between narrative construction and event sequence. Events such as the Dreyfus affair, Watergate, and the Rodney King beating become important plot elements for the different narratives of civil society and nation, and for this reason they can be extremely consequential for social outcomes. . . .

I argue for a more contextual approach to the study of civil society, one that takes into account its multiple public spheres and communities, the consequences of particular events and the different forms of their narration, and the consequences of these narrative understandings for other events. This requires, as Sewell (1992a, p. 487) has noted, an extended, in-depth, and empirical study of texts. In the analysis that follows I focus on two newspapers with different (but overlapping) readerships. By examining the different narratives they constructed about the Rodney King beating – in terms of characters, character attributes, plots, event linkages, and genres – I show how the two newspapers constructed different but overlapping narrative understandings about the crisis. I also show how certain events became crucial turning points for the different narratives of both newspapers, while other events had significance only for the African-American press. . . .

Narrative Tension and the Elaboration of the Crisis

With the event having been constructed as a crisis, it began to be represented through a tension between two competing narrative forms. On one side was a romantic "drama of redemption" pitting the heroic actors of the local government (the mayor and the City Council) against the antiheroic ones (Gates and the LAPD). In this narrative, which was employed by both the *Los Angeles Times* and the *Los Angeles Sentinel*, the heroic actors were not constructed through any sort of positive discourse, but rather through a semiotic opposition to Gates and the LAPD. Because Gates refused to hold his police officers accountable for their actions, and because he was coded by the counterdemocratic discourse of institutions, the remaining local governmental officials became the defenders of institutional legitimacy more or less by default. This occurred on several different levels. Semiotically, it operated through opposition, where every term implies and entails its opposite. In this case, symbolic opposition to Gates benefited the Mayor and the City Council. Politically, it worked because of the need for an identifiably legitimate authority.[2] This political dynamic was expressed quite well in a *Los Angeles Sentinel* editorial, which argued that "this community has had enough police brutality and if the chief of police won't stop it, then the commission must, and if not, the mayor and the City Council must take definitive action" (7 March 1991, p. A8).

In the *Los Angeles Sentinel*, however, the actual composition of the romantic narrative differed in important respects from that of the *Times*. An important reason for this was the construction of a second romantic narrative in which the African-American community itself was posited as the heroic actor. In this "romance of the community," the heroic actor was represented not through a mere semiotic opposition, but through actual and positive discourse. Employing a style common to the African-American press (cf. Wolseley 1971), the newspaper invoked the ideals of American society while criticizing that society as it actually existed. In opposition to mainstream society, the *Sentinel* represented the African-American community as the true voice of unity and morality, and hence as the only agent able to truly resolve the crisis. We can see the construction of this second romantic narrative in the following excerpts:

> Rarely, if ever, has an issue so united the Black community in the way the March 3 Rodney King incident has done. The savage beating of King has inspired Los Angeles' Black community to speak with one voice. (*Los Angeles Sentinel*, 14 March 1991, p. A1)

> We must not allow ourselves to be set apart in this battle. Justice must be served and we must, at least in part, be the instruments of that justice. (*Los Angeles Sentinel*, 28 March 1991, p. A7)

> The African-American community itself has a distinct role in the accountability equation. In fact, the community represents the proverbial bottom line: it is the ultimate determinant of values and enforcers of acceptable standards. (*Los Angeles Sentinel*, 11 April 1991, p. A6)

In this romantic narrative, the beating of Rodney King became a transformative event, unleashing the potential power of the African-American community. While Daryl Gates and the LAPD were still the villains of this narrative, there were new heroes.

In tension with the romantic narratives, both newspapers also used a tragic frame to interpret some of the events surrounding the crisis. In a tragic narrative, as Frye (1957, pp. 36–7, 282–7) notes, the drama must make a *tragic point*; that is, while the protagonist must be of a properly heroic stature, the development of the plot is one of ultimate failure. Thus, in the *Los Angeles Times* the public – what Sherwood (1994) has called the heroic actor of the "drama of democracy" – became represented as a series of factions, and it became more difficult to imagine a plot development where a new actor could successfully step in and do battle with Gates and the police department. Within the tragic genre, reaction to the beating was interpreted through a narrative of class, racial, and ethnic segregation rather than public unity. As an editorial in the *Los Angeles Times* lamented, "It is profoundly revealing that while middle-class viewers recoiled in horror at the brutal footage, the victim, like many others familiar with police behavior in poor and minority neighborhoods, considered himself lucky that the police did not kill him" (*Los Angeles Times*, 14 March 1991, p. B5).

These types of accounts in the *Los Angeles Times* represented a "tragedy of fate," in the aporetic sense of resigned acceptance, a tragedy pointing to an evil "already there and already evil" (Ricoeur 1967, p. 313). However, the tragic frame of the *Los Angeles Sentinel* diverged in important respects from such a tragedy of fate. The *Sentinel* combined elements of tragedy and irony, calling up other recent instances of brutality against African-Americans. News reports in the *Sentinel* juxtaposed the outrage and collective attention about the Rodney King beating with the relative lack of attention concerning another beating case whose trial had begun on the same day. The trial stemmed from the "Don Jackson case," a 1989 event where two Long Beach police officers were captured on videotape pushing an off-duty, African-

American police officer through a plateglass window, "followed by the sight of Jackson being slammed onto the hood of their patrol car, after a 'routine' traffic stop" (*Los Angeles Sentinel*, 7 March 1991, p. A1). While the *Los Angeles Times* had given the Don Jackson story significant coverage in 1989 (12 articles), it failed to make the textual attachment to the Rodney King beating in 1991. For the *Los Angeles Sentinel*, however, the Don Jackson story served as an important interpretive filter through which to view the Rodney King beating. Other historical events also found their way into the *Los Angeles Sentinel*'s coverage. In a feature interview, Brotherhood Crusade leader Danny Bakewell noted, "When I saw what happened to that brother on television, I thought I was watching a scene out of the distant past: a Ku Klux Klan lynch mob at work" (*Los Angeles Sentinel*, 14 March 1991, p. A5). By recalling other instances of brutality against African-Americans, writers for the *Los Angeles Sentinel* placed the event of the beating in the middle of a long and continuous narrative, rather than at the beginning of a new one.

It was unclear at this point which narrative form would prevail as the dominant understanding of the crisis in either newspaper. For both, the final act of the social drama would depend on the responses of political actors and on the interpretation of these actors' attempts to resolve the crisis. Even at this early point in the crisis, however, important differences were developing in the reports of the two newspapers. Specifically, the *Los Angeles Sentinel* constructed two competing romantic narratives and a more ironic-tragic narrative, both of which would have important consequences for subsequent news coverage...

With the crisis developing rapidly, members of the political elite launched investigations to try to maintain the romantic narrative (where they were the heroic figures) and to deflate the tragic one. Yet, just like the construction of the crisis, the success of these attempts was neither automatic nor guaranteed....

[N]one of the initial attempts to resolve the crisis were successful. The grand jury investigation was largely ignored by the press, the FBI probe was eventually de-emphasized after being criticized, and the conflict between the City Council and the Police Commission did little except hurt the mayor's approval ratings. News reports in the *Los Angeles Times* responded to these failed actions of the political elites by updating the two narrative constructions and shifting the relative importance accorded to each genre. On the one hand, reports from "civic leaders" strengthened the tragic narrative of factionalism, claiming that "the intense fight over Gates' tenure has further polarized the city, politicized the issue and obscured the fundamental questions of brutality, racism, and police training raised by the King beating" (*Los Angeles Times*, 1 April 1991, p. A13). At the same time as the tragic genre was reinforced, other reports weakened the romance of local government, noting with irony the lack of heroism among city leaders. As an editorial in the *Los Angeles Times* noted, "The Rodney King beating has brought to the surface ugly problems in Los Angeles: not only the allegations of police brutality, but the now exposed factionalism among races and ethnic groups and the tensions between longtime city powers who fear too much change and new line city powers who fear too little" (*Los Angeles Times*, 29 March 1991, p. B6). In this new plot, the event of the beating was not only linked to the problems of police brutality, but also to the weakness of local leaders....

The Christopher Commission and the Move Toward Resolution

Resolution of the crisis would, for the discursive community of the *Los Angeles Times*, require the creation of a new hero; for the *Los Angeles Sentinel*, it would require that this new hero, if not the African-American community itself, at least be attached to that community. The "hero" who was eventually to satisfy the conditions of both communities was the Christopher Commission and its "Report of the Independent Commission of the Los Angeles Police Department," released to the public on July 9, 1991. The Christopher Commission was composed of representatives from all institutional branches of "elite" civil society. It was cochaired by John Arguelles, a retired California State Supreme Court judge, and by Warren Christopher, a former deputy attorney general and deputy secretary of state. Also included in the commission were two university professors, a college president, three accomplished lawyers, the president of the Los Angeles County Bar Association, and a corporate executive.

Despite these symbolic resources, the Christopher Commission was not automatically cast in its ultimate role as romantic hero. It had originally been formed as two separate investigations: the Arguelles Commission, formed by Daryl Gates, and the Christopher Commission, instituted by Tom Bradley. Like the investigations preceding them, both commissions were initially represented in a negative light by the *Los Angeles Times* as being politically motivated and dependent. The Arguelles Commission was represented as being tied too closely to Gates, while the Christopher Commission was considered too close to Bradley. The decisive move toward symbolic resolution of the crisis came with the merging of the two commissions into an expanded Christopher Commission. As an event, the merging of the two commissions presented an opportunity for new narrations of the crisis to be made. Both Arguelles and Christopher made numerous public statements representing the merged commission as an independent, cooperative, and objective body whose orientation was directed toward the good of the public. They represented their merged commission as a movement away from the tragedy of factionalism and back toward the romance of local government. As the following excerpts demonstrate, their efforts were reflected in the *Los Angeles Times*:

> The heads of the panels... said they were seeking to distance themselves from the clash as the Police Commission forced Gates to take a leave. (*Los Angeles Times*, 5 April 1991, p. A23)

> "I think it would be good for everybody if we could come up with some kind of coordinated effort," said retired State Supreme Court Justice John Arguelles, the head of Gates' five-member civilian panel. "There are [now] two committees that might be perceived as having independent agendas that they might want to advance." (*Los Angeles Times*, 2 April 1991, p. A1)

> "In order to maximize the commission's contribution to the community," Christopher and Arguelles said in a joint statement, "we must concentrate on making an objective

and thorough study of the long-term issues without being drawn into the controversy over the tenure of Chief Gates."   (*Los Angeles Times*, 5 April 1991, p. A23)

In an environment dominated by satirical and tragic interpretations, even this merged commission was understood skeptically, and its report was forecast by some to be an "impressive study...that ends up just sitting on somebody's shelf" (*Los Angeles Times*, 11 April 1991, p. A10). Nevertheless, when the Christopher Commission's report was released on July 9 – completed "within a restricted time frame because delay would not be in the public interest"[3] – the density of media coverage about the crisis surged. In the *Los Angeles Times*, while there were three articles about the Rodney King crisis during the week before the release of the report, there were 48 articles in the subsequent week; in the *Los Angeles Sentinel*, the density of articles increased from three articles to nine over the same period of time. But the report did not only provoke a quantitative change in media discourse; it also engendered a qualitative shift. The event became a turning point for all of the narrative understandings of the Rodney King crisis. In the *Los Angeles Times*, it was interpreted through a religious metaphor of revelation strengthening the romantic narrative:

> Just as the Rodney G. King videotape gave the American public an unfiltered glimpse of police brutality, so did the Christopher Commission open a window Tuesday on the working lives of Los Angeles police, exposing strains of racism, violence, and callousness toward the public they are sworn to protect...Throughout the inquiry, both men said, they were acutely aware of the high expectations for their efforts. Arguelles talked of producing a report that would be seen as "visionary."   (*Los Angeles Times*, 10 July 1991, pp. A10, A17)

The *Los Angeles Times* began to interpret the release of the Christopher Commission report as a symbolic completion of the crisis begun by the videotape. If the videotape provided the beginning of the narrative, the report enabled its closure. With this interpretive shift the satirical and tragic frames disappeared from the reports of the *Los Angeles Times*. At this point, the discursive environment of the *Los Angeles Times* began to resemble a cultural situation that Turner (1969) has called "reaggregation." While authority figures had previously been represented as divided and politically motivated, they were now represented as being open and cooperative, unified in their support of the Christopher Commission report, and motivated by the duty of office and concern for the public. Attention also shifted back to Police Chief Gates, who was represented as increasingly ego driven and out of touch with the public. As the following news reports demonstrate, the sharp opposition drawn between Gates and the remaining political leaders helped to increase the legitimacy of those leaders:

> "It appears as though a pattern is beginning to develop at Parker Center to punish or harass those who cooperated with the Christopher Commission and to intimidate others from cooperating in the future," [City Councilman] Yaroslovsky said. "This is an untenable situation, which the Police Commission should immediately move to restore."   (*Los Angeles Times*, 16 July 1991, p. A7)

The councilmen's good faith should not be trifled with by Gates. He can either cooperate with the council members and business leaders who would try to work with him on a transition or he can try to fight the many lined up against him. (*Los Angeles Times*, 17 July 1991, p. B10)

Over a turbulent 10-day period, some of the most prominent political, business, and labor leaders wrestled with a difficult mission: how to persuade Police Chief Daryl Gates to commit to a retirement date. (*Los Angeles Times*, 24 July 1991, p. A1)

Former political adversaries, such as the Police Commission and the City Council, were now calling on one another to help in a common cause. Business and labor leaders, who had previously not been significant players in the social drama, were reported to be joining the unified effort. Articles in the *Los Angeles Times* reported that other area police departments, such as those in Pasadena, Long Beach, Santa Monica, Maywood, and the Los Angeles Sheriff's Office, were also conforming with the Christopher Commission reforms. Finally, when two of Gates's strongest supporters – councilmen John Ferraro and Joel Wachs – called for his resignation, the symbolization of political unity was virtually complete, at least for the *Los Angeles Times*....

For the *Los Angeles Times*, as I have suggested, this period witnessed a strong narrative consolidation into an exclusively romantic frame. Acting as a bridge to unify the previously divided members of the local government and the political elite the Christopher Commission was represented as an objective and "visionary" body enabling the unification and cooperation of local government leaders. At the same time, the unification of local government coincided with a strengthening opposition to Police Chief Gates. When Gates finally announced his resignation, the LAPD became purged of the figure around whom much of the symbolic pollution had concentrated. Public focus began to turn to the upcoming trial of the four indicted officers, the conviction of whom would signal complete redemption for the political leaders of Los Angeles, legitimacy for its institutions, and moral rejuvenation for its citizens. Rather than treating the trial as a separate event, the *Los Angeles Times* and its public understood it as the final chapter of the narrative, clearly expecting the result to be the conviction of the officers.[4] As for the other narrative forms that had previously been used by the *Los Angeles Times* – the tragedy of isolation and the satire of politicization – they appeared to disappear in a case of collective memory loss.

In the *Los Angeles Sentinel*, however, collective memory continued to play a significant role in the coverage of the crisis. We can see this from the earliest events leading up to the release of the Christopher Commission report. In its evaluations of the separate Christopher and Arguelles commissions, the *Sentinel* identified the latter with Gates and the former with Bradley and used the appropriate sides of the bifurcating discourse of civil society to interpret their actions. The *Sentinel* reported about the merging of the two commissions in a manner far different than the *Los Angeles Times*:

Earlier Gates said that his Arguelles Commission would cooperate with Bradley's Christopher Commission. Subsequent reports indicate that the Arguelles Commission has had difficulty in attracting panel members and that the two commissions would merge – a prospect not too much to the liking of the Brotherhood Crusades' Danny

Bakewell or acting Police Commission President Melanie Lomax. (*Los Angeles Sentinel*, 4 April 1991, p. A3)

The *Los Angeles Sentinel* interpreted the possibility of a merger between the two commissions as being necessitated by the weakness of the Arguelles Commission. In a direct metaphor of pollution, the Arguelles Commission was interpreted as something to be avoided, as a potential danger to the purity of the Christopher Commission.

Nevertheless, when the merged commission's report was released, the *Los Angeles Sentinel* described it as a "window of opportunity" and as an investigation of "extensiveness . . . forthrightness . . . and validity" (11 July 1991, p. A6). In this respect it mirrored the *Los Angeles Times*. At the same time, however, the *Sentinel* did not construct the commission report as a bridge toward the legitimation of local government leaders, but rather as a justification for the longstanding criticisms made by the African-American community. In this respect, the event of the Christopher Commission report was linked to the romance of the African-American community. John Mack, executive director of the Los Angeles Urban League, argued that the report "confirmed what we already know: that racism is rampant in the LAPD" (*Los Angeles Sentinel*, 11 July 1991, p. A15). By attaching the event to the romantic narrative of the African-American community, the *Sentinel* reinforced the heroic role of the black community at the same time that it extended such a role to the commission and its report. If local leaders wanted to be narrated into a heroic role by the *Sentinel*, they would have to include the African-American community in the resolution of the crisis and would have to recognize that community's collective memory.

Notably, the focus in the *Sentinel* was on the reform recommendations, the findings of bias, and the issue of racism, rather than on the unity of the political leadership in its quest to remove Gates. Rather than relying on sources of support from the political and business leadership, the *Sentinel*'s representation of support for the commission included City Councilman Michael Woo, Brotherhood Crusade leader Danny Bakewell, and the African-American Peace Officer Association, as well as "community leaders and various community coalitions long critical of Chief Gates and the practices and politics of the LAPD" (*Los Angeles Sentinel*, 18 July 1991, p. A1). The voices heard through the *Sentinel* did not readily forgive the political leaders, the police department, or "white society." They continued to represent the police department as exclusive and racist and to identify other area police departments (such as the Lynwood Sheriff's Office) as racist. The durable text of police oppression, always available for the *Sentinel*, was again brought forth as new incidents of brutality were revealed. As the following excerpts demonstrate, the *Los Angeles Sentinel* continued to represent the political system and mainstream society by using the antiheroic side of the discursive code:

After the Rodney King beating, the barrage of nationwide media publicity and public disgust lulled citizens into a false sense of pride and complacency, encouraging them to believe that impending recommendations on LAPD practices and politics would serve to turn the department's mentality around. Then along came the Vernell Ramsey case – another Black Foothill victim alleging excessive force by the LAPD. (*Los Angeles Sentinel*, 19 September 1991, p. A1)

Recent City Council debates – 13 so far – over Christopher Commission recommendations have led to a barrage of complaints from community leaders and various coalitions. One of the main arguments has been the issue of power. Critics charge that the City Council has too much and has become lackadaisical about responsibly exercising its duties. (*Los Angeles Sentinel*, 22 August 1991, p. A1)

Thus, there was no real narrative consolidation in the *Los Angeles Sentinel* after the release of the Christopher Commission report. The romance of the African-American community continued to be the dominant romantic genre for reporting about the crisis. It was supplemented by a "romance of the Christopher Commission," where the commission was constructed in relations of similarity to the African-American community instead of being attached to local government. Local government leaders, and the City Council in particular, were viewed largely as a threat to the resolution of the crisis. Similarly, the tragic-ironic narrative persisted. White citizens were interpreted as being not sufficiently concerned or vigilant enough to ensure that the reforms would be enacted. In other words, while the *Los Angeles Times* had narrated the event of the commission report as a link to political leadership and public unity, the *Los Angeles Sentinel* had narrated it as a link to African-American leadership and public complacency. In doing so, both newspapers were following the "narrative logic" that had developed during the course of events. . . .

In this study of the Rodney King crisis and its interpretation by the *Los Angeles Times* and *Los Angeles Sentinel*, I offer some suggestions about how to study the interplay between the analytic and concrete forms of culture, and I demonstrate how such an approach can help us to understand events, social actions, and the dynamics of cultural representation in civil society. First, I show how the cultural construction of social problems in civil society occurs in multiple media that are connected to different communities of discourse. It is not simply the case that a "social problem exists primarily in terms of how it is defined and conceived in society" (Blumer 1971, p. 300). This notion hypostatizes "society," "construction," and "problem" as though all were more unitary than they really are. The Rodney King crisis was socially constructed as several different problems in several different public spheres. In the *Los Angeles Times* it was constructed as a problem of police brutality, of factionalism, and of political divisiveness. In the *Los Angeles Sentinel* it was constructed as a problem of police brutality, of white insincerity, and of the need for African-American empowerment. The construction of these problems depended on the event, its narration by different social actors, and the ability of these actors to draw on codes and narratives that particular discursive communities found both plausible and dramatic. This finding supports a "public arenas" model of social problems (Hilgartner and Bosk 1988), at the same time that it reorients the model toward a recognition of multiple public spheres.

Second, by conceptualizing narratives and events in a relational manner, I show how interactional effects can have important consequences for social outcomes. Clearly, the event of the Rodney King beating had important consequences for subsequent narrative understandings about race relations and civil society. But the event had neither a unitary nor a necessary meaning. While it was constructed in the

Los Angeles Times as the beginning of a narrative of crisis, in the *Los Angeles Sentinel* it was inserted into the middle of an ongoing narrative about civil rights and police brutality. Furthermore, the meaning of the beating changed as new events were added to the various narrative constructions. Some events, such as the grand jury investigation, were "meaningless," in the sense that they were not significant for the narrative constructions of the crisis. This is noticeable in that the sequence of events following the grand jury investigation ultimately became very meaningful following the not-guilty verdicts for the four officers indicted in the original investigation. Other events, such as the FBI probe, were initially meaningful but were soon removed from the ongoing narrative constructions and thus made inconsequential. Still other events, such as the conflict between the Police Commission and City Council, changed the earlier meaning of the crisis. The point is that both meanings and outcomes depend on the *interaction* between events and their narrative understandings, a finding supported by related studies of collective action (see, e.g., Ellingson 1995; Kane 1994) and violence (e.g., Wagner-Pacifici 1986, 1994).

Finally, this study indicates that genre plays an important part in how events get narrated, linked to other events, and infused with social expectation. This is an important addition to narrative analysis and its focus on events, plots, and characters. Genre influences the expected outcome of a particular narrative construction by constructing a set of expectations for the hero and for the conclusion of the story. The "field" of genres surrounding a particular event influences social outcomes because of the way that it informs competing expectations. This is also true of other cultural structures, such as codes, idioms, and schemas. But the analysis of narrative and genre allows us to address more fully the relationship between the analytic properties of culture and their concrete articulation in real events. For this reason, a "narrative sociology" can help social scientists to better understand the dynamics of social process and social change.

Notes

1 The idea of imagined communities is borrowed from Anderson (1983).
2 Greenfeld (1992, p. 416) has illustrated how this dynamic worked in the 18th-century construction of an American nationalism and a revolutionary consciousness.
3 As stated on the cover sheet of the "Report of the Independent Commission on the Los Angeles Police Department."
4 Indeed, when the not-guilty verdicts were read in April 1992, the *Los Angeles Times* reported, "Outrage and indignation swept the city Wednesday as citizens rich and poor, black and white, struggled to reconcile the acquittals of four Los Angeles Police Department officers with the alarming, violent images captured on a late-night videotape" (30 April, p. A1).

Appendix Table A1   Chronology of the Rodney King Crisis

Date	Event
1991:	
March 3	Rodney King is beaten by members of the Los Angeles Police Department, an event recorded on videotape by amateur cameraman George Holliday.
March 6	Police Chief Daryl Gates calls the beating an "aberration."
March 11	A grand jury investigation is formed to look into the beating of Rodney King.
March 12	An FBI probe is formed to investigate the beating of Rodney King.
March 14	Four Los Angeles police officers are indicted for the beating of Rodney King.
March 30	Daryl Gates forms the Arguelles Commission to investigate the beating of Rodney King.
March 30	Tom Bradley forms the Christopher Commission to investigate the beating of Rodney King.
April 4	The Police Commission, on the urging of Mayor Tom Bradley, removes Daryl Gates from his position as police chief.
April 5	The Arguelles Commission and the Christopher Commission are merged into an expanded Christopher Commission.
April 6	The City Council, after criticizing the Police Commission's action, reinstates Daryl Gates to his position as police chief.
July 9	The Christopher Commission releases the results of its investigation, the "Report of the Independent Commission of the Los Angeles Police Department."
July 12	Daryl Gates announces that he will retire as police chief.
July 14	Daryl Gates announces that he might not retire until 1993.
July 17	City Councilmen John Ferraro and Joel Wachs make a public call for the resignation of Daryl Gates.
July 22	Daryl Gates announces that he will resign as police chief in April 1992.
1992:	
April 29	A Simi Valley jury acquits the officers charged with beating Rodney King. In the civil disturbances that ensue there are more than 11,000 arrests, 2,000 people are injured, and 58 people are killed.
June 6	Daryl Gates retires as chief of the Los Angeles Police Department and is replaced by Willie L. Williams.

References

Abbott, Andrew. 1988. "Transcending General Linear Reality," *Sociological Theory* 6: 169–86.

——. 1992. "From Causes to Events: Notes on Narrative Positivism." *Sociological Methods and Research* 20 (4): 428–55.

Alexander, Jeffrey. 1992. "Citizen and Enemy as Symbolic Classification: On the Polarizing Discourse of Civil Society." Pp. 289–308 in *Cultivating Differences: Symbolic Boundaries and the Making of Inequality*, edited by Michèle Lamont and Marcel Fournier. Chicago: University of Chicago Press.

Alexander, Jeffrey C., and Phillip Smith. 1993. "The Discourse of American Civil Society: A New Proposal for Cultural Studies." *Theory and Society* 22: 151–207.

Anderson, Benedict. 1983. *Imagined Communities: Reflections on the Origin and Spread of Nationalism*. London: Verso.

Blumer, Herbert. 1971. "Social Problems as Collective Behavior." *Social Problems* 18: 298–306.

Calhoun, Craig C. 1991. "Indirect Relationships and Imagined Communities: Large-Scale Social Integration and the Transformation of Everyday Life." Pp. 95–121 in *Social Theory for a Changing Society*, edited by P. Bourdieu and J. S. Coleman. Boulder, Colo.: Westview Press.

———. 1992. Introduction to *Habermas and the Public Sphere*, edited by C. Calhoun. Cambridge, Mass.: Harvard University Press.

———. 1993. "Civil Society and the Public Sphere." *Public Culture* 5 (2): 267–80.

———. 1994. "The Public Good as a Social and Cultural Project." Manuscript. University of North Carolina, Chapel Hill.

Cohen, Jean, and Andrew Arato. 1992. *Civil Society and Political Theory*. Cambridge, Mass.: MIT Press.

Darnton, Robert. 1975. "Writing News and Telling Stories." *Daedalus* 104 (2): 175–93.

Dayan, Daniel, and Elihu Katz. 1992. *Media Events*. Cambridge, Mass.: Harvard University Press.

Ellingson, Stephen. 1995. "Understanding the Dialectic of Discourse and Collective Action: Public Debate and Rioting in Antebellum Cincinnati." *American Journal of Sociology* 101: 100–44.

Etzioni, Amitai. 1995. "Old Chestnuts and New Spurs." Pp. 16–36 in *New Communitarian Thinking: Persons, Virtues, Institutions, and Communities*, edited by A. Etzioni. Charlottesville: University Press of Virginia.

Frye, Northrup. 1957. *Anatomy of Criticism*. Princeton, N.J.: Princeton University Press.

Greenfeld, Liah. 1992. *Nationalism: Five Roads to Modernity*. Cambridge, Mass.: Harvard University Press.

Hart, Janet. 1992. "Cracking the Code: Narrative and Political Mobilization in the Greek Resistance." *Social Science History* 16 (4): 631–68.

Hilgartner, Stephen, and Charles Bosk. 1988. "The Rise and Fall of Social Problems: A Public Arenas Model." *American Journal of Sociology* 94 (1): 53–78.

Hobsbawm, Eric, and Terence Ranger, eds. 1983. *The Invention of Tradition*. Cambridge: Cambridge University Press.

Jacobs, Ronald. 1996. "Producing the News, Producing the Crisis: Narrativity, Television, and News Work." *Media, Culture and Society* 18 (2): 373–97.

Kane, Anne. 1991. "Cultural Analysis in Historical Sociology: The Analytic and Concrete Forms of the Autonomy of Culture." *Sociological Theory* 9: 53–69.

———. 1994. *Culture and Social Change: Symbolic Construction, Ideology, and Political Alliance during the Irish Land War, 1879–1881*. Doctoral dissertation. University of California, Los Angeles, Department of Sociology.

Parsons, Talcott. 1971. *The System of Modern Societies*. Englewood Cliffs, N.J.: Prentice Hall.

Ricoeur, Paul. 1967. *The Symbolism of Evil*. Boston: Beacon Press.

Scannell, Paddy. 1995. "Media Events." *Media, Culture and Society* 17: 151–7.

Schudson, Michael. 1978. *Discovering the News*. New York: Basic.

———. 1982. "The Politics of Narrative Form: The Emergence of News Conventions in Print and Television." *Daedalus* 111 (4): 97–112.

———. 1992. "Was There Ever a Public Sphere? If So, When? Reflections on the American Case." Pp. 143–63 in *Habermas and the Public Sphere*, edited by C. Calhoun. Cambridge, Mass.: Harvard University Press.

Sewell, William H., Jr. 1992*a*. "Introduction: Narratives and Social Identities." *Social Science History* 16 (3): 479–89.

———. 1992*b*. "A Theory of Structure: Duality, Agency, and Transformation." *American Journal of Sociology* 98 (1): 1–29.

Sherwood, Steven. 1994. "Narrating the Social," *Journal of Narratives and Life Histories* 4 (1–2): 69–88.

Smith, Anthony. 1991. *National Identity*. New York: Penguin.

Somers, Margaret. 1992. "Narrativity, Narrative Identity, and Social Action: Rethinking English Working-Class Formation." *Social Science History* 16 (4): 591–630.

———. 1993. "Citizenship and the Place of the Public Sphere: Law, Community, and Political Culture in the Transition to Democracy." *American Sociological Review* 58 (5): 587–620.

———. 1995. "What's Political or Cultural about Political Culture and the Public Sphere? Toward an Historical Sociology of Concept Formation." *Sociological Theory* 13 (2): 113–44.

Steinmetz, George. 1992. "Reflections on the Role of Social Narratives in Working-Class Formation: Narrative Theories in the Social Sciences." *Social Science History* 16 (3): 489–516.

Taylor, Charles. 1991. "Modes of Civil Society." *Public Culture* 3 (1): 95–118.

———. 1995. "Liberal Politics and the Public Sphere." Pp. 183–217 in *New Communitarian Thinking: Persons, Virtues, Institutions, and Communities*, edited by A. Etzioni. Charlottesville: University Press of Virginia.

Turner, Victor. 1969. *The Ritual Process*. Chicago, Ill.: Aldine.

———. 1974. *Dramas, Fields and Metaphors*. Ithaca, N.Y.: Cornell University Press.

Wagner-Pacifici, Robin. 1994. *Discourse and Destruction: The City of Philadelphia versus MOVE*. Chicago: University of Chicago Press.

———. 1986. *The Moro Morality Play: Terrorism as Social Drama*. Chicago: University of Chicago Press.

Walzer, Michael. 1985. *Exodus and Revolution*. New York: Basic.

———. 1995. "The Communitarian Critique of Liberalism." Pp. 52–70 in *New Communitarian Thinking: Persons, Virtues, Institutions, and Communities*, edited by A. Etzioni. Charlottesville: University Press of Virginia.

Wolseley, Roland. 1971. *The Black Press, U.S.A.* Ames: Iowa State University Press.

Editor's Notes on Further Reading

Jacobs on Narratives and Public Events

Jacobs draws attention to the way different narrative constructions influence the understanding and evaluation of public events in his analysis of reporting about the political aftermath of the Rodney King beating in mainstream and African-American newspapers in Los Angeles. Narratives may differ in emplotment, character construction, and genre. In the full article, Jacobs analyzes such differences in the early construction of the event, and in failed attempts at resolution, as well as in the elaboration of the crisis and the move toward resolution discussed here.

For other studies of racial issues and the news see also excerpt from Hunt, this volume, and associated editor's note. Other work on news narratives includes Michael Schudson, "The Politics of Narrative Form: The Emergence of News Conventions in Print and Television," *Daedalus* 111 (1982): 97–112; Ronald Jacobs, "Producing the News, Producing the Crisis: Narrativity, Television, and News Work," *Media, Culture and Society* 18 (1996): 373–97;

Robert Karl Manoff, "Writing the News (By Telling the 'Story')," pp. 197–229 in Robert Karl Manoff and Michael Schudson, eds., *Reading the News* (New York: Pantheon, 1986); and Barbie Zelizer, "Achieving Journalistic Authority Through Narrative," *Critical Studies in Mass Communication* 7 (1990): 366–76. For more on news conventions and their history see Richard Kaplan, "The American Press and Political Community: Reporting in Detroit 1865–1920," *Media, Culture and Society* 19 (1997): 331–55; Michael Schudson, *Discovering the News* (New York: Basic Books, 1978); and Herbert Gans, *Deciding What's News* (New York: Vintage Books, 1979). For a classic semiotic analysis of conventions for news photos, see Stuart Hall, "The Determinations of News Photographs," pp. 176–90 in Stanley Cohen and Jock Young, eds., *The Manufacture of News: A Reader* (Beverley Hills: Sage, 1973).

Jacobs demonstrates the use of narrative analysis as another tool to unpack the ways meaning emerges from the internal structure of discourses; he incorporates binary code analysis (cf. Alexander and Smith, this volume) but focuses on sequencing conventions in narrative (cf. Cerulo, this volume.) On narrative analysis in sociology see, for instance, Roberto Franzosi, "Narrative Analysis – Or Why (And How) Sociologists Should Be Interested In Narrative," *Annual Review of Sociology* 24 (1998): 517–54; Ronald Jacobs and Philip Smith, "Romance, Irony, and Solidarity," *Sociological Theory* 15 (1997): 60–80; Margaret Somers, "Narrating and Naturalizing Civil Society and Citizenship Theory: The Place of Political Culture and the Public Sphere," *Sociological Theory* 13 (1995): 229–74; Steven Sherwood, "Narrating the Social," *Journal of Narratives and Life Histories* 4 (1994): 69–88; and William Sewell, "Introduction: Narratives and Social Identities," *Social Science History* 16 (1992): 479–89.

Part V

Social Change and Cultural Innovation

26 Constructing the Public Good: Social Movements and Cultural Resources

Rhys H. Williams

Introduction

Consider the following statements:

> What we can work for... is a nation where once again the Judeo-Christian ethic is the foundation for our politics, our judicial system, and our public morality; a nation not floating in the uncertain sea of humanism, but a country whose unmoving bedrock is Higher Laws.   (Randall Terry, founder of Operation Rescue, 1988: 178)

> [W]e take the position that the decision to bear a child... is a private decision – an ethical private decision – and the state has no [legitimate] interest in regulating it. [I]f your beliefs are contrary to abortion, then of course you can decide not to have an abortion.   (pro-choice activist quoted in Luker 1984: 184)

> "Life" includes the whole biosphere with its 30 million or so species. Only those who subscribe to a biocentric world view are entitled to call themselves a "right to life" movement... What is objectionable is the pronatalist spin put on... human reproduction, with no mention of the problems caused by too many people and by unwanted children.   (R. Wills Flowers, *The EarthFirst! Reader* 1991: 145)

These quotes are examples of political claims related to a particular public political issue, legalized abortion. Each claim has clear policy implications, familiar to those who have followed the issue. However, each claim is also undergirded by a particular notion of how life would be ordered in an ideal society. The claims are justified on these visions of the good society; they claim to speak to and for the "public good."

But the public good in each example is clearly different. The good society referred to by these different perspectives rests on different assumptions about societal order, the individual-community relationship, and human nature. Everyone is in favor of the public good, but just what constitutes that public good – or more accurately, *whose* public good is to be promoted – is a matter of political contention. The "good society," so often advocated by activists and scholars alike, is a stirring symbol of consensus, but its actual meaning is "essentially contested."

Rhetoric of the public good is used by members of the political establishment and challenger movements alike in the jockeying for political position. In the contemporary U.S. political climate, the charge of representing "special interests" is commonly hurled at political opponents (see Madsen 1991) – "we" represent the public good while "they" represent particularistic special interests. Challenger social movements are particularly vulnerable to such portrayals, as they lack the status quo's symbols of legitimacy – symbols expressly designed to associate establishment members with the idea of the "whole." Movements thus have an acute need for a plausible "public good" rhetoric.

This essay uses a particular substantive example – the rhetorical construction of the public good – to illustrate a theoretical point: the need to take culture and ideology seriously when studying social movements. Movement scholarship has begun to complement studies of resource mobilization with a focus on social movement culture (e.g., Buechler 1993; Morris and Mueller 1992). Recent concerns with culture have particularly related to the development of internal movement solidarity. I argue for pushing the concern with movement culture beyond its "internal" roles to its strategic and "external" uses. Movement rhetoric and ideology can be thought of as "cultural resources" and analyzed in many of the same ways as are the more conventional "structural" resources of money, members, and organizations. I make a brief conceptual case for considering cultural resources as part of movement "strategy" as well as "identity;" I then consider the "character" of cultural resources; and finally, I explore a specific cultural resource – the rhetoric of the "public good" – and the connections between collective action frames and the wider cultural repertoire.

Social Movements and Cultural Resources

Partly in response to the so-called "new social movements" (NSMs) in the United States and Western Europe, and partly in response to the pendulum-style inclinations in social research, resource mobilization theory's tendency to minimize the roles of ideology and culture has come under attack. Most attempts at reintegrating culture have centered on the production of solidarity within movements and the motivations for collective action. Included in this agenda is recognition of the expressive dimensions of many social movements' goals – that is, NSMs in particular have expressive and identity issues as explicit movement goals alongside the instrumental, power-oriented goals associated with conventional politics. Internal movement dynamics are a natural place for the study of movement culture, but cultural resources also have an external, strategic dimension. The important concept of "framing" (e.g., Edelman 1977; Goffman 1974; Snow et al. 1986) helps illuminate both processes. . . .

[M]any "constructionist" approaches continue to leave the field of the strategic or "external" dimensions of social movement activity to the analyses of structural resources such as money, member networks, and organizational power. Analyses of collective identity and empowerment have generally remained distinct from concerns with structural resources and organizational strategy – the stuff of political struggles. Thus Jean Cohen (1985) poses the theoretical challenge of NSMs as one that contrasts "strategy" with "identity." . . .

The "external" uses of a movement's cultural resources entail an understanding of movement culture not just as the *expressive* dimensions of action, but also as tools that groups wield more or less self-consciously in their social and political struggles. . . .

I view social movements as engaging in more or less rational pursuits of goals; in Swidler's (1986) terms I view movement culture primarily as a "tool kit" to be used by actors as situations warrant. Particular ways of talking about the public good are "tools" drawn from American political culture. And yet, the choice among strategies and the use of particular resources are not completely at the discretion of movement actors. Choice is also shaped by availability within historically situated social contexts. . . .

The Character of Cultural Resources

"Cultural resources" are the symbolic tools that movements wield in their efforts at social change, be they formal ideologies or symbolic-expressive actions. Cultural resources must be "carried" by social actors but are not merely passive reflections of deeper "interests." Because the symbols and ideologies that form cultural resources have an internal logic of their own they help construct interests and actions; culture shapes political contests even as it expresses them. Culture "holds" (or perhaps "molds") its social carriers even as those carriers hold and use cultural meanings (see Swidler 1986).

Cultural resources are analytically distinct from structural resources in two important ways: They are *contextual* and *public.* . . . The distinctive features of context and publicness offer both political efficacy and constraint. Due to their intense relationship to their contexts, cultural resources are volatile and must be constantly created and recreated. Due to their publicness, cultural resources are always liable to "get away from" the actors that first enter them into a debate. Publicness reinforces the contextual aspects of cultural resources. They cannot be bargained or traded as can capital, votes, or official positions. . . .

Social movements' rhetorical strategies have both internal and external consequences for the movement. Movement organizations must find ideological appeals that can mobilize action. Simultaneously, entrance into public political arenas requires legitimate cultural resources as a medium for power. Understanding movements' cultural resources requires an examination of the relationships among broad cultural contexts, strategically effective collective action frames, and the meso-level interpretive meaning-work done by specific movements. . . .

The versions of the public good presented here are drawn from the public accounts of movement activities – they are movements' attempts at presenting themselves and their cause to the body politic. While I focus on several specific movement organizations, due to the rich public material available about them, I emphasize that my interest at this point is on the construction of their visions of the good society, not the specific movement organizations themselves. Thus the media-based presentations of the movements are arguably the most important source of data.

I posit three ideal-types of the public/common good: the "covenant," "contract," and "stewardship" models. These are "theory-driven" categories developed out of my reading of U.S. cultural history and analysis of movement rhetorics. It is misleading to equate the rhetorical models with categories of movement "types." I present these three models as types of rhetorical strategy. It is the constructions of the public good – the cultural resource – not the movements themselves, that are covenantal, contractual, or stewardship based.

The Covenant Model

The first model of the public good is built on the traditional U.S. religious conception of the "moral community." This perspective views the nation as connected in a covenantal relationship with God – political reform becomes a necessary part of, and occasionally equivalent to, moral reform in accord with God's law (Platt and Williams 1988; Wald 1992). The common good is those social arrangements that are in accord with transcendent authority, corporately as well as in terms of individual action. In the main, individual preferences, wants, and choices are subordinated to the health of the moral community. The community stands before judgment as a collective, and thus there is an imperative to confront and repair injustice whether individuals are personally perpetrators or not. The root image of the good society is a version of the storied New England Covenant community.

Certainly there is variation within the covenant model of the common good. While this argument is often associated with the conservative groups of the so-called New Christian Right, political conservatism is not inherently connected to this model. Its defining feature is its reliance on transcendent authority for the model of human affairs, not the explicit content of its theology or ethics. For example, Epstein (1991: 195) notes that a significant wing of the nonviolent direct action movement was "religious, primarily Christian," and formed "a distinct community with its own organizations." They led protests against nuclear weapons in Connecticut and Washington State, and were the backbone of the Sanctuary movement for Central American refugees in California and Texas. The religious wing articulated a leftward politics built on "self-transformation through sacrifice" for a higher cause (Epstein 1991: 197). Whereas many factions of the direct action movement were focused on an exemplary politics that used self-realization as a political strategy, the religious community in the movement focused on "self-abnegation," the submission of personal interests to duties to a moral community (1991: 195–7; 210–26)....

The covenantal model of the public good is apparent in the rationale behind the anti-abortion group Operation Rescue. Founder Randall Terry's writings present a rationale for action built on a version of the covenanted community. Terry views stopping abortions as a necessary step in restoring the entire nation to a state of grace and thus avoiding God's wrath:

> Our once great nation...was born because of and founded on the concept of Higher Law; the belief that God, not man, was the Judge of the world, and that governments were accountable to Him, and that when they usurped His authority, they were no longer legitimate but tyrannical...   (Terry 1988: 283)

Terry calls abortion a "national sin" (1988: 142) for which the "entire nation suffers" (1988: 155). The nation as a whole is guilty, not only those directly involved. As a result, the entire nation is morally culpable....

Practical guides to organizing "rescues" are filled with the necessity for obedience to movement leadership. Only designated spokespersons are to talk with the press;

only demonstration leaders should know the location of the blockade before depart- ure for it; participants are told what the proper motivations for acting should be, what to bring (and what not to bring) to a blockade, how to behave when there and when arrested, even how to dress. Orderliness is stressed: "obedience to leadership is very important" (Terry 1988: 234); "follow every detail of the instructions given you by the rescue leadership" (1988: 236); "the attitude [should be] submissive, yet military and obligatory...we followed orders" (1988: 243). Military metaphors abound.

And yet, Operation Rescue is not organized very tightly at the national level. Affilia- ted chapters vary widely in their activities and coordination. In a sense, it is a mode of organization very much in keeping with the conservative Protestantism it now embo- dies. There is wide homogeneity in religious and social beliefs; attitudes toward what constitutes right behavior are exacting and stress uniformity. And yet there is a signific- ant degree of "congregational" autonomy in the actual operations. Many local chap- ters run largely independently, led by a charismatic authority figure. The covenant model of the public good that supports Operation Rescue's ideology has its sense of corporate morality and its tendency to give priority to the community over individual rights reflected in organizational characteristics of the movements and its activities.

The Contract Model

The second rhetorical model is a view of the public good built on ideas of rights, and justice defined as inclusion and participation in society. Expanding from the idea of society formed through a "social contract," the public good is the creation of an inclusive public through extension of full citizenship, political and economic, to all community members. "[J]ustice [is] a form of active participation in social life, while injustice is...a kind of exclusion from human community" (Hollenbach 1988: 218). Like the covenantal model, the contractual definition of the public good has a long and honored past in U.S. political culture, but several of its grounding assumptions differ from the covenant model....

The "shared conception" of the public good in the contractual model has changed from the covenant's religious-based sense of "duty" to the idea of individually held "rights." Society is a set of freely chosen relationships of formal equality. And the only truly authentic forms of community are those marked by voluntarism. If there is a root image for the contractual model of the good society it may well be a version of Jefferson's – and later the Populists' – yeoman farmer: rugged, neighborly, self- reliant, virtuous.

The contractual model's language of rights varies between the notion of liberty (the right to be left alone) and the notion of entitlement (the right to the means for achieving inclusion). Movements that have been most prone to this ideological strategy have been groups of the disenfranchised. From the colonial period forward, the notion of rights accruing to individuals that are unabridgeable by societal authorities has been a wedge into political life (see Rodgers 1987).

A contemporary example of the use of the rhetoric of citizenship rights justifying inclusion is the "environmental justice" ideology used by many local grassroots groups mobilizing against toxic contamination. Such groups are predominantly composed of ethnic minorities (due to the placement of toxic dumps and other ecological hazards) and have easily adapted the "rhetoric of dignity and full citizen-ship...preeminent in a range of 'rights' movements in the twentieth century" (Capek 1993:8). Inclusion into full status within the political community – symbo-lized here by the "American dream" of autonomy through home ownership – is the de facto vision of the good society.

Perhaps the most obvious example of the contract model of the public good is the "reproductive rights" ideology of the pro-choice movement. As Staggenborg (1991) notes, the pro-choice movement is composed of a variety of groups with differing interests. Indeed, much of the early agitation for the reform of abortion laws came from the population control movement. But as activists from the women's move-ment began to construct abortion as a "feminist" issue, the emphasis on reproductive rights came to dominate the public rhetoric:

> The National Women's Health Network opposes the...analysis which suggests that population control is an element in the movement for reproductive rights.... The NWHN does not support the population control analysis. It takes its stand on the inalienable right of each woman to control her body and her life. (NWHN Position Paper quoted in Staggenborg 1991: 113–14)

As this statement makes clear, the population control movement and the repro-ductive rights movement held different visions of the good society. The state control implicit in the population control movement's concerns with welfare and resource consumption was anathema to the civil liberties and individual rights thinking that formed the basis for a contractual model of society. Currently, groups such as the National Organization for Women (NOW) and the National Abortion Rights Action League (NARAL) call for a legal situation that leaves individual women unfettered in making their decisions whether to bear children: "Who Decides – You or Them?" is a phrase seen frequently on NARAL literature.

The "right to reproduce" is portrayed as a right accrued to women as individuals and it may not be abridged by any external group or institution. It considers the body as a person's property, and combines the defense of "property rights" with the more recent "right to privacy" (Glendon 1991). The popular slogans "keep your laws off my body," and "if you're against abortion, don't have one," represent the importance attached to individual independence from coercive external authority and the freedom of choice that goes with it; it is a call for an absolute guarantee of privacy (Wolfe 1992). The language of "duty" that animates Operation Rescue's construction of the relations between the individual and the community is countered with a rhetoric of "rights."...

However, for all the language about autonomy the contractual model's assump-tions about individual rights assume such rights exist within a community context that makes the resulting choices meaningful. Rights without the means for exercising them are empty at best. For example, the organizations that Staggenborg terms the "reproductive rights" wing of the pro-choice movement focus on women's health care issues in addition to abortion in order to produce a "comprehensive notion of 'choice'" (1991: 114)....

The Stewardship Model

Finally, there is a conception of the public good as "stewardship." Contemporary society is charged with the careful management of its resources and gifts for future benefit as well as current advantage. This is a common theme in many religious approaches to the world, and the root metaphor of the steward is alive in many U.S. churches and denominations. But it is not limited to religious organizations, per se, as its wide use in approaches to trusteeship and nonprofit organization management indicates.

The stewardship and covenant models of the public good are related due to their common focus on "duty," although this is manifested differently. The most distinctive differences in the two conceptions are found in the writings of one segment of the environmentalist movement – particularly those writing from what is often called a "deep ecology" perspective. Much of the deep ecology discourse is imbued with spiritual significance and often incorporates elements of non-Western (Nash 1989), or indigenous American (Albanese 1990) religious systems. However, the perspective stands apart from the predominant received traditions in U.S. Judeo-Christian thinking, as the latter have emphasized human dominion over nature. . . .

I am not claiming that the environmental *movement* is confined to a stewardship model of the public good; I am asserting that a common ideological theme used by certain movement factions or organizations is not shared with either the covenantal or contractual rhetorics. That is, their common good is not a religiously-based moral community, nor a society that nurtures individual rights and privileges. Nonetheless, stewardship rhetoric plays on a chord that is deep within U.S. culture, even if it has mostly been a minor chord. Both Nash (1989) and Albanese (1990) show that a form of "nature religion" is part of the U.S. cultural repertoire. The root societal image of the stewardship model is something of an organic rural commune, where harmony with nature is a necessary precondition for harmony among people.

The stewardship approach to the public good is apparent in some versions of the "biocentrism" that animates groups such as EarthFirst! and Trans-Species Unlimited. Central to stewardship thinking is the idea that humankind is not "privileged" vis-à-vis other life forms. Non-human life has intrinsic value unconnected to its human usefulness, and humans have no right to reduce non-human richness (Sessions and Naess 1991). Far from being granted dominion over nature and its products, humankind's only responsible and moral course of action is to consider first what is best for the planet, protecting ecosystems and bio-diversity as ends in themselves.

This is clearly illustrated by continuing an example used in the rhetorical models presented above: commentary on abortion as a political issue. "Stewardship" rhetoric focuses neither on the covenantal and religious question of when life begins nor on the contractual and political question of the balance of formal and substantive rights. Rather, abortion is discussed in connection with other forms of birth control and framed as an issue of population control – exactly what the ideology of reproductive rights has rejected:

> [L]iberals ... have made a critical error in tactics: they have rested their entire defense of legal abortion on the issue of a woman's right to choose – "pro-choice."   (Flowers 1991: 146)

The stewardship model's approach to abortion is to stress the burden on the planet of uncontrolled human reproduction. Controlling reproduction is both a personal and social responsibility as well as a political problem (Lyon 1991). Session and Naess (1991) put it programmatically:

> The flourishing of human life and cultures is compatible with a substantial decrease of the human population. The flourishing of non-human life requires such a decrease. (1991: 157)

The anti-abortion forces are called "the Spawning Lobby" and their holocaust imagery is turned around: "the real holocaust is what excess human breeding is doing to the rest of life" (Flowers 1991: 147)....

Thus, humans are not a privileged species; the good society will live in harmony with nature, not dominate it for its own purposes. Individual humans and *communities* must subordinate their wants to a common good that is planet-wide. Rhetorics along these lines are not concerned with bettering society as an end in itself; human society must change so that the biosphere, as an inherent value itself, can prosper. While this rhetoric expands radically the notion of community, it still embodies communalist arguments. It is a language of *communal* duties, distinct from the two rhetorical models offered above....

By offering a movement a positive evaluation of its own internal processes and purposes (it is "building community"), and by providing the movement with an ideologically potent symbol with which to organize its public rhetoric, "community" – or the "public good" – ties together the internal and the external dimensions of movement activity. The construction of community among movement members is a crucial part of collective action, whether done self-consciously or not. For many movements, it *is* their claim to a better way of organizing society. It is both strategy and identity.

And yet, simultaneously, a vision of the good society is a useful rhetorical tool in public politics. It gives the movement a claim to a moral high ground and it defuses questions of self-interest when the movement meets opposition. Further, public good rhetoric implicates bystanders in the movement's agenda, even if they are not directly involved in the issue at hand. That is, if a movement manages to create a "definitive" (meaning "effective") claim to the public good, bystander publics can only oppose the movement at the risk of a charge of "self-interest." The symbolic construction of community can thus mobilize movement members, help neutralize opponents, and elicit a general sympathy from neutral onlookers. Claims to embody community internally *and* calls for creating true community – or at least better community – in the wider society bring together a movement's most idealistic vision of itself with one of its most potent external ideological resources.

The relatively open content of the public good as a political symbol is an important macro condition in contemporary politics. Conceptual ambiguity means that as movements draw from the available cultural repertoire the resources for supplying specific content they must do considerable interpretive work. And the resulting "collective action frames" can vary considerably, even though their grounding symbols are drawn from a common societal "mentality" (Tarrow 1992). Effective rhetoric draws familiar elements from a common repertoire and uses them in new combinations or with innovative interpretations. Movements are "both consumers of existing cultural meanings and producers of new meanings" (Tarrow 1992: 189). Neither dimension alone is sufficient to produce a social movement culture.

Klandermans (1992) notes that movements do this meaning-work within a "multiorganizational field" of collective actors with varying alliances and conflicts. Thus in addition to negotiating the interplay of public discourse and interpersonal interactions, movements must operate within a competing field of rival meanings. Movements and their frames are shaped by "field dynamics" and must negotiate the macro–micro nexus at both the rhetorical and organizational levels. Movements must "maintain a delicate balance between the resonance of the movement's message with existing political culture and its promise of new departures" (Tarrow 1992: 197).

The cultural resources for constructing the common good are considerable, if not limitless. They provide an aura of legitimacy to the public purposes of a movement's agenda and provide part of the rationale for the movement's existence. These ideological resources are rooted in a cultural history that has generally moralized its political language (see, for example, Hollenbach 1988; Platt and Williams 1988; Wald 1992) and give movements the means for discussing the problems of the present within plans for a better future.

References

Albanese, Catherine L. 1990. *Nature Religion in American History: From the Algonkian Indians to the New Age*. Chicago: University of Chicago Press.

Buechler, Steven M. 1993. "Beyond resource mobilization? Emerging trends in social movement theory." *The Sociological Quarterly* 34:217–35.

Capek, Stella M. 1993. "The 'environmental justice' frame: A conceptual discussion and application." *Social Problems* 40:5–24.

Cohen, Jean 1985. "Strategy or identity: New theoretical paradigms and contemporary social movements." *Social Research* 52:663–716.

Edelman, J. Murray 1977. *Political Language: Words That Succeed and Policies That Fail*. New York: Academic Press.

——. 1988. *Constructing the Political Spectacle*. Chicago: University of Chicago Press.

Epstein, Barbara 1991. *Political Protest and Cultural Revolution: Nonviolent Direct Action in the 1970s and 1980s*. Berkeley: University of California Press.

Flowers, R. Wills 1991. "This is pro-life?" In *The EarthFirst! Reader*, ed. John Davis, 143–9. Salt Lake City: Gibbs-Smith Publishers.

Glendon, Mary Ann 1991. *Rights Talk: The Impoverishment of Political Discourse*. New York: The Free Press.

Goffman, Erving 1974. *Frame Analysis*. Cambridge, Mass.: Harvard University Press.

Hollenbach, David 1988. "Justice as participation: Public moral discourse and the U.S. economy." In *Community in America*, eds. Charles H. Reynolds and Ralph V. Norman, 217–29. Berkeley: University of California Press.

Klandermans, Bert 1992. "The social construction of protest and multiorganizational fields." In *Frontiers in Social Movement Theory*, eds. Aldon D. Morris and Carol McClurg Mueller, 77–103. New Haven: Yale University Press.

Luker, Kristin 1984. *Abortion and the Politics of Motherhood*. Berkeley: University of California Press.

Lyon, Leslie 1991. "Love your Mother – don't become one." In *The EarthFirst! Reader*, ed. John Davis, 152–4. Salt Lake City: Gibbs-Smith Publishers.

Madsen, Richard 1991. "Contentless consensus: The political discourse of a segmented society." In *America at Century's End*, ed. Alan Wolfe, 440–60. Berkeley: University of California Press.

Morris, Aldon D., and Carol McClurg Mueller, eds. 1992. *Frontiers in Social Movement Theory*. New Haven: Yale University Press.

Nash, Roderick 1989. *The Rights of Nature: A History of Environmental Ethics*. Madison: University of Wisconsin Press.

Platt, Gerald M., and Rhys H. Williams 1988. "Religion, ideology and electoral politics." *Society* 25:38–45.

Rodgers, Daniel T. 1987. *Contested Truths: Keywords in American Politics Since Independence*. New York: Basic Books.

Sessions, George, and Arne Naess 1991. "The basic principles of deep ecology." In *The EarthFirst! Reader*, ed. John Davis, 157–8. Salt Lake City: Gibbs-Smith Publishers.

Snow, David A., E. Burke Rochford, Jr., Steven K. Worden, and Robert D. Benford 1986. "Frame alignment processes, micromobilization, and movement participation." *American Sociological Review* 51:464–81.

Staggenborg, Suzanne 1991. *The Pro-Choice Movement: Organization and Activism in the Abortion Conflict*. New York: Oxford University Press.

Swidler, Ann 1986. "Culture in action: Symbols and strategies." *American Sociological Review* 51:273–86.

Tarrow, Sidney 1988. "Old movements in new cycles of protest." *International Social Movement Research* 1:281–304.

——. 1992. "Mentalities, political cultures, and collective action frames: Constructing meanings through action." In *Frontiers in Social Movement Theory*, eds. Aldon D. Morris and Carol McClurg Mueller, 174–202. New Haven: Yale University Press.

Terry, Randall A. 1988. *Operation Rescue*. Springdale, PA: Whitaker House.

Wald, Kenneth D. 1992. *Religion and Politics in the United States*. Second Edition. Washington, D.C.: Congressional Quarterly Press.

Wolfe, Alan 1992. "Is there an American social contract?" Paper presented to Institution for Social and Policy Studies Seminar on Inner City Poverty, Yale University, New Haven, Conn.

Editor's Notes on Further Reading

Williams on Ideals of the Public Good

Movements for social change require many practical resources, and as Rhys Williams argues, cultural resources like rhetorical frames must be counted among them. Analyzing accounts of a number of different social movements, he finds three distinct views of the ideal society which are used in movement arguments. The complete article also provides an overview of cultural analysis of social movements and further developments and illustrations from a variety of different movements across the political spectrum.

For more on the rhetoric of public debates see James Jasper, "The Politics of Abstractions: Instrumental and Moralist Rhetorics in Public Debates," *Social Research* 59 (1992): 315–44. For more on culture and social movements see Hank Johnston and Bert Klandermans, eds., *Social Movements and Culture* (Minneapolis: University of Minnesota Press, 1995), and excerpts from Eliasoph, Lichterman, and Swidler this volume. On the influential notion of cultural framing in protest see David Snow and Robert Benford, "Ideology, Frame Resonance, and Participant Mobilization," *International Social Movement Research* 1 (1988): 197–217 and Sydney Tarrow, "Mentalities, Political Cultures, and Collective Action Frames: Constructing Meanings Through Action," pp. 174–202 in Aldon Morris and Carol McClurg Mueller, eds., *Frontiers in Social Movement Theory* (New Haven and London: Yale University Press, 1992). For analysis, critique, and extension of framing theory see Rhys Williams and Robert Benford, "Two Faces of Collective Action Frames: A Theoretical Consideration," *Current Perspectives in Social Theory* 20 (2000): 127–51; Marc Steinberg, "The Talk and Back Talk of Collective Action: A Dialogic Analysis of Repertoires of Discourse Among Nineteenth-Century English Cotton Spinners," *American Journal of Sociology* 105 (1999): 736–80; Rhys Williams and Timothy Kubal, "Movement Frames and the Cultural Environment: Resonance, Failure, and the Boundaries of the Legitimate," *Research in Social Movements, Conflict and Change* 21 (1999): 225–48; Richard Wood, "Religious Culture and Political Action," *Sociological Theory* 17 (1999): 307–32; Marc Steinberg, "Tilting the Frame: Considerations on Collective Action Framing From a Discursive Turn," *Theory and Society* 27 (1998): 845–72; Mabel Berezin, "Politics and Culture: A Less Fissured Terrain," *Annual Review of Sociology* 23 (1997): 361–83; James Jasper, *The Art of Moral Protest: Culture, Biography, and Creativity in Social Movements* (Chicago: University of Chicago Press, 1997); Anne Kane, "Theorizing Meaning Construction in Social Movements: Symbolic Structures and Interpretation During the Irish Land War, 1879–1882," *Sociological Theory* 15 (1997): 249–76; Stephen Hart, "The Cultural Dimension of Social Movements: A Theoretical Reassessment and Literature Review," *Sociology of Religion* 57 (1996): 87–100; and Steven Ellingson, "Understanding the Dialectic of Discourse and Collective Action: Public Debate and Rioting in Antebellum Cincinnati," *American Journal of Sociology* 101 (1995): 100–44.

On cultural frames more generally see Erving Goffman, *Frame Analysis* (Cambridge, MA: Harvard University Press, 1974), and on the influential idea of culture as toolkit see Ann Swidler, "Culture in Action: Symbols and Strategies," *American Sociological Review* 51 (1986): 273–86.

27 The Search for Political Community: American Activists Reinventing Commitment

Paul Lichterman

Personalism and Political Commitment

A Common Complaint

Critics often say that too few Americans get politically involved. Active political commitment is declining, goes one familiar complaint, because people have become too concerned with their own personal fulfillment. Critics fear that the widespread emphasis on self-fulfillment is destroying traditional community ties that are necessary for active citizenship and the sacrifices that may accompany it. Calls to reestablish "a sense of community" continue to resound in academic criticism, political leaders' rhetoric, and everyday talk about what is wrong with contemporary US culture.

This book addresses the complaint about self-fulfillment and political commitment by exploring how different environmental activists practice their commitments to activism. Critics of the self-fulfillment ethos would not question that people can and do enter the political arena to win attention for their personal needs. The question is whether the self-fulfillment ethos necessarily detracts from a public-spirited politics, a politics that aims to secure a common, public good such as a safer environment for a wide community of citizens. Critics of modern US culture have often assumed that it takes certain kinds of communal bonds between people to nurture public-spirited commitments: they have advocated the kinds of ties that Americans in the past developed in local or perhaps national communities with shared civic or religious traditions that obligated community members to one another. People who grow up within such ties would find it easier, more natural to commit themselves to the public good than those who don't. These critics argue that the self-fulfillment ethos has weakened these communal ties. Modern society needs to reestablish the kind of community that will produce citizens with a sense of public obligation who stand up for standards and work for the common good.

Committed citizens have not completely disappeared, and some do belong to communities whose members share traditions and a sense of communal belonging. A good example is Mrs. Davis of Hillviewers Against Toxics. Toxic hazards from industrial plants ringing Hillview menaced largely low-income neighborhoods like Mrs. Davis' with the threat – occasionally realized – of a toxic fire or a slow, poisonous leak. Mrs. Davis did not, however, join her toxics group out of simple self-interest: she did not express concern about her neighborhood property values, and had so far escaped the chronic health problems that plagued some Hillview residents. Davis was new to grassroots activism, and looking for an organization to join when she attended her first Hillviewers Against Toxics (HAT) meeting. Conversations with her neighbors and the HAT staffperson made the anti-toxics struggle compelling to her.

An African-American woman in her forties, Mrs. Davis drew on communal traditions, a sense of belonging to the black Hillview community and to a broader community of African-American Christians, when she "went public" as an activist. When she ran for city council three years after joining HAT, several of her endorsement speakers, including her pastor and a member of a religious broadcasters association, spoke at length about her virtues as a Christian woman. Mrs. Davis did not often articulate a religious basis for her activism, and she did not always define her work as service to a specifically black community; she did not need to. She could take for granted a local moral universe of Christian charity and African-American communal service in which public-spirited good deeds made sense, were worthwhile. Of course, her community did not always live up to the standards its spokespersons set for it. HAT's staff-person asserted several times that his organization did what local churches should have been doing, had they not been worried about endangering the occasional economic or political support they received from Petrox, Hillview's largest taxpayer and a major target of HAT's anti-toxics efforts. Neither did Mrs. Davis' community-minded dedication keep her from eventually voicing dissatisfactions with the level of individual involvement that the HAT leadership allowed for members. The point is that Mrs. Davis lived within the kind of community ties that many critics of American individualism see as essential for public-spirited commitment, and threatened by the widespread quest for personal fulfillment.

Compare Carl of the Ridge Greens, an activist organization based about a half hour's drive from Hillview. Carl, like Mrs. Davis, had little experience with activism before getting involved with his organization. He had thought seriously about environmental and political issues, though, to the point of quitting his well-paying job in genetic engineering because of qualms about its moral and political implications. Carl followed political issues in the news with a passion and did not like most of what he learned. He figured, in fact, that conventional electoral politics would probably never raise the fundamental questions about corporate interests and environmental priorities that he found at the root of so much policy-making. The movement organizations he was familiar with went about "putting out fires" with single-issue political campaigns. He envisioned a popular movement that would publicize the fundamental questions about environmental priorities and social justice that smoldered behind any single issue. He wanted to be part of a movement that would let ordinary citizens voice alternatives to the usual answers given by big interests and single-issue agitators. He became more and more involved in community educating and occasional protests with the small US Green movement in hopes that it would provide one of those alternative voices, and was one of the key organizers in the successful effort to get the fledgling California Green Party on to the ballot in 1991.

Carl did not tap into the kinds of communal tradition that sustained Mrs. Davis. A white man in his thirties, son of liberal-minded and non-churchgoing college instructors, he did not nurture his political commitments with the sense of obligation to a particular people, community, or faith that Mrs. Davis had. No ready answer came to mind when I asked Carl what made him committed to activism; he supposed, after mulling it over, that his parents' fight against a color bar at their college may have inspired him. Carl's practice of political commitment grew out of a very personalized sense of political responsibility. A man who quit his job over its larger political implications – and screened future opportunities with a critical, political imagination – was one who assumed that individuals could and should exercise a great deal of political commitment in their own lives. Grassroots politics for Carl meant a highly participatory politics in which individuals could realize themselves, actualize themselves, as personal agents of social change both in activist organizations and in everyday life. Carl would have agreed with a former member of the Ridge Greens who declared that he "couldn't just be a little bit involved." Activism had to be self-fulfilling. Carl did not ease himself into political involvement by talking to local neighbors or accepting the tutelage of an organization staffperson. He practiced a self-propelled sense of social responsibility.

The terms of complaint about self-fulfillment make it hard to understand someone like Carl. Cultural analysts and critics have often argued that a widespread emphasis on personal fulfillment is incompatible with public, political commitments. This study challenges that argument. Rather than always weakening commitment, the culture of self-fulfillment has made possible in some settings a form of public-spirited political commitment that Carl and many others like him have practiced in a personalized, self-expressive way. In other words, some people's individualism supports rather than sabotages their political commitments. A culture of self-fulfillment may well have encouraged some Americans to turn away from political engagement and toward apolitical self-exploration or consumerism. But a strain of this culture has also enabled some activists to practice political commitments that include a strong critique of selfishness and acquistiveness. This study examines those activists' personalized form of commitment, and contrasts it with the more "community"-centered commitments that critics of individualism have upheld. . . .

"[P]ersonalism" refers to ways of speaking or acting which highlight a unique, personal self. Personalism supposes that one's own individuality has inherent value, apart from one's material or social achievements, no matter what connections to specific communities or institutions the individual maintains. Personalism upholds a personal self that lives with ambivalence towards, and often in tension with, the institutional or communal standards that surround it (Taylor 1991, 1989; Bellah *et al.* 1985; MacIntyre 1981; Rieff 1966). But we should not reduce personalism to its most selfish or privatizing manifestations: personalism does not necessarily deny the existence of communities surrounding and shaping the self, but it accentuates an individualized relationship to any such communities. In contrast with a political identity that is defined by membership in a local, national, or global polity, a traditional religious identity that gets realized in a fellowship of believers, or a communal identity that develops in relation to a specific community, the personal self gets developed by reflecting on individual biography, by establishing one's own individuality amidst an array of cultural, religious, or political authorities.

It is easy to assume that personalism is simply human nature. Isn't it just natural to want to develop one's individuality? Hasn't the main achievement of modern culture been a freeing of this natural, universal inclination from the constraints of tradition?

It is easy for many Americans to counterpose "natural" or "real" selves to social "constraints" outside the self because of a popular version of personalism that is widespread in the US cultural mainstream. Cross-cultural study makes clear that not all cultures place the emphasis on personal development and personalized initiative that many Americans now take for granted. Personalism is not a simple reflection of nature, but a way of defining and presenting the self. Developing individuality depends on interaction. There are norms for "expressing oneself," for being an individualist who can converse with others about personal feelings and experiences. Individuality does not pre-exist culture; it is a cultural accomplishment. Personalism develops in a kind of community in fact, one in which people create and practice norms of highly individualized expression. . . .

Speaking Out in Suburbia

Taking Risks

The Greens put on public education campaigns and attended demonstrations without worrying about whether they were sullying their reputations as respectable citizens. Going public was not nearly so easy for members of Airdale Citizens for Environmental Sanity (ACES). ACES had dedicated itself to sparking a critical public debate about environmental safety at a local firm, Microtechnologies Ltd. ("Microtech," or ML). The firm was a frequent military contractor, and secured a number of contracts for work related to upgrading US weapons systems. Work at Microtech resulted in highly toxic wastes, some of which had seeped into local groundwater, and the firm proposed to build an incinerator for disposing of them. A group of roughly six core members of the Airdale Citizens for Environmental Sanity (ACES) started a campaign to alert Airdale about the hazards of burning the wastes in the proposed incinerator. Most of Airdale did not care to listen, let alone debate the issue.

For ACES members, going public meant braving the withering stare of public opinion in Airdale, a small town of suburban-style neighborhoods about an hour's drive north of Ridgeville. The activists liked to tell newcomers the story of how someone at a public hearing on the incinerator had remarked, "There goes that crazy lady again," as the group's leading spokesperson, Laura, walked up to the microphone. Laura's son feared Laura would get arrested for her activism, leading to embarrassing consequences for him: "I have to go to school in this town." Other members thought they had paid with their local reputations for their association with ACES. One got dismissed by a neighboring city council as a mere anti-military "faddist" when he spoke on the incinerator issue. Another discovered that a few of her friendships may not survive her involvement in ACES. Another, finding herself on a dark street after an evening of door-to-door petitioning, flashed through her head spooky images of industry "whistle-blowers" who get stalked by company henchmen.

The chilly civic climate of suburban Airdale made activism feel risky if not scary for ACES members. As the largest single employer of Airdale residents, the Microtech plant helped keep criticism of its policies on ice. Yet with a core of seven members and a mailing list of other volunteers and supporters, ACES broke through the chill and became the regularly quoted local voice of dissent regarding Microtech policies. Environmentalists and local media too regarded them as a significant force behind the contractor's eventual decision to shelve plans for its proposed incinerator. The group moved on to confront other environmental hazards related to Microtech, and had existed for seven years by the end of my field research with them. How did these activists sustain their group and their commitment to the cause in a risky civic climate? Part of the answer involves understanding how personalism can sustain political commitment.

The culture of commitment in ACES was a hybrid of personalism and more communitarian practices and idioms ... Personalism, especially through the leader's strong influence, shaped the ways ACES organized itself and reached out to Airdale. At the same time ACES members rooted themselves in their local community milieu and defined their activism as in the "community interest," even when other Airdalers showed little interest in their project. Greens carried their commitments as individual political agents applying general Green principles to their locales and to national politics. ACES members situated themselves more in a specific community to begin with. Greens addressed cultural radicals in their locales, while ACES members addressed Airdale residents in general. Most members of ACES did not practice their commitments as highly individualized responsibilities. They acted much more *as group members* than as individual political actors who apply the precepts of a loose, national movement to their locale....

"Suburban" Culture in Airdale

Baumgartner characterized suburban culture in terms of a "moral minimalism" that keeps suburbanites out of each other's way and focused on their private affairs. The "weak" suburban moral order relies on few overt sanctions, and yet produces the much-criticized "controlled" feeling of suburban life that Baumgartner found in her own field site. ACES members saw themselves as having to deal with a lot of privatism and conflict avoidance in the course of publicizing environmental issues in Airdale. The relative lack of public, political engagement in Airdale, as much as the contractor's influence, shaped the way residents became activists in ACES. ACES members and supporters criticized the privatism in Airdale, but lived within it all the same.

It is important to establish first that ACES members did speak of Airdale as a kind of "suburb" rather than either an independent urban area or a self-sufficient community. On the first day that I volunteered for petitioning, I drove with Liz from one shopping mall to another to find shoppers that had not already been "saturated" by earlier petitioning efforts. Liz joked that I was getting a "tour of suburbia." "We don't have any fancy houses so we'll show you our shopping centers." John remarked that ACES had to "go to the people" in Airdale, which he and Liz both explained meant going to suburban-style shopping centers with large outdoor parking lots. Laura joked about a benefit concert for activist groups in metropolitan Ridgeville as "a chance to get out of Airdale for a night."

Both the politically radical and the more conservative members of ACES feared the consequences of being seen as bearers of public controversy. Every member I met imagined Airdalers would tag them with a wide variety of derogatory labels. Fending off expected derision was a regular part of being involved in ACES. One member, Rochelle, suggested that ACES not endorse a county nuclear-free zone initiative because she did not want them to look like "anti-nuke, peace kind of people." On another occasion she took pains to distance herself from Microtech's description of its opposition as a "nut fringe" based outside of Airdale. Jennie, another member who had become active in the incinerator campaign, told me "we are perceived as being these radical anarchists, but we are all concerned about our families." She insisted at a public hearing: "We're not flaky; we're people raising families and trying to live responsible lives." Liz argued the benefits of carefully crafted flyers for ACES: "We should hand out flyers that would really tell about what ACES is...more people would join our group if they don't think it's some radical-leftist organization." And Laura once said that flyer distributing was a good exercise because then Airdalers would see real people and not think ACES members were "monsters with two heads."

The activists did not seem worried that Airdalers attributed to them specific "anti-nuke" or "anarchist" or "radical-leftist" ideologies. Rather, these tags functioned to stigmatize people who, like monsters with two heads, disrupt routine public order with irrational controversy. In a "company town" situation like Gaventa's Appalachian valley, the stigmatizing tag "communist" might actually reflect, in however distorted a fashion, a threat to a company's specific economic interests. In Airdale, the tags "radical" or "leftist" or "communist" signified threats not just to economic or political interests but to a local civic milieu that prizes polite, circumspect comportment. "Making a scene" would challenge local morality almost as much as questioning the employer that helped to underwrite economic security in Airdale. This is the best way to understand Jennie's ambiguous couplet "radical anarchists"/ "concerned about our families." Jennie wanted to put across that it was possible to oppose the contractor without opposing "family values," the private bedrock of collective life in Airdale. Liz and Jack's frequent jokes and comments about "radical leftists" make sense in this light too....

No doubt the apprehensions in ACES did reflect real contacts between ACES and Airdale residents. But in a different "company town," resident activists might have found the strength to buck common opinion through a communal institution like a church, or a shared local culture that could inspire dissent. But in suburban Airdale, what residents shared most was privatism and an avoidance of public controversy. Of course suburbanites in Baumgartner's study or in Airdale might attend various churches or volunteer in service groups. But there are relatively few *publicly shared* cultural affiliations in a private-oriented suburban locale. Whether or not ACES activists personally upheld suburban civility norms, they lived in a situation with few widely shared bodies of folk wisdom or cultural authority that they could bring to ACES. Members found diverse sources for their activist identity. And as Laura summed up about the whole group:

> ACES is made up of what we have in common...Carrie is the society and religion coordinator at her church but doesn't come on with Christianity [at meetings], and I have certain spiritual commitments to peace, justice and the environment, but I don't come on strong with them at meetings. Sam has other things going on – everyone has other things going on too.

Without common, institutionalized cultural authorities to draw upon, ACES needed another basis of togetherness for individuals who all had "other things going on." So ACES drew on personalized notions of commitment that encouraged community members to speak out as empowered individuals.

Personalism and Leadership Among Suburban Activists

PERSONAL EXPRESSION AS AN OPTION, NOT A MANDATE

The ACES group culture combined an openness to personalized expression with a shared rootedness in Airdale. As the leading influence on the group, Laura structured ACES as a Green-style democracy of equal selves. For their part, other members considered ACES a group in which they could try out risky opinions in a safe atmosphere. But they did not assume the way Greens did that each individual carries an elaborately developed, individual political will. They "did their bit" for ACES and for Airdale with the good of the local community as their arbiter of worthwhile activism. Commitments made *as Airdale residents* did not require the special activist identity and lifestyle that Greens created in the absence of a shared sense of communal belonging. Personalism in ACES did not result in expectations about individual political virtuosity. Instead it created acceptance for different levels of individual engagement, including Laura's highly personalized – and time-consuming – engagement. ACES members were willing to let each other define different limits for involvement, and they were happy to let Laura lead them.

A shared respect for personal opinions enabled members to sustain disagreements. More than once, Laura interceded in a disagreement with an appeal to the equal validity of any sincerely held viewpoints. At one meeting, for instance, Margo and John sparred over how confrontational a stance the group should take towards the contractor:

JOHN insisted that ACES was not growing because members were so used to technical talk that "we don't talk about people." He concluded that it would be best if ACES was blunt and said that people working at the contractor were, in effect, "killers." Margo objected.
MARGO: "Well I do think . . . that you can polarize people, and the words you use are very important."
JOHN: "You hate the place!"
MARGO: "Well, I can say that here – I would never say that in public . . . I think there are many ways to approach this and they all need to be looked at."
LAURA   (broadening on Margo's statement): "All the voices need to be heard, everything needs to be said . . . It's a tapestry – you're not wrong and your way isn't the only right way. There is no one right way."
MARGO conceded that John "always brings up the moral issue" and "the moral issue is the basic issue."

No one offered a different moral argument than John's on how to frame the environmental hazards of work at Microtech. Laura's resolution was, in effect, definitive. Her resolution appealed to the intrinsic worth of all contributions and all contributors, rejecting a standard for judging between them.

A "tapestry" of self-expression was a suitable metaphor for external as well as internal relations. When the ACES agreed to help a metropolitan peace group plan a Peace Day rally for the Airdale area, Laura told ACES how different groups attending might engage in different activities. There were, for example, the "anarcho-punks" who might want to do civil disobedience and get arrested. "I want to validate that that's OK ... (because) that's what they do." Laura wanted to "validate" different people's conceptions of political action as intrinsically worthy – coming from within the person. There could be different activities, so that people whose idea of participation in the rally was "sitting" (she gestured a stiff pose with hands folded) could go to the event and so could people who intended to risk arrest for direct action.

Laura wanted to do more than create liberal tolerance for individual preferences in ACES. She assumed that group participation ought to include a lot of personalized expression. It surprised her, for instance, that I had characterized ACES after one of the general meetings as a "friendly" group:

LAURA: "I think we're not friendly enough. We should have more time for pro-
          cess."
PL: "What should people talk about?"
LAURA: "We should talk about *ourselves* ... how we feel about things." She gave
          an example of a man new to ACES who had previously worked in the
          weapons industry, saying that he must have feelings about the work but
          that there's so much business to get through, there is not enough time to
          talk about his feelings. "We mean to support him – we really are a
          supportive group – but there isn't enough time."

Like that of the Greens, Laura's everyday definition of participation included both political and personal expression without a strong division between the two. I commented once that I was struck at how a short, spontaneous exchange about American democracy and the cold war had erupted amid one of the general meetings. The meeting had included a lot of technical information about work at the contractor. Laura said "that kind of thing" needed to happen more often, because "that's what ACES exists for – to empower people." She continued, wondering whether meetings sometimes suffered from "fact overload" and suggested that meetings might strike a different balance between "facts" (technical presentations) and "emotional support." Talk about American democracy and emotional support were interchangeable in this definition of participation and "empowerment."

Personalist language certainly was not foreign to other members. Stacy, a newer member, conceived her own participation in ACES-related activity in terms of an inner, intuitive self. Carrie entered peace and environmental activism from experience in a church-based social action group that encouraged a very personalized way of adopting issues: her commitment to a "peaceable world" included family relations maintained through "conflict resolution" and "affirmation techniques" at home. Even John, steeped in both Catholic and union organizing traditions, was able to trade on notions from popular psychology – the idea of being "centered" as a person, for instance. He taught his catechism students that making the sign of the cross was also a symbolic way of "centering" oneself. Showing me how he crossed himself, he named the different hand positions: "Here, left, right – you're centered. See, Jesus was a Zen Buddhist." He said the kids really got it....

Empowerment as a Cultural Dilemma

ACES faced a predicament in trying to mobilize Airdale residents without simply scaring them off. Their predicament resulted not from a failure of commitment on their own part, then, but from a lack of shared bases for public-spirited, critical citizenship in their suburban culture. Members of ACES, like many residents of US suburbs perhaps, could not invoke publicly shared religious or communal sources of authority for undertaking collective action. In this milieu, personalist notions of community involvement sustained ACES in a number of ways. They enabled suburban activists to take risks in a group that was loose and welcoming enough of diverse individuals to make risk-taking more comfortable. One did not need to sever ties with the prevailing culture of privatism to join ACES. Prospective members would be welcomed into ACES on the basis of whatever (privately held) commitments had motivated them.

It would have been difficult at best for ACES members to recruit more aggressively than the personal "empowerment" theory would suggest. Aggressive mobilization for any controversial issue would have run the risk of seeming irrational to people whose shared culture consisted foremost in a dedication to private life. Appeals to economic self-interest or family health would not goad many local residents out of their privatism if these appeals could not be accompanied by well-publicized accounts of some toxic disaster already having taken a toll on local residents. ACES and other activists knew of "accidents" at Microtech over the years, but the effects of these accidents on residents' health could not be easily substantiated. On what basis, then, could an ACES neighborhood canvasser convince the person at the door to become involved in ACES?

"Empowerment" gave activists a way to talk about breaking suburban civility norms. Contesting suburban civility would mean awakening politically quiescent selves to a better, or more real, practice of selfhood. It meant contesting one kind of (privatized) individualism with another kind of individualism that actually enabled suburban residents to go public, each on an individual schedule, one by one. This kind of individualism empowered but also limited activism in Airdale: for people who believed that Airdalers suffered from individual, disempowered "mind-sets," a well-established organization with strong recruiting practices would not be part of the solution. For example, Laura once explained to me the ambivalence in ACES about getting an office front. On the one hand, the office would lend the group a "veneer of credibility." On the other hand, maintaining an office front would send the message that "ACES can do things" and detract from the goal of getting Airdalers to feel empowered, to "feel *they* can do things." She compared her preferred image of ACES with the Sierra Club's image, which to her said that "Sierra Club can do it." Attributing efficacy and responsibility to the organization would, in this view, only perpetuate the individual powerlessness and quiescence that ACES saw itself as challenging. So the empowerment theory directed attention toward awakening individual consciousness rather than expanding an organization.

Communitarian theorists might argue that ACES ought to have nurtured a political culture of "citizenship," avoiding notions of personal "empowerment" that limited the group's own growth and public visibility. For if everyone agreed on the goodness of good citizenship, then no one would fault ACES for aggressive recruiting and organization-building. The problem is that going public in ACES implied dissent from taken-for-granted notions of good citizenship in Airdale. "Good" local residents were "concerned about our families" as Jennie put it, and did not get involved in "flaky" or "radical" causes. The usual categories for talking about responsible citizenship in Airdale did not make much room for activists publicizing controversial issues in even the sincerest public interst. ACES could not simply neutralize skepticism about its efforts by claiming a moral high ground of citizenship. This is all the more the case when Microtech could already claim unimpeachable good citizenship by contributing to the national defense with its military contracts. ACES would, at least, need to make clear it was advocating a *different* or more "real" practice of good citizenship. This is in fact the route ACES took, legitimating itself by appealing to the "reality" of personal empowerment that breaks through constraining social conventions.

Further, the "good citizenship" of Liz, Rochelle, and Mrs. Starkey motivated them to get involved as helpful volunteers, but not as leaders in formulating strategy, confronting Microtech's management, or building ties to other activist groups. The empowerment theory limited the ACES' recruitment and its breadth of appeal, but it also gave Laura the means for making lasting, risky commitments that challenged local conceptions of (quiescent) good citizenship. Laura could sustain her leadership of ACES partly because she identified her commitments more strongly with a specific locale than did most Greens, but also because she had made her politics an ongoing part of her whole identity the way Greens did.

Communitarians held that personalism was inimical to pursuit of a common, public good. Yet, personalism allowed Laura and some other ACES members the freedom to contest privatism, in the public interest. In Airdale, personalist notions of empowerment and commitment gave at least some members of ACES the means to advocate for a new communal good – safety from military-related toxic wastes – a good that ACES claimed should concern everyone in Airdale, regardless of their employment. Rather than privatizing public issues, personalist culture gave activists a basis for working together and for trying to reach other Airdalers within local cultural constraints....

References

Baumgartner, M. 1988. *The Moral Order of a Suburb*. New York: Oxford University Press.
Bellah, Robert, Madsen, R., Sullivan, W., Swidler, A., and Tipton, S. 1985. *Habits of the Heart*. Berkeley: University of California Press.
Gaventa, John. 1980. *Power and Powerlessness*. Urbana: University of Illinois Press.
MacIntyre, Alasdair. 1981. *After Virtue*. Notre Dame, IN: University of Notre Dame Press.
Rieff, Philip. 1959. *Freud: The Mind of the Moralist*. New York: Viking Press.
——1966. *The Triumph of the Therapeutic: The Uses of Faith After Freud*. London: Chatto and Windus.

Suttles, Gerald. 1972. *The Social Construction of Communities*. Chicago: University of Chicago Press.
Taylor, Charles. 1989. *Sources of the Self: the Making of the Modern Identity*. Cambridge, MA: Harvard University Press.
—— 1991. *The Ethics of Authenticity*. Cambridge, MA: Harvard University Press.

Editor's Notes on Further Reading

Lichterman on Activist Cultures

Although individualism and community-mindedness are often thought to be contradictory, Lichterman's study identifies "personalized politics" as a type of public commitment which melds both in a way more appropriate to modern life (cf. Simmel, this volume) than either nostalgia for idealized community or simple self-absorption. Lichterman's extensive ethnographic observation of four environmental organizations compares groups like the Greens, which are grounded on a highly personalized sense of commitment, with more community-oriented groups grounded in neighborhood and church; the suburban group discussed in this excerpt combines both personalized and community-oriented commitments. The extended study also discusses the historical origins and class basis of personalized political commitment, and the significance of personalized politics for democratic theory and for social movements.

Other discussions of the opposition between individualism and commitment in American culture include, for example, Robert Wuthnow, *Acts of Compassion: Caring for Others and Helping Ourselves* (Princeton: Princeton University Press, 1991) and Robert Bellah, Richard Madsen, William Sullivan, Ann Swidler, and Steve Tipton, *Habits of the Heart* (Berkeley: University of California Press, 1985) and *The Good Society* (New York: Vintage, 1991). See also Charles Reynolds and Ralph Norman, eds., *Community in America: The Challenge of Habits of the Heart* (Berkeley: University of California Press, 1988). Different approaches to broadly related issues include Chantal Mouffe, ed., *Dimensions of Radical Democracy* (London: Verso, 1992), Amitai Etzioni, ed., *The Essential Communitarian Reader* (Lanham, MD: Rowman and Littlefield, 1998), and Orville Lee, "Culture and Democratic Theory: Toward a Theory of Symbolic Democracy," *Constellations* 5 (1998): 433–55.

Lichterman's emphasis on mundane practices as key to activist cultures differs somewhat from approaches (like Rhys Williams, this volume) which emphasize cultural frames in social movements: for more on movement culture as practice see Eliasoph, this volume, and accompanying editor's note, as well as Alberto Melucci, *Nomads of the Present: Social Movements and Individual Needs in Contemporary Society* (Philadelphia: Temple University Press, 1989); Lichterman, "Piecing Together Multicultural Community: Cultural Differences in Community Building Among Grass-Roots Environmentalists," *Social Problems* 42 (1995): 513–34; "Beyond the Seesaw Model: Public Commitment in a Culture of Self-Fulfillment," *Sociological Theory* 13 (1995): 275–300; "Talking Identity in the Public Sphere: Broad Visions and Small Spaces in Sexual Identity Politics," *Theory and Society* 28 (1999): 101–41; Mary Patillo-McCoy, "Church Culture as a Strategy of Action in the Black Community," *American Sociological Review* 63 (1998): 767–84; and Richard Wood, "Religious Culture and Political Action," *Sociological Theory* 17 (1999): 307–32. For methodological reflections see Michael Burawoy, "The Extended Case Method," *Sociological Theory* 16 (1998): 4–33, and Nina Eliasoph and Paul Lichterman, "'We Begin With Our Favorite Theory': Reconstructing the Extended Case Method," *Sociological Theory* 17 (1999): 228–34.

28 Cultural Power and Social Movements

Ann Swidler

Culture has always been important for the kinds of processes students of social movements study. But as culture moves to the forefront of social movement research, it is important to address directly the theories, methods, and assumptions different approaches to the sociology of culture carry with them.

I begin by reviewing the basic theoretical approaches in the sociology of culture and go on to suggest that traditional Weberian approaches, which focus on powerful, internalized beliefs and values held by individual actors (what I call culture from the "inside out") may ultimately provide less explanatory leverage than newer approaches that see culture as operating in the contexts that surround individuals, influencing action from the "outside in."

The sociology of culture contains two basic traditions, one deriving from Max Weber and the other from Emile Durkheim. Weber focused on meaningful action, and for him the fundamental unit of analysis was always the individual actor. Ideas, developed and promoted by self-interested actors (rulers seeking to legitimate their rule, elites attempting to justify their privileges, religious entrepreneurs seeking followers), come to have an independent influence on social action. People find themselves constrained by ideas that describe the world and specify what one can seek from it. Thus culture shapes action by defining what people want and how they imagine they can get it. Cultural analysis focuses on the complex systems of ideas that shape individuals' motives for action. In Weber's famous "switchman" metaphor:

> Not ideas, but material and ideal interests, directly govern men's conduct. Yet very frequently the 'world images' that have been created by 'ideas' have, like switchmen, determined the tracks along which action has been pushed by the dynamic of interest. 'From what' and 'for what' one wished to be redeemed and, let us not forget, 'could be' redeemed, depended on one's image of the world.   (1946a: 280)

Weber (1968, 1958) analyzed culture by trying to understand typical worldviews, like the Protestant one, that had shaped the motives of historically important groups. Identifying how a worldview motivates action – how one committed to it would act under its sway – *is* explanation in Weberian terms.

The second crucial strand in the sociology of culture comes from Durkheim. For Durkheim (1933, 1965), culture is constituted by "collective representations." These are not "ideas" in the Weberian sense. Collective representations may range from the vivid totemic symbol to moral beliefs to modern society's commitment to reason and individual autonomy (Durkheim 1973). Collective representations are not ideas developed by individuals or groups pursuing their interests. Rather, they are the vehicles of a fundamental process in which publicly shared symbols constitute social groups while they constrain and give form to individual consciousness (Durkheim

1965; Bellah 1973). Durkheim writes not of "ideas" and "world images" but of representations, rituals, and symbols. Symbols concretize "collective consciousness," making the animating power of group life palpable for its members. Symbols do not reflect group life; they constitute it.[1]

Talcott Parsons (1937) made a heroic attempt to synthesize Weber and Durkheim, taking from Weber the image of action as guided by culturally determined ends and from Durkheim the notion of culture as a shared, collective product. The end result was the Parsonian theory of "values," a term that played no important role for either Weber or Durkheim. For Parsons (1951, 1961), "values" are collectively shared ultimate ends of action. "Norms" are shared cultural rules that define appropriate means to attain valued ends. Parsons sees shared values as defining societies, making them what they are, just as Durkheim saw the totem as constituting the Aboriginal clan, making it a society. At the same time, Parsons sees values as governing action in very much the way Weber saw ideas as switchmen. But unlike Weber's concept of "ideas," Parsonian values are very general, abstract orientations of action, rather than the specific, historically grounded doctrines and worldviews that Weber thought shaped action (see Swidler 1986).

Despite its logical appeal and distinguished theoretical ancestry, the Parsonian theory of values was never very successful as a guide to research.[2] Renewed interest in culture emerged from the Parsonian legacy but moved in a different direction. Clifford Geertz (1973), a student of Parsons, followed Weber in much of his substantive work but broke with the Weberian foundations of Parsons's theory of action.[3] He did so by altering both the question and the methods of cultural studies. Influenced by semiotic approaches to language and symbols, Geertz argued that culture should be studied for its meanings and not for its effects on action. He also shifted methodological focus, arguing that the proper object of cultural study is not meanings in people's heads but publicly available symbols – rituals, aesthetic objects, and other "texts."

Despite Geertz's debt to Weber, the effect of the Geertzian revolution in anthropology, history, and literary studies has been to break with the Weberian problematic. Rather than looking at the ideas that motivate individual actors (or even collections of individual actors), Geertz's followers examine public symbols and ritual experiences (see Keesing 1974). Culture cannot be used to explain individual action or even group differences in behavior. Attention does not focus primarily on ideas, belief systems, or dogmas, but on other properties of culture, especially the mood or tone that a "cultural system" gives to daily life through its symbolic vocabulary and through the ritual experiences it makes available (Geertz 1973, 1976). Culture constitutes "humanness" itself as well as the social world: "Man is an animal suspended in webs of significance he himself has spun" (Geertz 1973: 5). If culture influences action, then, it is not by providing the ends people seek, but by giving them the vocabulary of meanings, the expressive symbols, and the emotional repertoire with which they can seek anything at all.

The Revolution in Cultural Studies

Since the mid-1960s, when Geertz's influence began to be felt (with the original publication of "Religion as a Cultural System" in 1966), three dramatic developments have transformed cultural studies. They can best be summarized as public-ness, practices, and power.

Culture as Public Symbols

Geertz's work fundamentally redefined the object of cultural analysis, revitalizing the practice of cultural studies.[4] Geertz shifted attention from a question that cultural analysts could rarely answer satisfactorily – How does a person's culture actually influence his or her actions – to one that was guaranteed to produce satisfying and even dazzling results: What does this cultural text, ritual, or practice mean to the people who use, perform, or live it? From Geertz's (1973) unpacking of the multistranded meanings of a Balinese cockfight to a historian unraveling the meaning of a ritual or folk tale (Davis 1975; Darnton 1984) to a literary critic finding deeper cultural patterns that animated Shakespeare's plays (Greenblatt 1980), the technique is similar. Identify a cultural text and then situate it in the rich web of associated cultural practices, beliefs, social structural realities, folk experiences, and so forth that allow its hearers, practitioners, or devotees to find it meaningful. Meaning itself is defined as context, as the other practices in which a text or ritual is embedded. This redefinition of the object of cultural analysis subtly altered what culture was understood to be. The focus on public vehicles of meaning reduced the need to investigate what any given individual or group actually felt or thought. Indeed, public symbols displayed a system of mean-ings, what some would call a semiotic code, rather than ideas that were in any person's head. The semiotic code was in some sense external to, or at least independ-ent of, the minds of particular individuals. No longer the study of an ineffable subjectivity, the study of culture could now be grounded in accessible public objects.

The focus on public symbols also avoided the question of whether culture is necessarily shared or consensual. Durkheim and Parsons had been forced by the logic of their arguments to claim that cultural meanings were universally shared. But this claim did not hold up empirically. Public symbols, on the other hand, are clearly shared by the people who use them or form around them, and the question of whether these symbols' wider context of meaning is really shared seems unimportant. The analyst's task is to understand a formerly opaque ritual or prac-tice through its context, and that exercise itself seemingly confirms that the context that has made its meaning comprehensible to the analyst also accounts for the ritual's ability to animate its practitioners or devotees.

Focusing on public ideas or texts also reshapes how one describes culture's influence on history. Rather than looking, as Weber did, for the ideas that motivated particular historical actors, the analyst traces changes in the cultural context within which all actors operated. Weber looked for ideas that directed the operation of "material and ideal interests." Contemporary culture analysts trace shifts in "dis-courses," the larger contexts of meanings within which any particular ideas or interests can be formulated (see Wuthnow 1987, 1989).

Practices

Cultural analysts have externalized the locus of culture in another way, by moving it from the mind's interior (ideas and mental representations) to social practices. The focus on practice has been widespread, from the attempt to revise the Marxian model of culture as "superstructure" (Williams 1973) to the efforts of Pierre Bourdieu and Michel Foucault to locate culture in embodied and institutionalized practices. Indeed, along with the terms *text* and *discourse*, the concept of "practice" is the hallmark of the new approaches in the sociology of culture.[5]

The concept of practice or practices differs from older conceptions of culture in two important ways. First, in reaction against the Durkheimian tradition, it emphasizes human agency. Pierre Bourdieu's *Outline of a Theory of Practice* (1977) conceives of culture not as a set of rules, but as deeply internalized habits, styles, and skills (the "habitus") that allow human beings to continually produce innovative actions that are nonetheless meaningful to others around them. For Bourdieu, active human beings continually recreate culture. They do not dutifully follow cultural rules, but energetically seek strategic advantage by using culturally encoded skills. Because access to those skills is differentially distributed, people's strategic efforts reproduce the structure of inequality (even if the players of the game are slightly rearranged).

Second, locating culture in social practices ties the study of culture to the analysis of institutions. Here the most important innovator is Michel Foucault. Foucault analyzes how systems of categories and distinctions are enacted and made real in institutional practices. For example, the practices that, after the sixteenth century, came to differentiate the sane from the mad – exclusion and confinement in asylums, or the diagnostic criteria later used by psychologists and others in the human sciences – are sets of cultural rules made real by being used to categorize and control human beings (Foucault 1965, 1978).

Foucault's arguments resemble Durkheim's insistence that rituals demarcate cultural boundaries and make symbolic truths real. But Foucault does not emphasize exotic ritual and symbol, nor the shared mental representations that unify a society's members. Rather, Foucault shifts attention to institutions, which use power to enact rules that construct human beings ("the subject") and the social world (Foucault 1983).

Power

The third important element in rethinking culture is a focus on power and inequality (Lamont and Wuthnow 1990). Max Weber (1968) always noted how the struggle for power shaped ideas, arguing that the interests of powerful groups had lasting influence on the shape of a culture. But he was interested in how ideas originally created to serve the powerful came to have a life of their own, constraining rulers as well as those they ruled, forcing elites to preserve their legitimacy by making good on their status claims and leading religious specialists to become preoccupied with distinctively religious problems.

Contemporary theorists instead see culture as itself a form of power. Foucault (1980), for example, analyzes how new kinds of knowledge and associated practices (such as measuring, categorizing, or describing objects of knowledge) in effect construct new sites where power can be deployed. New disciplines, such as psychoanalysis, construct new loci such as the unconscious, new subjectivities, where power can be exercised (and also where resistance can emerge). Foucault (1977, 1983) eliminates the question of who has power, leaving aside the role of interested agents, to emphasize instead that each cultural formation, each technique of power, has a history of its own, and that different actors adopt these techniques for different purposes. Since cultural practices, categories, and rules are enactments of power, Foucault does not think of culture as being used by the powerful to maintain their power. Rather, he thinks of power itself as practices that deploy knowledge to constitute human beings as the subjects of that knowledge.

Pierre Bourdieu focuses less on power than on inequality. He emphasizes that people differ not only in their cultural resources but also in the skill with which they deploy those resources. Bourdieu's (1984) special contribution is to show how deeply inequalities between the more and less privileged penetrate persons, constituting the fundamental capacities for judgment, aesthetic response, social ease, or political confidence with which they act in the world. Actors use culture in creative ways to forward their own interests in a system of unequal power, but the effect of that struggle is to reproduce the basic structure of the system....

Culture and Social Movements

Turning Culture Inside Out

There is now an abundance of work – that of Foucault and Bourdieu, but also many others (Wuthnow 1987; Sewell 1985, 1990, 1992) – arguing that culture constitutes social experience and social structure, that culture should be seen as socially organized practices rather than individual ideas or values, that culture can be located in public symbols and rituals rather than in ephemeral subjectivities, and that culture and power are fundamentally linked. Yet these more global approaches to the study of culture can also be difficult to grasp firmly, either theoretically or empirically. It would be ideal to marry Weber's concrete, grounded style of causal argument to Durkheim's understanding of the irreducibly collective, encompassing nature of culture.[6]

One new approach to understanding how culture shapes social movements involves rethinking how culture works. Most culture theory assumes that culture has more powerful effects where it is deeper – deeply internalized in individual psyches, deeply integrated into bodies and habits of action, or deeply embedded in taken-for-granted "mentalities." But at least some of the time, culture may have more powerful effects when it is on the "outside," not deeply internalized or even deeply meaningful. Variations in the ways social contexts bring culture to bear on action may do more to determine culture's power than variations in how deeply culture is held. And study of these social contexts may prove a fruitful direction for integrating culture into social movement research.

For Weber's actor-based sociology of ideas, culture has more influence when it is clearer, more coherent, and more deeply held. Protestantism had more influence on economic action than any other faith because its rationalized doctrine cut off "magical paths" to salvation, because it held that salvation was demonstrated in worldly action, and because it demanded that the intensely believing faithful rigorously regulate every aspect of daily life. Although Durkheim's model of culture was different from Weber's, he also held that culture had its greatest effects when it was most deeply part of the collective consciousness. Only universally shared, actively practiced, vivid symbols could constrain individual passions and impose a social reality on individual consciousness.

To analyze culture's power to affect action, independent of whether it is deeply held (either in the sense of deeply internalized, taken-for-granted practices like the habitus or in the sense of deeply held beliefs like those of Weber's Protestant saints), we may focus on three sources of cultural power: codes, contexts, and institutions. In each case we will see how the culture's effects on action can operate from the outside in, as social processes organize and focus culture's effects on action.

CODES

The notion of culture as a semiotic code has been one of the hallmarks of the new cultural studies. But the notion of semiotic code, by analogy with the deep structures that organize language, usually refers to deeply held, inescapable relationships of meaning that define the possibilities of utterance in a cultural universe. Deep, unspoken, and pervasive equals powerful.

Some codes are not deep, however, and not in the least invisible. A perfect example is provided by Theodore Caplow's (1982, 1984) study of Christmas gift giving in Middletown. In an article with the compelling title "Rule Enforcement without Visible Means," Caplow (1984) makes the point precisely. Caplow finds that middle-class Americans do not "believe in" Christmas gift giving. They criticize the commercialization of Christmas; they consider buying Christmas gifts an unpleasant burden; they think most gifts are a waste of money; they often do not like the gifts they receive; and they are unhappy with much of what they buy for others. Thus, Caplow asks, why do they give Christmas gifts, spending a considerable share of their disposable income, if they do not believe in it? Why does the practice persist without normative support and even in the face of widespread criticism?

Caplow uses data on actual gift giving to argue that Christmas gift giving constitutes a semiotic code (that is, a set of relationally defined meanings) in which the relative value of the gifts a person gives others signals the relative importance with which she or he holds those others. Not to give a gift would, independent of the intentions of the giver, be interpretable as a sign that one did not value the (non) recipient. What governs action in this case, then, is not individuals' internalized beliefs, but their knowledge of what meanings their actions have for others.[7]

Speaking of semiotic codes may seem to take us right back into the thickets of French structuralist theories or into a search for the deep underlying meanings that animate Geertzian "cultural systems." But semiotic codes can be much more discrete, more superficial, and sometimes more contested or political than semioticians usually imply. For example, when florists and confectioners try to increase their business by announcing National Secretaries' Week, few are presumably moved by deep belief in the principles that lie behind the announcement. But if every newspaper in the country is for weeks blanketed with advertisements implying that bosses who appreciate their secretaries will give them flowers and take them out to lunch, both secretaries and their employers may be, at the least, uncomfortable about what signals their actions will send. An employer may well think that for twenty-five dollars it is not worth the risk of hurting the secretary's feelings; and even a secretary who has disdain for the occasion may feel offended, or at least ambivalent, if it is ignored.

Much of our cultural politics is fought out on precisely such terrain. Let us imagine that a national secretaries' union launches a "Bread Not Roses" campaign, so that for employers to offer flowers without a raise is redefined as a sign of contempt. This would be a direct use of culture to influence action, not so much by shaping beliefs as by shaping the external codes through which action is interpreted. These are cultural power struggles, in which publicity can be a potent weapon even if no deeper persuasion occurs.

Even without conscious efforts at publicity, one of the most important effects social movements have is publicly enacting images that confound existing cultural codings. From the punk subculture's deliberate embrace of "ugly" style (meant to muddle standard status codings [Hebdige 1979]) to the Black Panthers' display of militant, disciplined, armed black revolutionaries to the New Left spectacle of middle-class college students being beaten by police (Gitlin 1980), altering cultural codings is one of the most powerful ways social movements actually bring about change.

Recent American gender politics exhibit similar redefinitions of the cultural codes that signal masculinity and femininity. Increasingly in films (a perfect example is *Working Girl*) toughness and ambition are coded as part of earthy, sexy femininity, while classical feminine weakness, lace, and fluffy pillows are identified with a manipulative, dishonest antifemininity. In the same spirit, the very word *macho* makes the traditional hallmarks of masculinity seem suspect – signs of insecurity or weakness. The recent Disney classic *Beauty and the Beast* offers a wonderfully muscled, powerful, handsome antihero, Gaston, who is made utterly ridiculous as he carefully examines his appearance in every mirror he passes. In contrast, the Beast wins Beauty's love through his gentle awkwardness, his eagerness to please her, his love of books, and his distaste for violence. These cultural reworkings may sometimes change people's values or give them new role models. But more important, such cultural recodings change understandings of how behavior will be interpreted by others. If traditional feminine helplessness starts to look manipulative and controlling, and if masculine dominance starts to look pathetically self-absorbed, then men and women do not have to convert to find themselves meeting a new standard. Men may continue to aspire to masculinity and women to femininity, but the content those ideals encode has changed. . . .

CONTEXTS

One of the persistent difficulties in the sociology of culture is that culture influences action much more powerfully at some moments than at others. I have argued elsewhere (Swidler 1986), for example, that explicit cultural ideologies emerge during "unsettled" historical periods when such coherent, systematic worldviews can powerfully influence their adherents. But sometimes even fully articulated ideologies do not predict how people will act (as the many examples of co-optation, of movements that sell out their principles, or of leaders who betray revolutions attest). And at other times, even inchoate or contradictory worldviews powerfully affect action. To better understand such variations in culture's influence, we need to think more carefully about the specific contexts in which culture is brought to bear.

The contexts in which ideas operate can give them coherence and cultural power. "Context" in the first instance means the immediate, face-to-face situation – whether actors are meeting in public forums such as mass meetings or legislatures where issues are debated and decided. In such settings, the dynamics of the meeting itself can give ideas a coherent, systematic influence, even when the individual participants are confused and ambivalent. Second, context can mean the more general situation of conflict or accommodation, polarization and alliance formation, crisis or politics as usual.

The effect of context is evident in many ordinary political and work activities. In academia, for example, one may be confused or ambivalent about an issue – how good a job candidate's work is, whether a colleague merits tenure, whether a departmental decision is genuinely feminist. But in a meeting where sides polarize, where one group defines the issue one way and their antagonists define it in another, these ambiguities fall by the wayside. When politics polarize and alliances are at stake, the public culture crystallizes. Ideas that may have had only loose associations become part of a unified position; other ideas, which may originally have been intermingled with the first set, become clearly opposed. To back the side one supports comes to mean holding a particular ideological line, casting one's lot with a given framing of the situation. It is the conflict itself, the need to separate allies from foes and the need to turn general predispositions into specific decisions, that structures ideological debate.

Certain contexts, particularly those that are important in many social movements, give culture a coherent organization and consistent influence that it normally lacks in the minds of most individuals. This accounts for some of the difficulty in trying to pin down just where and why culture makes a difference in social action (see, for an example, the revealing debate between Sewell [1985] and Skocpol [1985] on the role of culture in the French revolution). If we think of culture either in the Weberian sense, as ideas deeply internalized in individual psyches, or in the more recent semiotic sense as broad, encompassing discourses that shape all social discussion in a given historical era, we will miss the more specific ways cultural power varies by context. . . .

Social movements play out in contexts such as revolutionary committees, public meetings, and constituent assemblies, where stakes are high, risks are great, and political alliances are both essential and uncertain. . . .[S]pecific political contexts lead actors to draw lines of ideological division sharply, to develop the action implications of their ideological stances, and to make adherence to one side or another of a debate an important sign of alliance or opposition. As the song says, "Which side are you on?"

INSTITUTIONS

To explain how culture can have consistent effects on action even when people's beliefs are inconsistent, ambiguous, or lightly held, I have suggested that semiotic codes and political contexts can make ideas and symbols culturally constraining, irrespective of whether people believe them. Institutions can have similar effects, by another route.

Institutions are well-established, stable sets of purposes and rules backed by sanctions. One example is legally structured marriage. Others, less formal but no less powerful, are the employment relationship and the established norms about buying and selling that define consumer transactions.[9]

Institutions create obdurate structures that are both constraints and opportunities for individuals. For sociologists of culture, what is interesting about institutions is that individuals create culture around their rules. Individuals can then come to act in culturally uniform ways, not because their experiences are shared, but because they must negotiate the same institutional hurdles.[10]

For example, in a college where students must have a major in order to graduate, they need to be able to answer the question, What do you plan to major in? They may also ask themselves and each other, What am I interested in? because the institution contains the presumption that focused interests guide the choice of major. Moreover, students may develop cultural lore about how to select a major, identities based around the choice of major, and categorizations of others ("techies" versus "fuzzies") on the basis of their majors. In a similar way, the American institution of voting presumes that citizens have ideas or opinions about public issues. Those who do not have opinions or ideas may feel that they are missing some crucial ingredient of self-hood. The tasks an institution requires make sense only if people have or can develop corresponding orientations. Widely shared cultural accounts for those orientations ensue, creating collective consistencies and resonances that the actors might not possess otherwise.

Similarly, the cultures of social movements are shaped by the institutions the movements confront. Different regime types and different forms of repression generate different kinds of social movements with differing tactics and internal cultures. Dominant institutions also shape the movements' deeper values. The most obvious case is the institution of suffrage itself. From Chartism to women's suffrage to the civil rights movement, Western democracies have witnessed the drama of people denied suffrage organizing extra-legal protest to batter their way into the system, making claims for equal dignity and equal moral personhood. In such systems, to be a legitimate political actor is to be one who can vote....

[P]erhaps [the] search for a popular culture that could support activism starts in the wrong place. How people organize the cultural resources at their disposal depends very much on the kinds of institutional challenges they face.

Conclusion

I began this essay by stressing the two great wellsprings from which much of contemporary culture theory derives. In a sense Weber and Durkheim still define the range of alternatives available to sociologists who want to use culture to explain things. I have suggested that while the Weberian image of culture as belief carried by committed individual actors seems easier to work with, recent developments in cultural studies have moved in a more Durkheimian direction, seeing culture as constitutive, inherently collective, imbedded in symbols and practices, and necessarily infused with power (see Alexander 1988). But culture in this sense – public practices infused with power – can also be extremely hard to grasp concretely. Indeed, too-easy embrace of the notion that culture is ubiquitous and constitutive can undermine any explanatory claims for culture. Then emphasis on culture becomes a species of intellectual hand waving, creating a warm and cozy atmosphere, while other factors continue to carry the real explanatory weight.

I have tried to offer four concrete suggestions about how culture might be conceived as a global, collective property without becoming only a diffused mist within which social action occurs. I have argued first that, to think more powerfully about culture, we must entertain the possibility that culture's power is independent of whether or not people believe in it. I have then gone on to suggest that culture can have powerful influence if it shapes not individuals' own beliefs and aspirations, but their knowledge of how others will interpret their actions.

My third suggestion is that students of culture in general, and social movement scholars in particular, need to pay close attention to the public contexts in which cultural understandings are brought to bear. Reminding ourselves of the power that meetings and other group forums have to crystallize ideological splits and recode public speech and action, I suggest that culture can have consistent, coherent effects on action in particular contexts even if individuals and groups are divided and inconsistent in their beliefs.

Finally, I have suggested that institutions structure culture by systematically patterning channels for social action. In a sense this simply reinforces the insights of the "political process" model of social movements, which notes that movements respond to the wider structure of political constraints and opportunities (McAdam 1982). But I have tried to push the cultural dimension of such processes, arguing that even cultural patterns that appear to be independent inventions (or innate needs) of individuals or groups can be produced or reproduced by the challenges with which institutions confront actors. Thus many movements may invent simultaneously what seem to be common cultural frames (like the many rights movements of the 1960s or the identity movements of the 1980s). But these need not be matters either of independent discovery or of cultural contagion. Rather, they may be common responses to the same institutional constraints and opportunities.

Rethinking how culture might work from the outside in is a large task. I do not think the suggestions I have made here about codes, contexts, and institutions are the only ways the issue might be approached. But I am convinced that if interest in culture is restricted to studying the inner meaning systems of deeply committed activists, or if culture is relegated to a vague – if "constitutive" – penumbra, we will sacrifice more incisive ways of thinking about its power.

Notes

1   See the analysis of Durkheim's view of symbols as constitutive in Bellah 1973.
2   The two major lines of empirical work on values are the anthropological, comparing values of different social groups (Kluckhohn and Strodtbeck 1961), and the social-psychological, comparing the values of individuals (Rokeach 1973).

3 Geertz's early classic, *The Religion of Java* (1960), is overtly Weberian in inspiration and execution, tracing the influence of differing religious ethics on economic action. Geertz (1966) also emphasizes the problem of theodicy (explaining suffering and injustice in the world God controls), which was central to Weber's analysis of the dynamics of religious change. And Geertz has returned repeatedly to the problem of rationalization in non-Western religious traditions (1968, 1973).

4 See Keesing 1974 for a detailed treatment of this issue.

5 See Sherry Ortner's (1984) insightful and entertaining analysis of shifts in culture theory, "Theory in Anthropology Since the Sixties."

6 This is the theoretical strategy Randall Collins (1981, 1988) has called "microtranslation." The theorist attempts to provide concrete, individual-level causal imagery even for macro or global causal processes, without making the micro reductionist claim that the underlying causal dynamics operate at the micro level.

7 Careful readers of Weber will note that such an explanation of action is perfectly compatible with his theoretical orientation. "Social action" is, after all, action whose "subjective meaning takes account of the behavior of others and is thereby oriented in its course" (Weber 1968: 4). Weber (1946b) also argued clearly that the Protestant sects continued to influence action long after intense belief had faded because members knew that sect membership gave visible social testimony to their worthiness. Nonetheless, Weber and most of his followers have been preoccupied with the inner workings of the religious psyche rather than with more external forms of cultural power.

8 William Sewell Jr. (1985, 1990) analyzes how dramatic social movements shift an entire pattern of public discourse and thus remake future forms of collective action.

9 See Jepperson 1991 and Scott 1992 for fuller treatments of institutions and problems of institutional analysis.

10 I develop this argument more fully for the case of marriage in *Talk of Love: How Americans Use Their Culture* (Chicago: University of Chicago Press, 2001).

References

Alexander, Jeffrey C., ed. 1988. *Durkheimian Sociology: Cultural Studies*. New York: Cambridge University Press.

Bellah, Robert N. 1973. Introduction to *Emile Durkheim on Morality and Society*, edited by Robert Bellah. Chicago: University of Chicago Press.

Bourdieu, Pierre. 1984. *Distinction: A Social Critique of the Judgement of Taste*, translated by R. Nice. Cambridge, Mass.: Harvard University Press.

——. 1977. *Outline of a Theory of Practice*. Cambridge: Cambridge University Press.

Caplow, Theodore. 1984. "Rule Enforcement without Visible Means: Christmas Gift Giving in Middletown." *American Journal of Sociology* 89: 1306–23.

——. 1982. "Christmas Gifts and Kin Networks." *American Sociological Review* 47: 383–92.

Collins, Randall. 1988. "The Micro Contribution to Macro Sociology." *Sociological Theory* 6 (Fall): 242–53.

——. 1981. "On the Microfoundations of Macrosociology." *American Journal of Sociology* 86: 984–1014.

Darnton, Robert. 1984. *The Great Cat Massacre and Other Episodes in French Cultural History*. New York: Basic Books.

Davis, Natalie Zemon. 1975. *Society and Culture in Early-Modern France*. Stanford, Calif.: Stanford University Press.

Durkheim, Emile. 1973. "Individualism and the Intellectuals." In *Emile Durkheim on Morality and Society*, edited by R. N. Bellah. Chicago: University of Chicago Press.

Durkheim, Emile. 1965, 1961 [1915]. *The Elementary Forms of the Religious Life*. Translated by Joseph Ward Swain. New York: Free Press.

——. 1933. *The Division of Labor in Society*. New York: Free Press.

Foucault, Michel. 1983. "Afterword: The Subject and Power." In *Michel Foucault: Beyond Structuralism and Hermeneutics*. Edited by Hubert Dreyfus and Paul Rabinow. Chicago: University of Chicago Press.

——. 1980. *Power/Knowledge: Selected Interviews and Other Writings, 1972–1977*, edited by Colin Gordon. New York: Pantheon.

——. 1978. *The History of Sexuality*. Vol. 1. London: Penguin.

——. 1977. *Discipline and Punish*. New York: Vintage.

——. 1965. *Madness and Civilization: A History of Insanity in the Age of Reason*. New York: Random House.

Geertz, Clifford. 1976. "Art as a Cultural System." *Modern Language Notes* 91: 1473–99.

——. 1973. *The Interpretation of Cultures*. New York: Basic Books.

——. 1968. *Islam Observed: Religious Development in Morocco and Indonesia*. New Haven, Conn.: Yale University Press.

——. 1966. "Religion as a Cultural System." In *Anthropological Approaches to the Study of Religion*, edited by Michael Baston. London: Tavistock.

——. 1960. *The Religion of Java*. New York: Free Press of Glencoe.

Gitlin, Todd, 1980. *The Whole World Is Watching*. Berkeley and Los Angeles: University of California Press.

Greenblatt, Stephen. 1980. *Renaissance Self-Fashioning: From More to Shakespeare*. Chicago: University of Chicago Press.

Hebdige, Dick. 1979. *Subculture: The Meaning of Style*. London: Methuen.

Jepperson Ronald L. 1991. "Institutions, Institutional Effects, and Institutionalism." In *The New Institutionalism in Organizational Analysis*, edited by Walter W. Powell and Paul DiMaggio. Chicago: University of Chicago Press.

Keesing, Roger M. 1974. "Theories of Culture." In *Annual Review of Anthropology* 3. Palo Atto: Annual Reviews.

Kluckhohn, Florence R., and Fred Strodtbeck. 1961. *Variations in Value Orientations*. New York: Row, Peterson.

Lamont, Michèle, and Robert Wuthnow. 1990. "Betwixt and Between: Recent Cultural Sociology in Europe and the United States." In *Frontiers of Social Theory: The New Synthesis*, edited by George Ritzer. New York: Columbia University Press.

McAdam, Doug. 1982. *Political Process and the Development of Black Insurgency 1930–1970*. Chicago: University of Chicago Press.

Ortner, Sherry, 1984. "Theory in Anthropology since the Sixties." *Comparative Studies in Society and History* 26: 126–66.

Parsons, Talcott. 1961. "An Outline of the Social System." In *Theories of Society*, edited by T. Parsons et al. New York: Free Press.

——. 1951. *The Social System*. Glencoe, Ill.: Free Press.

——. 1937. *The Structure of Social Action*. New York: Free Press.

Rokeach, Milton. 1973. *The Nature of Human Values*. New York: Free Press.

Scott, W. Richard. 1992. "Institutions and Organizations: Toward a Theoretical Synthesis." Unpublished paper, Department of Sociology, Stanford University.

Sewell, William H. Jr. 1992. "A Theory of Structure: Duality, Agency, and Transformation." *American Journal of Sociology* 98: 1–29.

——. 1990. "Collective Violence and Collective Loyalties in France: Why the French Revolution Made a Difference." *Politics and Society* 18, no. 4: 527–52.

——. 1985. "Ideologies and Social Revolutions: Reflections on the French Case." *Journal of Modern History* 57: 57–85.

——. 1980. *Work and Revolution in France*. Cambridge University Press.

Skocpol, Theda. 1985. "Cultural Idioms and Political Ideologies in the Revolutionary Reconstruction of State Power: A Rejoinder to Sewell." *Journal of Modern History* 57: 86–96.

Swidler, Ann. 2001. *Talk of Love: How Americans Use Their Culture*. Chicago: University of Chicago Press.

——. 1986. "Culture in Action: Symbols and Strategies." *American Sociological Review* 51: 273–86.

Weber, Max. 1968 [1920–22]. *Economy and Society: An Outline of Interpretive Sociology*. Berkeley: University of California Press.

——. 1958 [1904–5]. *The Protestant Ethic and the Spirit of Capitalism*. New York: Scribner's.

——. 1946a [1922–23]. "The Social Psychology of the World Religions." In *From Max Weber*, edited by H. H. Gerth and C. W. Mills. New York: Oxford University Press.

——. 1946b [1922–23]. "The Protestant Sects and the Spirit of Capitalism." In *From Max Weber*, edited by H. H. Gerth and C. W. Mills. New York: Oxford University Press.

Williams, Raymond. 1973. "Base and Superstructure in Marxist Cultural Theory." *New Left Review* 82 (November–December): 3–16.

Wuthnow, Robert. 1987. *Meaning and Moral Order: Explanations in Cultural Analysis*. Berkeley: University of California Press.

Editor's Notes on Further Reading

Swidler on How Culture Works

Culture is often thought to influence action through internalized individual beliefs and norms. Against this, Swidler makes the important and sometimes counterintuitive argument that culture is influential through mechanisms external to the individual: interactional and institutional contexts carry expectations about others' beliefs which influence action. In the full article she argues that social movements may influence social change by recoding traditional symbols and by creating contexts which sharpen inchoate beliefs.

For the general theoretical context of this argument see excerpts from work by Geertz, Bourdieu, Alexander and Smith, Sewell, and Wuthnow, and related editor's notes, this volume; for an alternative view of how culture affects individual beliefs and norms, see excerpt from Schudson, this volume. For an influential argument against the impact of cultural values and in favor of cultural repertoires of strategies of action, and arguing for different mechanisms of cultural influence in settled and unsettled times, see Ann Swidler, "Culture in Action: Symbols and Strategies," *American Sociological Review* 51 (1986): 273–86. On long-term cultural persistence see Ann Swidler, "Inequality and American Culture: The Persistence of Voluntarism," pp. 294–314 in Gary Marks and Larry Diamond, eds., *Reexamining Democracy: Essays in Honor of Seymour Martin Lipset* (Newbury Park, CA: Sage, 1992).

Swidler's approach emerges from her investigations of American culture and society; see, for instance, Ann Swidler, *Organization Without Authority: Dilemmas of Social Control in Free Schools* (Cambridge, MA: Harvard University Press, 1979); Robert Bellah, Richard Madsen, William Sullivan, Ann Swidler, and Steve Tipton, *Habits of the Heart: Individualism and Commitment in American Life* (Berkeley: University of California Press, 1985) and *The Good Society* (New York: Vintage, 1991); Ann Swidler and Jorge Arditi, "The New Sociology of Knowledge," *Annual Review of Sociology* 20 (1994): 305–29; Claude Fischer, Michael Hout, Martin Sanchez Jankowski, Samuel Lucas, Ann Swidler, and Kim Voss, *Inequality by Design: Cracking the Bell Curve Myth* (Princeton: Princeton University Press, 1996); and Ann Swidler, *Talk of Love: How Americans Use Their Culture* (Chicago: University of Chicago Press, 2001).

29 A Theory of Structure: Duality, Agency, and Transformation

William H. Sewell, Jr.

Why Structural Change Is Possible

It is, of course, entirely proper for Bourdieu to insist on the strong reproductive bias built into structures – that is the whole point of the structure concept and part of what makes the concept so essential for theorizing social change. After all, as Renato Rosaldo (1980) and Marshall Sahlins (1981, 1985) have brilliantly demonstrated, the same reproductive biases of structures that explain the powerful continuities of social relations also make it possible to explain the paths followed in episodes of social change. What gets Bourdieu off the track is his unrealistically unified and totalized concept of habitus, which he conceptualizes as a vast series of strictly homologous structures encompassing all of social experience. Such a conceptualization, which Bourdieu in fact shares roughly with many structurally inclined theorists, cannot explain change as arising from within the operation of structures. It is characteristic that many structural accounts of social transformation tend to introduce change from outside the system and then trace out the ensuing structurally shaped changes, rather than showing how change is generated by the operation of structures internal to a society. In this respect, Marshall Sahlins's (1981) analysis of how Captain Cook's voyages affected the Hawaiians is emblematic. It is my conviction that a theory of change cannot be built into a theory of structure unless we adopt a far more multiple, contingent, and fractured conception of society – and of structure. What is needed is a conceptual vocabulary that makes it possible to show how the ordinary operations of structures can generate transformations. To this end, I propose five key axioms: the multiplicity of structures, the transposability of schemas, the unpredictability of resource accumulation, the polysemy of resources, and the intersection of structures.

The multiplicity of structures. – Societies are based on practices that derive from many distinct structures, which exist at different levels, operate in different modalities, and are themselves based on widely varying types and quantities of resources. While it is common for a certain range of these structures to be homologous, like those described by Bourdieu in *Outline of a Theory of Practice*, it is never true that all of them are homologous. Structures tend to vary significantly between different institutional spheres, so that kinship structures will have different logics and dynamics than those possessed by religious structures, productive structures, aesthetic structures, educational structures, and so on. There is, moreover, important variation even within a given sphere. For example, the structures that shape and constrain religion in Christian societies include authoritarian, prophetic, ritual, and theoretical modes. These may sometimes operate in harmony, but they can also lead to sharply conflicting claims and empowerments. The multiplicity of structures means that the knowledgeable social actors whose practices constitute a society are far more versatile than Bourdieu's account of a universally homologous habitus would imply: social actors are capable of applying a wide range of different and even incompatible schemas and have access to heterogeneous arrays of resources.

The transposability of schemas. – Moreover, the schemas to which actors have access can be applied across a wide range of circumstances. This is actually recognized by Bourdieu, but he has not, in my opinion, drawn the correct conclusions from his insight. Schemas were defined above as generalizable or transposable procedures applied in the enactment of social life. The term "generalizable" is taken from Giddens; the term "transposable," which I prefer, is taken from Bourdieu.[1] At one point Bourdieu defines habitus as "a system of lasting transposable dispositions which, integrating past experiences, functions at every moment as a *matrix of perceptions, appreciations, and actions* and makes possible the achievement of infinitely diversified tasks, thanks to analogical transfers of schemas permitting the solution of similarly shaped problems" (1977, p. 83; emphasis in original).

The slippage in this passage occurs in the final phrase, "permitting the solution of similarly shaped problems." Whether a given problem is similarly shaped enough to be solved by analogical transfers of schemas cannot be decided in advance by social scientific analysts, but must be determined case by the actors, which means that there is no fixed limit to the possible transpositions. This is in fact implied by the earlier phrase, "makes possible the achievement of infinitely diversified tasks." To say that schemas are transposable, in other words, is to say that they can be applied to a wide and not fully predictable range of cases outside the context in which they are initially learned. This fits with what we usually mean by knowledge of a rule or of some other learned procedure. In ordinary speech one cannot be said to really *know* a rule simply because one can apply it mechanically to repeated instances of the same case. Whether we are speaking of rules of grammar, mathematics, law, etiquette, or carpentry, the real test of knowing a rule is to be able to apply it successfully in *unfamiliar* cases. Knowledge of a rule or a schema by definition means the ability to transpose or extend it – that is, to apply it creatively. If this is so, then *agency*, which I would define as entailing the capacity to transpose and extend schemas to new contexts, is inherent in the knowledge of cultural schemas that characterizes all minimally competent members of society.[2]

The unpredictability of resource accumulation. – But the very fact that schemas are by definition capable of being transposed or extended means that the resource consequences of the enactment of cultural schemas is never entirely predictable. A joke told to a new audience, an investment made in a new market, an offer of marriage made to a new patriline, a cavalry attack made on a new terrain, a crop planted in a newly cleared field or in a familiar field in a new spring – the effect of these actions on the resources of the actors is never quite certain. Investment in a new market may make the entrepreneur a pauper or a millionaire, negotiation of a marriage with a new patriline may result in a family's elevation in status or its extinction in a feud, planting a crop in the familiar field may result in subsistence, starvation, or plenty. Moreover, if the enactment of schemas creates unpredictable quantities and qualities of resources, and if the reproduction of schemas depends on their continuing validation by resources, this implies that schemas will in fact be differentially validated when they are put into action and therefore will potentially be subject to modification. A brilliantly successful cavalry attack on a new terrain may change the battle plans of subsequent campaigns or even theories of military tactics; a joke that draws rotten tomatoes rather than laughter may result in the suppression of a category of jokes from the comedian's repertoire; a succession of crop failures may modify routines of planting or plowing.[3]

The polysemy of resources. – The term polysemy (or multiplicity of meaning) is normally applied to symbols, language, or texts. Its application to resources sounds like a contradiction in terms. But, given the concept of resources I am advocating here, it is not. Resources, I have insisted, embody cultural schemas. Like texts or ritual performances, however, their meaning is never entirely unambiguous. The form of the factory embodies and therefore teaches capitalist notions of property relations. But, as Marx points out, it can also teach the necessarily social and collective character of production and thereby undermine the capitalist notion of private property. The new prestige, wealth, and territory gained from the brilliant success of a cavalry charge may be attributed to the superior discipline and élan of the cavalry officers and thereby enhance the power of an aristocratic officer corps, or it may be attributed to the commanding general and thereby result in the increasing subordination of officers to a charismatic leader. Any array of resources is capable of being interpreted in varying ways and, therefore, of empowering different actors and teaching different schemas. Again, this seems to me inherent in a definition of agency as the capacity to transpose and extend schemas to new contexts. Agency, to put it differently, is the actor's capacity to reinterpret and mobilize an array of resources in terms of cultural schemas other than those that initially constituted the array.

The intersection of structures. – One reason arrays of resources can be interpreted in more than one way is that structures or structural complexes intersect and over-lap. The structures of capitalist society include both a mode of production based on private property and profit and a mode of labor organization based on workplace solidarity. The factory figures as a crucial resource in both of these structures, and its meaning and consequences for both workers and managers is therefore open and contested. The intersection of structures, in fact, takes place in both the schema and the resource dimensions. Not only can a given array of resources be claimed by different actors embedded in different structural complexes (or differentially claimed by the same actor embedded in different structural complexes), but schemas can be borrowed or appropriated from one structural complex and applied to another. Not only do workers and factory owners struggle for control of the factory, but Marx appropriates political economy for the advancement of socialism.

Structures, then, are sets of mutually sustaining schemas and resources that empower and constrain social action and that tend to be reproduced by that social action. But their reproduction is never automatic. Structures are at risk, at least to some extent, in all of the social encounters they shape – because structures are multiple and intersecting, because schemas are transposable, and because resources are polysemic and accumulate unpredictably. Placing the relationship between resources and cultural schemas at the center of a concept of structure makes it possible to show how social change, no less than social stasis, can be generated by the enactment of structures in social life.

Notes

1 To generalize a rule implies stating it in more abstract form so that it will apply to a larger number of cases. The verb "transpose" implies a concrete application of a rule to a new case, but in such a way that the rule will have subtly different forms in each of its applications. This is implied by three of the *Oxford English Dictionary's* (1971, s.v. "transpose") definitions: "To remove from one place or time to another; to transfer, shift," "to alter the order of or the position of in a series ... to interchange," and, in music, "to put into a different key." *Transposer*, in French (which was of course the language in which Bourdieu wrote), also has an even more appropriate meaning: "faire changer de forme ou de contenu en faisant passer dans un autre domaine," (to cause something to change in form or content by causing it to pass into another domain, *Le Petit Robert* [1984, s.v. "transposer"]). I would like my use of *transpose* to be understood as retaining something of this French meaning.
2 Here my thinking has been influenced by Goran Therborn (1980, esp. pp. 15–22).
3 Although Marshall Sahlins (1981, 1985) does not explicitly include resources in his definition of structure, my argument here runs closely parallel to his. Sahlins argues that "in action in the world – technically, in acts of reference – the cultural categories acquire new functional values" because the categories are "burdened with the world" (1985, p. 138). This burdening of categories with the world is a matter of schemas being changed by the unanticipated effects of action on the resources that sustain the schemas.

References

Bourdieu, Pierre. 1977. *Outline of a Theory of Practice*. Cambridge: Cambridge University Press.
——. 1988. *Homo Academicus*, translated by Peter Collier. Stanford, Calif.: Stanford University Press.
Giddens, Anthony. 1984. *The Constitution of Society: Outline of the Theory of Structuration*. Berkeley and Los Angeles: University of California Press.
Oxford English Dictionary. 1971. *The Compact Edition of the Oxford English Dictionary*. Oxford: Oxford University Press.
Le Petit Robert. 1984. *Le Petit Robert: Dictionnaire alphabétique et analogique de la langue française*. Paris: Le Robert.
Rosaldo, Renato. 1980. *Ilongot Headhunting, 1883–1974: A Study in Society and History*. Stanford, Calif.: Stanford University Press.
Sahlins, Marshall. 1976. *Culture and Practical Reason*. Chicago: University of Chicago Press.
——. 1981. *Historical Metaphors and Mythical Realities*. Ann Arbor: University of Michigan Press.
——. 1985. *Islands of History*. Chicago: University of Chicago Press.
Therborn, Goran. 1980. *The Ideology of Power and the Power of Ideology*. London: Verso.

Editor's Notes on Further Reading

Sewell on Cultural Schemas and Structural Change

How is social change possible when social structures pattern and constrain human action? In part, Sewell attacks this classic question by including a cultural dimension – schemas – in his concept of social structure, and by giving important theoretical weight to the cultural point that meanings for the same thing may vary (polysemy). In the full article he redefines the idea of social structure as combining cultural schemas and resources, develops a theory of human agency as inherent in structures, and articulates how social structures differ in depth and range. Of particular interest here is the way qualities of culture help make social structures changeable.

Sewell builds on and critiques work of Anthony Giddens and Pierre Bourdieu: see for example Anthony Giddens, *The Constitution of Society: Outline of the Theory of Structuration* (Berkeley: University of California Press, 1984) and Pierre Bourdieu, *Outline of a Theory of Practice* (Cambridge: Cambridge University Press, 1977). Related theoretical reflections include Sewell, "The Concept(s) of Culture," pp. 35–61 in Victoria Bonnell and Lynn Hunt, eds., *Beyond the Cultural Turn: New Directions in the Study of Society and Culture* (Berkeley: University of California Press, 1999); "Historical Events as Transformations of Structures: Inventing Revolution at the Bastille," *Theory and Society* 25 (1996): 841–81; and Sewell "Ideologies and Social Revolutions: Reflections on the French Case," and Theda Skocpol, "Cultural Idioms and Political Ideologies in the Revolutionary Reconstruction of State Power: A Rejoinder to Sewell," *The Journal of Modern History* 57 (1985): 57–85, 86–96.

On the general issue of structure, culture, continuity, and change see also excerpts from work by Shils, Williams, Bourdieu, Schudson, Swidler, and Wuthnow, this volume, as well as Mustafa Emirbayer and Ann Mische, "What is Agency?" *American Journal of Sociology* 103 (1998): 962–1023; Bennett Berger, *An Essay on Culture: Symbolic Structure and Social Structure* (Berkeley: University of California Press, 1995); S. N. Eisenstadt, "Culture and Social Structure Revisited," pp. 280–305 in *Power, Trust, and Meaning: Essays in Sociological Theory and Analysis* (Chicago and London: University of Chicago Press, 1995), and other essays in that volume; Mustafa Emirbayer and Jeff Goodwin, "Network Analysis, Culture, and the Problem of Agency," *American Journal of Sociology* 99 (1994): 1411–54; Douglas Porpora, "Cultural Rules and Material Relations," *Sociological Theory* 11 (1993): 212–29; Gene Burns, "Materialism, Ideology, and Political Change," pp. 248–62 in Robert Wuthnow, ed., *Vocabularies of Public Life: Empirical Essays in Symbolic Structure* (London and New York: Routledge, 1992); Anne Kane, "Cultural Analysis in Historical Sociology: The Analytic and Concrete Forms of the Autonomy of Culture," *Sociological Theory* 9 (1991): 53–69; Margaret Archer, *Culture and Agency* (Cambridge and New York: Cambridge University Press, 1988); and Gary Alan Fine and Sherryl Kleinman, "Network and Meaning: An Interactionist Approach to Structure," *Symbolic Interaction* 6 (1983): 97–110.

30 Communities of Discourse: Ideology and Social Structure in the Reformation, the Enlightenment, and European Socialism

Robert Wuthnow

Environments, Institutions, Actions

The sociological tradition . . . has generally emphasized the so-called material conditions of the social environment as possible sources of cultural change. In this tradition economic activities, modes of production, demographic patterns, urbanization, class relations, income levels, and the like have been given special attention. The emphasis on these material conditions rests, in addition to whatever theoretical framework may be invoked, on at least three practical considerations: that material conditions are sufficiently distinguishable from cultural phenomena that one is unlikely to become involved in purely tautological arguments by attempting to establish the influence of one on the other; that societies and individuals are relatively dependent on their capacity to extract resources from the material environment and are, therefore, likely to be affected in significant ways by their relations to this environment; and that material conditions, by their very materiality, are likely to have left traces of themselves, thereby facilitating the task of empirical reconstruction. In arguing for both a broader conception of environmental conditions, especially one that includes intellectual precedents and implicit features of the cultural tradition, and a more empirical or behavioral concept of culture itself, some of these practical advantages may be diminished. Nevertheless, the general value of paying attention to the broad environmental conditions under which ideological change comes about would appear to remain beyond dispute.

Environmental conditions, as the term has been used in this study, consist of economic, political, and cultural resources, characterized in terms of overall levels, distributions, and rates of change that determine the nature of broad societal patterns. Unlike more specific concepts, such as bourgeoisie or urbanization, that are intended to denote actual historical formations, the idea of environmental conditions is a purely sensitizing device free of historical content. It therefore requires operationalization in more concrete terms in specific historical settings. As a general category of social factors, however, it points toward the probable importance of economic resources that affect capacities to engage in culture production; political resources such as guarantees of intellectual freedom, legal guarantees underlying relevant contracts and property relations, and the prestige or legitimacy that political entities may be capable of bestowing on cultural products; communication technologies such as river transportation, postal services, printing, bookshops, or electronic media that influence genres of cultural production and their capacity to reach particular audiences; and cultural resources such as shared languages, literacy, religious and ethnic traditions, and orientations toward particular values. In the case of the Reformation, for instance, the specific manifestations of these general conditions that proved relevant to the analysis include the cultural uniformity that spanned most of Europe as a result of the historic influences of Christianity, the existence of printing and of rising levels of literacy, the prevalence of agrarian modes of economic production, the continent's division into numerous political entities that were often in conflict with one another, a gradual rise in population, expansion in trade, and correlative increases in prices and the circulation of money.

In the cases considered, several points about these environmental conditions appear worth emphasizing. Of particular importance, insofar as ideology is conceived of as the result of a process of production, is the extent to which broad social environments function as pools of resources. Changes in population, trading networks, wages and price levels have all been considered in this manner, as have such relevant conditions as literacy rates, military obligations, levels of national political integration, and tensions within the religious sphere. Treating these conditions as resources has placed emphasis on their potential for altering or maintaining the specific contexts in which ideological production takes place. Changes in the profitability of particular commodities thus become important, for instance, insofar as these changes permit some actors involved in the production of ideology greater latitude in making decisions. This view is, of course, quite different from a perspective that understands ideology to be merely a constitutive element of the broad social environment. It also differs from a purely structural approach that emphasizes certain tacit homologies between environmental conditions and their associated ideologies. In this cases ideology is shaped directly and determinatively by the social environment. Conceiving of environments as resources adds an element of indeterminacy. Resources affect the range of ideologies that are likely to be produced, but these resources are also channeled by the more proximate contexts in which ideological production occurs.

Another point is that the abstract notion of environmental resources takes on meaning only in specific historical settings. What constitutes a relevant resource in one setting clearly may not be an important factor in another setting. The economic changes that permitted towns to fortify themselves against surrounding nobility clearly had greater relevance in the sixteenth century than in the eighteenth or nineteenth centuries. It also bears noting, however, that this very lack of conceptual specificity has advantages in pointing toward a wide variety of relevant resources. Not only can the role of economic conditions and class relations be considered, but also the influences of intellectual antecedents, prevailing literary genres, precedents for voicing dissent, and so on. The concept of environmental conditions thus subsumes the more generalized, implicit, embedded features of culture that have been emphasized in other perspectives.

Broad changes in dominant ideologies such as those associated with the Reformation, the Enlightenment, and socialism appear to have been facilitated by overall increases in the level of resources available in the social environment. Demographic, commercial, and political expansion opened the way for new elites to gain power and for new mechanisms of ideological production to emerge without fundamentally undermining established institutions (until later in the process). The effects of resource expansion were, however, mediated. They did not facilitate new ideologies simply by altering the outlooks of disaggregated individuals. Nor did their effects occur uniformly. Changes in resources were decisively channeled by preexisting patterns of social relations, by the particular kinds of resources available, and by prevailing modes of appropriating and distributing resources.

The critical mediating connection between shifts in environmental conditions and changes in ideology appears in all three of the episodes examined to have been the specific institutional contexts in which ideologies were produced, disseminated, and authorized. None of these ideologies sprang into bloom on a thousand hilltops as if scattered there by the wind. They grew under the careful cultivation of particular movements that arose in specific places and that bore specific relations to their surroundings. The Reformation grew in urban pulpits, within certain ranks of the clergy, and in the offices of some ecclesiastical and secular hierarchies; the Enlightenment in salons, academies, bureaus, and universities; the socialist movement in party offices, legislative halls, and clandestine associations. Broadly speaking, institutional contexts are the organizational positions and relations that form the matrix in which ideas are produced and disseminated, including the relations between these organizations and other institutions in the broader environment.

The study of the institutional contexts of ideological production must focus first on the producers themselves: their numbers, conditions of work, sources of patronage, and channels of communication. Second, it must focus on the immediate audiences toward which ideological production is directed: their size and social composition, the channels connecting them with producers, the resources they can place at the disposal of producers, and the limitations they can impose. Finally, it must focus on the broader web of institutional linkages in which these specific activities are embedded: relations with established culture producing institutions, relations with agencies of the state, informal relations with ruling elites, integration into market relations and patronage networks, vulnerability to institutional schisms. These, much more so than the general spirit of the times or even the specific conditions under which culture producers' personalities are shaped, constitute the immediate contexts in which ideology is produced. It is in these contexts that particular forms of patronage can facilitate one kind of ideology more than another, or that audiences with particular grievances can gain the attention of writers capable of articulating these grievances, or that literary markets sizable enough to sustain an interactive and competitive community of literary producers can be created.

Within these institutional contexts ideology is generated and shaped, not all at once but through a series of action sequences. These are the work of historical agents. Their activities occur within the structural constraints of the institutional arrangements to which they are exposed. But within these constraints discretion is exercised, and variability in the cultural products that emerge is the inevitable result. The producers of ideology and those in a position to channel it in one direction or another respond to specific pressures, to crises, to demands that must be met if further crises are to be avoided. These responses occur in time; they follow

one another and depend on the precedents and limitations set by their own pre-
decessors.

The ideologies that result from these processes are likely, over time, to bend in the
direction of the resources and situational constraints that went into their formation.
They may not, however, reflect the interests of their creators. The decisions from
which they emanate are more likely to be made with partial knowledge of the
immediate situation, with an even more limited knowledge of the future, and with
the intention of resolving short-term crises more than perpetuating long-term
interests.

The idea of action sequences also points toward a reciprocal influence (a kind of
feedback mechanism) of ideas on the social environment. If, as I have suggested, the
social environment consists of resources, then ideology may be recognized as one of
the ways in which actors attempt to gain control over these resources. Ideologies are
seldom neutral with respect to the distribution of resources. Rather than merely
describing the environment, ideologies specify how social resources should be distributed. Claims are made on authorities; scripts are provided that become operative
in situations of decision making; standards are set forth for evaluating the propriety
of behavior. If an ideology succeeds in becoming institutionalized, therefore, it may
play a decisive role in acting back on its environment. This, of course, becomes the
point at which to consider the processes involved in articulating a distinct relation
between an ideology and its environment.

Production, Selection, Institutionalization

It has been suggested that cultural change comes about as a result of relatively
abrupt, episodic ideological innovations, such as those associated with the Reformation, the Enlightenment, and socialism, in addition to the more gradual, incremental
migration of outlooks that has often been described in the literature. In these
episodes of marked ideological innovation, the conjuncture of changing resources
and shifting institutional contexts can be seen clearly. The resulting ideological
change does not, however, consist of a simple replacement of an old ideology by a
new one. The process, as I have suggested, can be divided into three phases or
subprocesses.

The production phase is characterized by an increase in the overall range of
variation in ideological forms. Older, well-established forms continue but are
faced with deviant alternatives, some of which will eventually fail while others
will eventually triumph. The heightened degree of diversity may be evident along a
number of dimensions: substantive or thematic emphases, modes of ideological
production, genres, distinct charismatic leaders and devotees of a particular ideological orientation, ritual practices. In the Reformation this diversity was evident in
an expanded array of biblical interpretations, views of the sacraments, styles of worship, and charismatic figures whose names came to symbolize clusters of alternative
beliefs and practices. In the Enlightenment a heightened variety of ideological forms
became evident in the use of alternative genres, in an enlarged number of literary and
scientific topics, in the increasing range of media and sources of, patronage and
again in the proliferation of charismatic figures with distinct ideological positions.

The socialist movement demonstrated a similar proliferation of charismatic figures, a variety of programmatic emphases, experimentation with new genres of discourse, and the adoption of a wide range of discursive vehicles. The accepted ideas of the past were confronted not so much by a single innovative revelation as by many ideological contenders. Permutations compounded, and their advocates often found themselves at odds with one another as much as with the more traditional ideological practices.

All three periods were characterized by a combination of circumstances that expanded the opportunities available for this kind of diversity to be produced. Economic expansion alone contributed to an increasing availability of patronage, opportunities for a larger number of talented writers or speakers to pursue careers in theology or literature or politics, and an enlarged segment of the population with requisite literacy levels or excess income to devote to books, newspapers, and the support of literary associations. In addition, changing configurations of power among fractions of the ruling elite created stalemates that prevented established cultural authorities from repressing the new alternatives, or expanded the variety of patrons from whom support could be obtained or of officials from whom protection could be sought. Changing configurations of power also created structural ambiguities that appear to have encouraged efforts to redefine prevailing ideologies. In the Reformation these ambiguities were evident in uprisings within the lower strata of the towns and cities, in the relations between state officials and the land-owning elite, and in the relations among the leading regimes. In the Enlightenment a critical source of ambiguity lay in the altered balance of power between central bureaucracies and representative bodies and in the heterarchic structure of patronage networks and state agencies. The socialist movement grew in response to ambiguities created by competition between liberal republican parties and monarchic aristocratic parties and by the numeric increases evident in the working class itself. Combined with the resources and de facto opportunities to respond to these ambiguities, circumstances of these kinds became rife with competing communities of discourse.

As the historical evidence has indicated, heightened levels of ideological diversity in these periods, once produced, also became subject to processes of social selection. Certain variants gradually proved more successful at securing resources under particular circumstances, while other contenders gradually fell by the wayside or became relegated to relatively small, marginalized niches. These processes were evident in the trajectories of Lutheranism, Calvinism, Catholicism, and the various Anabaptist sects during the Reformation. Local circumstances reinforced different religious tendencies in different parts of Europe. In the Enlightenment local conditions favored more philosophic orientations in some areas and technical orientations in others. Socialist leaders found some contexts more conducive to revolutionary rhetoric, others to reformist coalitions.

In each instance the very possibility of selective processes coming into being was contingent on two decisive characteristics of the broader society. It was contingent on preexisting ideological diversity, for without heightened variation in ideological forms, fewer options for selection would have been present. It was also contingent on the relation I have emphasized between resources and ideological production. Were ideologies simply the private ruminations of individuals, any number of conceivable permutations could coexist in happy mutual accommodation. But to be produced, ideologies require resources and, in turn, specify how resources ought to be used. Thus, the various purveyors of ideologies in each of these periods were indeed one another's competitors. Ideologies that secured the necessary resources flourished; others declined.

The competition on which selective processes rested also depended on several broad features of the social environment in which these ideological movements developed. One was the relative ease with which communication occurred. Without it, the Reformation or the Enlightenment or socialism would not have been a single movement with internal competition but a congeries of separate movements. In a general sense, communication in each instance was facilitated by the fact that Europe, even by the sixteenth century, had achieved a remarkable degree of economic integration, was criss-crossed with an increasing amount of trade and travel, and enjoyed a single religious heritage that, despite language differences, provided common values and interests. At the same time, it was also crucial that Europe consisted of a heterogeneous array of local and regional niches. It was possible in all three periods for leaders of ideological movements to gain control over needed resources by adapting to certain of these niches. This adaptation furthered the overall ideological diversity of each period and yet facilitated the survival quotient of the movement as a whole by linking it to a broader array of conditions. None of the three movements depended only on the success or failure of a particular regime.

In addition to the selective processes that connected specific ideological variants with specific geographic locations, more general selective processes are also evident in the three movements. Dependent as they were on the state for patronage of all kinds, the leaders of each movement found themselves constrained by the interests of state officials. This did not mean that state officials encouraged only those ideologies that aggrandized their regimes or adopted ideologies that legitimated the broader class interests on which their power was based. But it did mean, in nearly all instances, that officials were more likely to bestow resources on ideological movements that posed no immediate challenge to their authority and that enhanced their own capacity in the short term to make decisions. Henry VIII's Reformation placed the ecclesiastical hierarchy under the crown's control but militated against Lollardy and other heresies that demanded greater lay control over the church. Town magistrates in central Europe for the most part followed courses of action that they hoped would quiet popular dissent and avoid intervention by outside regimes. The Enlightenment writers produced works of virtually every conceivable kind, but the works that gained them prominence, patronage, and appointments to prestigious academies were more likely to emphasize moral and utilitarian themes, appeal to highbrow aesthetic tastes, and disguise more critical themes in satire and historical treatises than to cater openly to the masses or encourage blatant dissent. Even the socialists, whose revolutionary rhetoric posed direct challenges to the established order, produced an ideology prior to the First World War that largely favored parliamentary debate, moderate reform, and cooperation with the state in achieving legislation favorable to the working classes. At a more general level, we have also seen examples of the degree to which rational procedures for the conduct of scholarly business, rational forms of discourse, utilitarian criteria of evaluation, and universalistic appeals were reinforced by the movements' association with the state.

The fact that selective processes occurred in the context of relatively high levels of ideological diversity and structural ambiguity also resulted in some tendencies for genres of discourse capable of expressing this diversity and ambiguity to be reinforced. For instance, Reformation discourse tended to favor the homily, the tract, and verse-by-verse commentary, all of which were suited to discrete observations about contemporary events, to a greater extent than the more systematically integrated theological tome. Enlightenment literature gradually turned away from the more constricted forms of epic poetry and classical drama and experimented with epistolary fiction, travelogues, and the novel. Socialist writers found advantages in formulating programs around seriatim lists of demands, disaggregated theses, and short polemical tracts and newspaper commentaries. In each instance, a symbolic differentiation also occurred between these more practical modes of discourse and the theoretical treatises that defined the movement's ideology in more abstract terms.

As these examples indicate, selective processes involve the active efforts of ideological producers as well as the effects of impersonal social mechanisms. But in both ways, selective processes draw ideological manifestations into closer articulation with their social contexts and demonstrate the shaping influences of these contexts. Processes of institutionalization, in contrast, point more toward ideologies gaining the capacity to shape their own destinies, as it were, and even to have an effect on the social contexts in which they occur. Institutionalization is characterized by an increasing level of differentiation between other arenas of social activity and those in which ideology is produced. In this process the producers of ideology gain a greater degree of autonomy in setting their own standards of evaluation. This autonomy, together with a more highly developed system of internal communication and greater routinization of the means by which resources are channeled toward ideological production, generally implies a stronger sense of stability for the resulting ideologies.

Institutionalization implies that ideas become embedded in concrete communities of discourse rather than floating freely in the creative minds of their inventors. Despite the loftiness of its ideals, the Enlightenment was grounded firmly in the concrete activities of writers and patrons, publishers and booksellers, the gatherings in salons and academies, classrooms, libraries, and laboratories. So were the ideals of the Protestant reformers and revolutionary Marxists. Indeed, a distinguishing feature of each of the periods examined was that new ideas ceased to be the sporadic contributions of a few inventive minds and became the regular products of social organizations devoted to their cultivation and dissemination. Reading clubs, academies, salons, university chairs, book fairs, subscription lists, and periodicals, in this sense, gauge the success of the Enlightenment as much as do the more ethereal virtues of rationality, skepticism, empiricism, and freedom.

Yet institutionalization also implies the emancipation of ideas from the social contexts in which they are embedded. Clergy made Scripture the measure of their authority, writers their own standards of aesthetic virtue, and revolutionaries the deterministic movement of material conditions that only they and their disciples could claim to understand. Discourse contemporizes itself by addressing concrete issues of collective importance, but it also refers reflexively to its own central themes. The competition separating different wings of the movement is not resolved by fiat but is allowed to continue, thereby necessitating further discourse and ensuring the perpetuation of its own production. Discretion in the interpretation of dogma is enjoined, giving it flexibility in adapting to unforeseen situations. At the same time, responsibility, deliberation, ritual enactments, festivals, and gatherings are prescribed, increasing the likelihood that fellow producers and their audiences will sustain contact with one another and acquire a tangible identity that reinforces the more abstract levels of their discourse.

Institutionalization, therefore, overlaps with the processes of production and selection but also plays a distinct role in ideological innovation. Like production and selection, it results from the actions of culture producers and involves not only responses to social conditions but also adaptations of the internal structure of discourse itself. It strengthens an ideology's capacity to withstand subsequent changes in its social environment. But it also depends on an appropriate combination of social circumstances. In each of the cases examined, broader expansion in the resource environment made possible an increase in the range of ideologies produced and a more dependable assortment of patronage networks, publishing arrangements, recruitment mechanisms, and offices for culture producers. The relative abundance of resources also made possible an extended period of internal competition which encouraged higher overall levels of ideological productivity. More important perhaps, the particular distribution of these resources among fractions of the ruling elite opened up zones of activity that were relatively free of control by established cultural institutions: urban pulpits, state-initiated academies, working-class political parties. Divisions within religious institutions and other established cultural organizations and in the ruling elite more generally also created conditions that culture producers could exploit to gain greater control over their own affairs. In each case these favorable conjunctures were relatively short-lived, lasting no more than a few generations, but new ideas became sufficiently institutionalized that they could not be ignored in the more turbulent times that followed.

Discursive Fields and Figural Action

The content of ideology in each of these instances was thus shaped in a variety of ways by the social circumstances in which it appeared. To pin down these relations more specifically, I have drawn attention to the connections among social horizons, discursive fields, and figural action. Examining these connections necessitates shifting the primary focus of attention to the discursive texts in which an ideology is expressed. All the foregoing is required in order to grasp the conditions of which the experienced social horizons of culture producers are composed, but the clues for linking these horizons to the internal composition of texts themselves come largely from a different source. They come from structuralist and formalist methods of literary analysis: from Bakhtin, Todorov, Althusser, Jameson, and others.

Linking the internal structure of discourse with the social contexts of its production must also be understood in relation to the problem of articulation that was raised at the outset. Efforts to identify direct homologies between belief systems and the experienced world, such as those prevailing in standard approaches to the sociology of knowledge, have generally proven theoretically sterile and empirically futile. That ideologies should bear the decisive imprint of class relations, authority structures, or some other feature of the social environment has proven impossible to defend in the face of the vast creative variety that characterizes culture production. At the same time, a distinctly inferior theoretical position is taken if one asserts that culture production is free of all social influences or related to social contexts only in idiosyncratic ways. If ideologies are produced, rather than merely happening by some subjective process, then they are produced in time and space, and these coordinates limit the horizons from which resources can be obtained. Some degree of articulation with these horizons seems inevitable. And yet some degree of disarticulation seems equally inevitable, particularly if the ideologies under consideration have any continuing appeal. This delicate balance between articulation and disarticulation is, of course, partly achieved by the process of institutionalization, insofar as this process places culture producers within a tangible social setting and yet emancipates them from some of the constraints of the surrounding social environment. It is, however, a balance that depends on the more dynamic interaction between experience and discourse as well.

The ideologies purveyed by the Reformation, the Enlightenment, and socialism constitute a distinct mode of discourse: not only are they ideologies that attempt to persuade (for example, in contrast with discourse aimed merely at description, factual communication, or entertainment), but they are also the work of oppositional movements. Through the processes of production, selection, and institutionalization, they generated an enlarged range of ideas and significantly challenged those of established cultural institutions. To a degree more pronounced than in other forms of discourse, therefore, questions of authority, of sacralization and desacralization, and of opposing views play a prominent role in these ideologies.

Beyond the usual binary categories evident in all discourse, the ideologies of the Reformation, the Enlightenment, and Marxism, it has been argued, display a distinct oppositional structure characterized by such polarities as ecclesiastical tradition versus scriptural authority, inherited knowledge versus nature, and capitalist society versus the vision of a classless community. These are not single polarities but an oppositional form to which symbols of a wide variety become attached. Nor are they simple oppositions that only negate each other; they anchor widely separated ends of a continuum, thereby defining a space or field in which discourse can be framed.

The origins of these discursive fields, it appears, can be traced to various intellectual precedents rather than being attributable entirely to the creative work of leading figures of the Reformation, the Enlightenment, or socialism. Nevertheless, these figures appear to have sharpened the rhetorical use to which such oppositions were put, and in so doing effected a greater degree of articulation between them and contemporary social circumstances. In part, the creation of a distinct discursive field appears to have constructed an alternative source of authority with which to challenge the authority of prevailing ideas. But elements of the experienced social context can also be found at each end of the discursive continuum. The social setting in which ideologies were produced was sufficiently heterogeneous that both negative and positive models could be found. Luther attached the church and the nobility to the negative end of his discursive fields but found positive examples in the actions of some rulers and his fellow reformers. Rousseau criticized the pretensions of courtly society and modeled republican ideals after his native city of

Geneva. Marx and Engels castigated the hypocrisy of bourgeois society and extrapolated from economic trends to predict the numerical superiority of the working classes.

In each instance the raw materials of social experience were lifted directly, as it were, and placed into the symbolic frameworks that made up the new ideologies. Movement leaders themselves evoked responses from other actors in their social milieu, and these responses provided grist for the mills that ground out ideological statements. This was one of the ways in which the movements' own action sequences fed back into the formulation and reformulation of movement discourse. Social experience became incorporated as elements of movement ideology, thus forging a higher degree of articulation between ideology and social conditions. As it was incorporated, though, it was also transformed by the other symbolic materials to which it was related. Marxist characterizations of the bourgeois family were not simply factual descriptions; they took on meaning as negative anchors in Marxist discourse, were associated with more trenchant criticisms of bourgeois society, and provided examples of exploitation and oppression. The same was true of Voltaire's satire and Calvin's polemics.

The central concepts that grew from each ideological movement were not modeled directly after the activities of some concrete status group or rising social class but were figural actions that depended on the discursive fields in which they were framed. Luther's and Calvin's admonitions concerning faith, worship, the calling, individual moral responsibility, and even the righteous conduct of rulers were seldom defenses of behavior they witnessed directly in their social environment. These admonitions focused on figural or representative characters and behavior. The legitimation of the reformers' own behavior or that of their secular patrons was sometimes in question, to be sure. But just as frequently this behavior provided instances for making points about the validity of the theological tenets at issue rather than the other way around.

The main role filled by formulations of figural action was to resolve the tensions built into the discursive fields of the ideological system itself. Rather than simply holding up a positive ideal against the negative circumstances of the experienced world, movement leaders provided more subtle and complex examples of behavior that remained in the experienced world and yet aspired to higher ideals. The very problems that inspired discussions of the righteous individual, the enlightened person of liberty, or the valorized revolutionary proletarian were set by the discursive fields in which these discussions were framed.

The moral constructs that specified models for behavior, therefore, were at least one significant step removed from the immediate social experience from which movement leaders produced their ideas. They grew out of this experience but were mediated by the symbolic frameworks in which they were placed. They were as much, or more, dependent on an ideological structure as they were on their social contexts. They consisted of representative actions and characters, and their generality was contingent on the symbolic space that removed them from concrete events. They provided models that could be emulated long after the specific events had changed – models of the righteous individual, the conscientious bourgeois, the heroic worker. These models were loosely recognizable within their immediate contexts of origin because of the tangible examples that were used in formulating the relevant discursive fields. But they were also disarticulated from these contexts. And this degree of disarticulation permitted them to function as some of the more abiding elements of modern culture.

The most general lesson to be learned from these considerations, it appears, is to situate the study of cultural change within a multifactoral perspective that emphasizes both the tangible social contexts in which culture is produced and the internal structures of the resulting cultural products. Shifts in broad environmental conditions influence the supply and distribution of social resources on which the production of ideology depends. Of special importance are the institutional arrangements that channel these resources and set the constraints that limit the activities of culture producers, their audiences, and patrons. The conditions that shape the various subprocesses involved in cultural change must also be distinguished, especially those augmenting the range of variability in ideological production, those selectively furthering particular ideological orientations in some contexts and impeding the survival of others, and those affecting the institutionalization of ideological forms. These influences, moreover, appear to function not as mechanical processes but as part of a dynamic sequence of action in which culture producers and other relevant agents respond to their circumstances. Part of this response involves modifications to the structure of ideology itself, which at the same time draw on features of the experienced social context and remove ideology from the immediate limitations of this context. The shaping of ideology is thus historically contingent. Certain relevant factors can be identified for bringing these contingencies into sharper relief, but no single overarching framework can be imposed apart from the specific historical conditions of cultural change themselves.

Editor's Notes on Further Reading

Wuthnow on Ideological Innovation

The classic question of how ideas are related to their surrounding social environments, and the related issue of how new ideas emerge, is addressed in depth in Wuthnow's extensive study of three periods of important cultural innovation in the West (the Reformation, the Enlightenment, and nineteenth-century socialism). In this excerpt he summarizes his findings about the factors to be considered in explaining any period of cultural innovation. The larger study develops further the nature of "articulation" between ideas and social environments, shows how this problem was addressed in classical sociological theory, and provides historical accounts of each period. The research shows how the key factors he identifies explain variation in the extent to which each movement succeeded in different places.

Most recent work challenges or refines the idea that there is any simple reflection between ideas and social environments – a view most explicit in older Marxist theories of culture but also evident in many functionalist theories – see Nicholas Abercrombie, Stephen Hill, and Bryan Turner, *The Dominant Ideology Thesis* (London: George Allen and Unwin, 1980). Other important reflections on the theory of ideology and its developments include Terry Eagleton, *Ideology: An Introduction* (London and New York: Verso, 1991); John Thompson, *Ideology and Modern Culture* (Stanford: Stanford University Press, 1990); Alvin Gouldner, *The Dialectic of Ideology and Technology: The Origins, Grammar, and Future of Ideology* (New York: Seabury Press, 1976); and the essays in Richard Münch and Neil Smelser, eds., *Theory of Culture* (Berkeley: University of California Press, 1992). For an overview of the "problem of articulation" see Lyn Spillman, "Culture, Social Structure, and Discursive Fields," *Current Perspectives in Social Theory* 15 (1995): 129–54.

Reflection on the relations between ideas and their social environments is a central theme of cultural sociology, evident in excerpts throughout this volume: for other approaches to this issue see especially excerpts from work of Schudson, Swidler, and Sewell. Wuthnow's model includes attention to most of the sorts of factors discussed in previous sections. His emphasis on the way particular institutions mediate ideological outcomes is echoed in selections in Part III: see for instance Griswold on the impact of copyright law, Peterson on musical innovation, or Larson on professional context. Further, his emphasis on discursive fields, and the complex, contingent use of underlying binary categories, echoes work on the internal structures of culture excerpted in Part IV: see for instance Alexander and Smith on binary codes or Cerulo on narrative sequences. For earlier work see also Robert Wuthnow, ed., *Vocabularies of Public Life: Empirical Essays in Symbolic Structure* (London and New York: Routledge, 1992); Robert Wuthnow, *Meaning and Moral Order: Explorations in Cultural Analysis* (Berkeley: University of California Press, 1987); Robert Wuthnow, "State Structures and Ideological Outcomes," *American Sociological Review* 50 (1985): 799–821; and Robert Wuthnow, James Davison Hunter, Albert Bergesen, and Edith Kurzweil, *Cultural Analysis: The Work of Peter L. Berger, Mary Douglas, Michel Foucault, and Jürgen Habermas* (Boston and London: Routledge and Kegan Paul, 1984).

31 Postmodernism, or The Cultural Logic of Late Capitalism

Fredric Jameson

[T]he general thesis of Mandel's book *Late Capitalism*, [is] that there have been three fundamental moments in capitalism, each one marking a dialectical expansion over the previous stage: these are market capitalism, the monopoly stage or the stage of imperialism, and our own – wrongly called postindustrial, but what might better be termed multinational capital. I have already pointed out that Mandel's intervention in the postindustrial involves the proposition that late or multinational or consumer capitalism, far from being inconsistent with Marx's great 19th-century analysis, constitutes on the contrary the purest form of capital yet to have emerged, a prodigious expansion of capital into hitherto uncommodified areas. This purer capitalism of our own time thus eliminates the enclaves of precapitalist organization it had hitherto tolerated and exploited in a tributary way: one is tempted to speak in this connection of a new and historically original penetration and colonization of Nature and the Unconscious: that is, the destruction of precapitalist third world agriculture by the Green Revolution, and the rise of the media and the advertising industry. At any rate, it will also have been clear that my own cultural periodization of the stages of realism, modernism and postmodernism is both inspired and confirmed by Mandel's tripartite scheme....

It is therefore in terms of that enormous and threatening, yet only dimly perceivable, other reality of economic and social institutions that in my opinion the postmodern sublime can alone be adequately theorized.

Post-Modernism and the City

I want to sketch the analysis of a full-blown postmodern building – a work which is in many ways uncharacteristic of that postmodern architecture whose principal names are Robert Venturi, Charles Moore, Michael Graves, and more recently Frank Gehry, but which to my mind offers some very striking lessons about the originality of postmodernist space. Let me amplify the figure which has run through the preceding remarks, and make it even more explicit: I am proposing the motion that we are here in the presence of something like a mutation in built space itself. My implication is that we ourselves, the human subjects who happen into this new space, have not kept pace with that evolution; there has been a mutation in the object, unaccompanied as yet by any equivalent mutation in the subject; we do not yet possess the perceptual equipment to match this new hyperspace, as I will call it, in part because our perceptual habits were formed in that older kind of space I have called the space of high modernism. The newer architecture therefore stands as something like an imperative to grow new organs, to expand our sensorium and our body to some new, as yet unimaginable, perhaps ultimately impossible, dimensions.

The Bonaventura Hotel

The building whose features I will very rapidly enumerate in the next few moments is the Bonaventura Hotel, built in the new Los Angeles downtown by the architect and developer John Portman, whose other works include the various Hyatt Regencies, the Peachtree Center in Atlanta, and the Renaissance Center in Detroit. I have mentioned the populist aspect of the rhetorical defence of postmodernism against the elite (and Utopian) austerities of the great architectural modernisms: it is generally affirmed, in other words, that these newer buildings are popular works on the one hand; and that they respect the vernacular of the American city fabric on the other, that is to say, that they no longer attempt, as did the masterworks and monuments of high modernism, to insert a different, a distinct, an elevated, a new Utopian language into the tawdry and commercial sign-system of the surrounding city, but rather, on the contrary, seek to speak that very language, using its lexicon and syntax as that has been emblematically 'learned from Las Vegas'.

On the first of these counts, Portman's *Bonaventura* fully confirms the claim: it is a popular building, visited with enthusiasm by locals and tourists alike (although Portman's other buildings are even more successful in this respect). The populist insertion into the city fabric is, however, another matter, and it is with this that we will begin. There are three entrances to the *Bonaventura*, one from Figueroa, and the other two by way of elevated gardens on the other side of the hotel, which is built into the remaining slope of the former Beacon Hill. None of these is anything like the old hotel marquee, or the monumental porte-cochère with which the sumptuous buildings of yesteryear were wont to stage your passage from city street to the older interior. The entryways of the *Bonaventura* are as it were lateral and rather backdoor affairs: the gardens in the back admit you to the sixth floor of the towers, and even there you must walk down one flight to find the elevator by which you gain access to the lobby. Meanwhile, what one is still tempted to think of as the front entry, on Figueroa, admits you, baggage and all, onto the second-storey shopping balcony, from which you must take an escalator down to the main registration desk. More about these elevators and escalators in a moment. What I first want to suggest about these curiously unmarked ways-in is that they seem to have been imposed by some new category of closure governing the inner space of the hotel itself (and this over and above the material constraints under which Portman had to work). I believe that, with a certain number of other characteristic postmodern buildings, such as the *Beaubourg* in Paris, or the Eaton Centre in Toronto, the *Bonaventura* aspires to being a total space, a complete world, a kind of miniature city (and I would want to add that to this new total space corresponds a new collective practice, a new mode in which individuals move and congregate, something like the practice of a new and historically original kind of hyper-crowd). In this sense, then, ideally the mini-city of Portman's *Bonaventura* ought not to have entrances at all, since the entryway is always the seam that links the building to the rest of the city that surrounds it: for it does not wish to be a part of the city, but rather its equivalent and its replacement or substitute. That is, however, obviously not possible or practical, whence the deliberate downplaying and reduction of the entrance function to its bare minimum. But this disjunction from the surrounding city is very different from that of the great monuments of the International Style: there, the act of disjunction was violent, visible, and had a very real symbolic significance – as in Le Corbusier's great *pilotis* whose gesture radically separates the new Utopian space of the modern from the degraded and fallen city fabric which it thereby explicitly repudiates (although the gamble of the modern was that this new Utopian space, in the virulence of its Novum, would fan out and transform that eventually by the very power of its new spatial language). The Bonaventura, however, is content to 'let the fallen city fabric continue to be in its being' (to parody Heidegger); no further effects, no larger protopolitical Utopian transformation, is either expected or desired.

This diagnosis is to my mind confirmed by the great reflective glass skin of the *Bonaventura*, whose function I will now interpret rather differently than I did a moment ago when I saw the phenomenon of reflexion generally as developing a thematics of reproductive technology (the two readings are however not incompatible). Now one would want rather to stress the way in which the glass skin repels the city outside; a repulsion for which we have analogies in those reflector sunglasses which make it impossible for your interlocutor to see your own eyes and thereby achieve a certain aggressivity towards and power over the Other. In a similar way, the glass skin achieves a peculiar and placeless dissociation of the *Bonaventura* from its neighbourhood: it is not even an exterior, inasmuch as when you seek to look at the hotel's outer walls you cannot see the hotel itself, but only the distorted images of everything that surrounds it.

Now I want to say a few words about escalators and elevators: given their very real pleasures in Portman, particularly these last, which the artist has termed 'gigantic kinetic sculptures' and which certainly account for much of the spectacle and the excitement of the hotel interior, particularly in the Hyatts, where like great Japanese lanterns or gondolas they ceaselessly rise and fall – given such a deliberate marking and foregrounding in their own right, I believe one has to see such 'people movers' (Portman's own term, adapted from Disney) as something a little more than mere functions and engineering components. We know in any case that recent architectural theory has begun to borrow from narrative analysis in other fields, and to attempt to see our physical trajectories through such buildings as virtual narratives or stories, as dynamic paths and narrative paradigms which we as visitors are asked to fulfil and to complete with our own bodies and movements. In the *Bonaventura*, however, we find a dialectical heightening of this process: it seems to me that the escalators and elevators here henceforth replace movement but also and above all designate themselves as new reflexive signs and emblems of movement proper (something which will become evident when we come to the whole question of what remains of older forms of movement in this building, most notably walking itself). Here the narrative stroll has been underscored, symbolized, reified and replaced by a transportation machine which becomes the allegorical signifier of that older promenade we are no longer allowed to conduct on our own: and this is a dialectical intensification of the autoreferentiality of all modern culture, which tends to turn upon itself and designate its own cultural production as its content.

I am more at a loss when it comes to conveying the thing itself, the experience of space you undergo when you step off such allegorical devices into the lobby or atrium, with its great central column, surrounded by a miniature lake, the whole positioned between the four symmetrical residential towers with their elevators, and surrounded by rising balconies capped by a kind of greenhouse roof at the sixth level. I am tempted to say that such space makes it impossible for us to use the language of volume or volumes any longer, since these last are impossible to seize. Hanging streamers indeed suffuse this empty space in such a way as to distract systematically and deliberately from whatever form it might be supposed to have; while a constant busyness gives the feeling that emptiness is here absolutely packed, that it is an element within which you yourself are immersed, without any of that distance that formerly enabled the perception of perspective or volume. You are in this hyperspace up to your eyes and your body; and if it seemed to you before that that suppression of depth I spoke of in postmodern painting or literature would necessarily be difficult to achieve in architecture itself, perhaps you may now be willing to see this bewildering immersion as the formal equivalent in the new medium.

Yet escalator and elevator are also in this context dialectical opposites; and we may suggest that the glorious movement of the elevator gondolas is also a dialectical compensation for this filled space of the atrium – it gives us the chance at a radically different, but complementary, spatial experience, that of rapidly shooting up through the ceiling and outside, along one of the four symmetrical towers, with the referent, Los Angeles itself, spread out breathtakingly and even alarmingly before us. But even this vertical movement is contained: the elevator lifts you to one of those revolving cocktail lounges, in which you, seated, are again passively rotated about and offered a contemplative spectacle of the city itself, now transformed into its own images by the glass windows through which you view it.

Let me quickly conclude all this by returning to the central space of the lobby itself (with the passing observation that the hotel rooms are visibly marginalized: the corridors in the residential sections are low-ceilinged and dark, most depressingly functional indeed; while one understands that the rooms are in the worst of taste). The descent is dramatic enough, plummeting back down through the roof to splash down in the lake; what happens when you get there is something else, which I can only try to characterize as milling confusion, something like the vengeance this space takes on those who still seek to walk through it. Given the absolute symmetry of the four towers, it is quite impossible to get your bearings in this lobby; recently, colour coding and directional signals have been added in a pitiful and revealing, rather desperate attempt to restore the coordinates of an older space. I will take as the most dramatic practical result of this spatial mutation the notorious dilemma of the shopkeepers on the various balconies: it has been obvious, since the very opening of the hotel in 1977, that nobody could ever find any of these stores, and even if you located the appropriate boutique, you would be most unlikely to be as fortunate a second time; as a consequence, the commercial tenants are in despair and all the merchandise is marked down to bargain prices. When you recall that Portman is a businessman as well as an architect, and a millionaire developer, an artist who is at one and the same time a capitalist in his own right, one cannot but feel that here too something of a 'return of the repressed' is involved.

So I come finally to my principal point here, that this latest mutation in space – postmodern hyperspace – has finally succeeded in transcending the capacities of the individual human body to locate itself, to organize its immediate surroundings perceptually, and cognitively to map its position in a mappable external world. And I have already suggested that this alarming disjunction point between the body and its built environment – which is to the initial bewilderment of the older modernism as the velocities of space craft are to those of the automobile – can itself stand as the symbol and analogue of that even sharper dilemma which is the incapacity of our minds, at least at present, to map the great global multinational and decentred communicational network in which we find ourselves caught as individual subjects.

The New Machine

But as I am anxious that Portman's space not be perceived as something either exceptional or seemingly marginalized and leisure-specialized on the order of Disneyland, I would like in passing to juxtapose this complacent and entertaining (although bewildering) leisure-time space with its analogue in a very different area, namely the space of postmodern warfare, in particular as Michael Herr evokes it in his great book on the experience of Vietnam, called *Dispatches*. The extraordinary linguistic innovations of this work may still be considered postmodern, in the eclectic way in which its language impersonally fuses a whole range of contemporary collective idiolects, most notably rock language and Black language: but the fusion is dictated by problems of content. This first terrible postmodernist war cannot be told in any of the traditional paradigms of the war novel or movie – indeed that breakdown of all previous narrative paradigms is, along with the breakdown of any shared language through which a veteran might convey such experience, among the principal subjects of the book and may be said to open up the place of a whole new reflexivity. Benjamin's account of Baudelaire, and of the emergence of modernism from a new experience of city technology which transcends all the older habits of bodily perception, is both singularly relevant here, and singularly antiquated, in the light of this new and virtually unimaginable quantum leap in technological alienation: 'He was a moving-target-survivor subscriber, a true child of the war, because except for the rare times when you were pinned or stranded the system was geared to keep you mobile, if that was what you thought you wanted. As a technique for staying alive it seemed to make as much sense as anything, given naturally that you were there to begin with and wanted to see it close; it started out sound and straight but it formed a cone as it progressed, because the more you moved the more you saw, the more you saw the more besides death and mutilation you risked, and the more you risked of that the more you would have to let go of one day as a "survivor". Some of us moved around the war like crazy people until we couldn't see which way the run was taking us anymore, only the war all over its surface with occasional, unexpected penetration. As long as we could have choppers like taxis it took real exhaustion or depression near shock or a dozen pipes of opium to keep us even apparently quiet, we'd still be running around inside our skins like something was after us, ha ha, La Vida Loca. In the months after I got back the hundreds of helicopters I'd flown in began to draw together until they'd formed a collective metachopper, and in my mind it was the sexiest thing going; saver-destroyer, provider-waster, right hand-left hand, nimble, fluent, canny and human; hot steel, grease, jungle-saturated canvas webbing, sweat cooling and warming up again, cassette rock and roll in one ear and door-gun fire in the other, fuel, heat, vitality and death, death itself, hardly an intruder.'

In this new machine, which does not, like the older modernist machinery of the locomotive or the airplane, represent motion, but which can only be represented *in motion*, something of the mystery of the new postmodernist space is concentrated.

The Abolition of Critical Distance

The conception of postmodernism outlined here is a historical rather than a merely stylistic one. I cannot stress too greatly the radical distinction between a view for which the postmodern is one (optional) style among many others available, and one which seeks to grasp it as the cultural dominant of the logic of late capitalism: the two approaches in fact generate two very different ways of conceptualizing the phenomenon as a whole, on the one hand moral judgements (about which it is indifferent whether they are positive or negative), and on the other a genuinely dialectical attempt to think of our present time in History. . . .

[W]hat we have been calling postmodernism is inseparable from, and unthinkable without the hypothesis of, some fundamental mutation of the sphere of culture in the world of late capitalism, which includes a momentous modification of its social function. Older discussions of the space, function or sphere of culture (most notably Herbert Marcuse's classic essay on 'The Affirmative Character of Culture') have insisted on what a different language would call the 'semi-autonomy' of the cultural realm: its ghostly, yet Utopian, existence, for good or ill, above the practical world of the existent, whose mirror image it throws back in forms which vary from the legitimations of flattering resemblance to the contestatory indictments of critical satire or Utopian pain.

What we must now ask ourselves is whether it is not precisely this 'semi-autonomy' of the cultural sphere which has been destroyed by the logic of late capitalism. Yet to argue that culture is today no longer endowed with the relative autonomy it once enjoyed as one level among others in earlier moments of capitalism (let alone in pre-capitalist societies), is not necessarily to imply its disappearance or extinction. On the contrary: we must go on to affirm that the dissolution of an autonomous sphere of culture is rather to be imagined in terms of an explosion: a prodigious expansion of culture throughout the social realm, to the point at which everything in our social life – from economic value and state power to practices and to the very structure of the psyche itself – can be said to have become 'cultural' in some original and as yet untheorized sense. This perhaps startling proposition is, however, substantively quite consistent with the previous diagnosis of a society of the image or the simulacrum, and a transformation of the 'real' into so many pseudo-events.

It also suggests that some of our most cherished and time-honoured radical conceptions about the nature of cultural politics may thereby find themselves outmoded. However distinct those conceptions may have been – which range from slogans of negativity, opposition, and subversion to critique and reflexivity – they all shared a single, fundamentally spatial, presupposition, which may be resumed in the equally time-honoured formula of 'critical distance'. No theory of cultural politics current on the Left today has been able to do without one notion or another of a certain minimal aesthetic distance, of the possibility of the positioning of the cultural act outside the massive Being of capital, which then serves as an Archimedean point from which to assault this last. What the burden of our preceding demonstration suggests, however, is that distance in general (including 'critical distance' in particular) has very precisely been abolished in the new space of postmodernism. We are submerged in its henceforth filled and suffused volumes to the point where our now postmodern bodies are bereft of spatial coordinates and practically (let alone theoretically) incapable of distantiation; meanwhile, it has already been observed how the prodigious new expansion of multinational capital ends up penetrating and colonizing those very pre-capitalist enclaves (Nature and the Unconscious) which offered extraterritorial and Archimedean footholds for critical effectivity. The shorthand language of 'cooptation' is for this reason omnipresent on the Left; but offers a most inadequate theoretical basis for understanding a situation in which we all, in one way or another, dimly feel that not only punctual and local countercultural forms of cultural resistance and guerrilla warfare, but also even overtly political interventions like those of *The Clash*, are all somehow secretly disarmed and reabsorbed by a system of which they themselves might well be considered a part, since they can achieve no distance from it. . . .

The Need for Maps

But if all this is so, then at least one possible form of a new radical cultural politics becomes evident: with a final aesthetic proviso that must quickly be noted. Left cultural producers and theorists particularly those formed by bourgeois cultural traditions issuing from romanticism and valorizing spontaneous, instinctive or unconscious forms of 'genius' – but also for very obvious historical reasons such as Zhdanovism and the sorry consequences of political and party interventions in the arts – have often by reaction allowed themselves to be unduly intimidated by the repudiation, in bourgeois aesthetics and most notably in high modernism, of one of the age-old functions of art – namely the pedagogical and the didactic. The teaching function of art was, however, always stressed in classical times (even though it there mainly took the form of *moral* lessons); while the prodigious and still imperfectly understood work of Brecht reaffirms, in a new and formally innovative and original way, for the moment of modernism proper, a complex new conception of the relationship between culture and pedagogy. The cultural model I will propose similarly foregrounds the cognitive and pedagogical dimensions of political art and culture, dimensions stressed in very different ways by *both* Lukács *and* Brecht (for the distinct moments of realism and modernism, respectively).

We cannot, however, return to aesthetic practices elaborated on the basis of historical situations and dilemmas which are no longer ours. Meanwhile, the conception of space that has been developed here suggests that a model of political culture appropriate to our own situation will necessarily have to raise spatial issues as its fundamental organizing concern. I will therefore provisionally define the aesthetic of such new (and hypothetical) cultural form as an aesthetic of *cognitive mapping*. . . .

An aesthetic of cognitive mapping – a pedagogical political culture which seeks to endow the individual subject with some new heightened sense of its place in the global system – will necessarily have to respect this now enormously complex representational dialectic and to invent radically new forms in order to do it justice. This is not, then, clearly a call for a return to some older kind of machinery, some older and more transparent national space, or some more traditional and reassuring perspectival or mimetic enclave: the new political art – if it is indeed possible at all – will have to hold to the truth of postmodernism, that is, to say, to its fundamental object – the world space of multinational capital – at the same time at which it achieves a breakthrough to some as yet unimaginable new mode of representing this last, in which we may again begin to grasp our positioning as individual and collective subjects and regain a capacity to act and struggle which is at present neutralized by our spatial as well as our social confusion. The political form of postmodernism, if there ever is any, will have as its vocation the invention and projection of a global cognitive mapping, on a social as well as a spatial scale.

Editor's Notes on Further Reading

Jameson on Postmodern Culture

Some of the most significant and pervasive cultural innovations in the late twentieth century have been characterized as "postmodern." Here, literary theorist Fredric Jameson summarizes his thesis that postmodern culture should be situated historically as the dominant culture expressing the signifying practices and sensibilities generated by contemporary global capitalism, and illustrates it with his famous architectural exemplar of the Bonaventure Hotel in Los Angeles. The full essay treats more extensively some features of postmodern culture, such as an emphasis on pastiche, a focus on images, dissociation between meaning and emotional attachment, and ahistoricism. Jameson's argument here bears comparison with Simmel's characterization of modern culture, Horkheimer and Adorno's critique of the modern culture industry, and Larson's investigation of the specific professional context generating postmodern architecture in the United States, all excerpted in this volume.

This essay is collected with other work of related interest in Fredric Jameson, *Postmodernism, or, The Cultural Logic of Late Capitalism* (Durham: Duke University Press, 1991). See also Michael Hardt and Kathi Weeks, eds., *The Jameson Reader* (Malden, MA and Oxford: Blackwell, 2000); Fredric Jameson and Masao Miyoshi, eds., *The Cultures of Globalization* (Durham: Duke University Press, 1998); and Fredric Jameson, *The Cultural Turn: Selected Writings on the Postmodern 1983–1998* (London and New York: Verso, 1998). Important earlier works include Jameson, "Postmodernism and Consumer Society," in Hal Foster, ed., *The Anti-Aesthetic: Essays on Postmodern Culture* (Port Townsend, WA: Bay Press, 1983); *The Political Unconscious: Narrative as a Socially Symbolic Act* (Ithaca: Cornell University Press, 1981); and *Marxism and Form: Twentieth-Century Dialectical Theories of Literature* (Princeton: Princeton University Press, 1971). For review essays which address links between textual and social analysis see Jameson, "On Goffman's *Frame Analysis*" *Theory and Society* 3 (1976): 119–33, "Ideology, Narrative Analysis, and Popular Culture," *Theory and Society* 4 (1977): 543–59; "On *Habits of the Heart*," pp. 97–113 in Charles Reynolds and Ralph Norman, eds., *Community in America: The Challenge of Habits of the Heart* (Berkeley: University of California Press, 1988); and "Culture and Finance Capital," *Critical Inquiry* 24 (1997): 246–65.

Some commentary on this essay and Jameson's work more generally can be found in Perry Anderson, *The Origins of Postmodernity* (London: Verso, 1998); Sean Homer, *Fredric Jameson: Marxism, Hermeneutics, Postmodernism* (New York: Routledge, 1998); M. Gottdiener, *Postmodern Semiotics: Material Culture and the Forms of Postmodern Life* (Oxford and Cambridge, MA: Blackwell, 1995), pp. 122–4; Steven Best and Douglas Kellner, *Postmodern Theory: Critical Interrogations* (New York: The Guilford Press, 1991), pp. 182–92; Lidia Curti, "What is Real and What is Not: Female Fabulations in Cultural Analysis," pp. 134–53 in Lawrence Grossberg, Cary Nelson, and Paula Treichler, eds., *Cultural Studies* (New York and London: Routledge, 1992); and Charles Bernstein, "Centering the Postmodern," *Socialist Review* 17 (1987): 45–56.

Influential statements on postmodernism include Andreas Huyssen, "Mapping the Postmodern," *New German Critique* 33 (1984): 5–52; Jean Baudrillard, *Selected Writings*, Mark Poster, ed. (Stanford: Stanford University Press, 1988) and *Simulacra and Simulation*, trans. Sheila Faria Glaser (Ann Arbor: University of Michigan Press, 1994); and Jean-François Lyotard, *The Postmodern Condition: A Report on Knowledge*, trans. Geoff Bennington and Brian Massumi (Minneapolis: University of Minnesota Press, 1984). For a useful introduction see Tim Woods, *Beginning Postmodernism* (Manchester and New York: Manchester University Press, 1999).

By linking the postmodern aesthetic to changes in capitalism Jameson bridges the textual and the social in ways which challenge both postmodern literary theorists and sociologists. A more direct challenge to postmodern theory is Jürgen Habermas, "Modernity vs. Postmodernity," *New German Critique* 22 (1981): 3–14; on this challenge see Scott Lash, "Postmodernity and Desire," *Theory and Society* 14 (1985): 1–33, and works by Foster, and Best and Kellner cited above. Other important commentary on modernism, postmodernism and their social contexts includes Paul Rabinow, "Representations are Social Facts: Modernism and Postmodernism in Anthropology," pp. 234–61 in James Clifford and George Marcus, eds., *Writing Culture: The Poetics and Politics of Ethnography* (Berkeley: University of California Press, 1986); David Harvey, *The Condition of Postmodernity* (Oxford and Cambridge, MA: Basil Blackwell, 1989); Scott Lash, *Sociology of Postmodernism* (London and New York: Routledge, 1990); Scott Lash and Jonathan Friedman, eds., *Modernity and Identity* (Oxford and Cambridge, MA: Blackwell, 1992); Steven Seidman, ed., *The Postmodern Turn: New Perspectives on Social Theory* (Cambridge and New York: Cambridge University Press, 1994); Linda Nicholson and Steven Seidman, eds., *Social Postmodernism: Beyond Identity Politics* (Cambridge and New York: Cambridge University Press, 1995); Charles Lemert, *Postmodernism is Not What You Think* (Malden, MA and Oxford: Blackwell, 1997); and works by Best and Kellner, and Gottdiener, cited above. Two otherwise different studies examining postmodernism empirically are Barry Schwartz, "Postmodernity and Historical Reputation: Abraham Lincoln in Late Twentieth-Century American Memory," *Social Forces* 77 (1998): 63–103, and George Lipsitz, *Dangerous Crossroads: Popular Music, Postmodernism, and the Poetics of Place* (London and New York: Verso, 1994).

Index

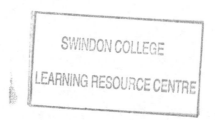